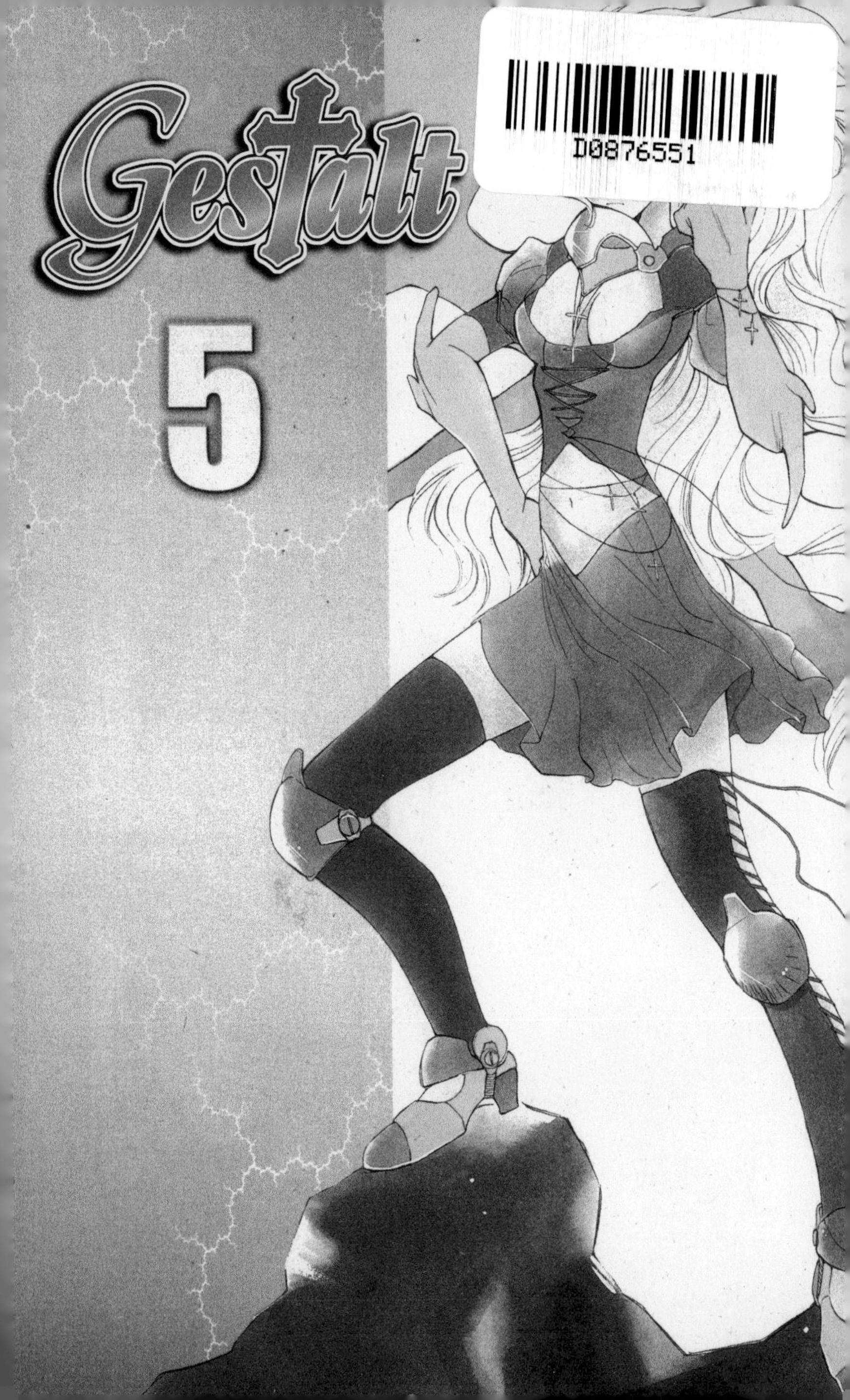
Gestalt
5

CONTENTS

Legend of the Great Beast

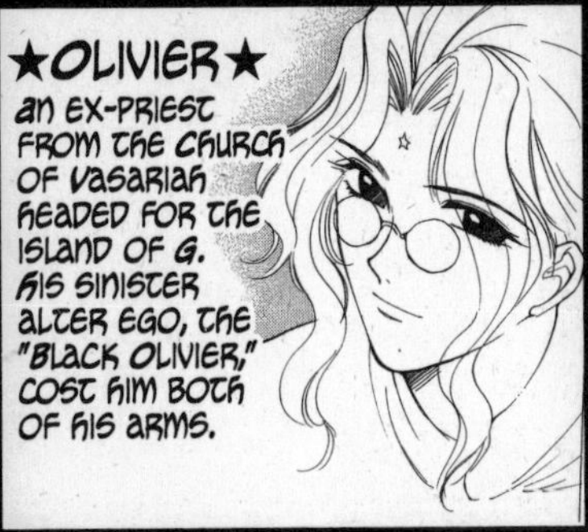
★OLIVIER★
AN EX-PRIEST FROM THE CHURCH OF VASARIAH HEADED FOR THE ISLAND OF G. HIS SINISTER ALTER EGO, THE "BLACK OLIVIER," COST HIM BOTH OF HIS ARMS.

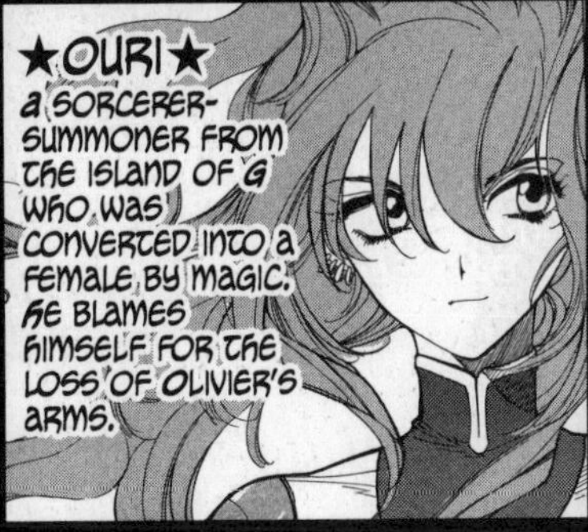
★OURI★
A SORCERER-SUMMONER FROM THE ISLAND OF G WHO WAS CONVERTED INTO A FEMALE BY MAGIC. HE BLAMES HIMSELF FOR THE LOSS OF OLIVIER'S ARMS.

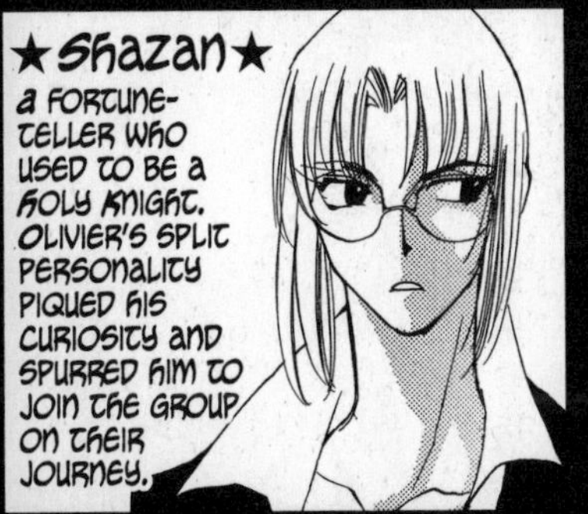
★SHAZAN★
A FORTUNE-TELLER WHO USED TO BE A HOLY KNIGHT. OLIVIER'S SPLIT PERSONALITY PIQUED HIS CURIOSITY AND SPURRED HIM TO JOIN THE GROUP ON THEIR JOURNEY.

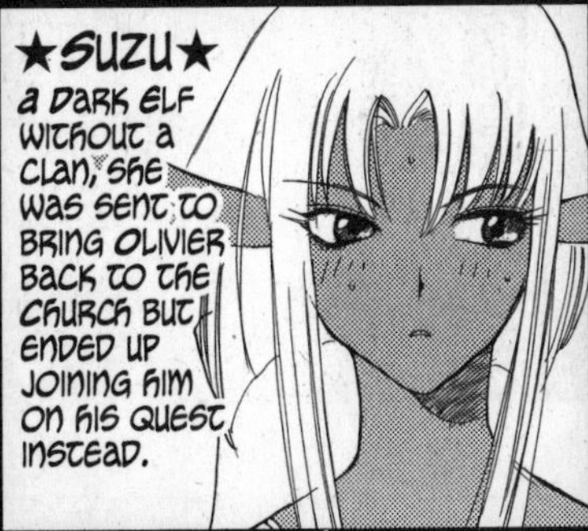
★SUZU★
A DARK ELF WITHOUT A CLAN, SHE WAS SENT TO BRING OLIVIER BACK TO THE CHURCH BUT ENDED UP JOINING HIM ON HIS QUEST INSTEAD.

CHARACTERS

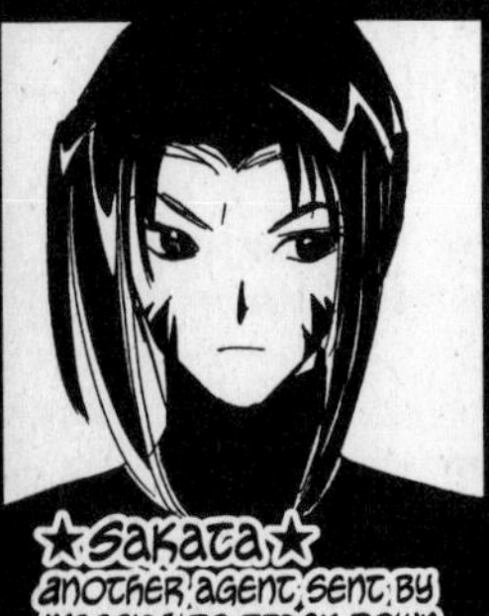
★SAKATA★
ANOTHER AGENT SENT BY MESSIAH TO TRACK DOWN AND RETURN OLIVIER. SHE DOESN'T WORK WELL WITH OTHERS...

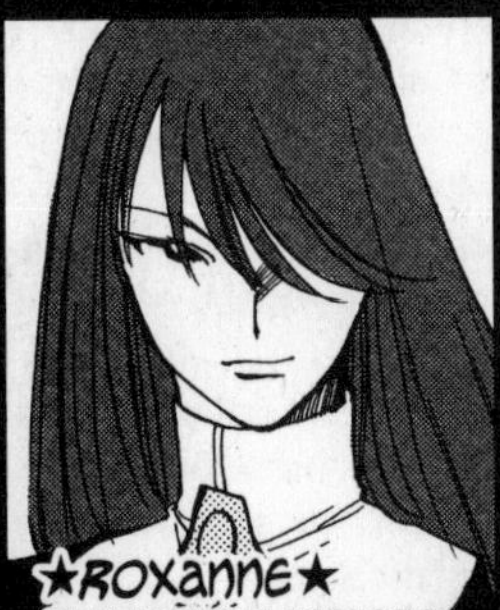
★ROXANNE★
A MYSTERIOUS ASSASSIN WHO PLACED A CURSE ON OURI. SEIZING OLIVIER IS HER TRUE GOAL.

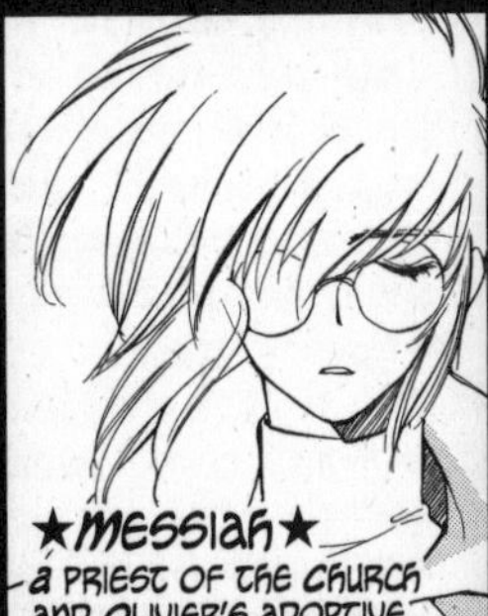
★MESSIAH★
A PRIEST OF THE CHURCH AND OLIVIER'S ADOPTIVE FATHER. HE WANTS TO KEEP OLIVIER FROM REACHING G, EVEN IF HE MUST USE FORCE.

G e s t a l t

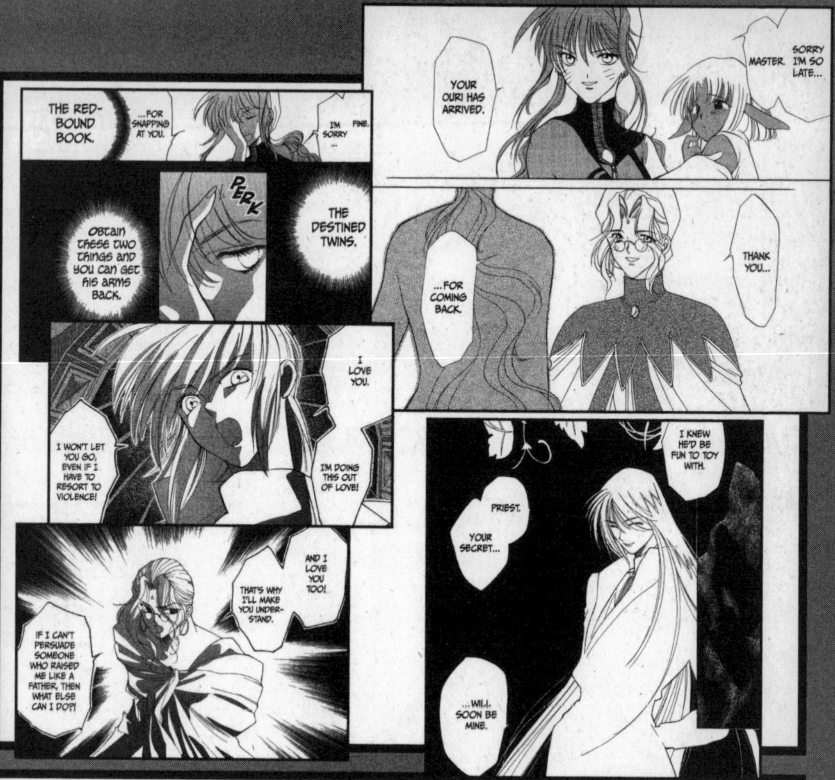
SORRY I'M SO LATE...
MASTER.
YOUR OURI HAS ARRIVED.
FINE.
I'M SORRY ...
...FOR SNAPPING AT YOU.
THE RED-BOUND BOOK.
THANK YOU...
...FOR COMING BACK.
THE DESTINED TWINS.
PERK
OBTAIN THESE TWO THINGS AND YOU CAN GET HIS ARMS BACK.
I LOVE YOU.
I'M DOING THIS OUT OF LOVE!
I WON'T LET YOU GO, EVEN IF I HAVE TO RESORT TO VIOLENCE!
I KNEW HE'D BE FUN TO TOY WITH.
PRIEST.
YOUR SECRET...
...WILL SOON BE MINE.
AND I LOVE YOU TOO!
THAT'S WHY I'LL MAKE YOU UNDER-STAND.
IF I CAN'T PERSUADE SOMEONE WHO RAISED ME LIKE A FATHER, THEN WHAT ELSE CAN I DO?!

Olivier was a priest of the Church of Vasariah until the day he fled the order to pursue the forbidden island of G. On his journey, he saves a slave girl named Ouri who is actually a sorcerer from the island of G. "She" is also actually a man, handicapped with a new body as part of a savage combat game against his siblings. Ouri quickly becomes smitten with Olivier and puts the game on hold to accompany him on his journey. The two are soon joined by Suzu and Shazan, as they all make their way to G.

On their way, the villainous "Black Olivier" surfaces again and commits the heinous act of destroying the priest's arms. Ouri feels inconsolably responsible for this and abandons the team to mourn by himself.

Without Ouri, the others almost fall prey to a sick-minded feudal lord's plot to sell Olivier's body on the black market. Thankfully, a newly resolved Ouri returns to save them in the nick of time.

Meanwhile, a dark figure named Roxanne shows interest in Olivier's secret alter ego and places a curse on Ouri before disappearing from sight.

Hoping to find a way of restoring Olivier's lost arms, our heroes go to meet Olivier's foster father but are shocked when they're met by an enraged Messiah who refuses to let Olivier leave!

THE STORY SO FAR

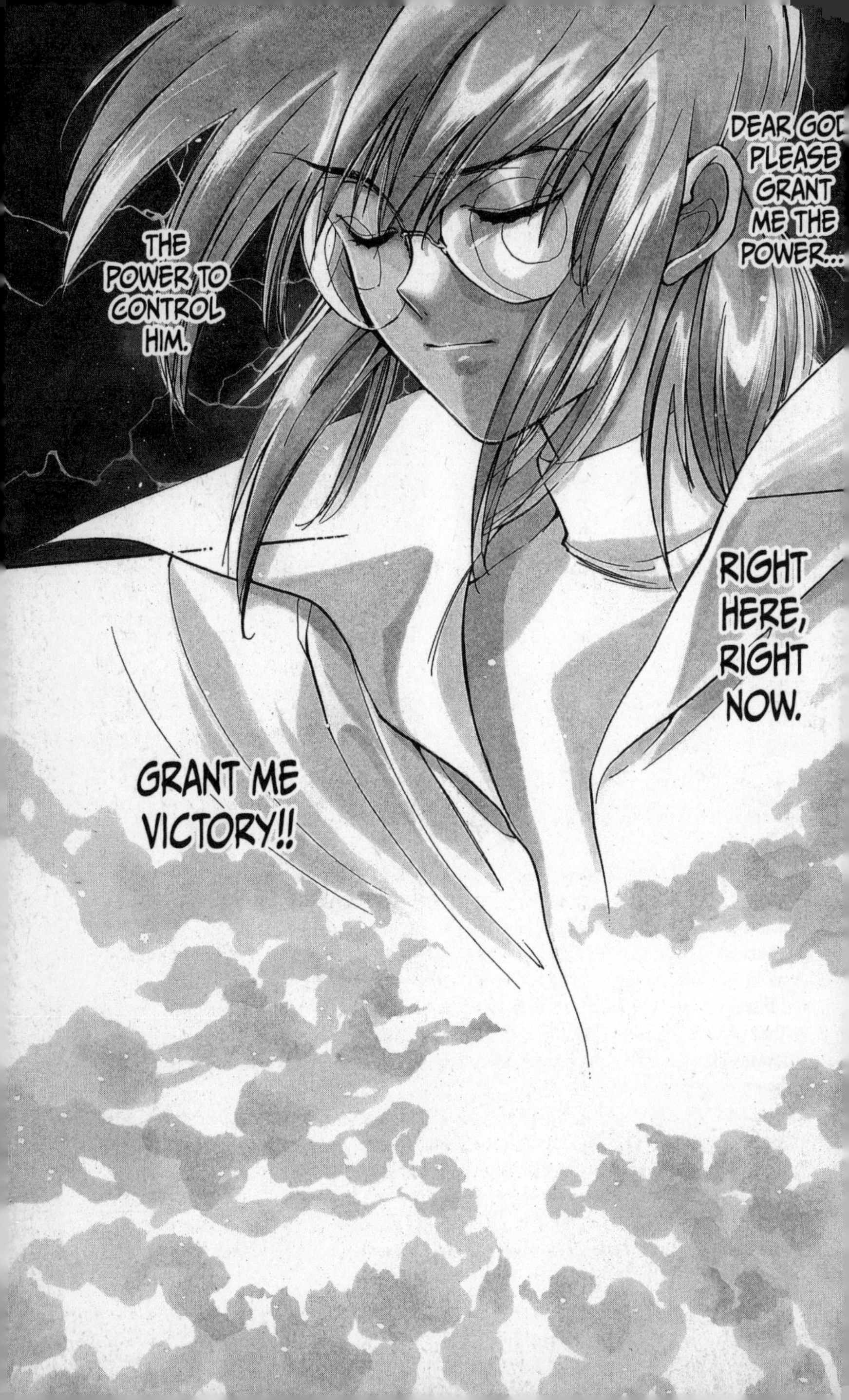
DEAR GOD PLEASE GRANT ME THE POWER...
THE POWER TO CONTROL HIM.
RIGHT HERE, RIGHT NOW.
GRANT ME VICTORY!!

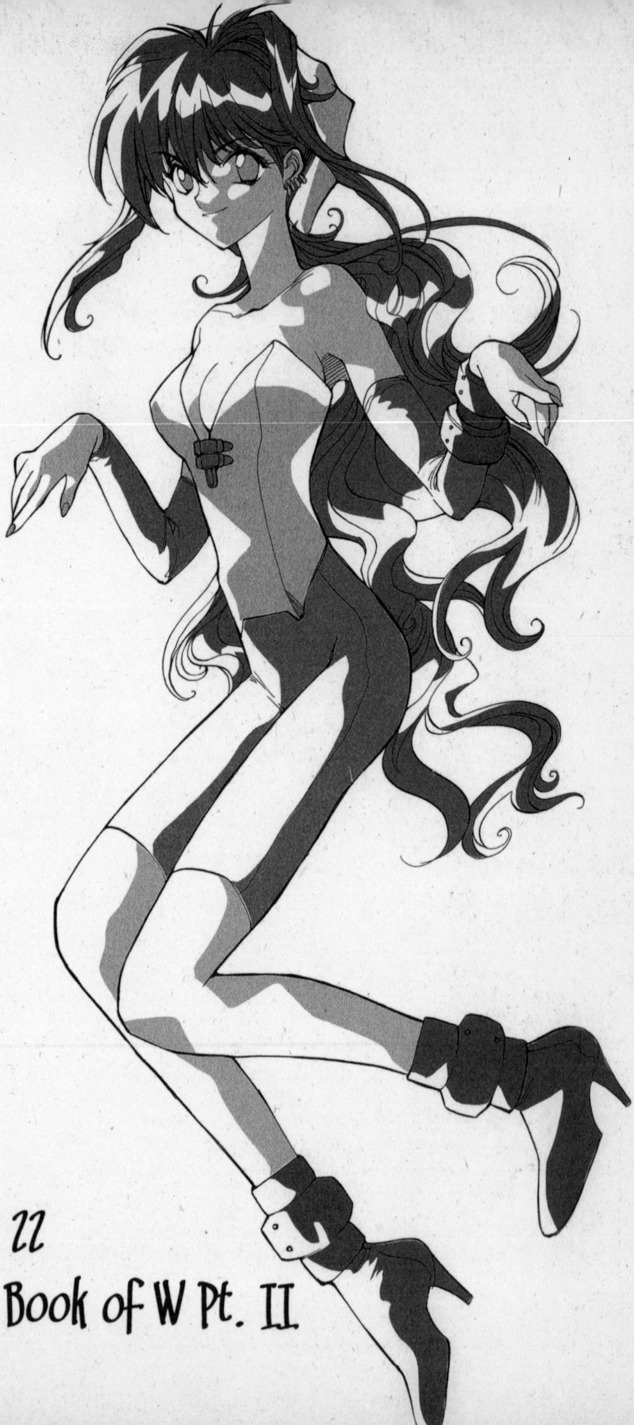

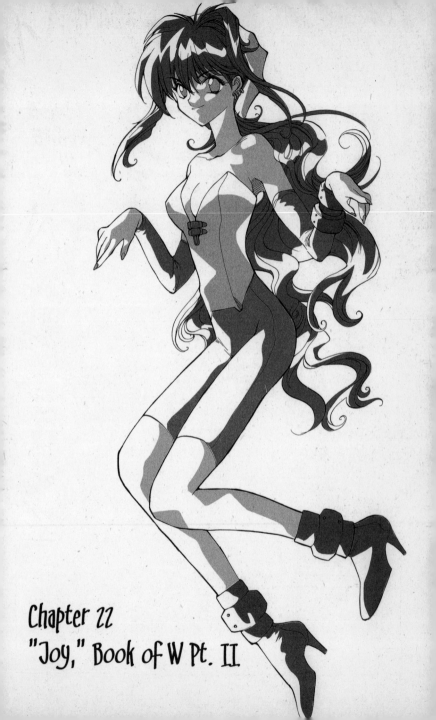

Chapter 22
"Joy," Book of W Pt. II

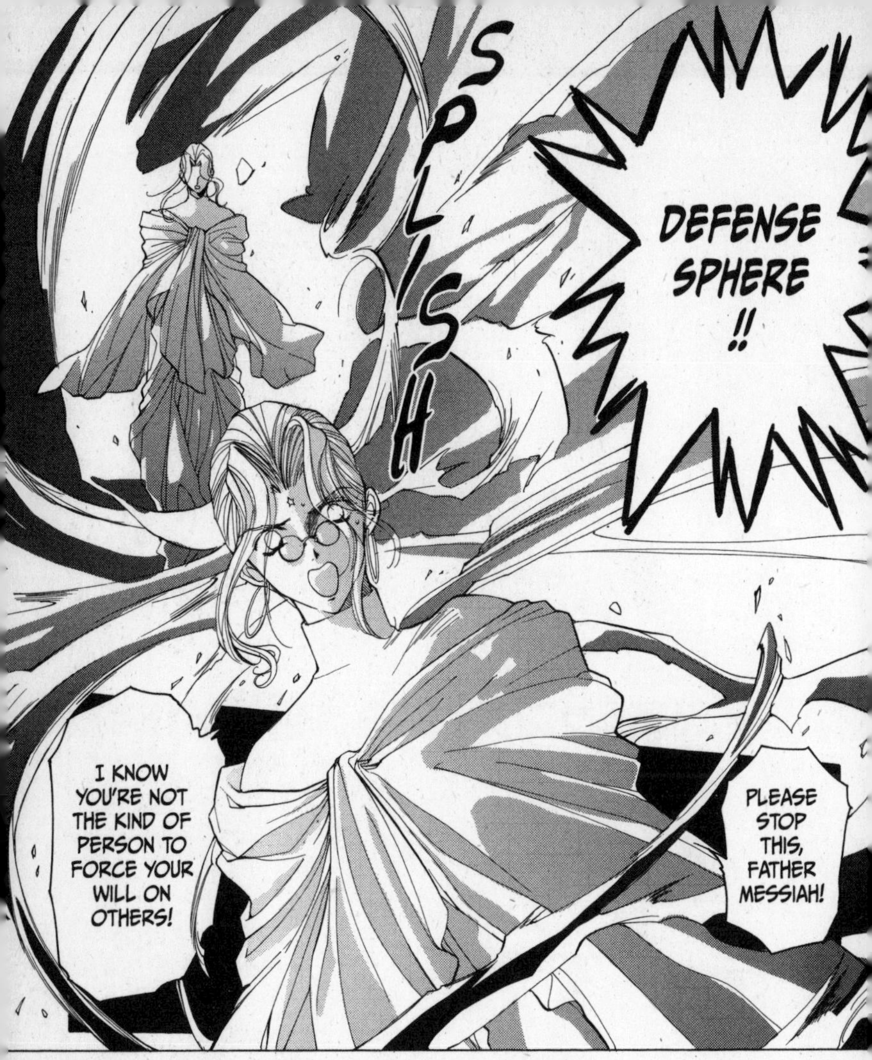
DEFENSE SPHERE!!
SPLISH
PLEASE STOP THIS, FATHER MESSIAH!
I KNOW YOU'RE NOT THE KIND OF PERSON TO FORCE YOUR WILL ON OTHERS!

Summary Space ①

This space is usually filled with "The Story So Far" when the chapter is serialized in the magazine, but my editor insisted I write something profound in here instead...!

So yeah... We sure had a lotta snow this year.

WOOO——

It's usually the editor's job to write the copy for openings to manga like this anyway.

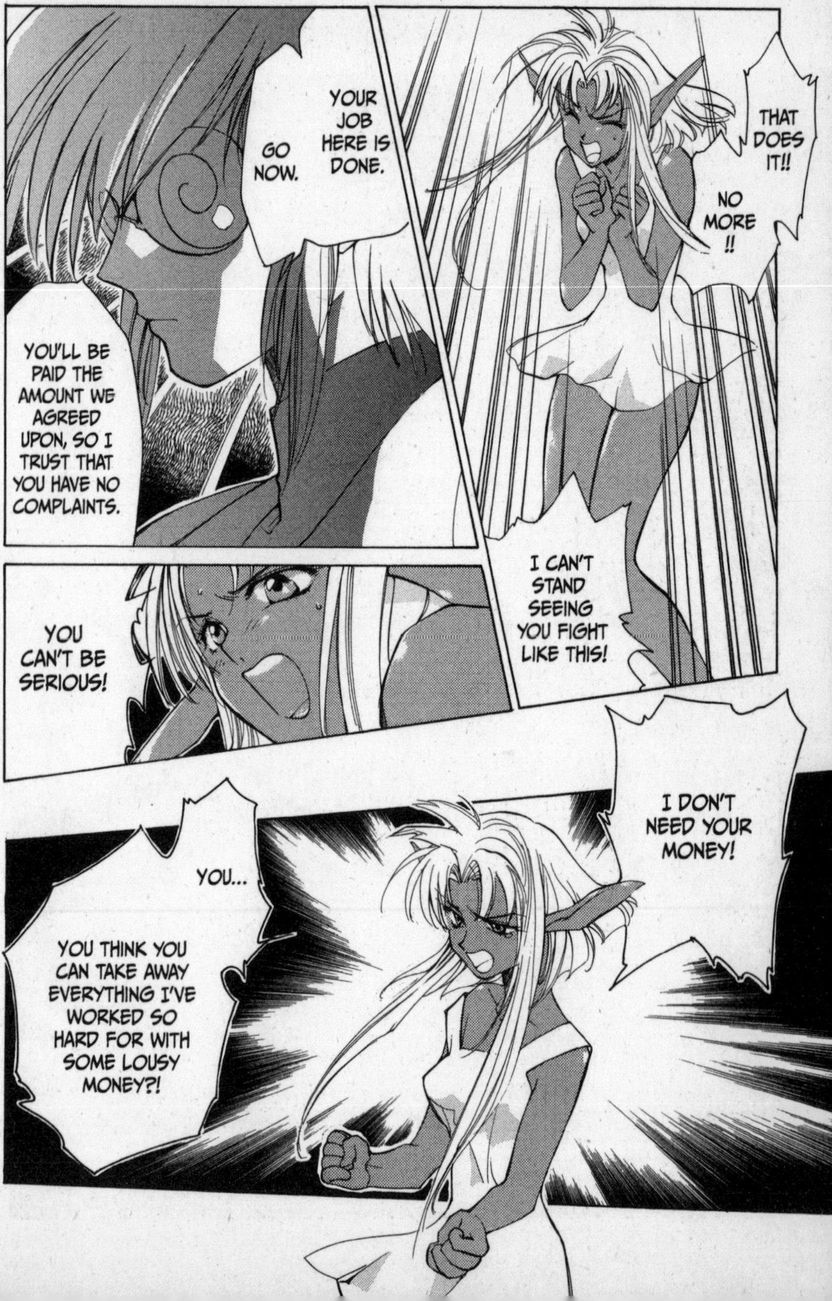
THAT DOES IT!!
NO MORE !!
I CAN'T STAND SEEING YOU FIGHT LIKE THIS!
YOUR JOB HERE IS DONE.
GO NOW.
YOU'LL BE PAID THE AMOUNT WE AGREED UPON, SO I TRUST THAT YOU HAVE NO COMPLAINTS.
YOU CAN'T BE SERIOUS!
I DON'T NEED YOUR MONEY!
YOU...
YOU THINK YOU CAN TAKE AWAY EVERYTHING I'VE WORKED SO HARD FOR WITH SOME LOUSY MONEY?!

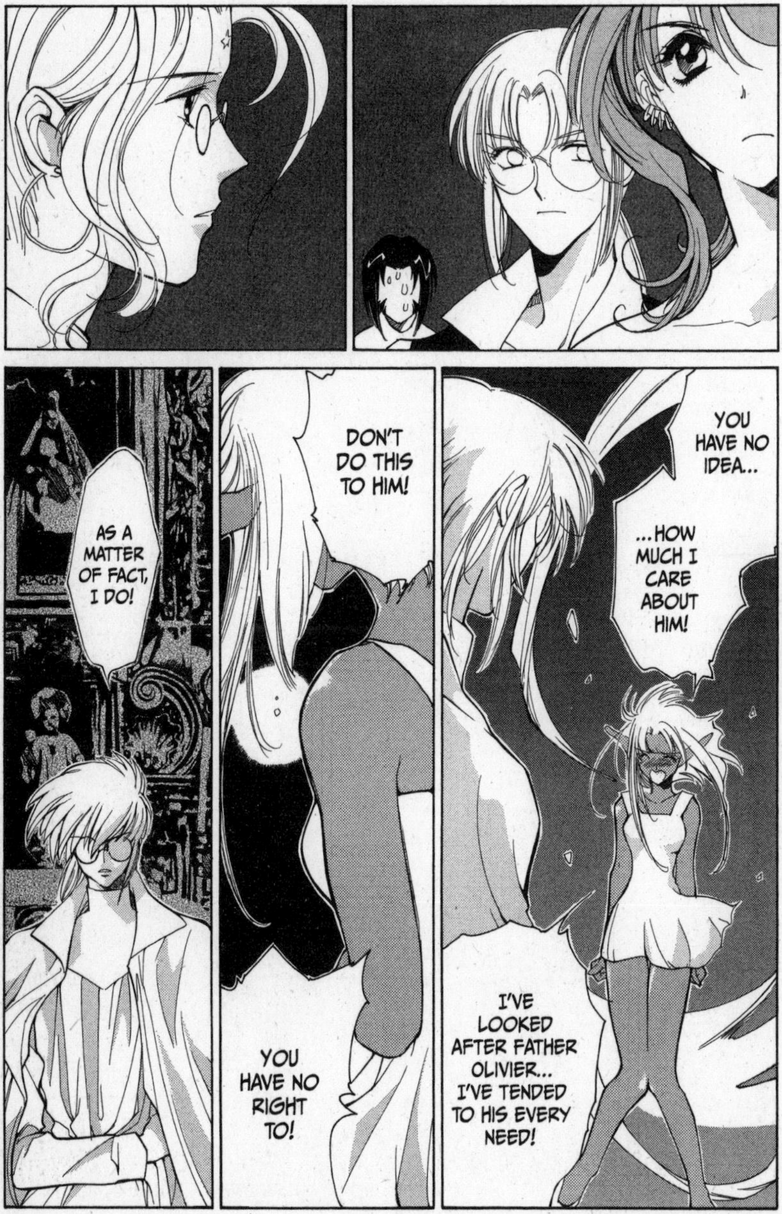
YOU HAVE NO IDEA...
...HOW MUCH I CARE ABOUT HIM!
I'VE LOOKED AFTER FATHER OLIVIER... I'VE TENDED TO HIS EVERY NEED!
DON'T DO THIS TO HIM!
YOU HAVE NO RIGHT TO!
AS A MATTER OF FACT, I DO!

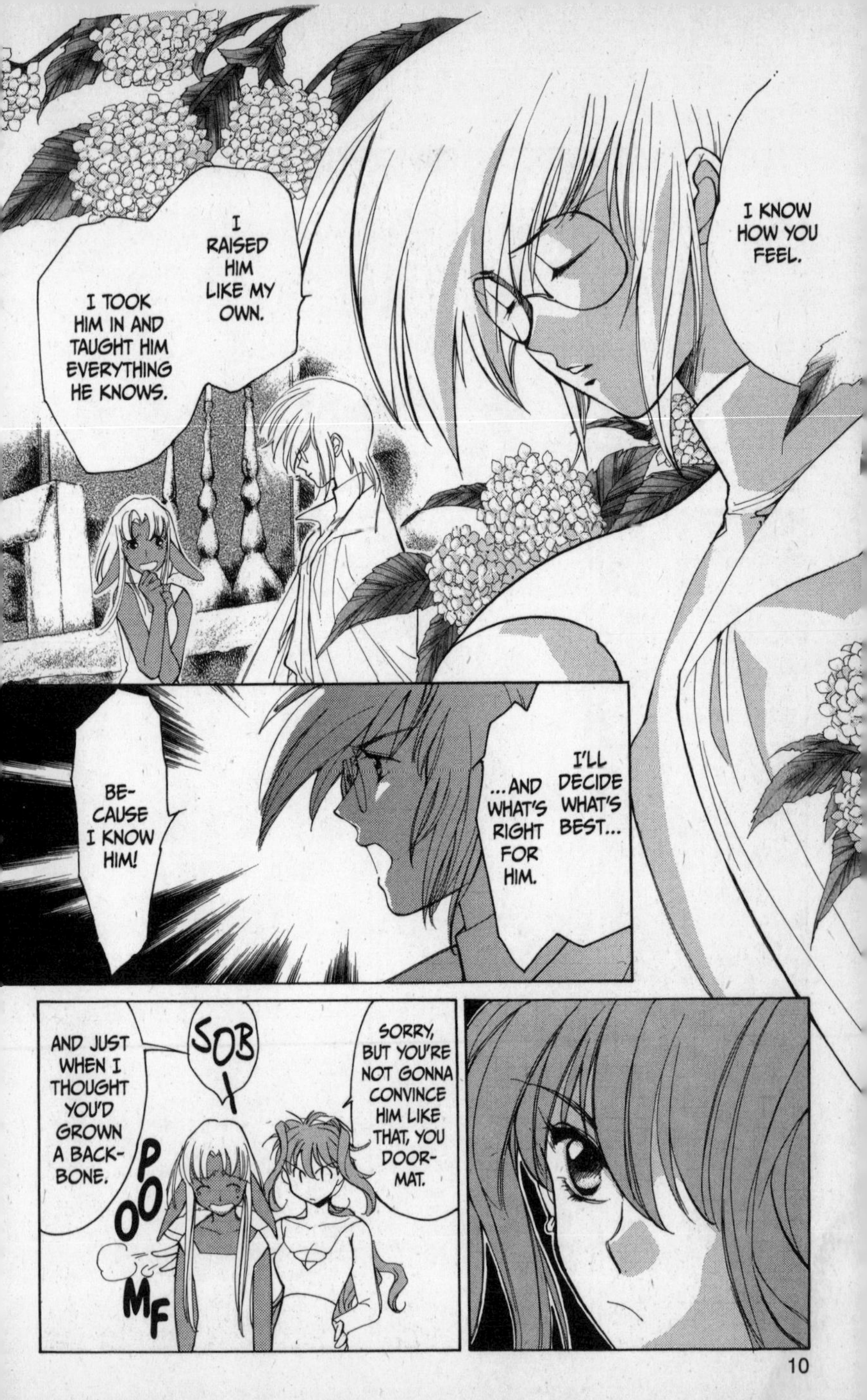

I KNOW HOW YOU FEEL.
I RAISED HIM LIKE MY OWN.
I TOOK HIM IN AND TAUGHT HIM EVERYTHING HE KNOWS.
I'LL DECIDE WHAT'S BEST...
...AND WHAT'S RIGHT FOR HIM.
BE-CAUSE I KNOW HIM!
SORRY, BUT YOU'RE NOT GONNA CONVINCE HIM LIKE THAT, YOU DOOR-MAT.
SOB
AND JUST WHEN I THOUGHT YOU'D GROWN A BACK-BONE.
POOOMF

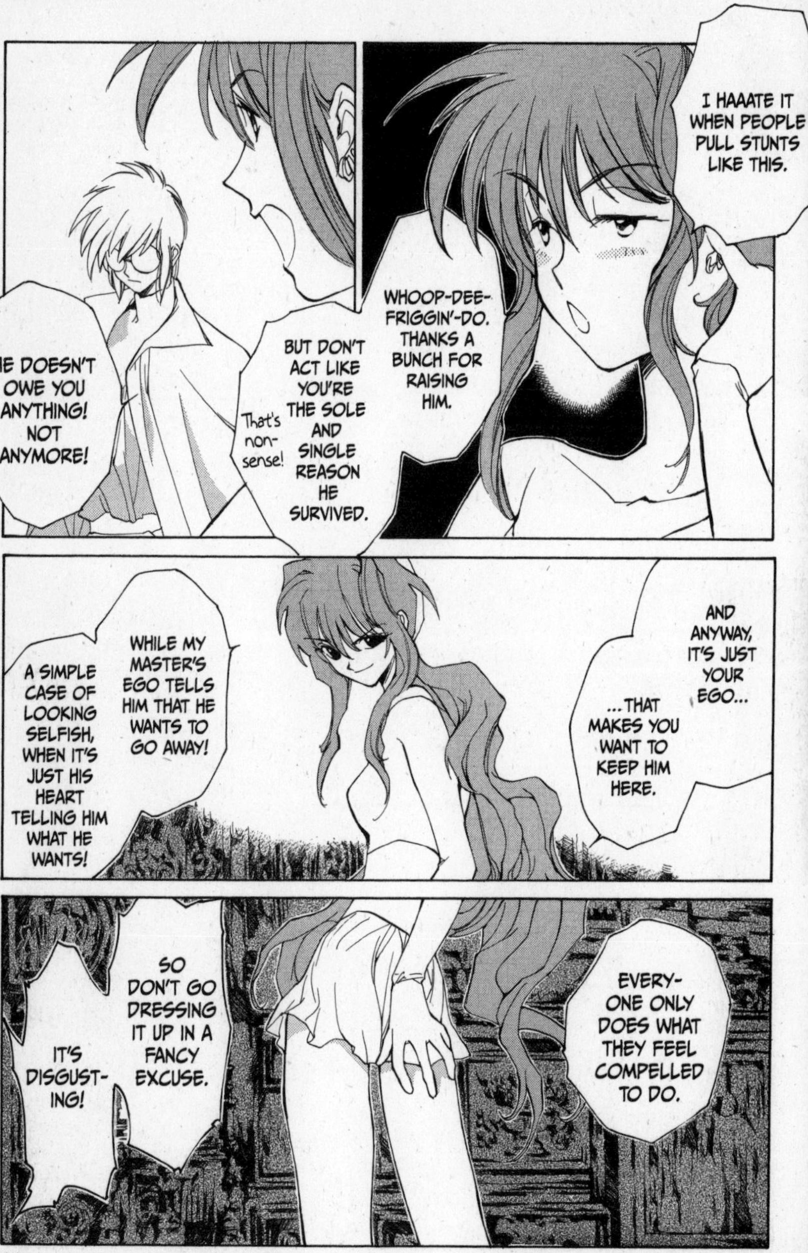
I HAAATE IT WHEN PEOPLE PULL STUNTS LIKE THIS.
WHOOP-DEE-FRIGGIN'-DO. THANKS A BUNCH FOR RAISING HIM.
BUT DON'T ACT LIKE YOU'RE THE SOLE AND SINGLE REASON HE SURVIVED.
That's non-sense!
HE DOESN'T OWE YOU ANYTHING! NOT ANYMORE!
AND ANYWAY, IT'S JUST YOUR EGO...
...THAT MAKES YOU WANT TO KEEP HIM HERE.
WHILE MY MASTER'S EGO TELLS HIM THAT HE WANTS TO GO AWAY!
A SIMPLE CASE OF LOOKING SELFISH, WHEN IT'S JUST HIS HEART TELLING HIM WHAT HE WANTS!
EVERY-ONE ONLY DOES WHAT THEY FEEL COMPELLED TO DO.
SO DON'T GO DRESSING IT UP IN A FANCY EXCUSE.
IT'S DISGUST-ING!

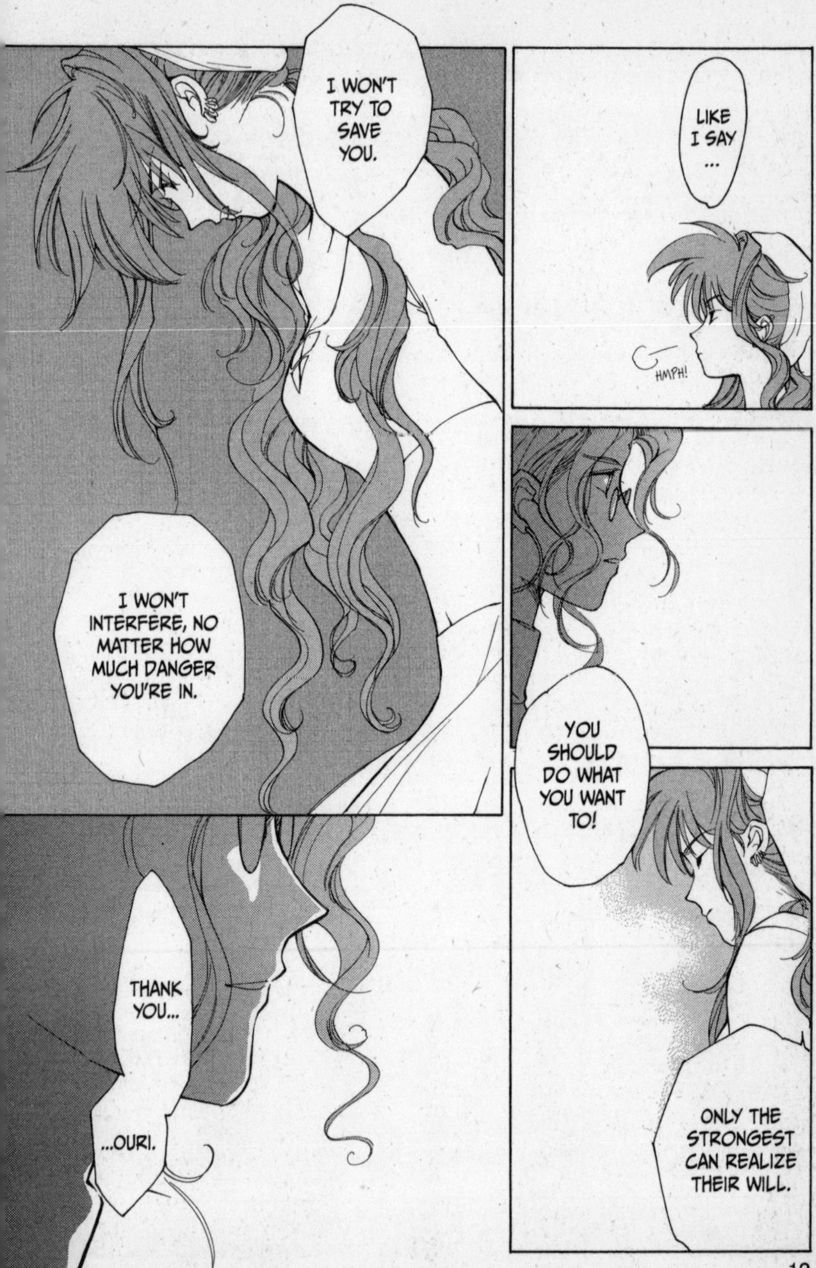
LIKE I SAY ...
HMPH!
YOU SHOULD DO WHAT YOU WANT TO!
ONLY THE STRONGEST CAN REALIZE THEIR WILL.
I WON'T TRY TO SAVE YOU.
I WON'T INTERFERE, NO MATTER HOW MUCH DANGER YOU'RE IN.
THANK YOU...
...OURI.

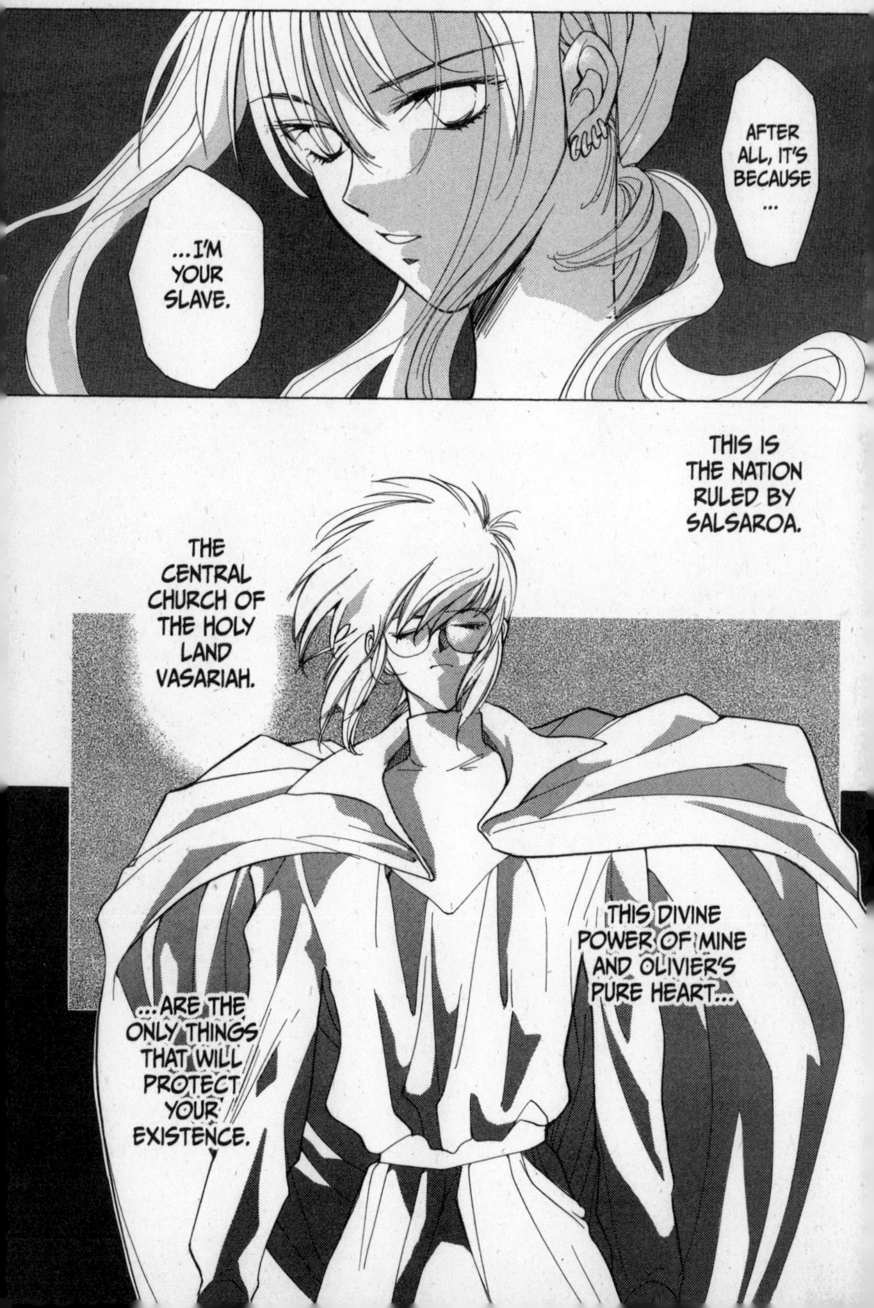
AFTER ALL, IT'S BECAUSE ...
...I'M YOUR SLAVE.
THIS IS THE NATION RULED BY SALSAROA.
THE CENTRAL CHURCH OF THE HOLY LAND VASARIAH.
THIS DIVINE POWER OF MINE AND OLIVIER'S PURE HEART...
...ARE THE ONLY THINGS THAT WILL PROTECT YOUR EXISTENCE.

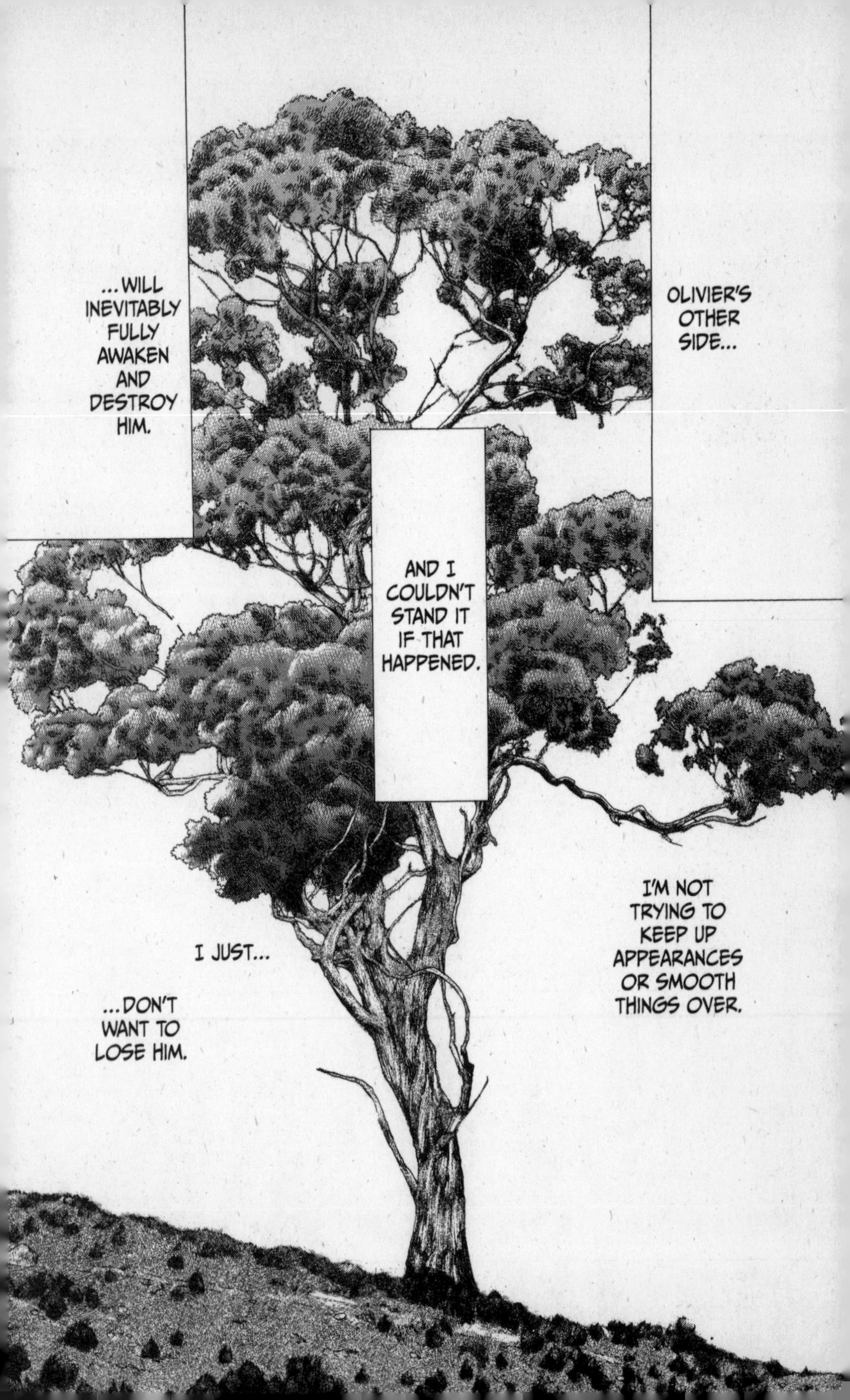
OLIVIER'S OTHER SIDE...
...WILL INEVITABLY FULLY AWAKEN AND DESTROY HIM.
AND I COULDN'T STAND IT IF THAT HAPPENED.
I'M NOT TRYING TO KEEP UP APPEARANCES OR SMOOTH THINGS OVER.
I JUST...
...DON'T WANT TO LOSE HIM.

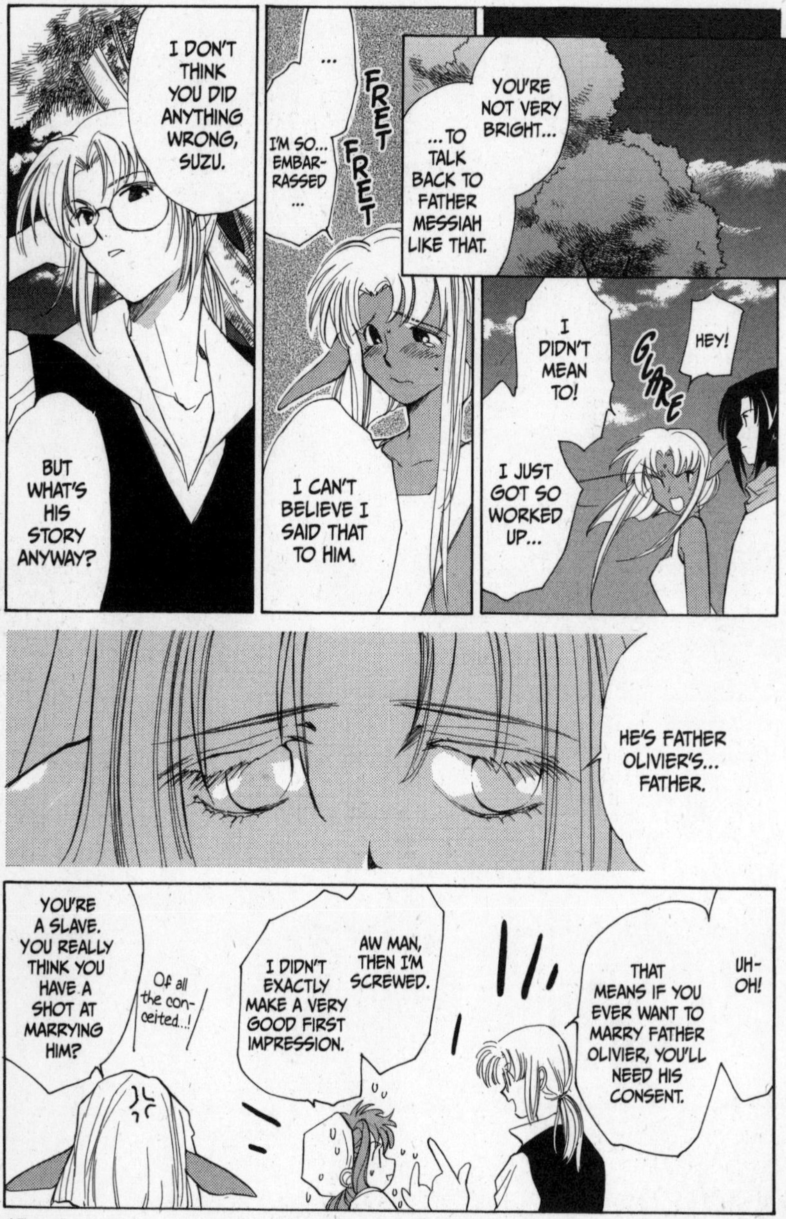
YOU'RE NOT VERY BRIGHT...
...TO TALK BACK TO FATHER MESSIAH LIKE THAT.
HEY!
GLARE
I DIDN'T MEAN TO!
I JUST GOT SO WORKED UP...
...
FRET FRET
I'M SO... EMBARRASSED...
I CAN'T BELIEVE I SAID THAT TO HIM.
I DON'T THINK YOU DID ANYTHING WRONG, SUZU.
BUT WHAT'S HIS STORY ANYWAY?
HE'S FATHER OLIVIER'S... FATHER.
UH-OH!
THAT MEANS IF YOU EVER WANT TO MARRY FATHER OLIVIER, YOU'LL NEED HIS CONSENT.
AW MAN, THEN I'M SCREWED.
I DIDN'T EXACTLY MAKE A VERY GOOD FIRST IMPRESSION.
Of all the conceited...!
YOU'RE A SLAVE. YOU REALLY THINK YOU HAVE A SHOT AT MARRYING HIM?

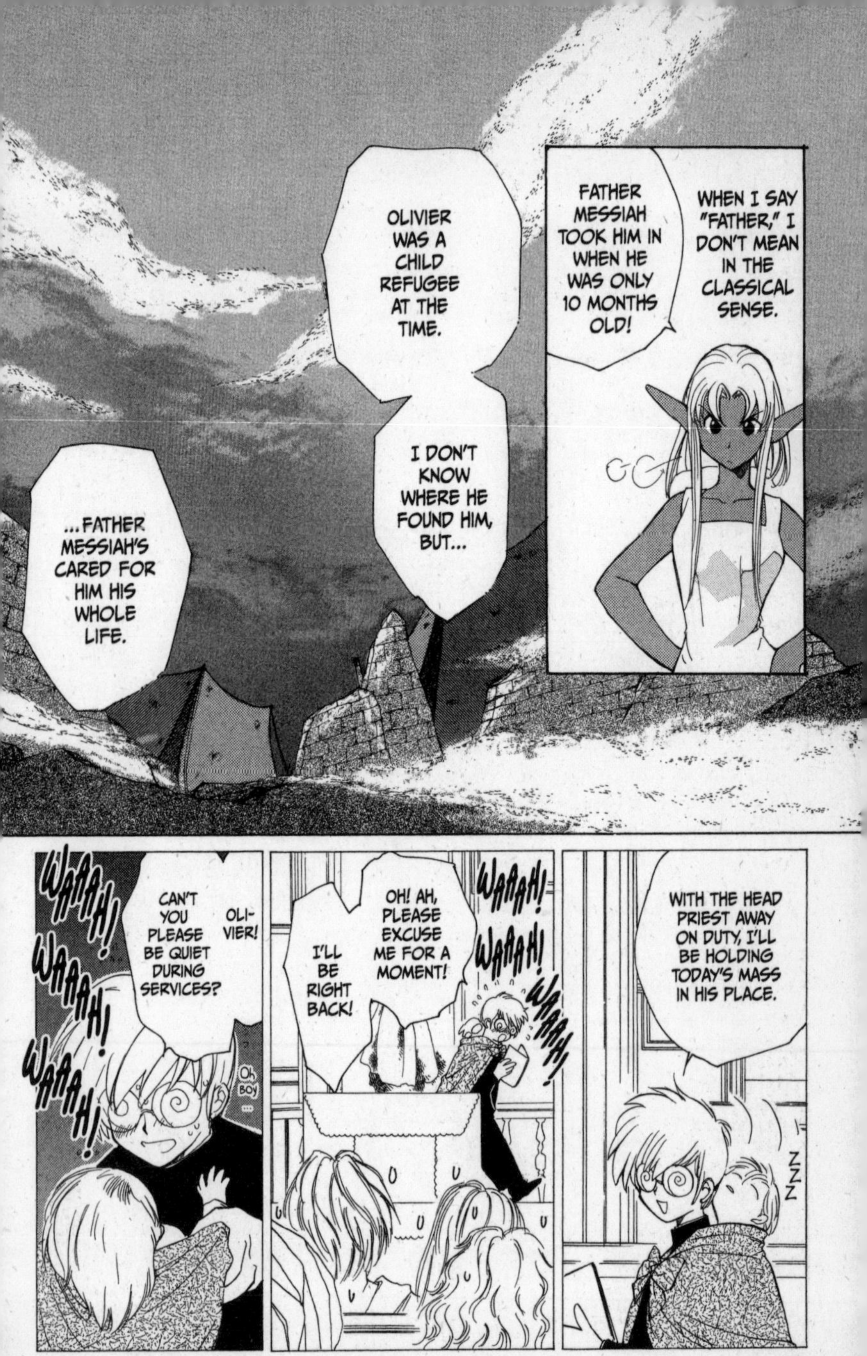
WHEN I SAY "FATHER," I DON'T MEAN IN THE CLASSICAL SENSE.
FATHER MESSIAH TOOK HIM IN WHEN HE WAS ONLY 10 MONTHS OLD!
OLIVIER WAS A CHILD REFUGEE AT THE TIME.
I DON'T KNOW WHERE HE FOUND HIM, BUT...
...FATHER MESSIAH'S CARED FOR HIM HIS WHOLE LIFE.
WITH THE HEAD PRIEST AWAY ON DUTY, I'LL BE HOLDING TODAY'S MASS IN HIS PLACE.
ZZZ
WAAAH! WAAAH! WAAAH!
OH! AH, PLEASE EXCUSE ME FOR A MOMENT!
I'LL BE RIGHT BACK!
OLI- VIER!
CAN'T YOU PLEASE BE QUIET DURING SERVICES?
Oh boy...
WAAAH! WAAAH! WAAAH!

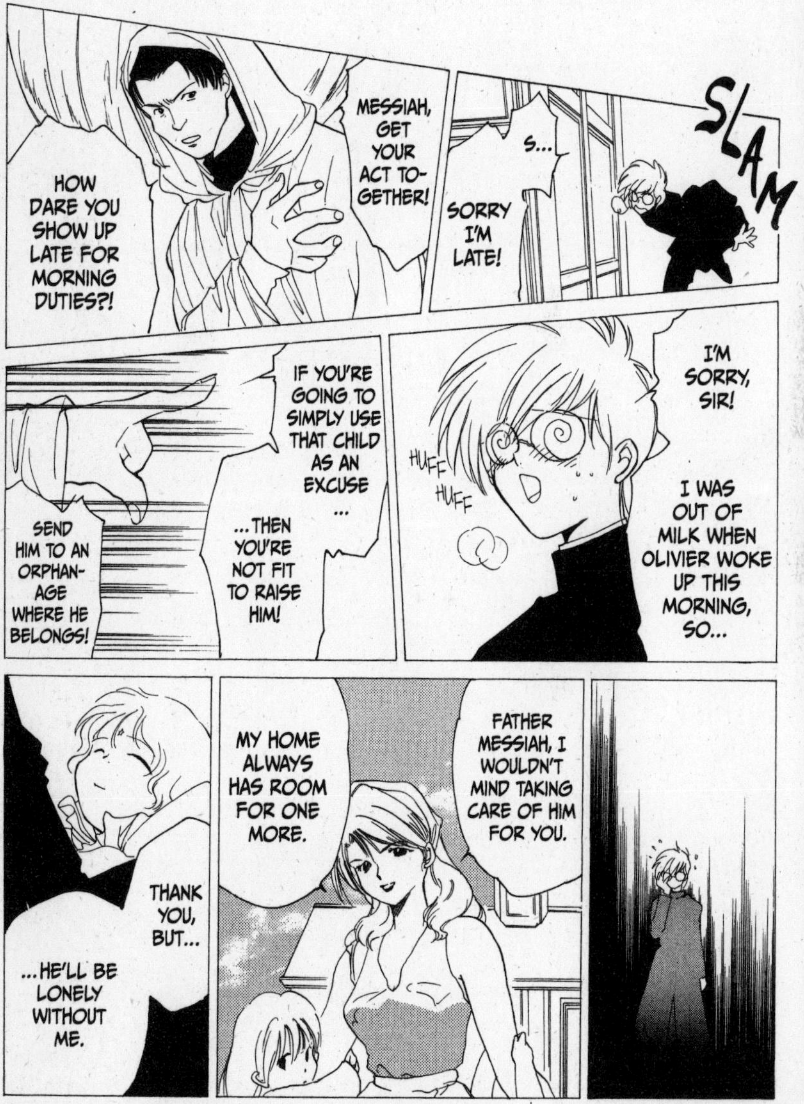
SLAM
S...
SORRY I'M LATE!
MESSIAH, GET YOUR ACT TOGETHER!
HOW DARE YOU SHOW UP LATE FOR MORNING DUTIES?!
I'M SORRY, SIR!
HUFF HUFF
I WAS OUT OF MILK WHEN OLIVIER WOKE UP THIS MORNING, SO...
IF YOU'RE GOING TO SIMPLY USE THAT CHILD AS AN EXCUSE...
...THEN YOU'RE NOT FIT TO RAISE HIM!
SEND HIM TO AN ORPHANAGE WHERE HE BELONGS!
FATHER MESSIAH, I WOULDN'T MIND TAKING CARE OF HIM FOR YOU.
MY HOME ALWAYS HAS ROOM FOR ONE MORE.
THANK YOU, BUT...
...HE'LL BE LONELY WITHOUT ME.

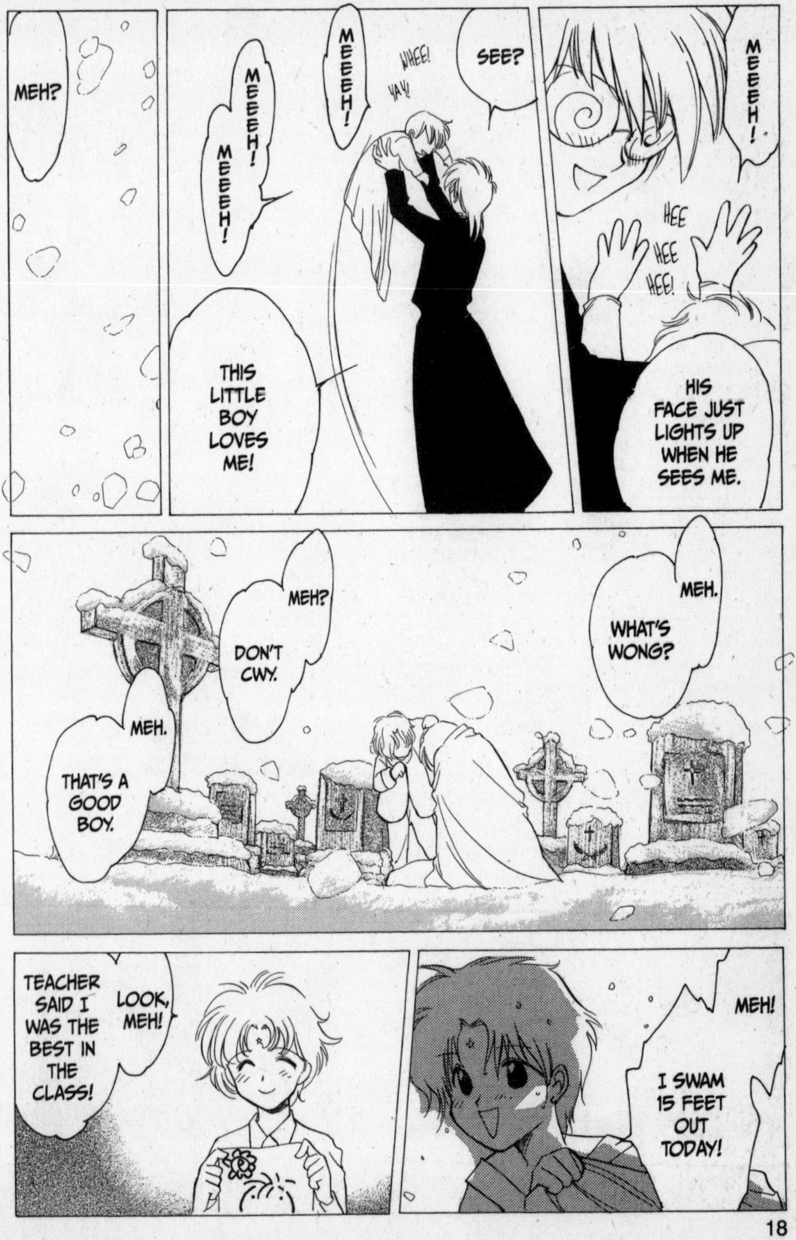
MEEEH!
HEE HEE HEE!
HIS FACE JUST LIGHTS UP WHEN HE SEES ME.
SEE?
WHEE!
YAY!
MEEEH!
MEEEH!
MEEEH!
THIS LITTLE BOY LOVES ME!
MEH?
MEH.
WHAT'S WONG?
MEH?
DON'T CWY.
MEH.
THAT'S A GOOD BOY.
MEH!
I SWAM 15 FEET OUT TODAY!
LOOK, MEH!
TEACHER SAID I WAS THE BEST IN THE CLASS!

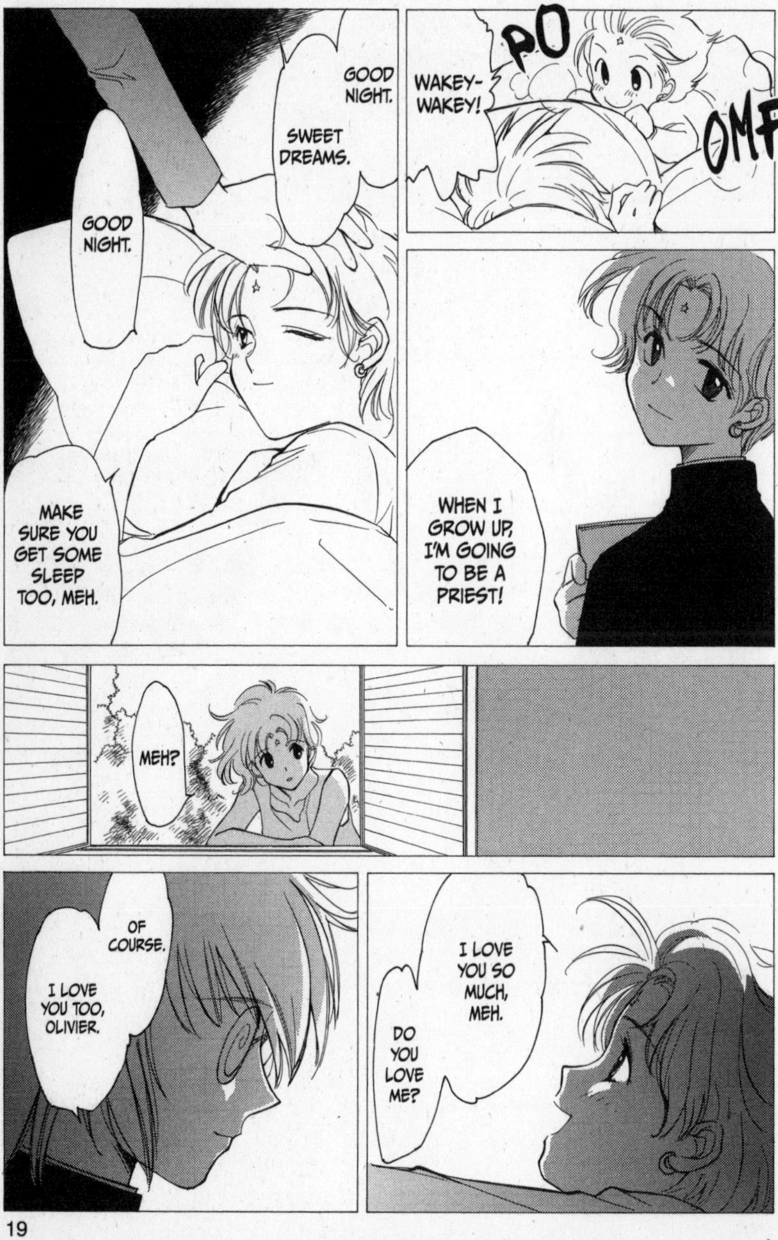
PO
OMF
WAKEY-WAKEY!
WHEN I GROW UP, I'M GOING TO BE A PRIEST!
GOOD NIGHT.
SWEET DREAMS.
GOOD NIGHT.
MAKE SURE YOU GET SOME SLEEP TOO, MEH.
MEH?
I LOVE YOU SO MUCH, MEH.
DO YOU LOVE ME?
OF COURSE.
I LOVE YOU TOO, OLIVIER.

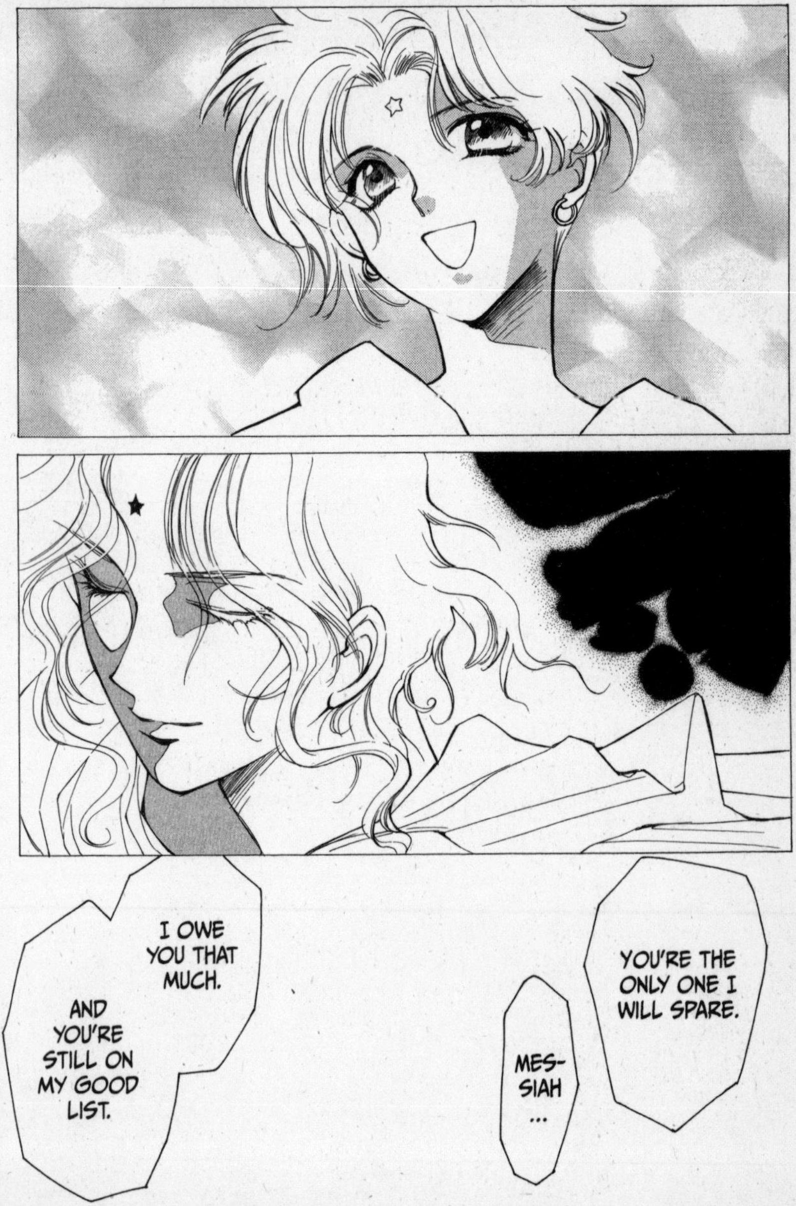
YOU'RE THE ONLY ONE I WILL SPARE.
MES-SIAH ...
I OWE YOU THAT MUCH.
AND YOU'RE STILL ON MY GOOD LIST.

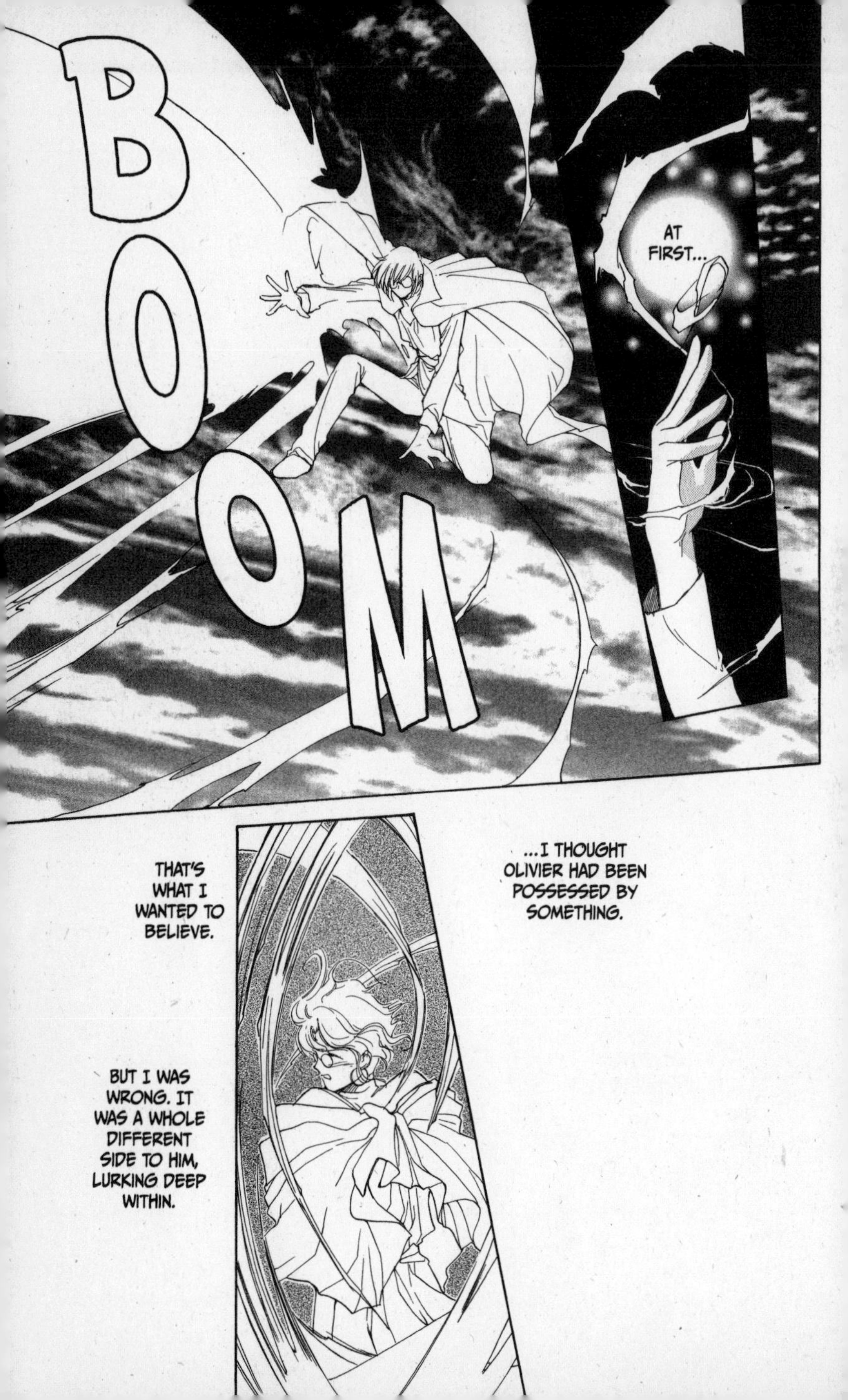
AT FIRST...
BOOM
...I THOUGHT OLIVIER HAD BEEN POSSESSED BY SOMETHING.
THAT'S WHAT I WANTED TO BELIEVE.
BUT I WAS WRONG. IT WAS A WHOLE DIFFERENT SIDE TO HIM, LURKING DEEP WITHIN.

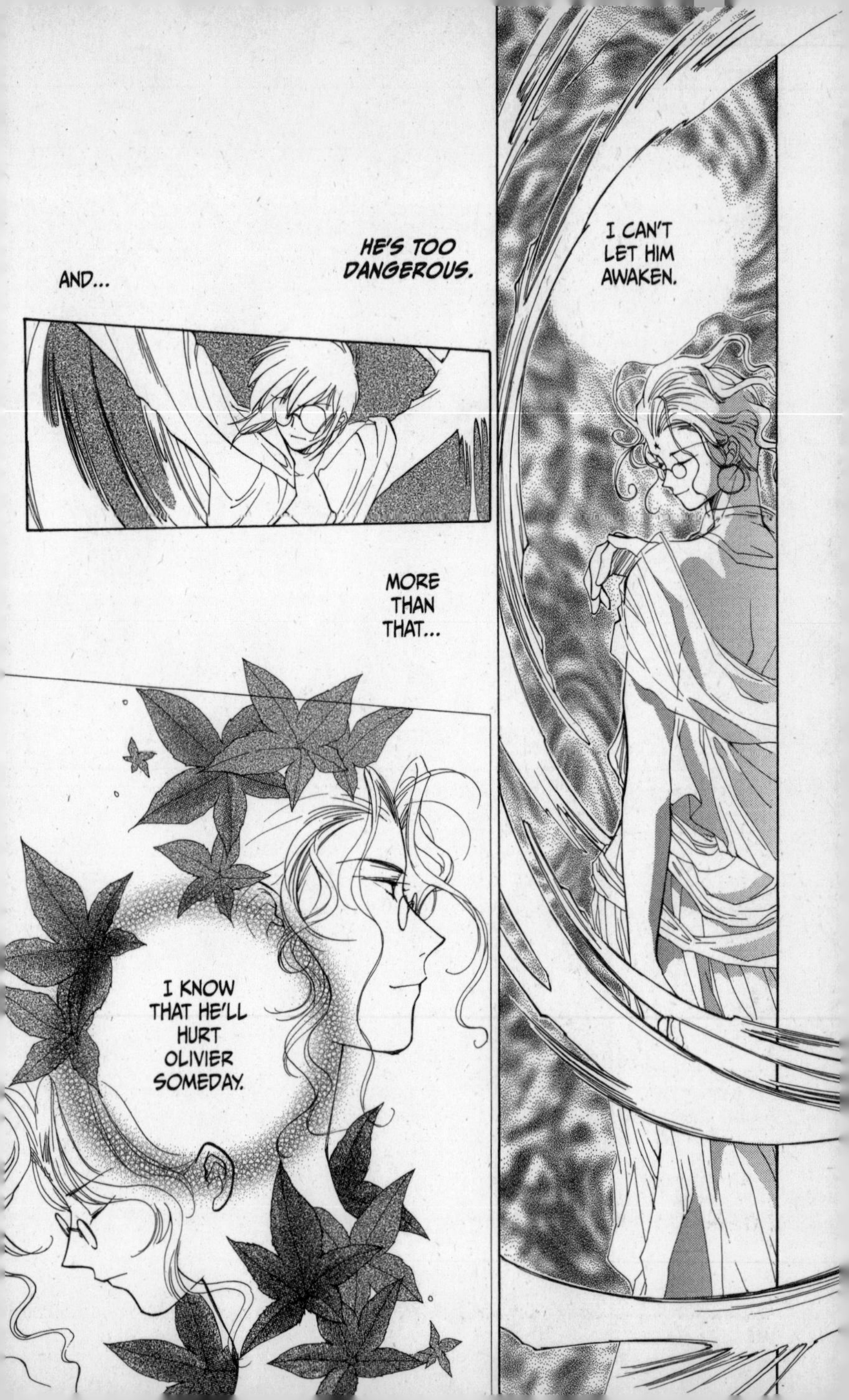
I CAN'T LET HIM AWAKEN.
HE'S TOO DANGEROUS.
AND...
MORE THAN THAT...
I KNOW THAT HE'LL HURT OLIVIER SOMEDAY.

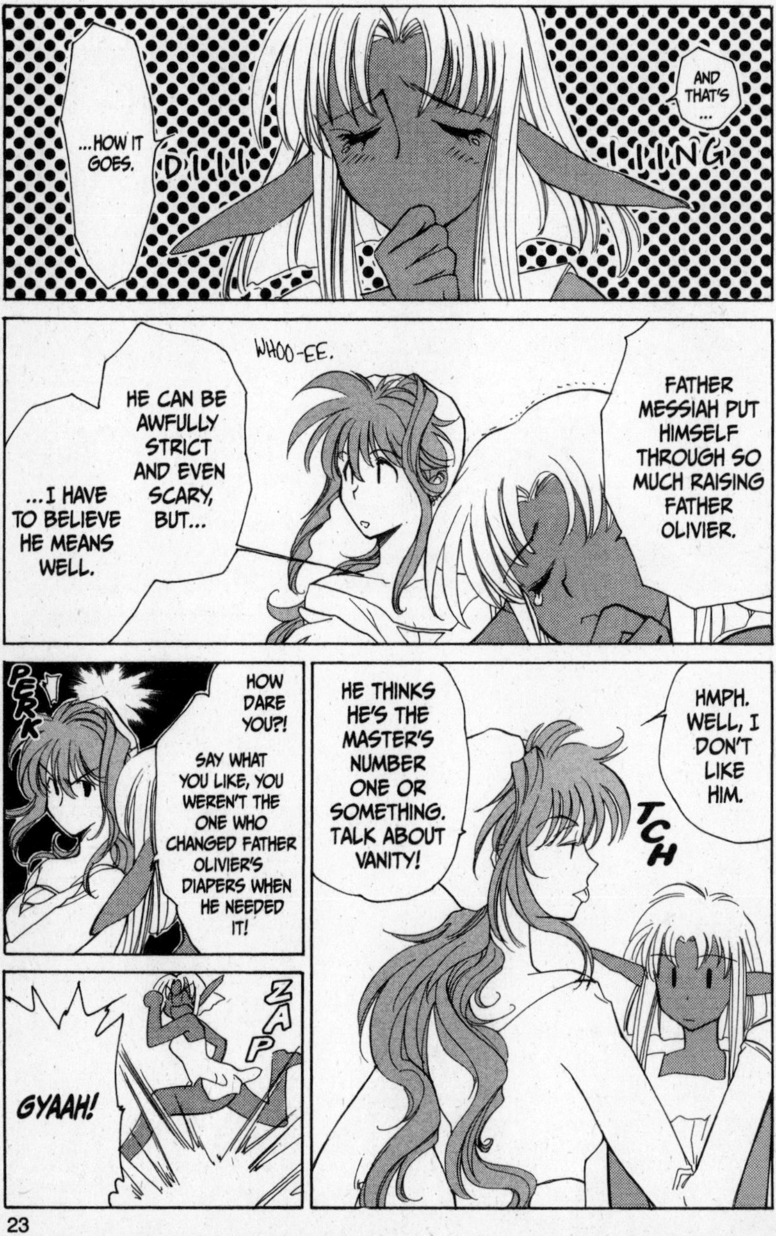
AND THAT'S ...
DIIII IIING
...HOW IT GOES.
FATHER MESSIAH PUT HIMSELF THROUGH SO MUCH RAISING FATHER OLIVIER.
WHOO-EE.
HE CAN BE AWFULLY STRICT AND EVEN SCARY, BUT...
...I HAVE TO BELIEVE HE MEANS WELL.
HMPH. WELL, I DON'T LIKE HIM.
TCH
HE THINKS HE'S THE MASTER'S NUMBER ONE OR SOMETHING. TALK ABOUT VANITY!
HOW DARE YOU?!
SAY WHAT YOU LIKE, YOU WEREN'T THE ONE WHO CHANGED FATHER OLIVIER'S DIAPERS WHEN HE NEEDED IT!
PERK
ZAP
GYAAH!

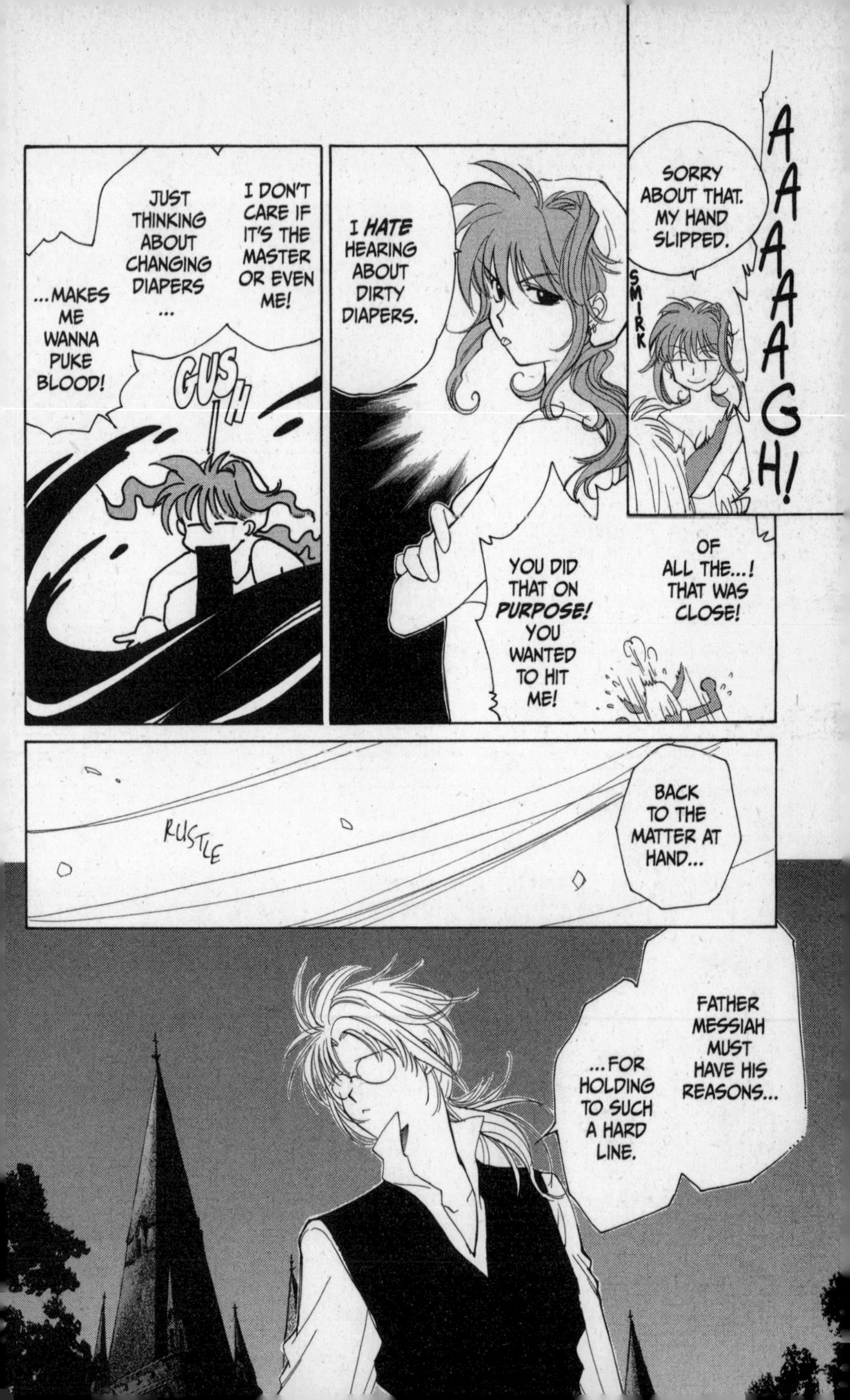
AAAAAAGH!
SORRY ABOUT THAT. MY HAND SLIPPED.
SMIRK
OF ALL THE...! THAT WAS CLOSE!
YOU DID THAT ON *PURPOSE!* YOU WANTED TO HIT ME!
I *HATE* HEARING ABOUT DIRTY DIAPERS.
I DON'T CARE IF IT'S THE MASTER OR EVEN ME!
JUST THINKING ABOUT CHANGING DIAPERS...
...MAKES ME WANNA PUKE BLOOD!
GUSH
BACK TO THE MATTER AT HAND...
RUSTLE
FATHER MESSIAH MUST HAVE HIS REASONS...
...FOR HOLDING TO SUCH A HARD LINE.

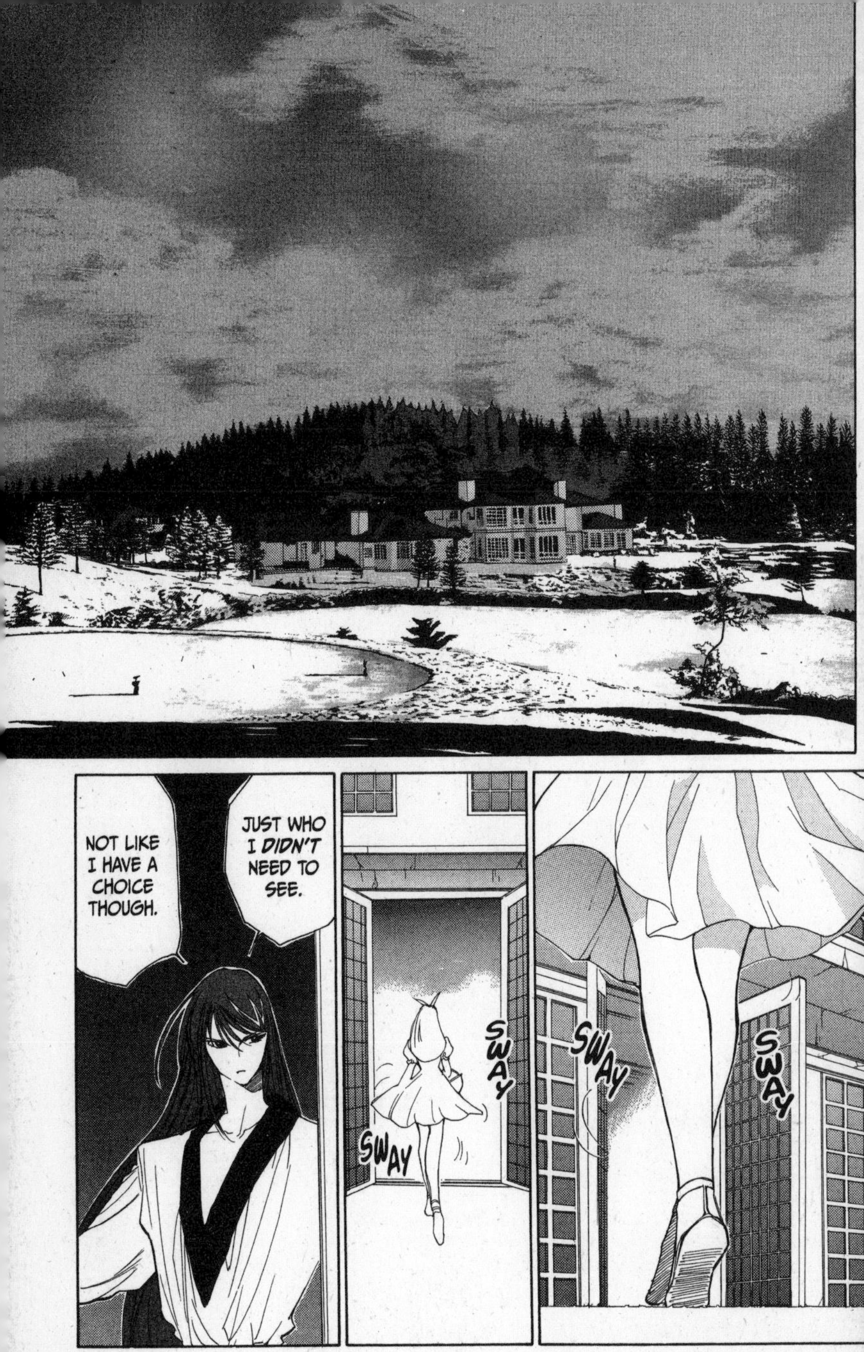
SWAY
SWAY
SWAY
SWAY
JUST WHO I *DIDN'T* NEED TO SEE.
NOT LIKE I HAVE A CHOICE THOUGH.

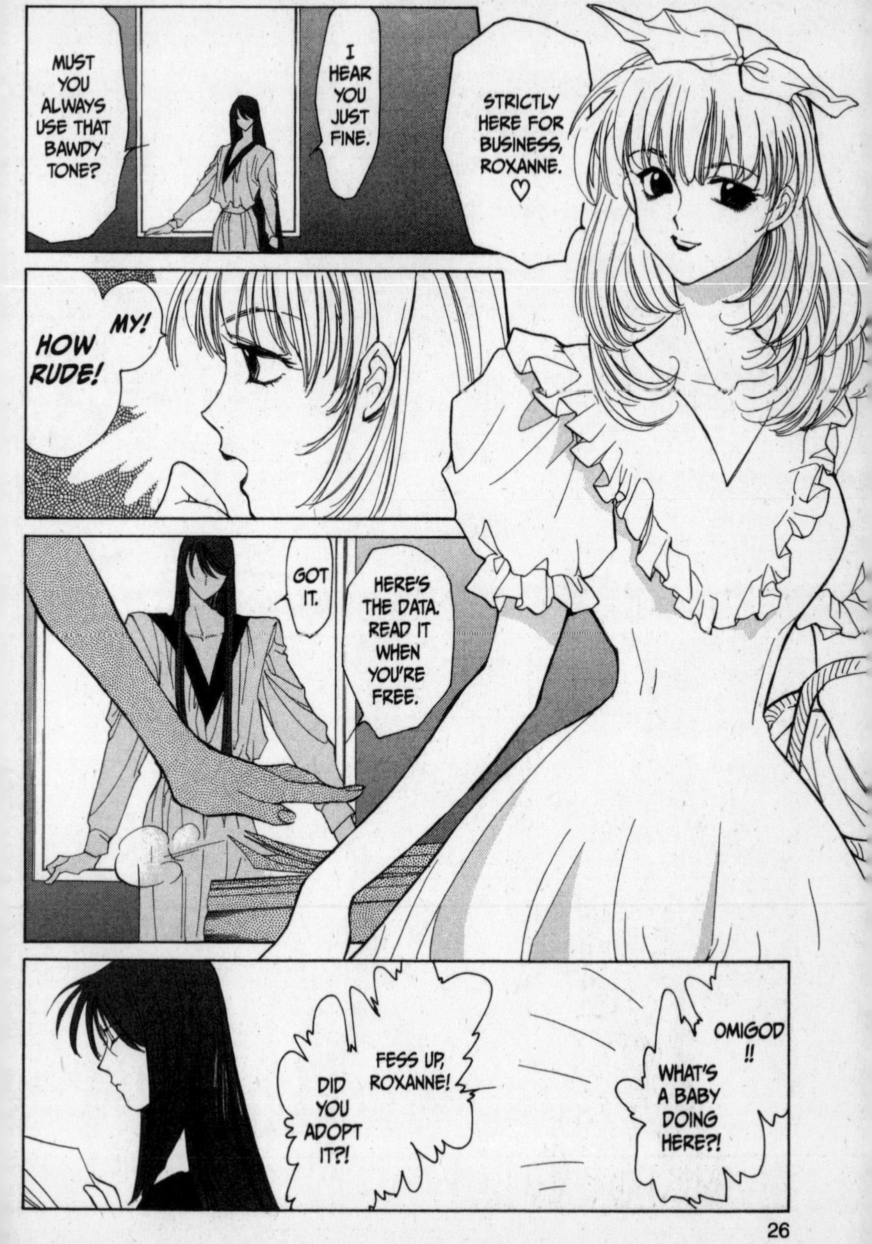
STRICTLY HERE FOR BUSINESS, ROXANNE. ♡
I HEAR YOU JUST FINE.
MUST YOU ALWAYS USE THAT BAWDY TONE?
MY! HOW RUDE!
HERE'S THE DATA. READ IT WHEN YOU'RE FREE.
GOT IT.
OMIGOD!!
WHAT'S A BABY DOING HERE?!
FESS UP, ROXANNE!
DID YOU ADOPT IT?!

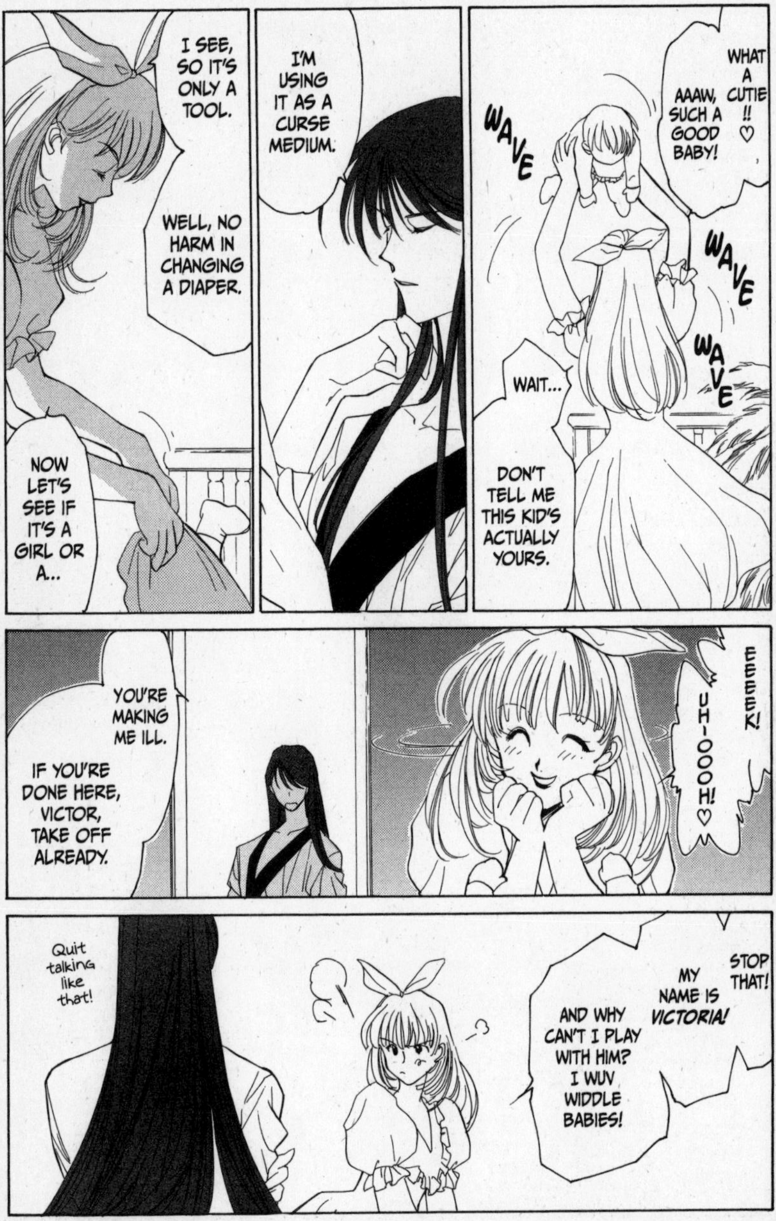
WHAT A CUTIE!! ♡
AAAW, SUCH A GOOD BABY!
WAVE
WAVE
WAVE
WAIT...
DON'T TELL ME THIS KID'S ACTUALLY YOURS.
I'M USING IT AS A CURSE MEDIUM.
I SEE, SO IT'S ONLY A TOOL.
WELL, NO HARM IN CHANGING A DIAPER.
NOW LET'S SEE IF IT'S A GIRL OR A...
EEEEK!
UH-OOOOH! ♡
YOU'RE MAKING ME ILL.
IF YOU'RE DONE HERE, VICTOR, TAKE OFF ALREADY.
STOP THAT!
MY NAME IS *VICTORIA!*
AND WHY CAN'T I PLAY WITH HIM? I WUV WIDDLE BABIES!
Quit talking like that!

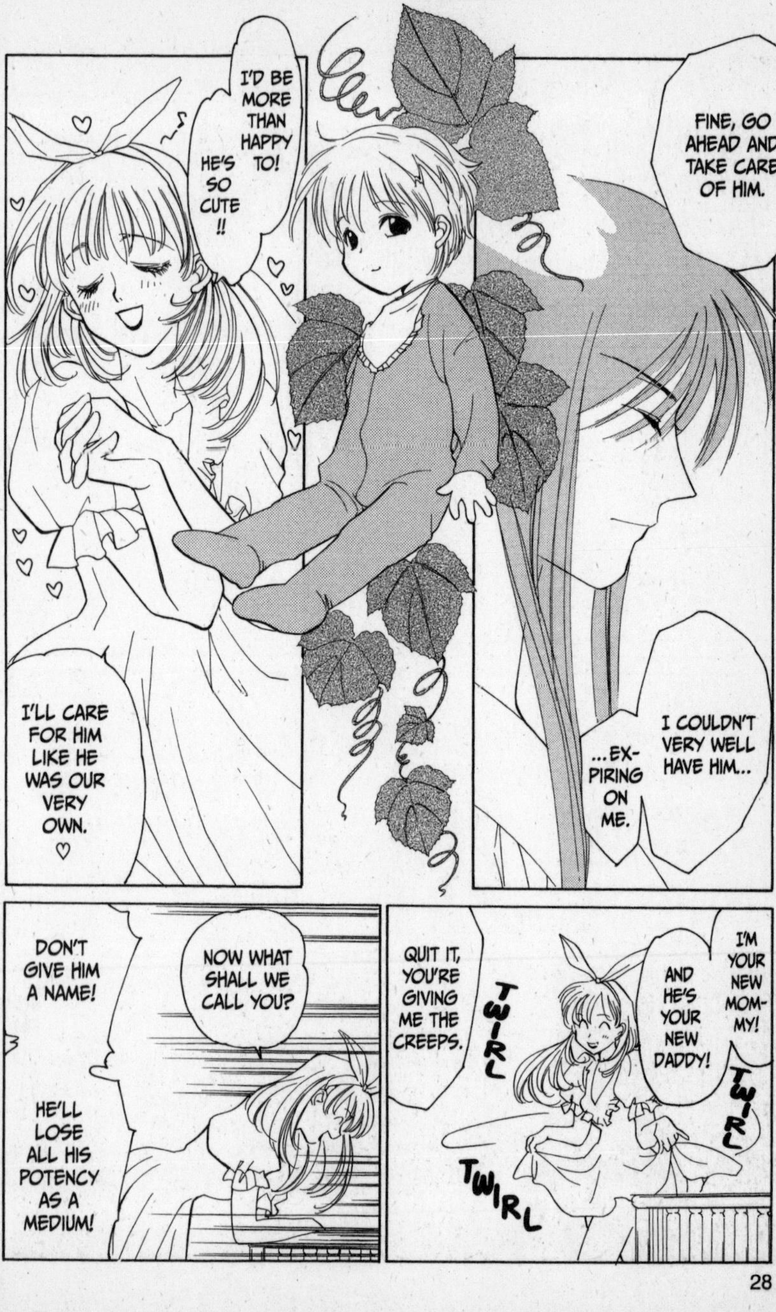
FINE, GO AHEAD AND TAKE CARE OF HIM.
I COULDN'T VERY WELL HAVE HIM...
...EX-PIRING ON ME.
I'D BE MORE THAN HAPPY TO!
HE'S SO CUTE!!
I'LL CARE FOR HIM LIKE HE WAS OUR VERY OWN. ♡
I'M YOUR NEW MOM-MY!
AND HE'S YOUR NEW DADDY!
TWIRL
TWIRL
QUIT IT, YOU'RE GIVING ME THE CREEPS.
TWIRL
NOW WHAT SHALL WE CALL YOU?
DON'T GIVE HIM A NAME!
HE'LL LOSE ALL HIS POTENCY AS A MEDIUM!

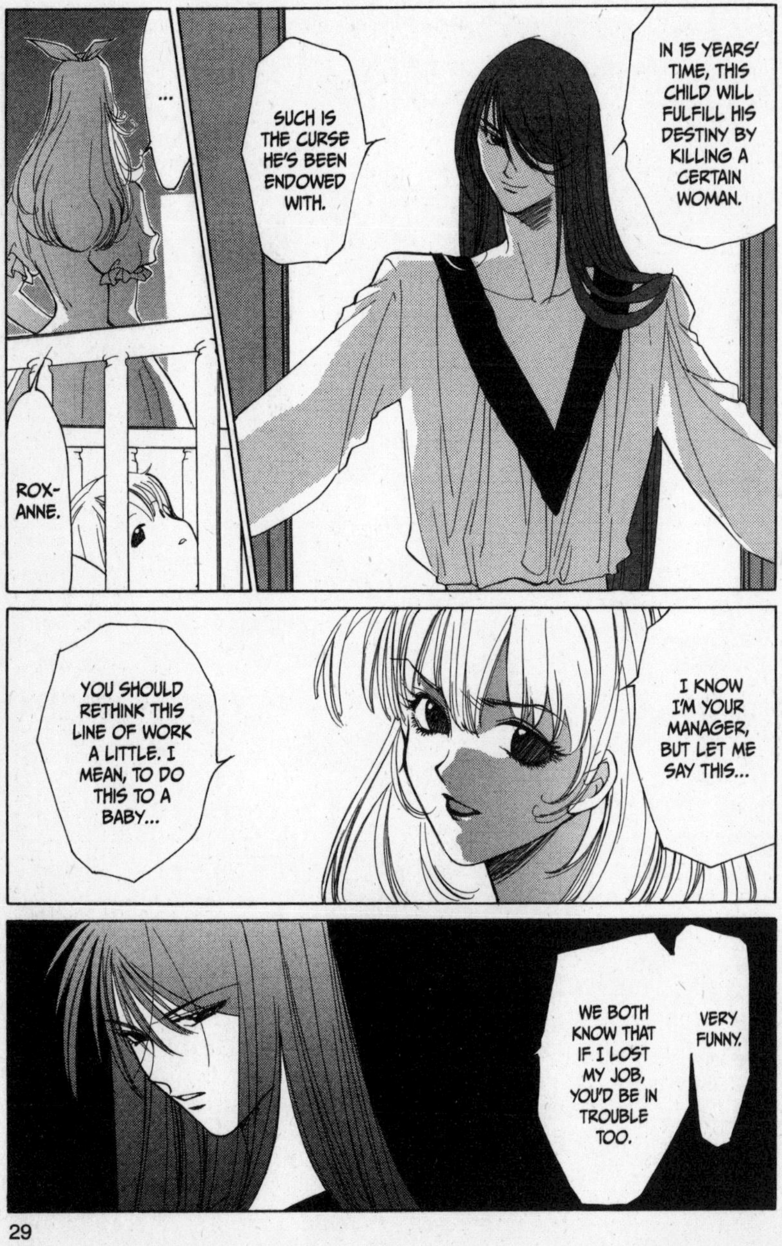
IN 15 YEARS' TIME, THIS CHILD WILL FULFILL HIS DESTINY BY KILLING A CERTAIN WOMAN.
SUCH IS THE CURSE HE'S BEEN ENDOWED WITH.
...
ROX-ANNE.
I KNOW I'M YOUR MANAGER, BUT LET ME SAY THIS...
YOU SHOULD RETHINK THIS LINE OF WORK A LITTLE. I MEAN, TO DO THIS TO A BABY...
VERY FUNNY.
WE BOTH KNOW THAT IF I LOST MY JOB, YOU'D BE IN TROUBLE TOO.

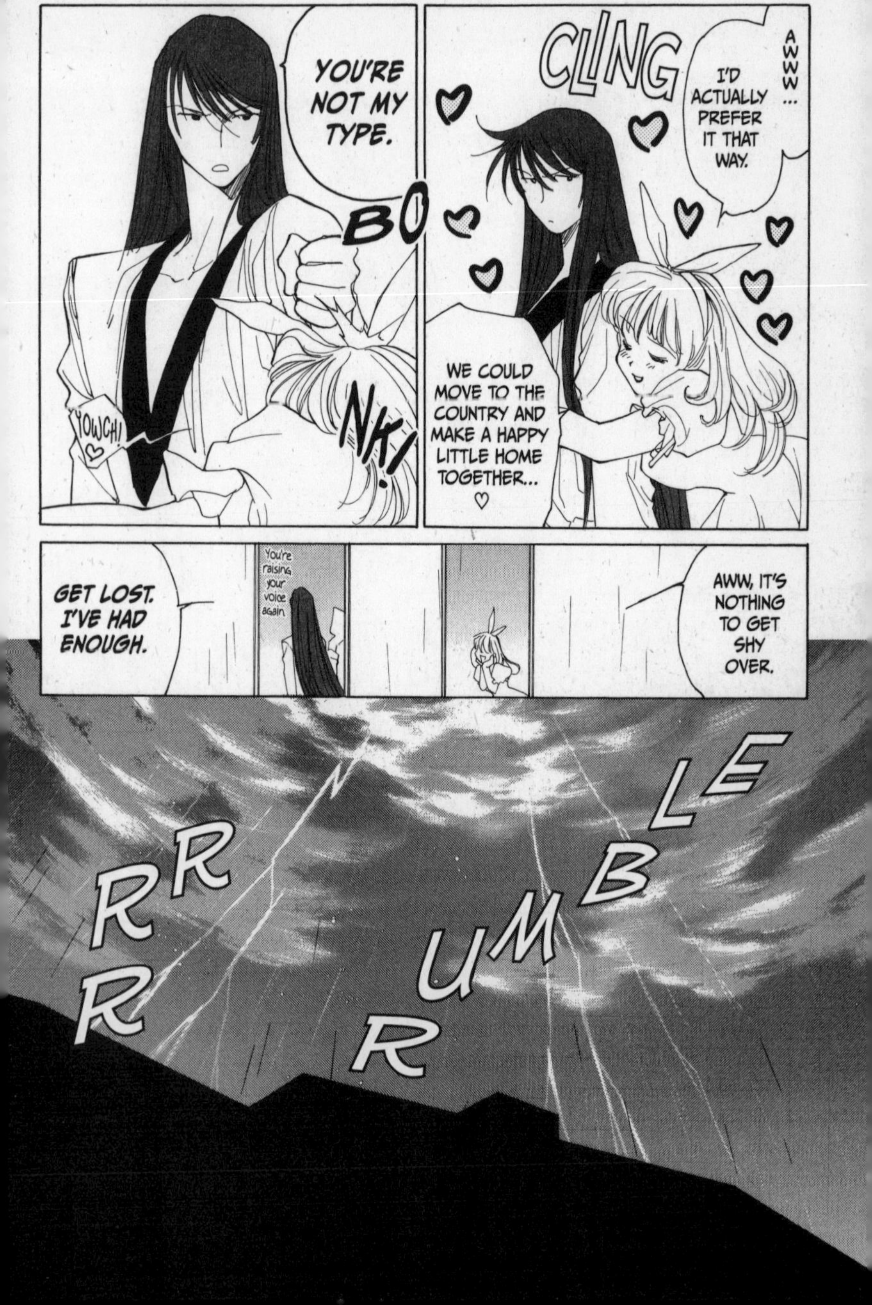
AWWW...
I'D ACTUALLY PREFER IT THAT WAY.
CLING
WE COULD MOVE TO THE COUNTRY AND MAKE A HAPPY LITTLE HOME TOGETHER... ♡
YOU'RE NOT MY TYPE.
BONK!
YOWCH! ♡
AWW, IT'S NOTHING TO GET SHY OVER.
You're raising your voice again
GET LOST. I'VE HAD ENOUGH.
RRRR
RUMBLE

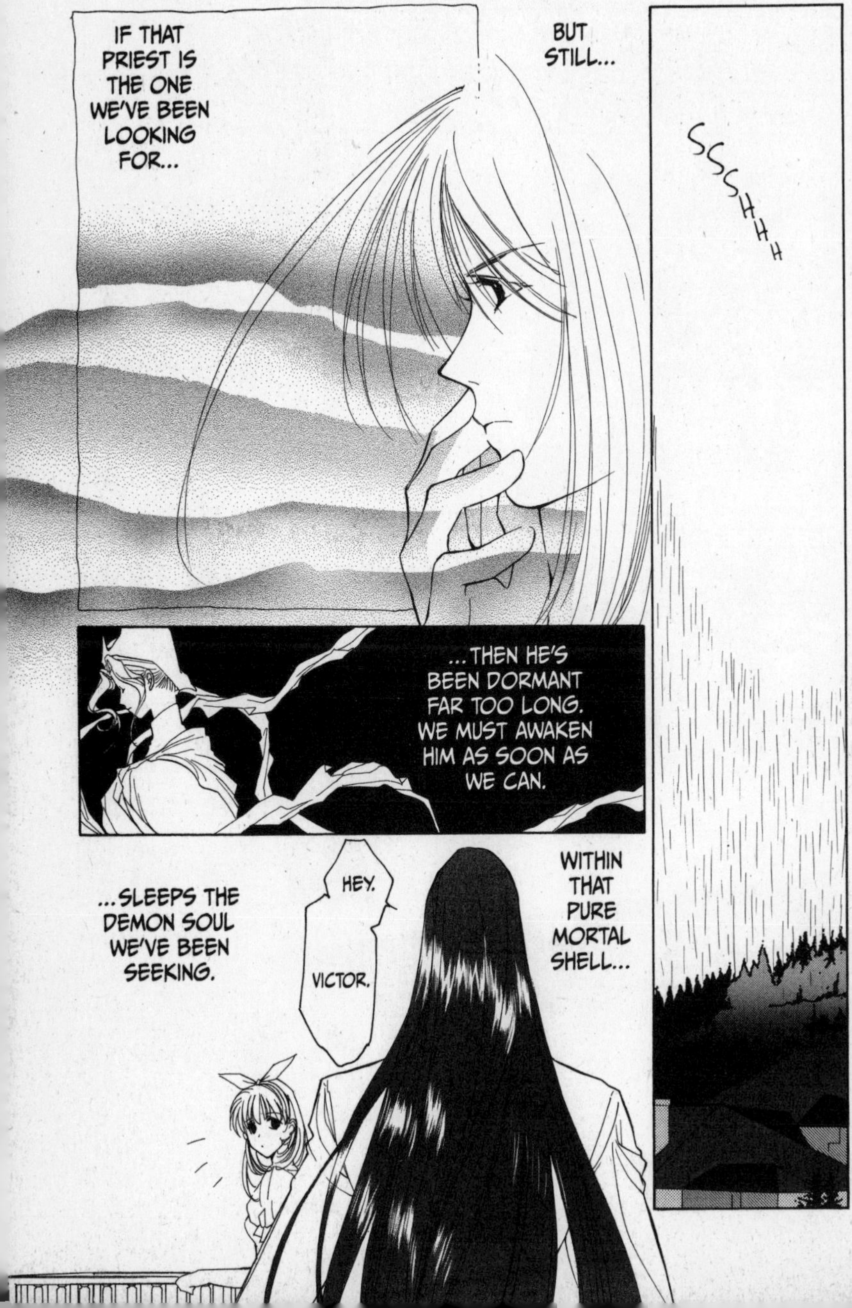
SSSHHH
BUT STILL...
IF THAT PRIEST IS THE ONE WE'VE BEEN LOOKING FOR...
...THEN HE'S BEEN DORMANT FAR TOO LONG. WE MUST AWAKEN HIM AS SOON AS WE CAN.
WITHIN THAT PURE MORTAL SHELL...
HEY.
VICTOR.
...SLEEPS THE DEMON SOUL WE'VE BEEN SEEKING.

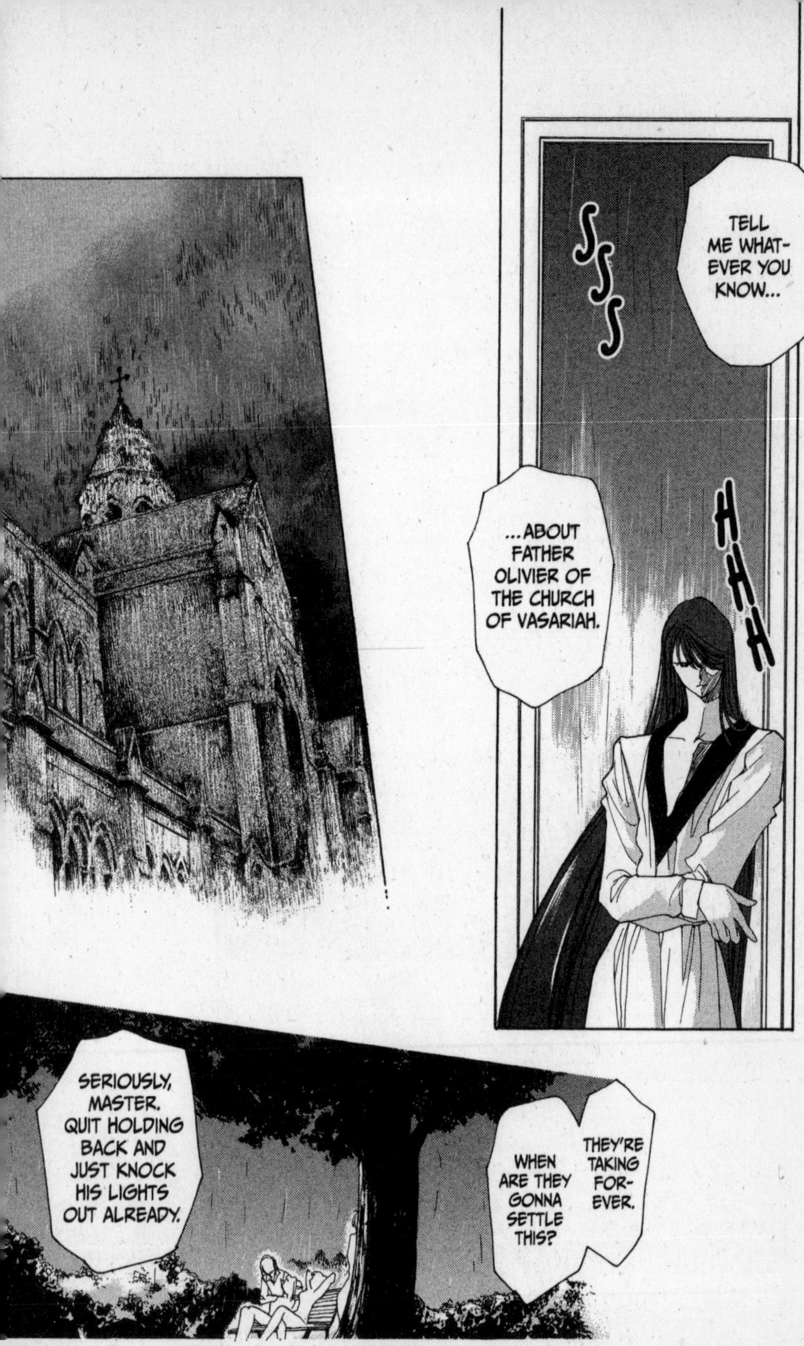
TELL ME WHAT-EVER YOU KNOW...
SSS
...ABOUT FATHER OLIVIER OF THE CHURCH OF VASARIAH.
HHHH
THEY'RE TAKING FOR-EVER.
WHEN ARE THEY GONNA SETTLE THIS?
SERIOUSLY, MASTER. QUIT HOLDING BACK AND JUST KNOCK HIS LIGHTS OUT ALREADY.

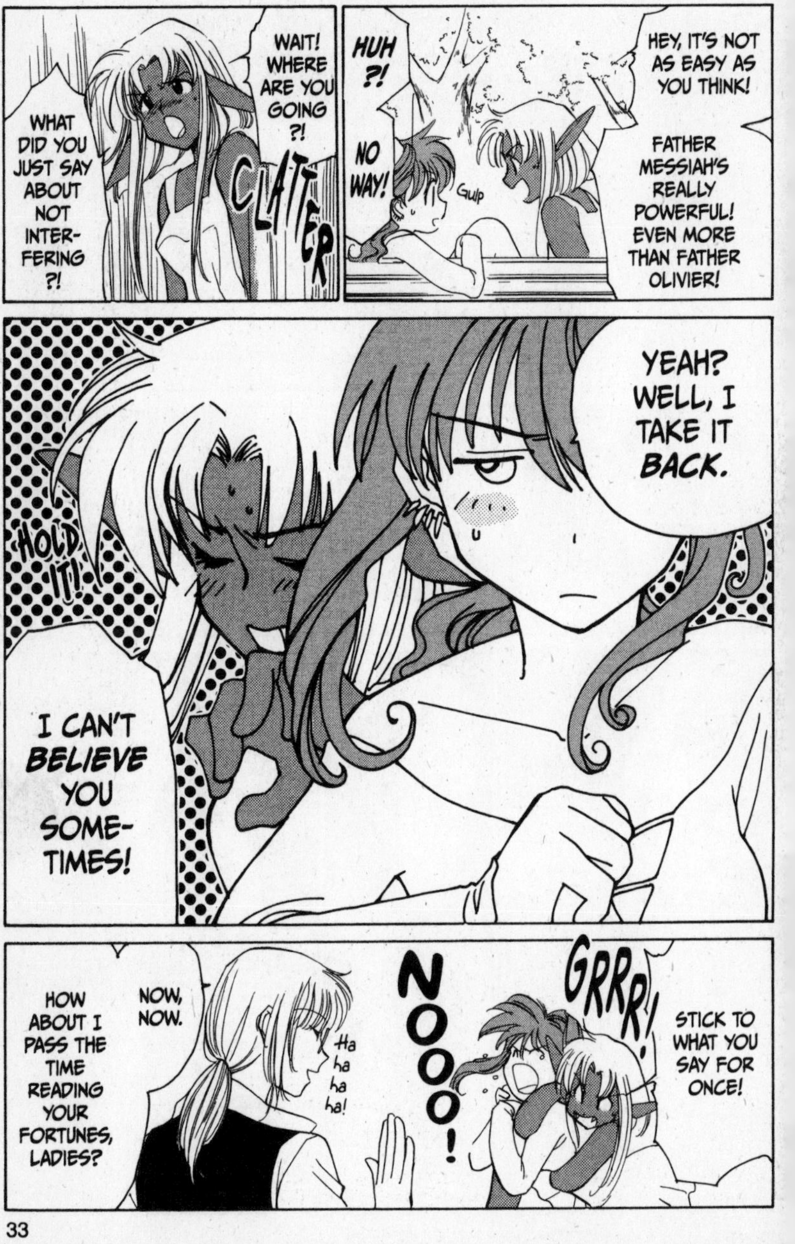
HEY, IT'S NOT AS EASY AS YOU THINK!
FATHER MESSIAH'S REALLY POWERFUL! EVEN MORE THAN FATHER OLIVIER!
HUH?!
NO WAY!
Gulp
WAIT! WHERE ARE YOU GOING?!
CLATTER
WHAT DID YOU JUST SAY ABOUT NOT INTERFERING?!
YEAH? WELL, I TAKE IT BACK.
HOLD IT!
I CAN'T BELIEVE YOU SOMETIMES!
STICK TO WHAT YOU SAY FOR ONCE!
GRRR!
NOOO!
Ha ha ha ha!
NOW, NOW.
HOW ABOUT I PASS THE TIME READING YOUR FORTUNES, LADIES?

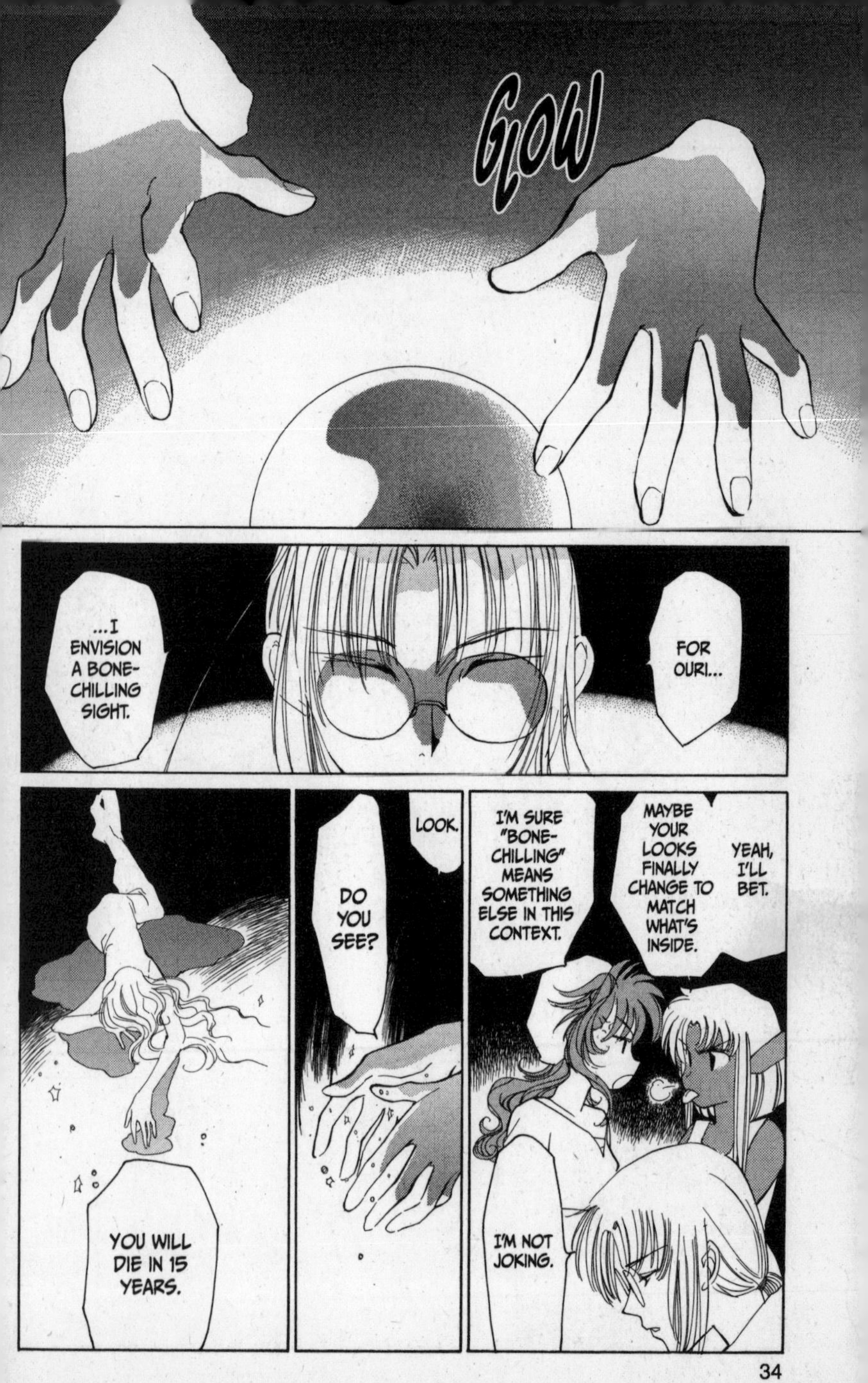
GLOW
FOR OURI...
...I ENVISION A BONE-CHILLING SIGHT.
YEAH, I'LL BET.
MAYBE YOUR LOOKS FINALLY CHANGE TO MATCH WHAT'S INSIDE.
I'M SURE "BONE-CHILLING" MEANS SOMETHING ELSE IN THIS CONTEXT.
I'M NOT JOKING.
LOOK.
DO YOU SEE?
YOU WILL DIE IN 15 YEARS.

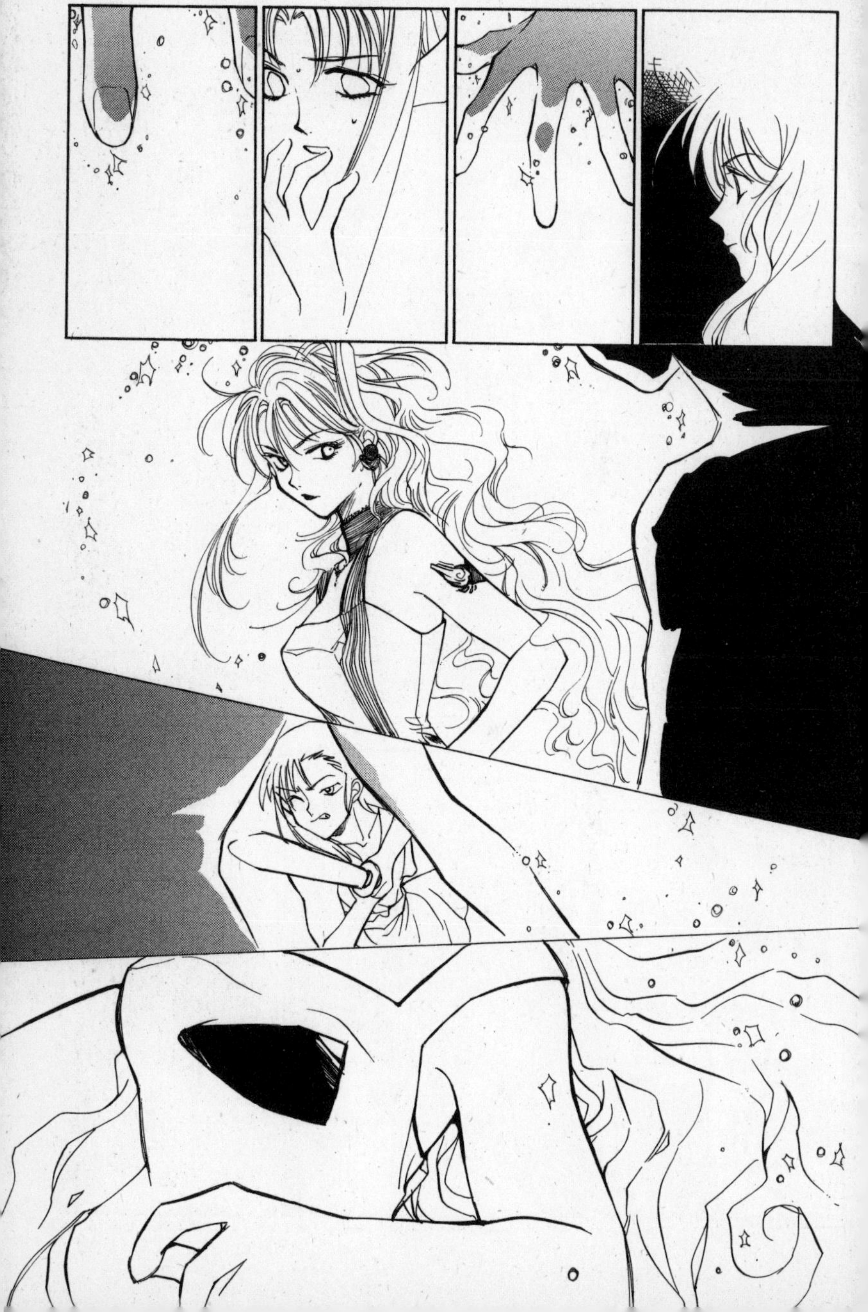

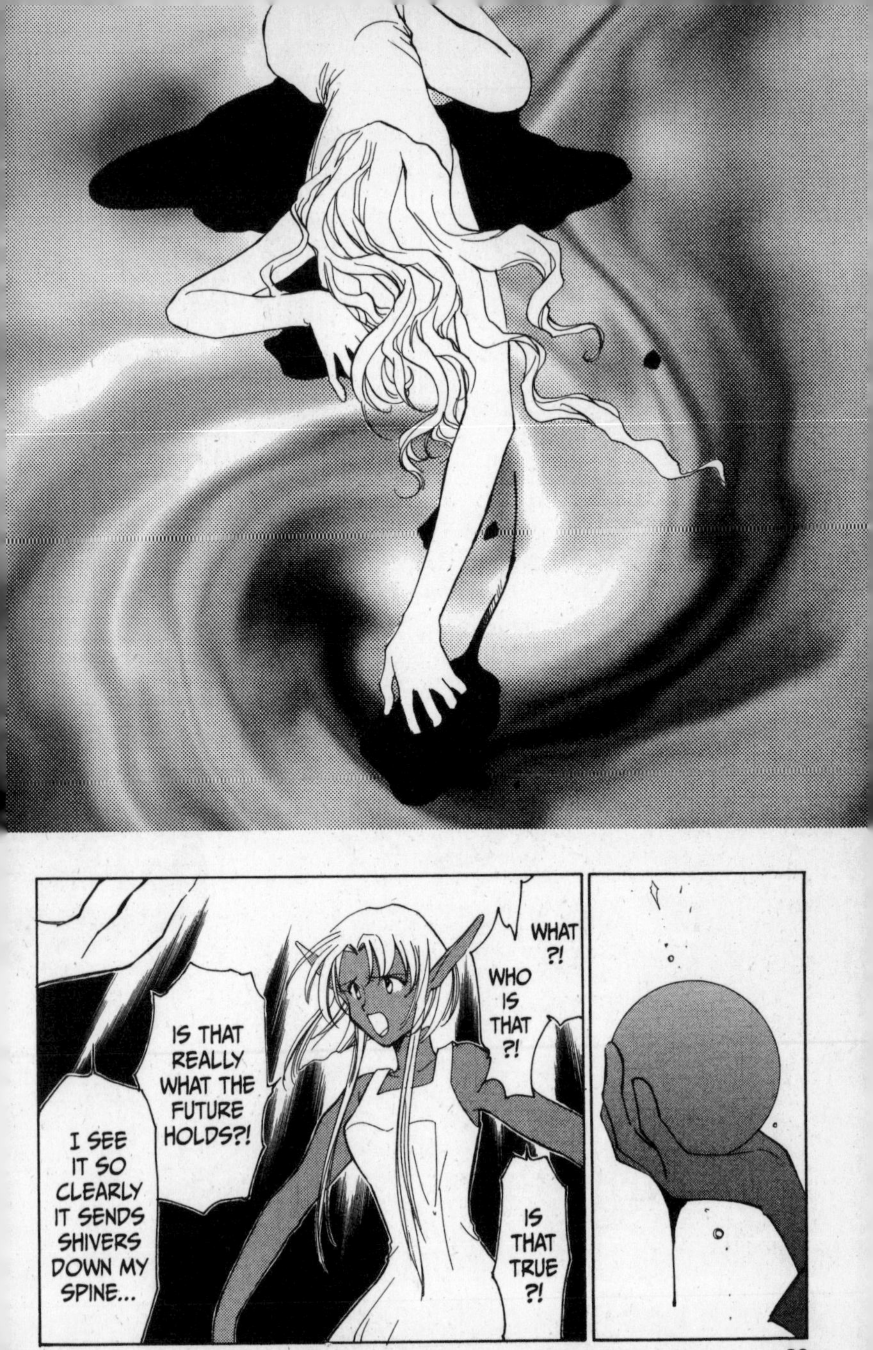
WHAT?!
WHO IS THAT?!
IS THAT TRUE?!
IS THAT REALLY WHAT THE FUTURE HOLDS?!
I SEE IT SO CLEARLY IT SENDS SHIVERS DOWN MY SPINE...

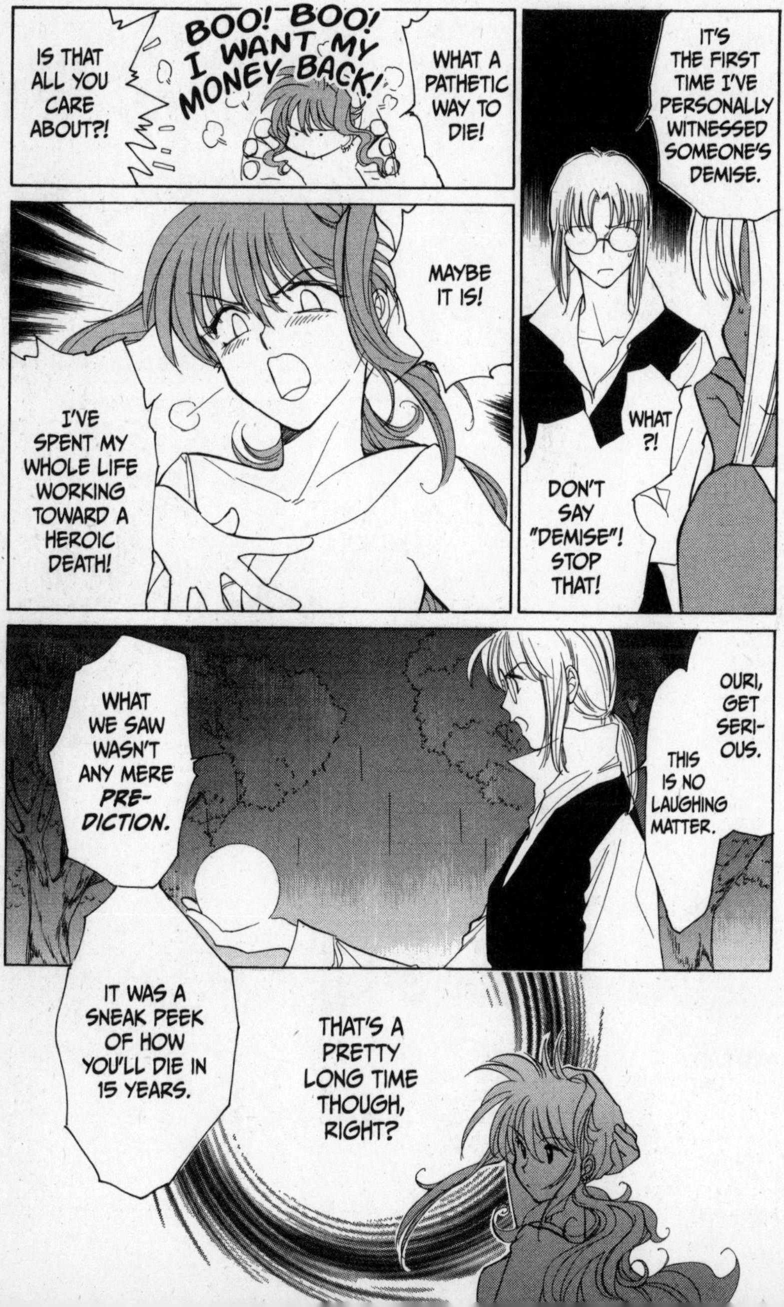
IT'S THE FIRST TIME I'VE PERSONALLY WITNESSED SOMEONE'S DEMISE.
WHAT?!
DON'T SAY "DEMISE"! STOP THAT!
WHAT A PATHETIC WAY TO DIE!
BOO! BOO! I WANT MY MONEY BACK!
IS THAT ALL YOU CARE ABOUT?!
MAYBE IT IS!
I'VE SPENT MY WHOLE LIFE WORKING TOWARD A HEROIC DEATH!
OURI, GET SERI-OUS.
THIS IS NO LAUGHING MATTER.
WHAT WE SAW WASN'T ANY MERE *PRE-DICTION.*
IT WAS A SNEAK PEEK OF HOW YOU'LL DIE IN 15 YEARS.
THAT'S A PRETTY LONG TIME THOUGH, RIGHT?

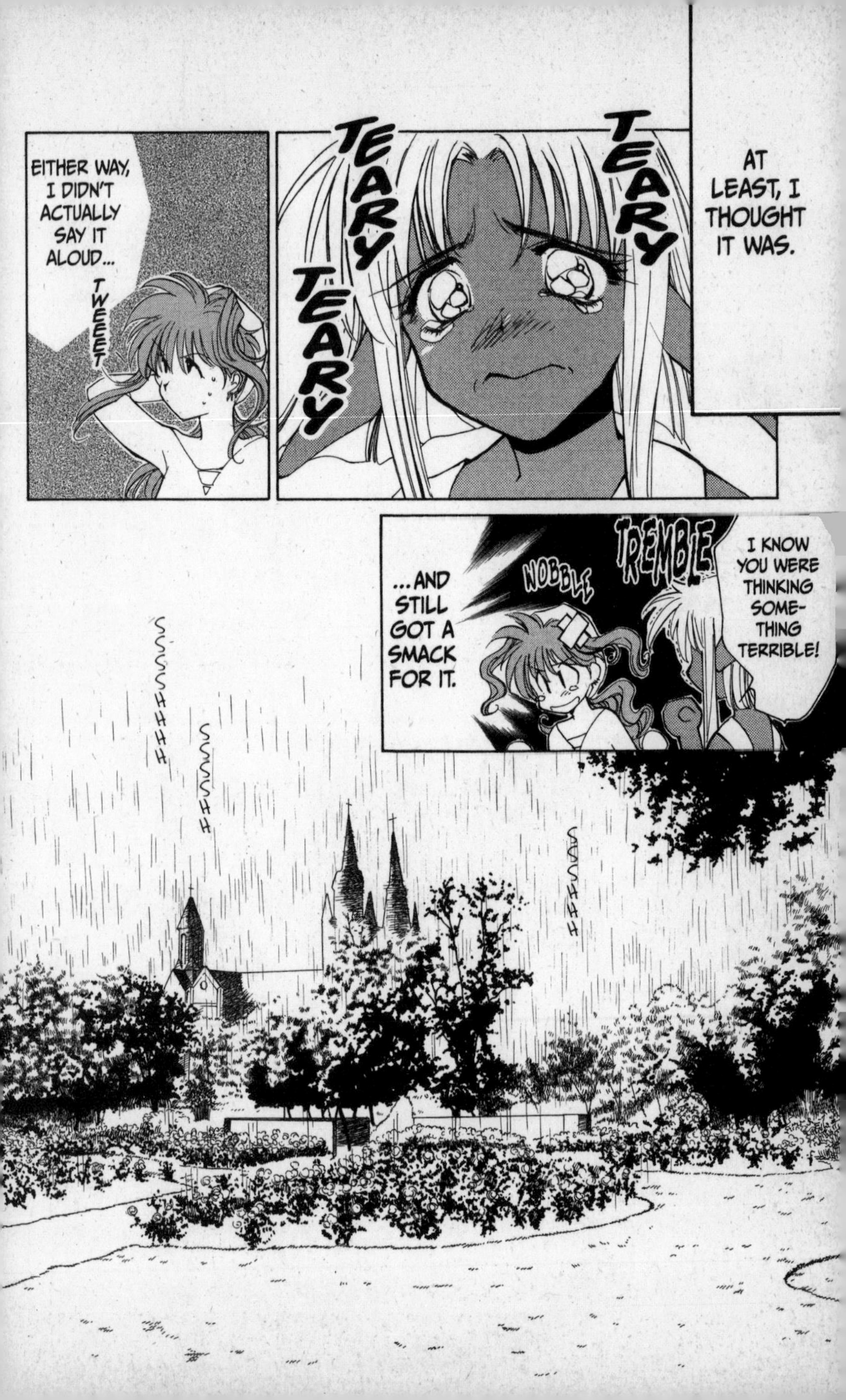
AT LEAST, I THOUGHT IT WAS.
TEARY TEARY
TEARY
EITHER WAY, I DIDN'T ACTUALLY SAY IT ALOUD...
TWEEEET
I KNOW YOU WERE THINKING SOME-THING TERRIBLE!
TREMBLE
WOBBLE
...AND STILL GOT A SMACK FOR IT.
SSSSHHHH
SSSSHH
SSSSHHH

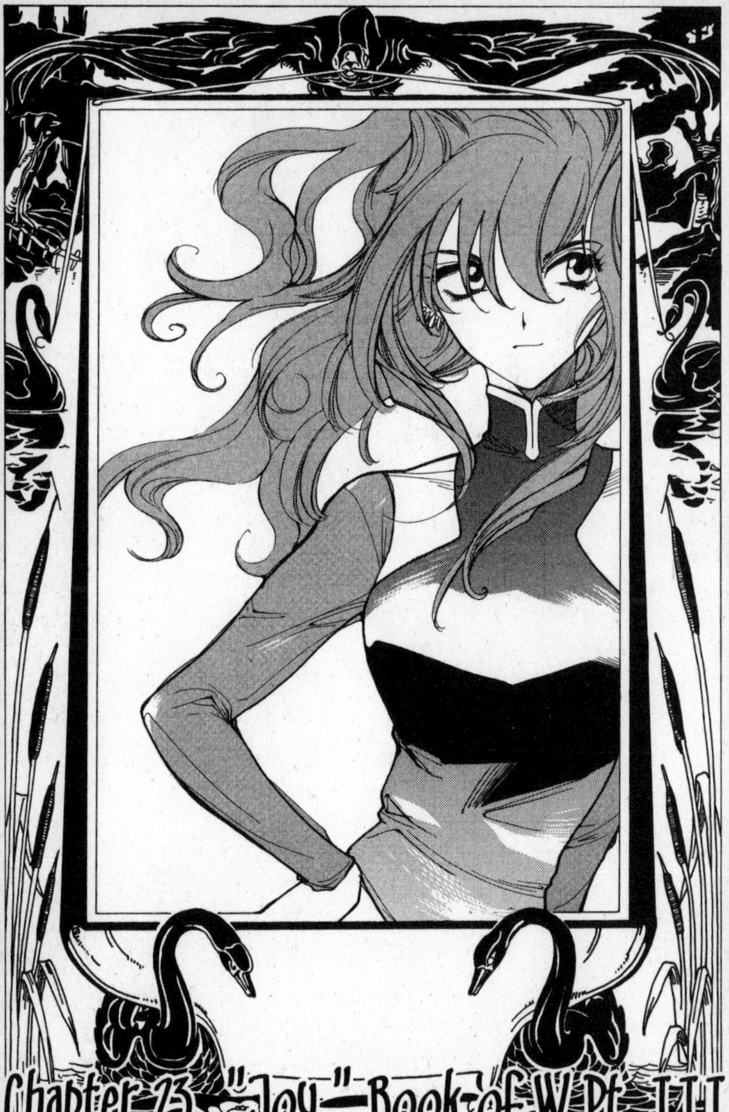

Chapter 23 "Joy," Book of W Pt. III

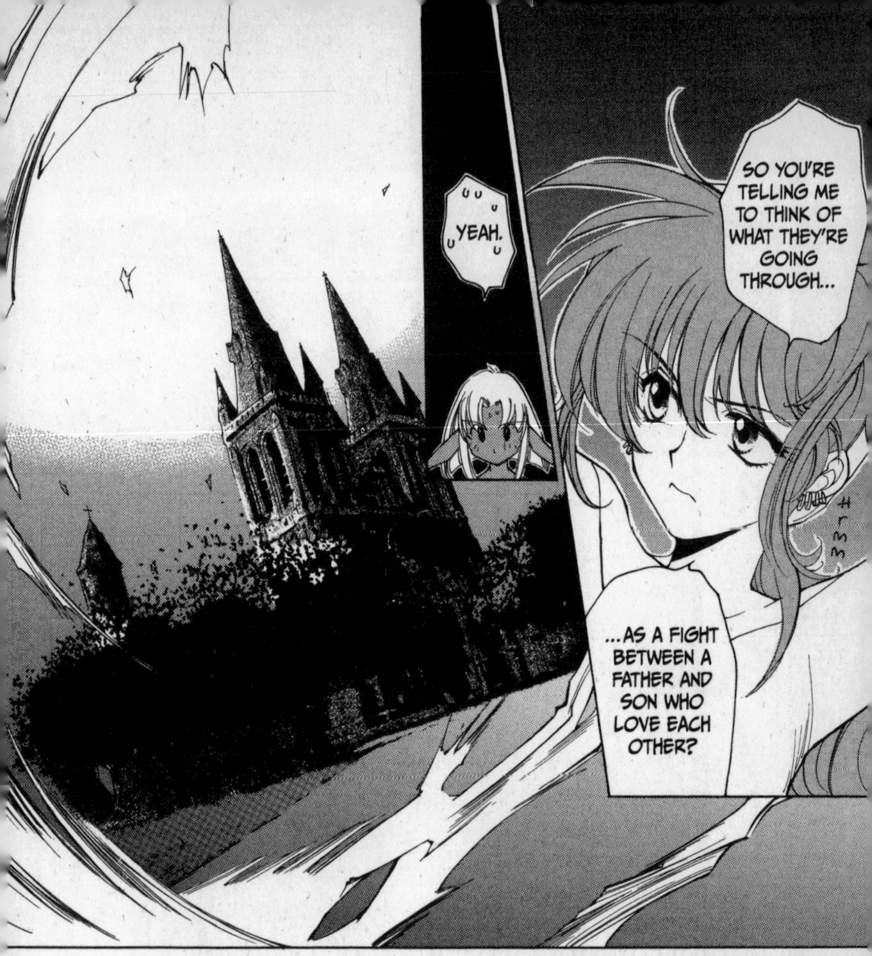
SO YOU'RE TELLING ME TO THINK OF WHAT THEY'RE GOING THROUGH...
...AS A FIGHT BETWEEN A FATHER AND SON WHO LOVE EACH OTHER?
hrmm
YEAH.

Summary Space ②

This year I went abroad a few times to take photos as drawing references and the like.

The shot of this church was actually taken on my trip to Australia with Yumi Tamura-san. Tamu-san, let's go again together sometime. ♥

Apparently koalas have really nervous temperaments, so it's not a good idea to try to hold them or anything. At the same time, the government protects them so well, there's a bit of an overpopulation problem... which means they've gone and stripped all the eucalyptus trees bare of leaves!! So as you can see, Australia has its own problems to deal with.

Basara will begin airing in April 1998 on TV Kanagawa! I hope you all watch it since I'll be watching it too.

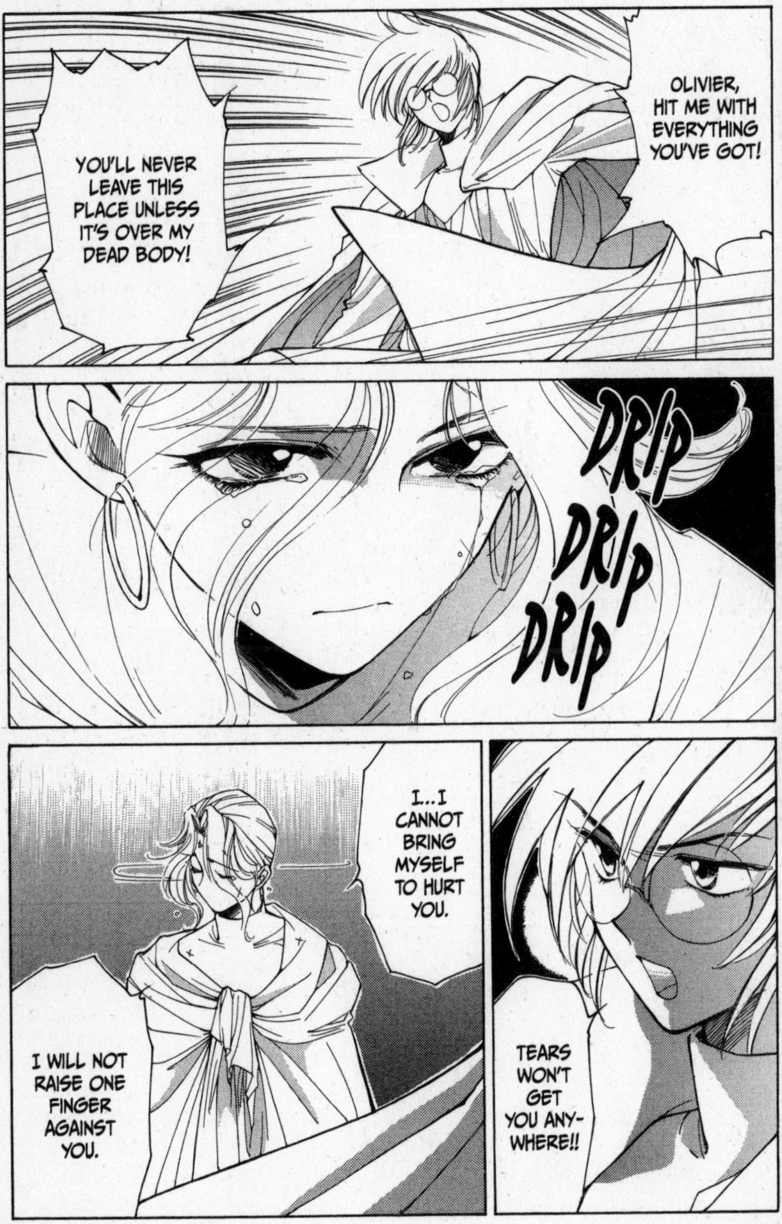
OLIVIER, HIT ME WITH EVERYTHING YOU'VE GOT!
YOU'LL NEVER LEAVE THIS PLACE UNLESS IT'S OVER MY DEAD BODY!
DRIP DRIP DRIP
TEARS WON'T GET YOU ANY-WHERE!!
I...I CANNOT BRING MYSELF TO HURT YOU.
I WILL NOT RAISE ONE FINGER AGAINST YOU.

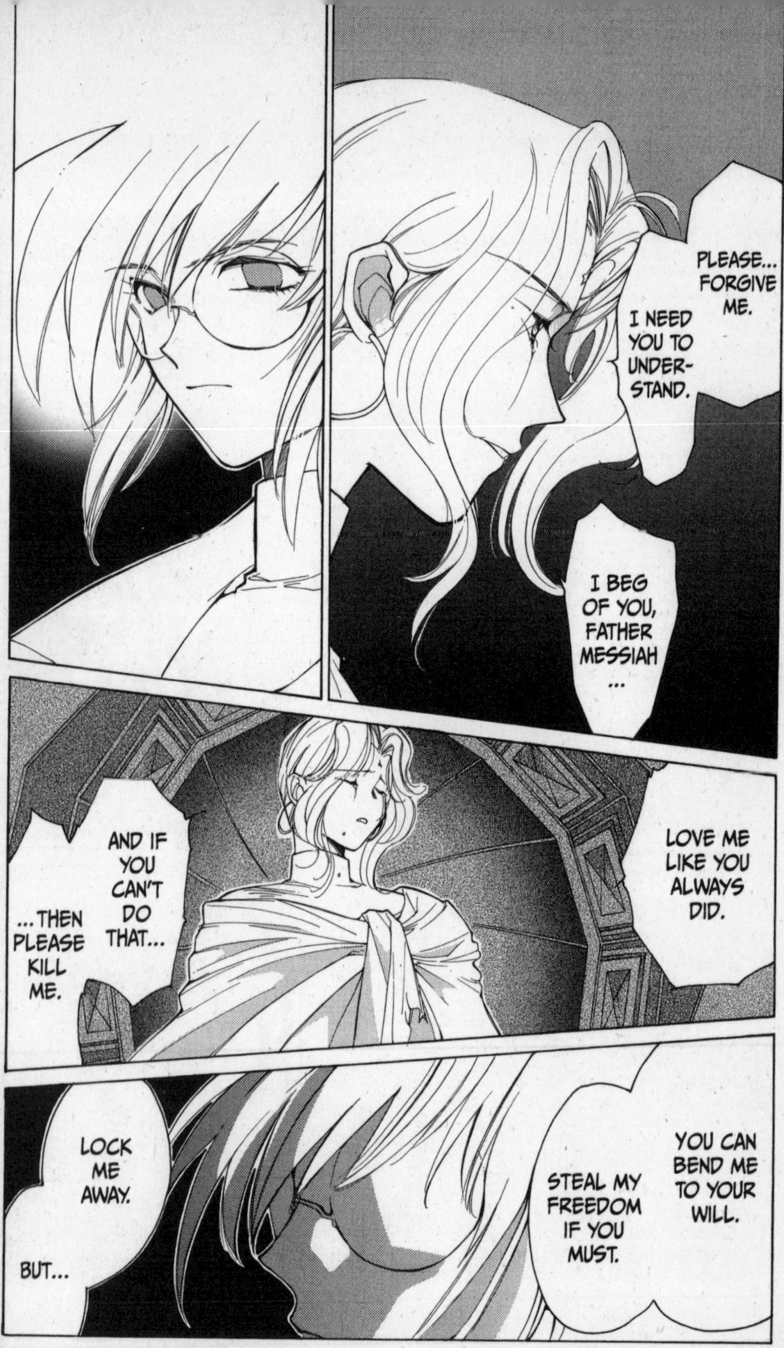
PLEASE... FORGIVE ME.
I NEED YOU TO UNDERSTAND.
I BEG OF YOU, FATHER MESSIAH ...
LOVE ME LIKE YOU ALWAYS DID.
AND IF YOU CAN'T DO THAT...
...THEN PLEASE KILL ME.
YOU CAN BEND ME TO YOUR WILL.
STEAL MY FREEDOM IF YOU MUST.
LOCK ME AWAY.
BUT...

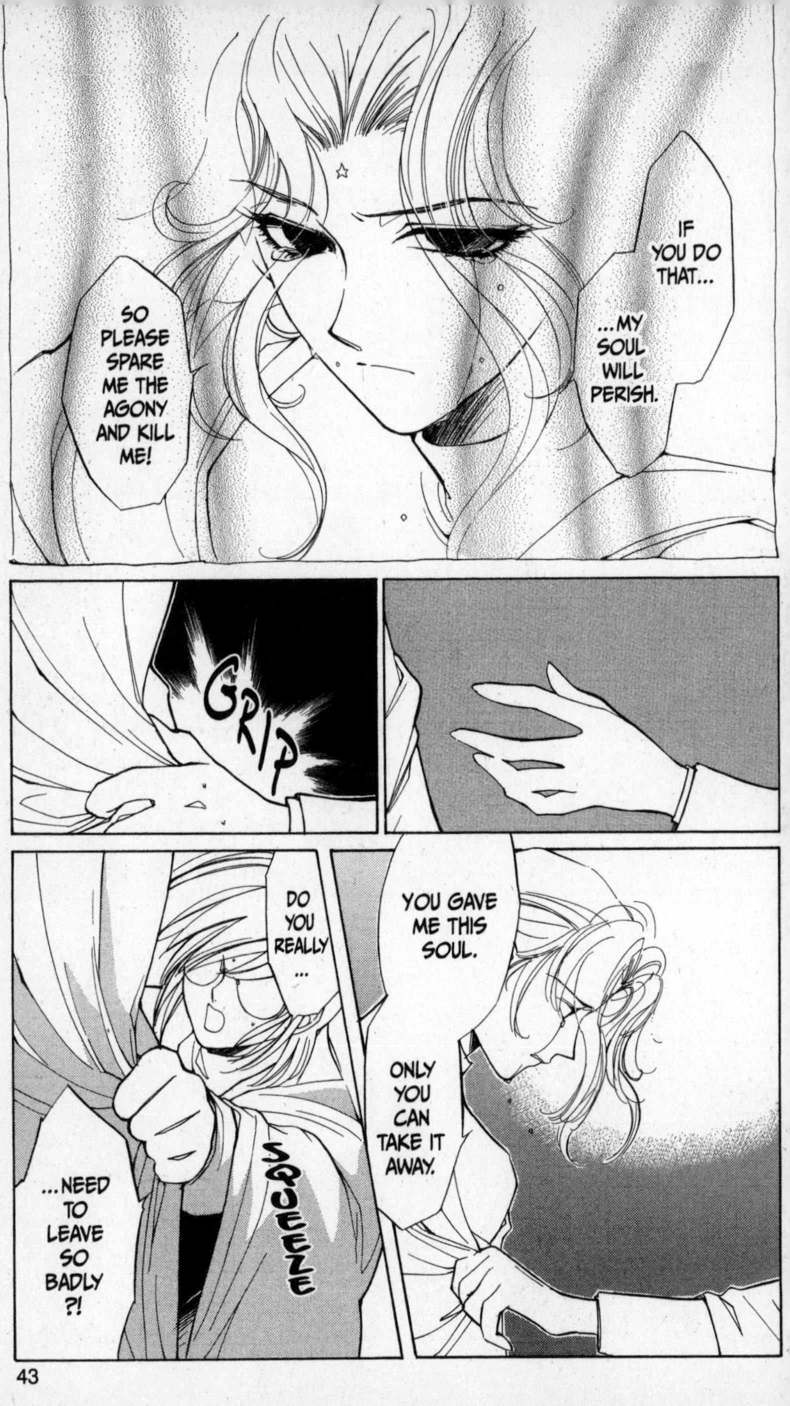
IF YOU DO THAT...
...MY SOUL WILL PERISH.
SO PLEASE SPARE ME THE AGONY AND KILL ME!
GRIP
YOU GAVE ME THIS SOUL.
ONLY YOU CAN TAKE IT AWAY.
DO YOU REALLY ...
...NEED TO LEAVE SO BADLY?!
SQUEEZE

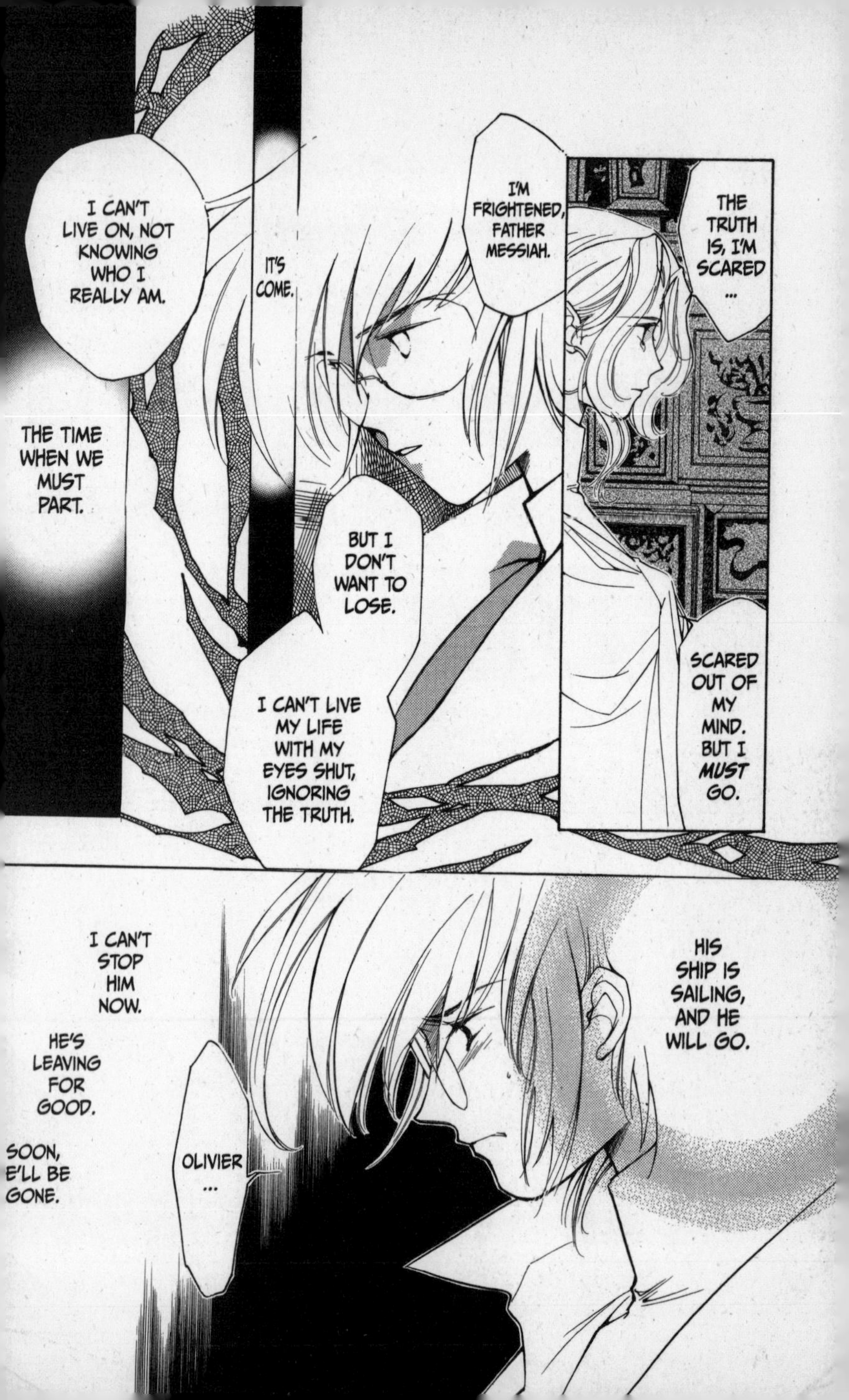
THE TRUTH IS, I'M SCARED ...
SCARED OUT OF MY MIND. BUT I *MUST* GO.
I'M FRIGHTENED, FATHER MESSIAH.
IT'S COME.
BUT I DON'T WANT TO LOSE.
I CAN'T LIVE MY LIFE WITH MY EYES SHUT, IGNORING THE TRUTH.
I CAN'T LIVE ON, NOT KNOWING WHO I REALLY AM.
THE TIME WHEN WE MUST PART.
HIS SHIP IS SAILING, AND HE WILL GO.
I CAN'T STOP HIM NOW.
HE'S LEAVING FOR GOOD.
SOON, E'LL BE GONE.
OLIVIER ...

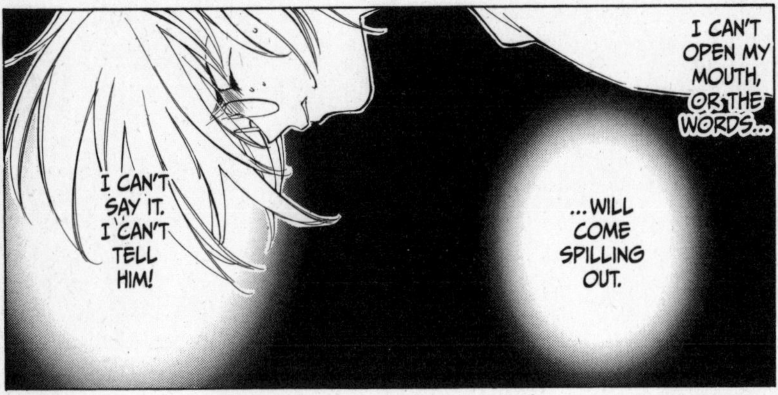
I CAN'T OPEN MY MOUTH, OR THE WORDS...
...WILL COME SPILLING OUT.
I CAN'T SAY IT. I CAN'T TELL HIM!

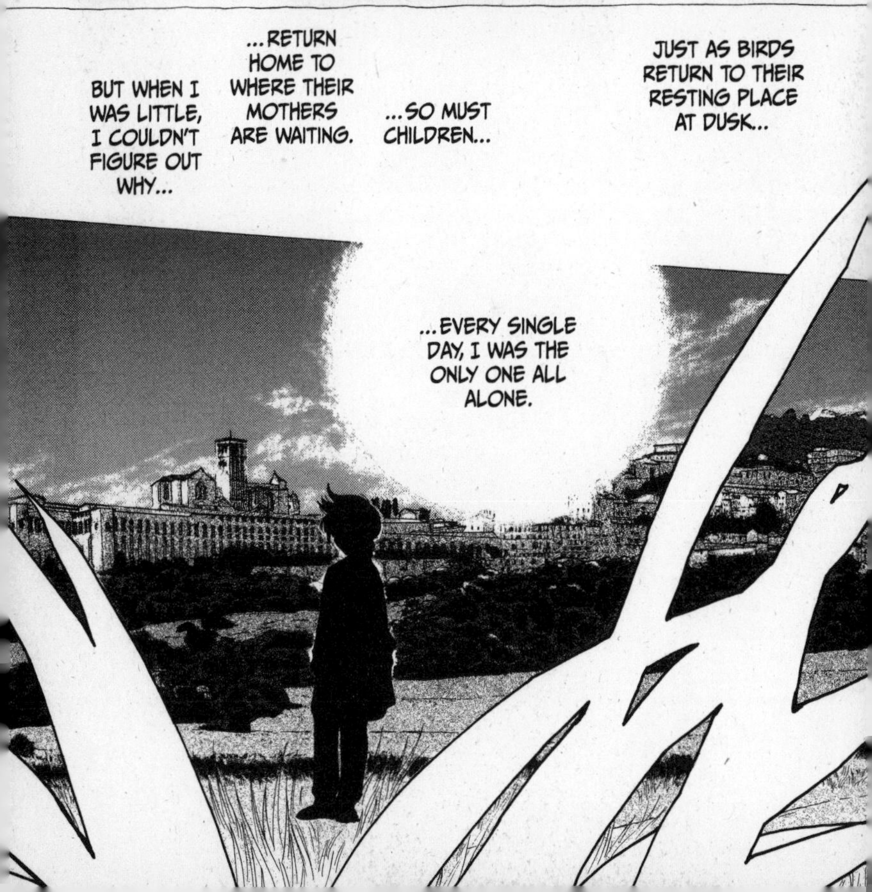
JUST AS BIRDS RETURN TO THEIR RESTING PLACE AT DUSK...
...SO MUST CHILDREN...
...RETURN HOME TO WHERE THEIR MOTHERS ARE WAITING.
BUT WHEN I WAS LITTLE, I COULDN'T FIGURE OUT WHY...
...EVERY SINGLE DAY, I WAS THE ONLY ONE ALL ALONE.

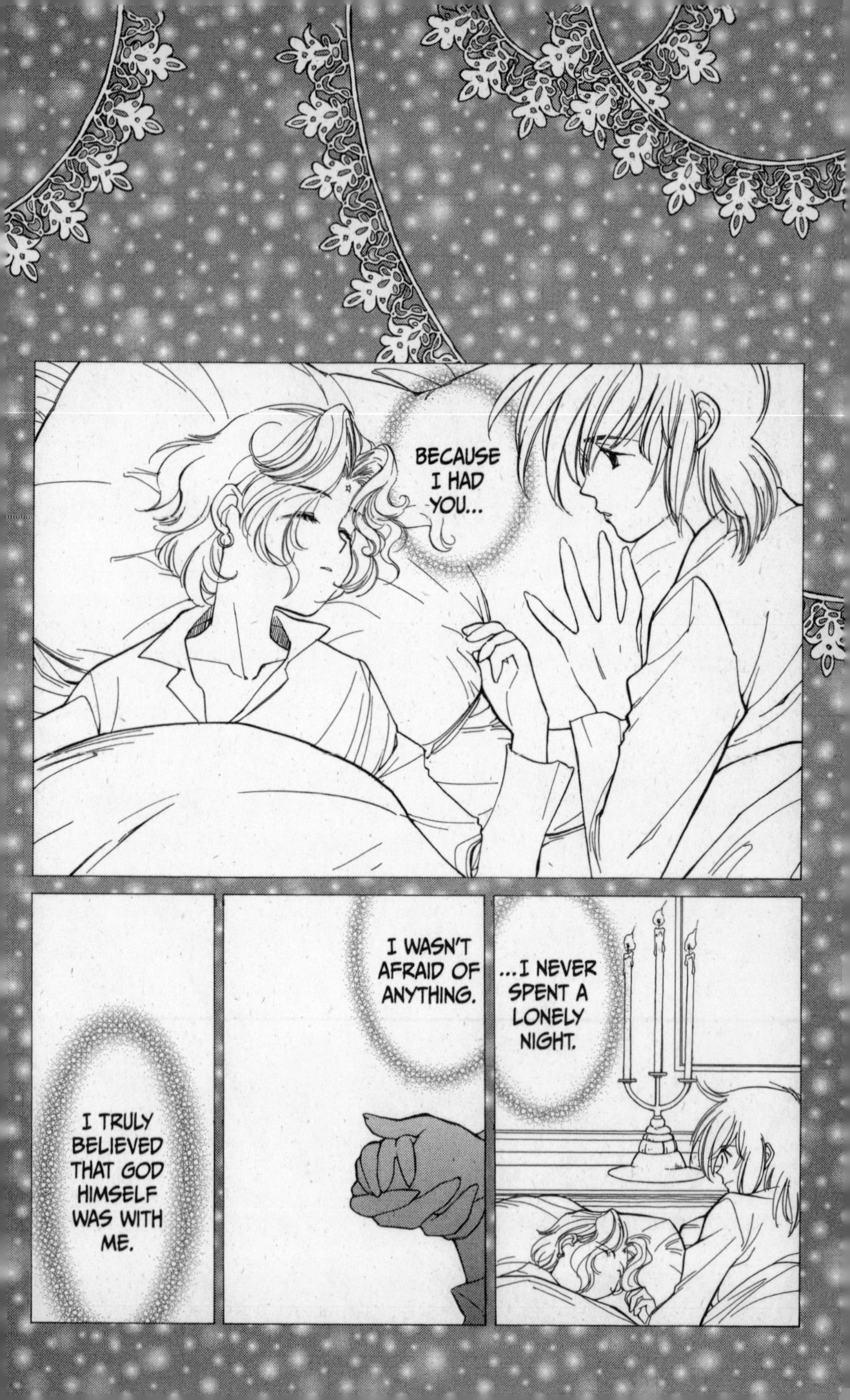
BECAUSE I HAD YOU...
...I NEVER SPENT A LONELY NIGHT.
I WASN'T AFRAID OF ANYTHING.
I TRULY BELIEVED THAT GOD HIMSELF WAS WITH ME.

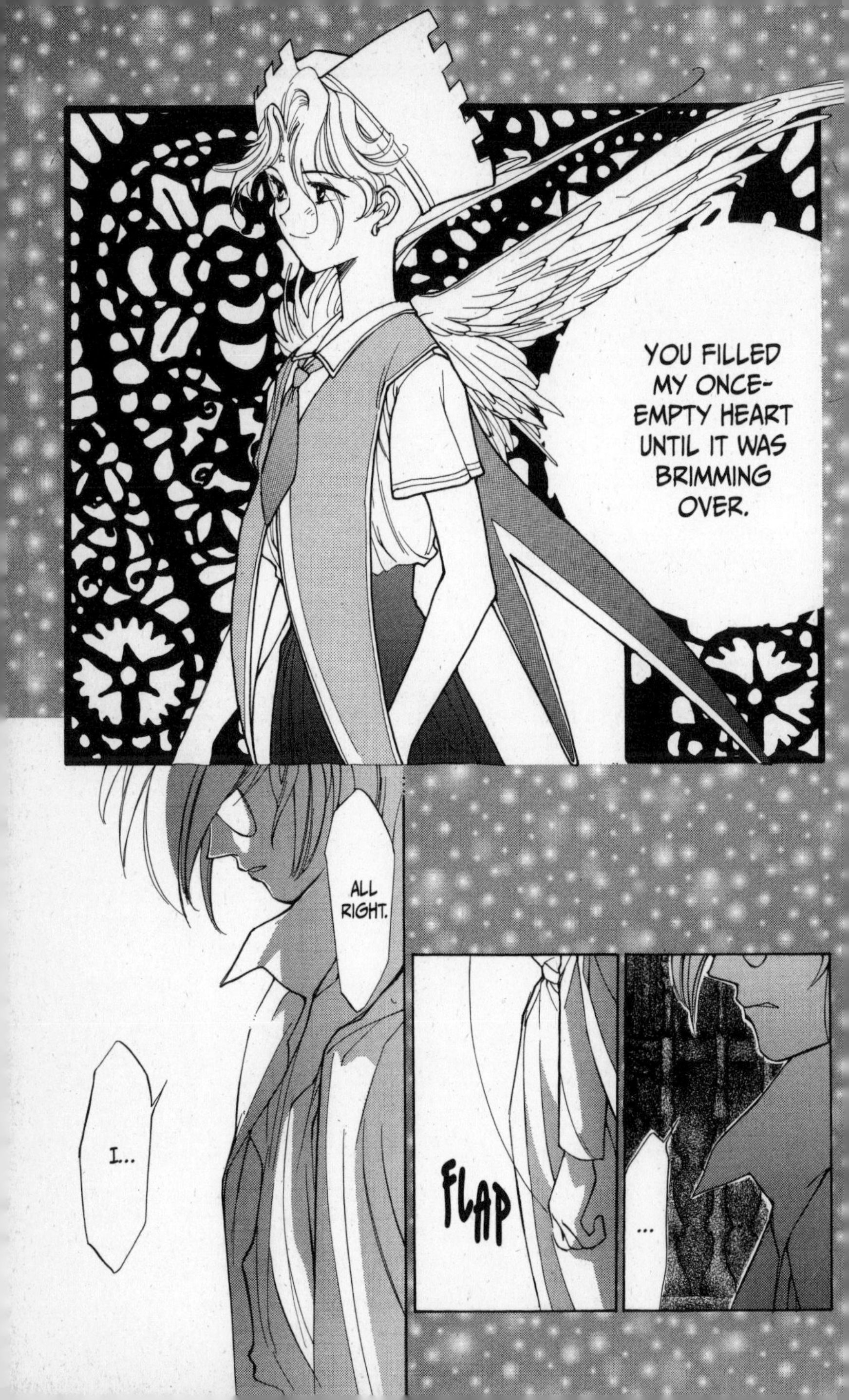
YOU FILLED MY ONCE-EMPTY HEART UNTIL IT WAS BRIMMING OVER.
...
FLAP
ALL RIGHT.
I...

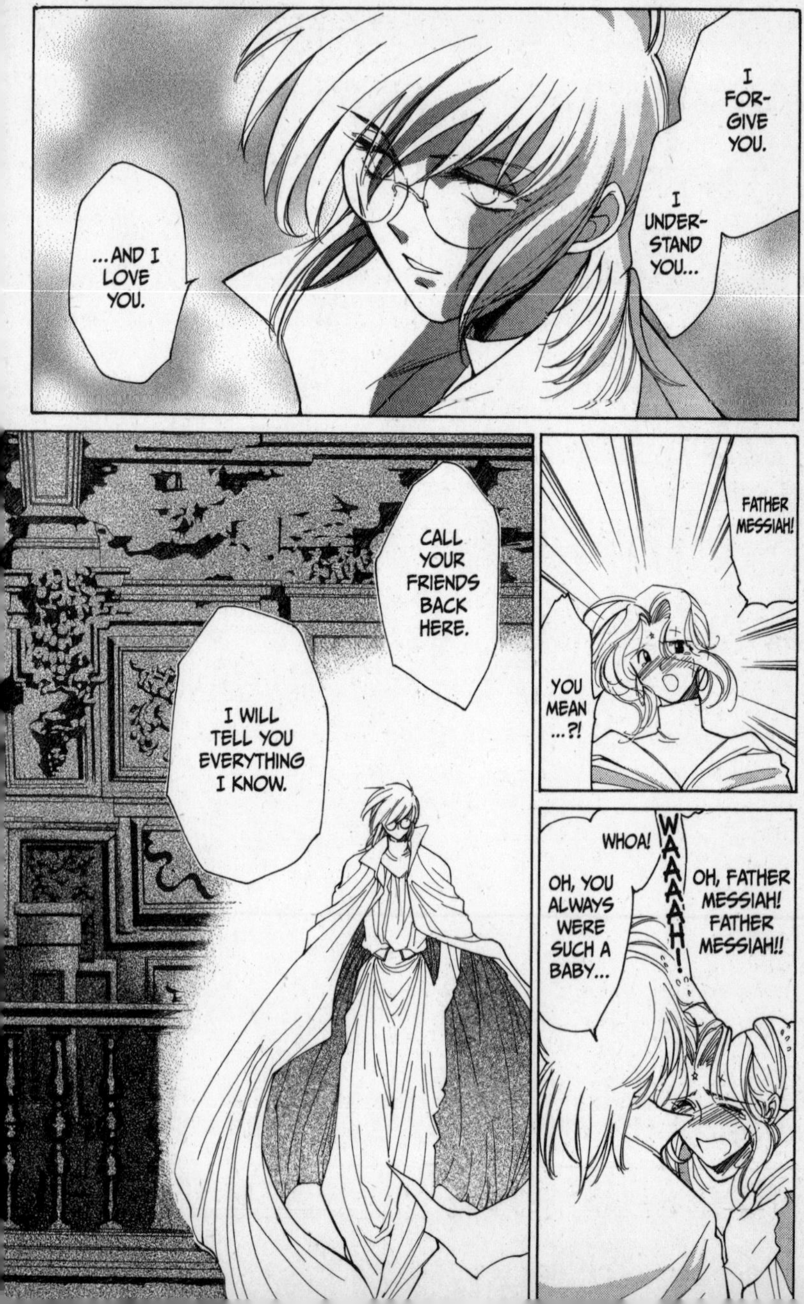
I FORGIVE YOU.
I UNDERSTAND YOU...
...AND I LOVE YOU.
FATHER MESSIAH!
YOU MEAN ...?!
WAAAAH!!
OH, FATHER MESSIAH! FATHER MESSIAH!!
WHOA!
OH, YOU ALWAYS WERE SUCH A BABY...
CALL YOUR FRIENDS BACK HERE.
I WILL TELL YOU EVERYTHING I KNOW.

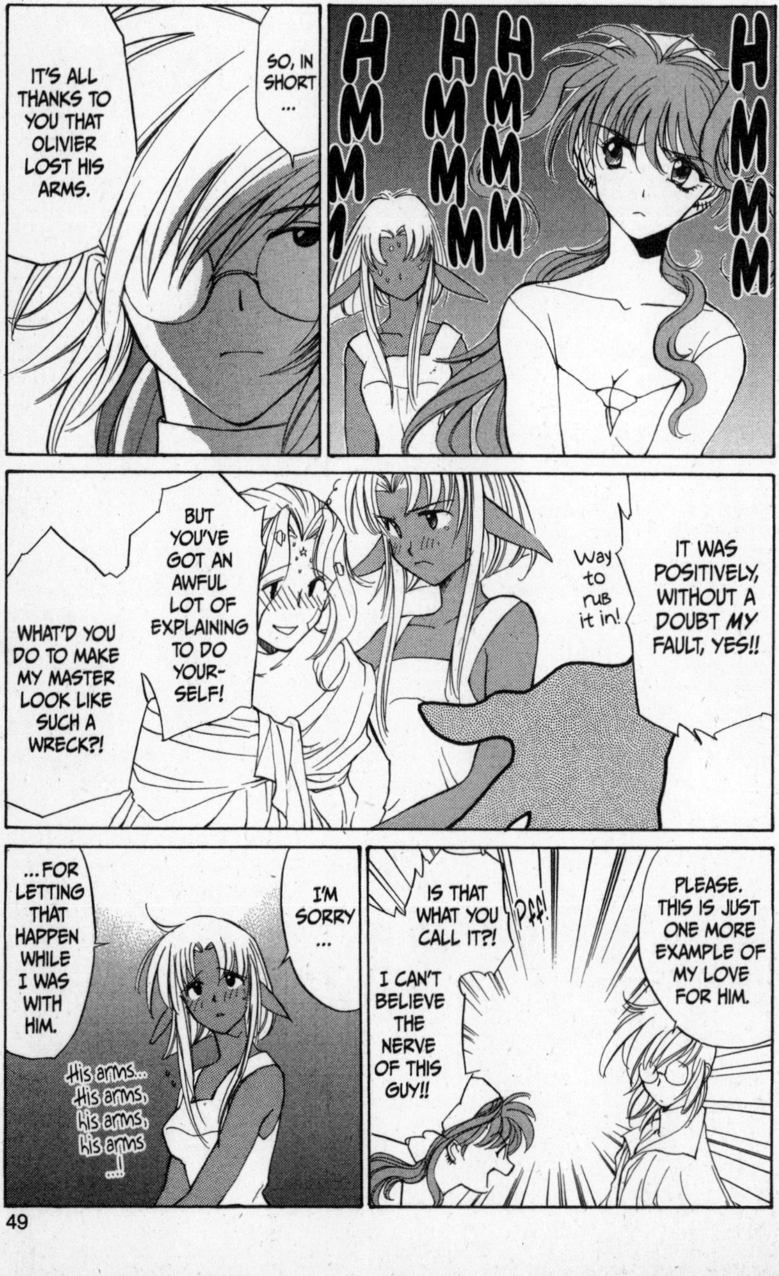
HMMMMM
HMMMMM
HMMMM
HMMM
SO, IN SHORT ...
IT'S ALL THANKS TO YOU THAT OLIVIER LOST HIS ARMS.
IT WAS POSITIVELY, WITHOUT A DOUBT *MY* FAULT, YES!!
Way to rub it in!
BUT YOU'VE GOT AN AWFUL LOT OF EXPLAINING TO DO YOURSELF!
WHAT'D YOU DO TO MAKE MY MASTER LOOK LIKE SUCH A WRECK?!
PLEASE. THIS IS JUST ONE MORE EXAMPLE OF MY LOVE FOR HIM.
Pff!
IS THAT WHAT YOU CALL IT?!
I CAN'T BELIEVE THE NERVE OF THIS GUY!!
I'M SORRY ...
...FOR LETTING THAT HAPPEN WHILE I WAS WITH HIM.
His arms... His arms, his arms, his arms ...!

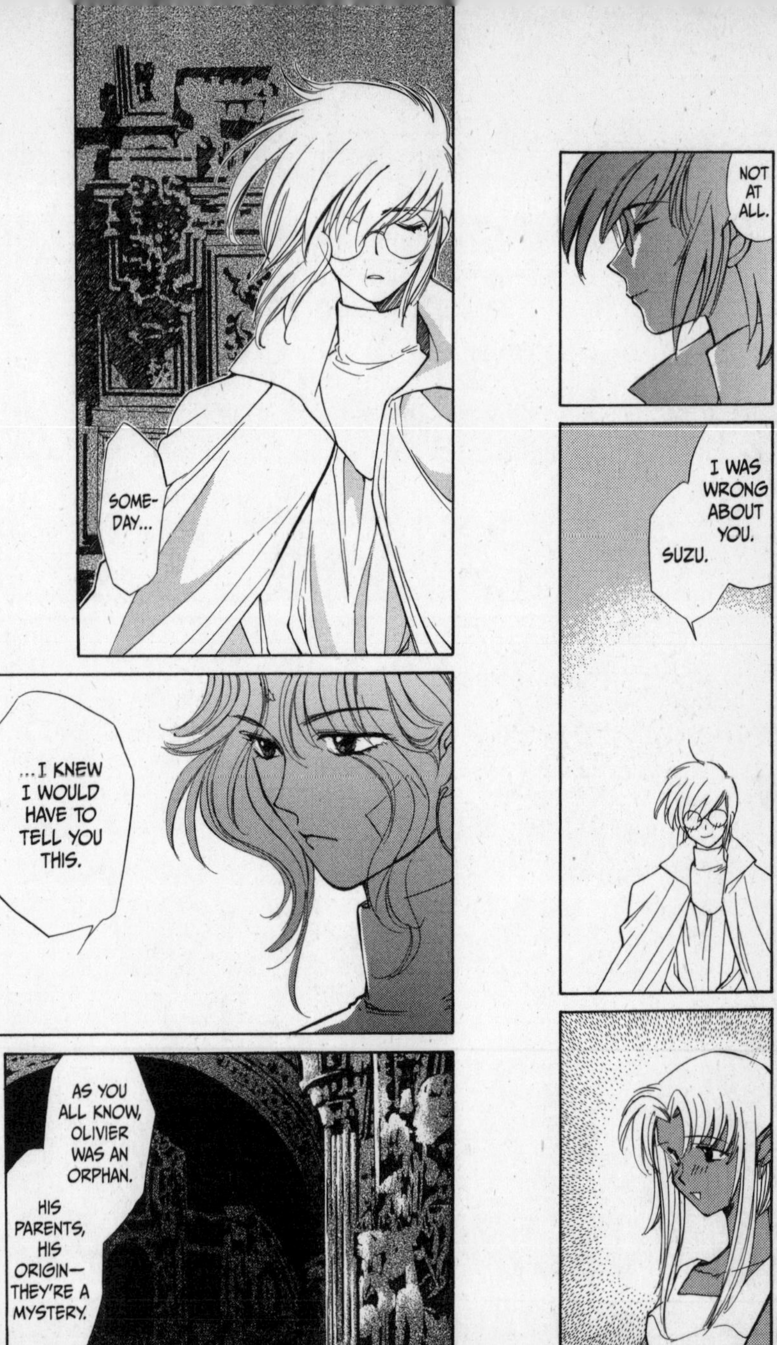
NOT AT ALL.
I WAS WRONG ABOUT YOU.
SUZU.
SOME-DAY...
...I KNEW I WOULD HAVE TO TELL YOU THIS.
AS YOU ALL KNOW, OLIVIER WAS AN ORPHAN.
HIS PARENTS, HIS ORIGIN—THEY'RE A MYSTERY.

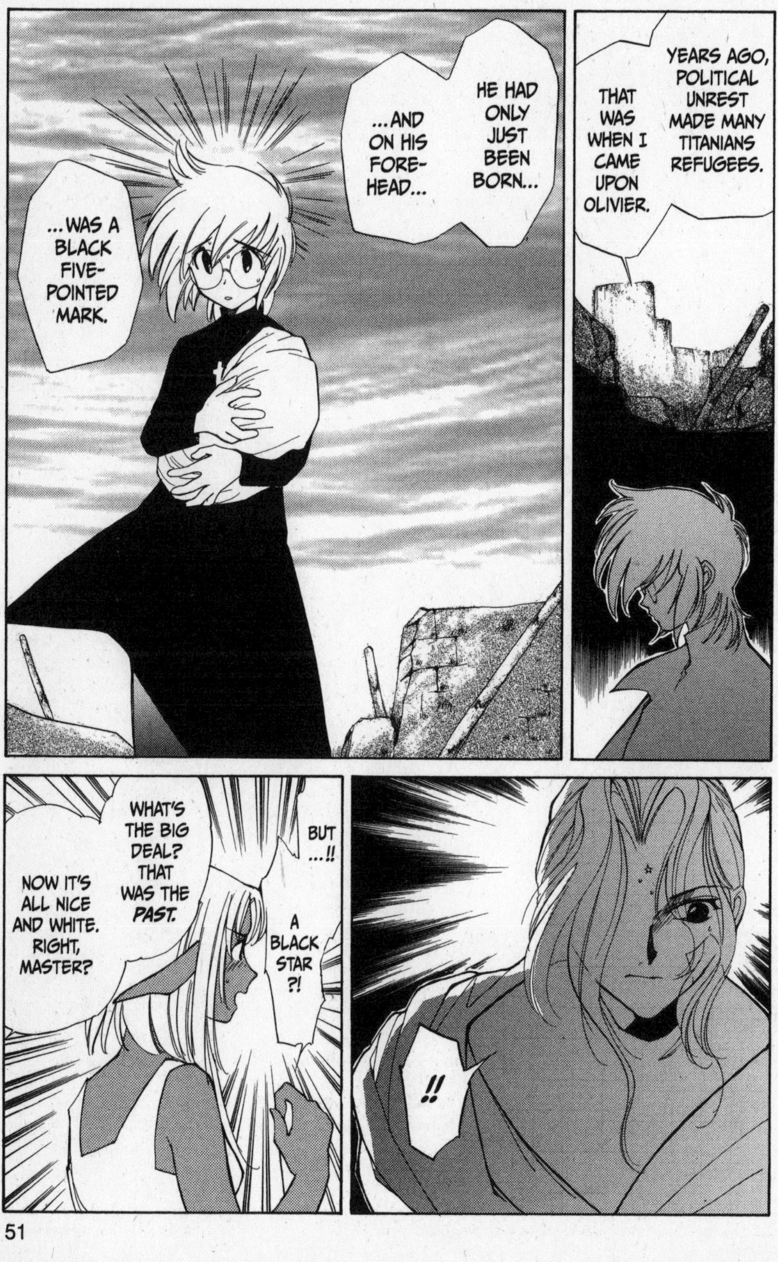
YEARS AGO, POLITICAL UNREST MADE MANY TITANIANS REFUGEES.
THAT WAS WHEN I CAME UPON OLIVIER.
HE HAD ONLY JUST BEEN BORN...
...AND ON HIS FORE-HEAD...
...WAS A BLACK FIVE-POINTED MARK.
!!
BUT...!!
A BLACK STAR?!
WHAT'S THE BIG DEAL? THAT WAS THE *PAST.*
NOW IT'S ALL NICE AND WHITE. RIGHT, MASTER?

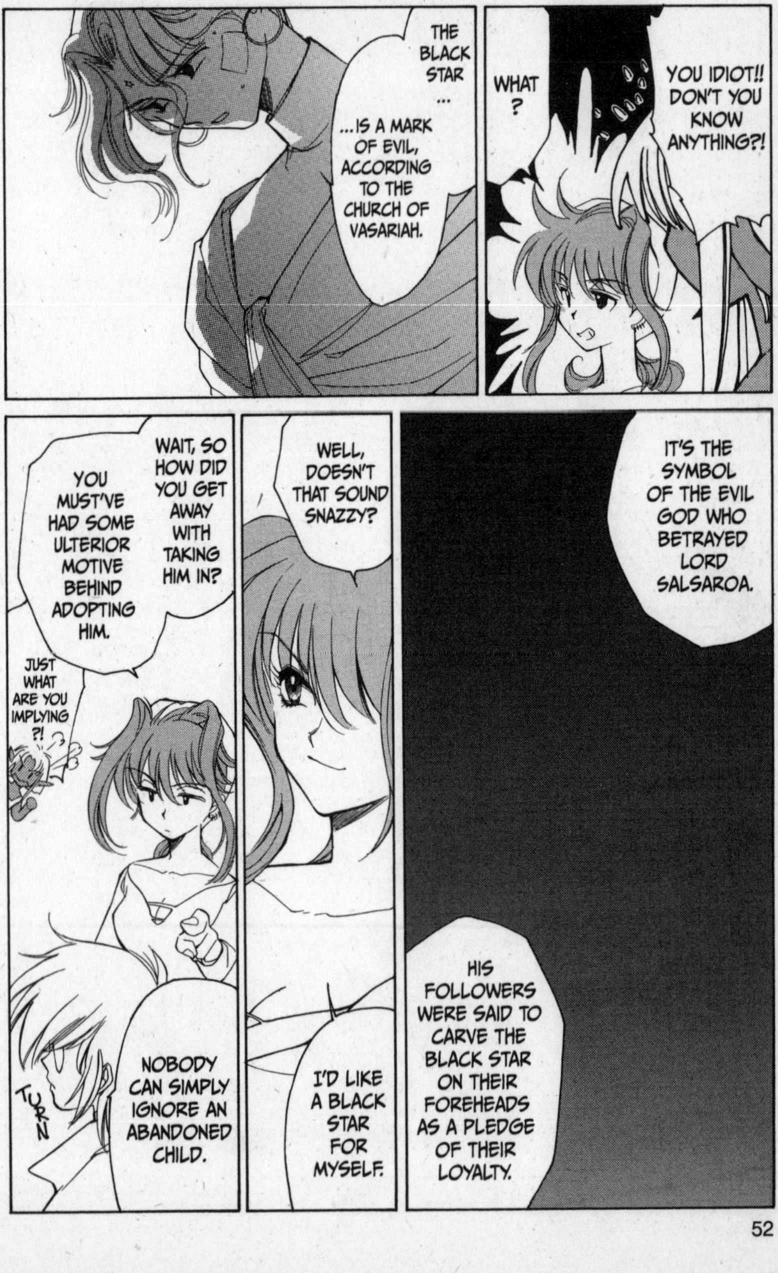
YOU IDIOT!! DON'T YOU KNOW ANYTHING?!
WHAT?
THE BLACK STAR...
...IS A MARK OF EVIL, ACCORDING TO THE CHURCH OF VASARIAH.
IT'S THE SYMBOL OF THE EVIL GOD WHO BETRAYED LORD SALSAROA.
HIS FOLLOWERS WERE SAID TO CARVE THE BLACK STAR ON THEIR FOREHEADS AS A PLEDGE OF THEIR LOYALTY.
WELL, DOESN'T THAT SOUND SNAZZY?
I'D LIKE A BLACK STAR FOR MYSELF.
WAIT, SO HOW DID YOU GET AWAY WITH TAKING HIM IN?
YOU MUST'VE HAD SOME ULTERIOR MOTIVE BEHIND ADOPTING HIM.
JUST WHAT ARE YOU IMPLYING?!
NOBODY CAN SIMPLY IGNORE AN ABANDONED CHILD.
TURN

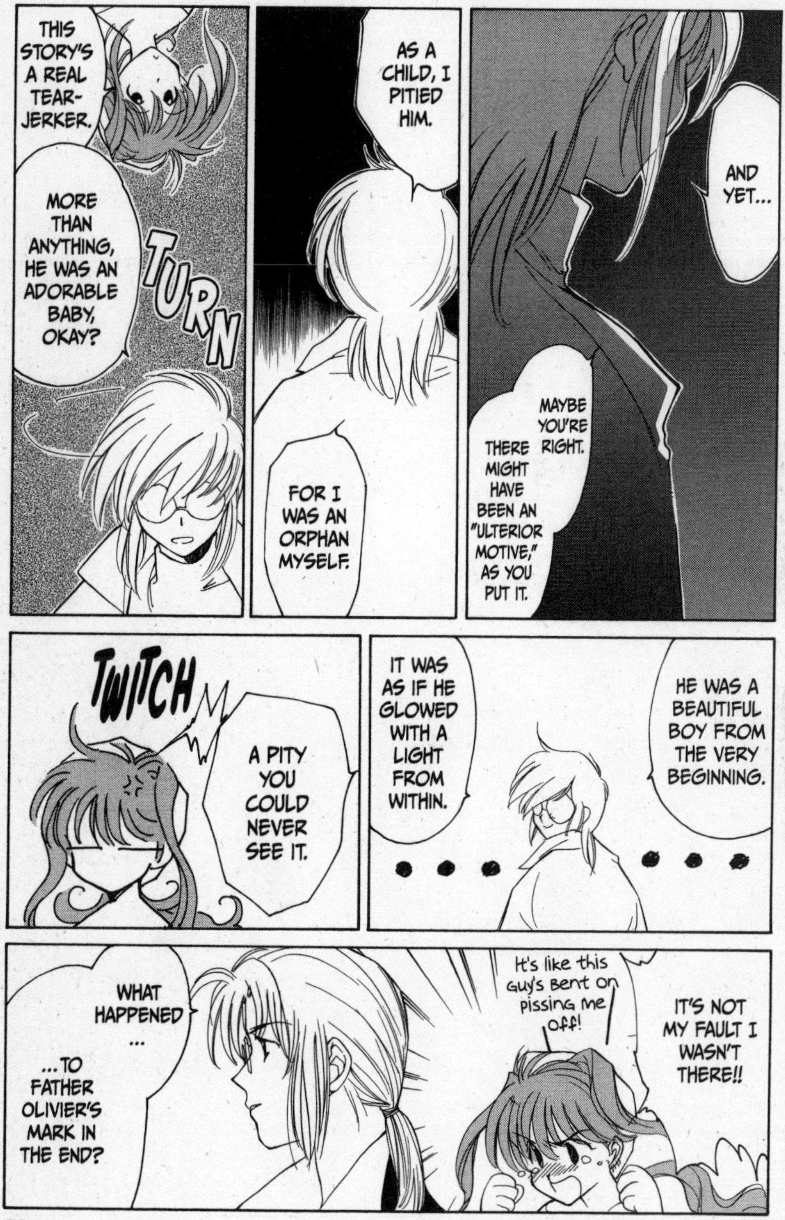

AND YET...
MAYBE YOU'RE RIGHT. THERE MIGHT HAVE BEEN AN "ULTERIOR MOTIVE," AS YOU PUT IT.
AS A CHILD, I PITIED HIM.
FOR I WAS AN ORPHAN MYSELF.
THIS STORY'S A REAL TEAR-JERKER.
MORE THAN ANYTHING, HE WAS AN ADORABLE BABY, OKAY?
TURN
HE WAS A BEAUTIFUL BOY FROM THE VERY BEGINNING.
IT WAS AS IF HE GLOWED WITH A LIGHT FROM WITHIN.
. . . . . .
A PITY YOU COULD NEVER SEE IT.
TWITCH
IT'S NOT MY FAULT I WASN'T THERE!!
It's like this Guy's Bent on pissing me off!
WHAT HAPPENED ...
...TO FATHER OLIVIER'S MARK IN THE END?

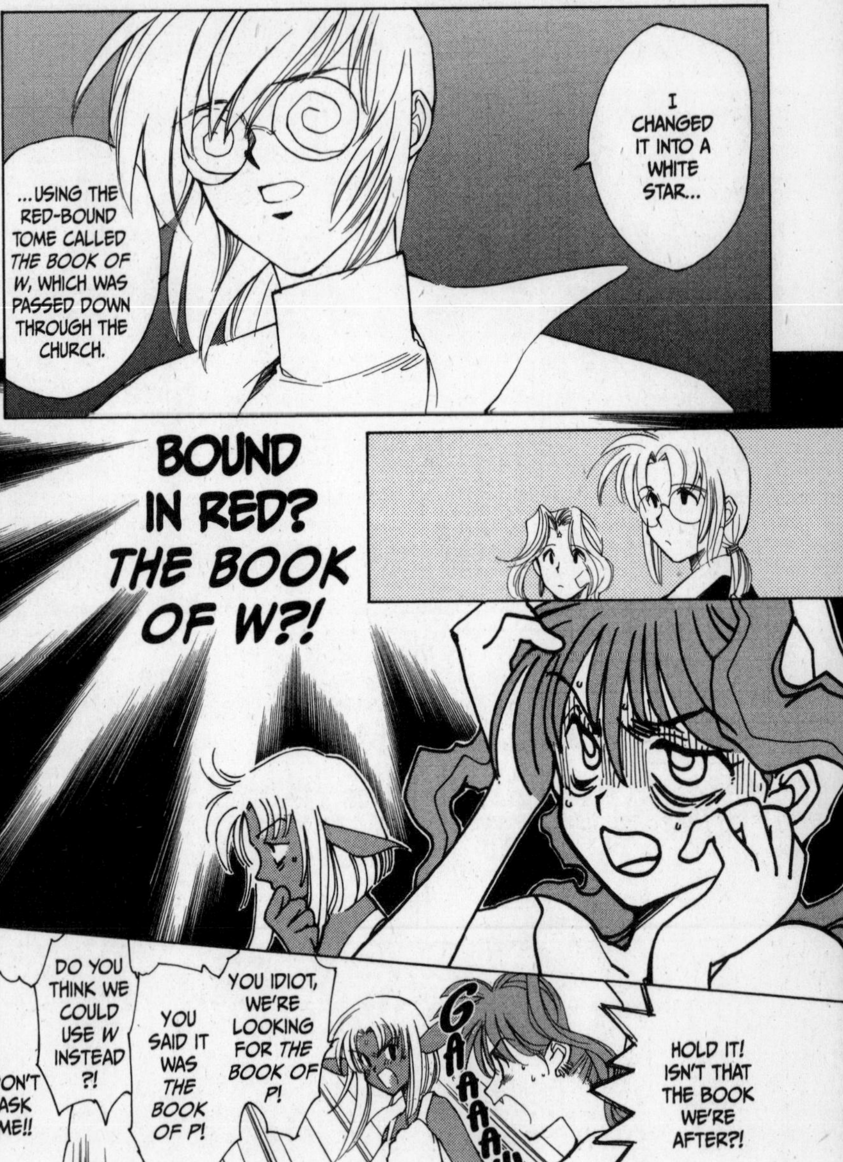
I CHANGED IT INTO A WHITE STAR...
...USING THE RED-BOUND TOME CALLED *THE BOOK OF W*, WHICH WAS PASSED DOWN THROUGH THE CHURCH.
BOUND IN RED? *THE BOOK OF W*?!
HOLD IT! ISN'T THAT THE BOOK WE'RE AFTER?!
GAAAAH!
YOU IDIOT, WE'RE LOOKING FOR *THE BOOK OF P*!
YOU SAID IT WAS *THE BOOK OF P*!
DO YOU THINK WE COULD USE *W* INSTEAD?!
DON'T ASK ME!!

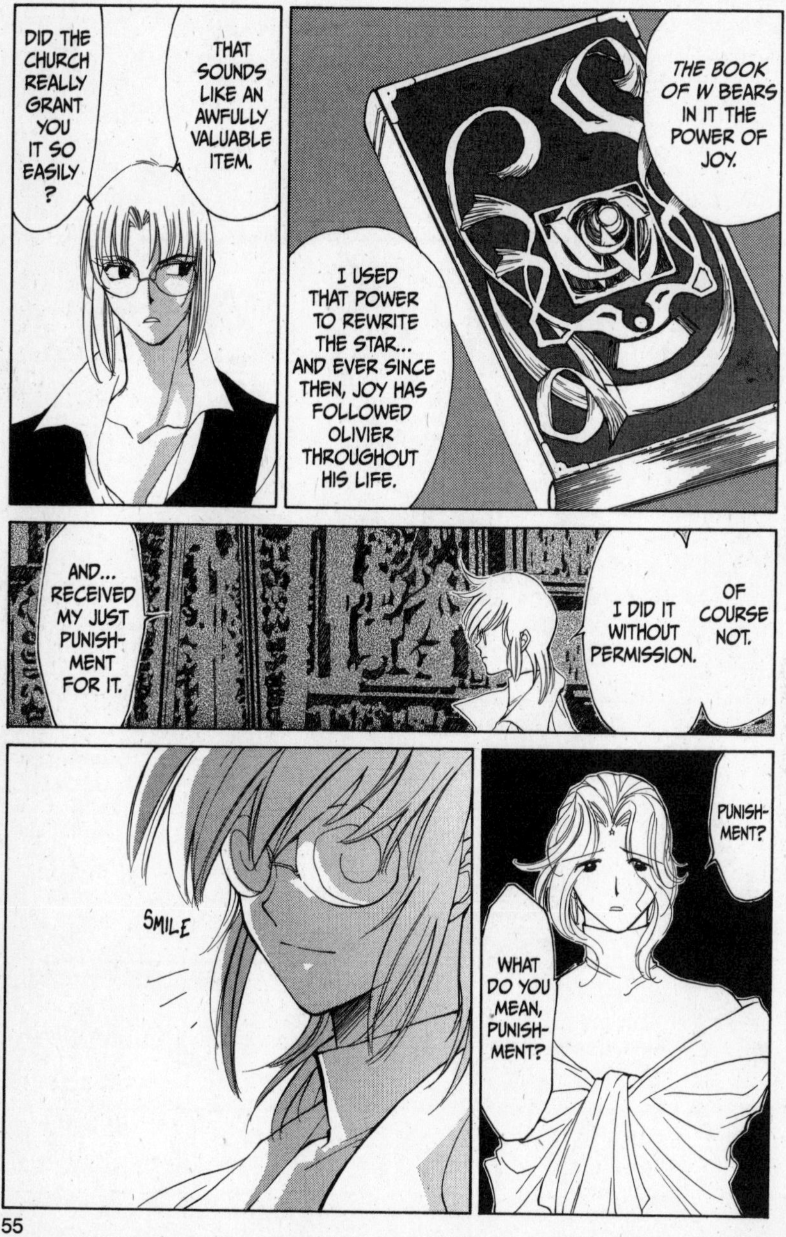
THE BOOK OF W BEARS IN IT THE POWER OF JOY.
I USED THAT POWER TO REWRITE THE STAR... AND EVER SINCE THEN, JOY HAS FOLLOWED OLIVIER THROUGHOUT HIS LIFE.
THAT SOUNDS LIKE AN AWFULLY VALUABLE ITEM.
DID THE CHURCH REALLY GRANT YOU IT SO EASILY?
OF COURSE NOT.
I DID IT WITHOUT PERMISSION.
AND... RECEIVED MY JUST PUNISHMENT FOR IT.
PUNISHMENT?
WHAT DO YOU MEAN, PUNISHMENT?
SMILE

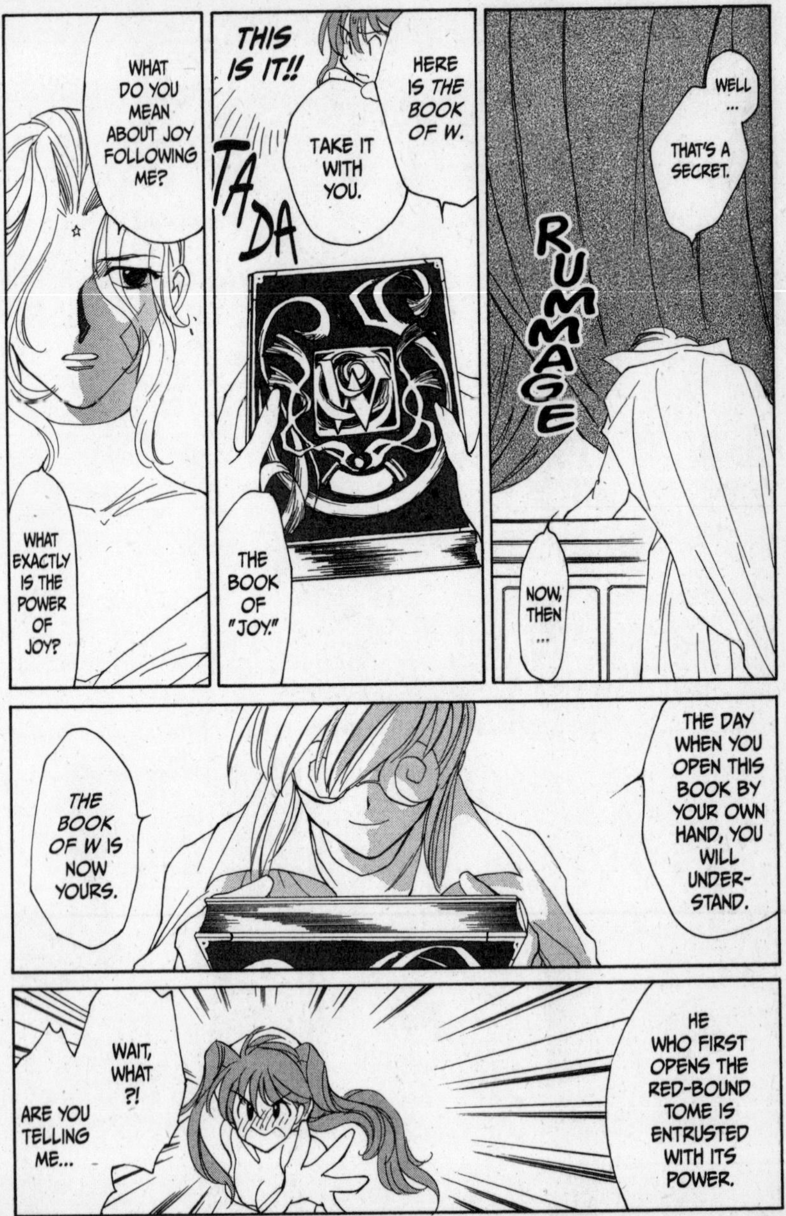
WELL ... THAT'S A SECRET.
RUMMAGE
NOW, THEN ...
HERE IS THE BOOK OF W.
THIS IS IT!!
TAKE IT WITH YOU.
TA DA
THE BOOK OF "JOY."
WHAT DO YOU MEAN ABOUT JOY FOLLOWING ME?
WHAT EXACTLY IS THE POWER OF JOY?
THE DAY WHEN YOU OPEN THIS BOOK BY YOUR OWN HAND, YOU WILL UNDER-STAND.
THE BOOK OF W IS NOW YOURS.
HE WHO FIRST OPENS THE RED-BOUND TOME IS ENTRUSTED WITH ITS POWER.
WAIT, WHAT ?!
ARE YOU TELLING ME...

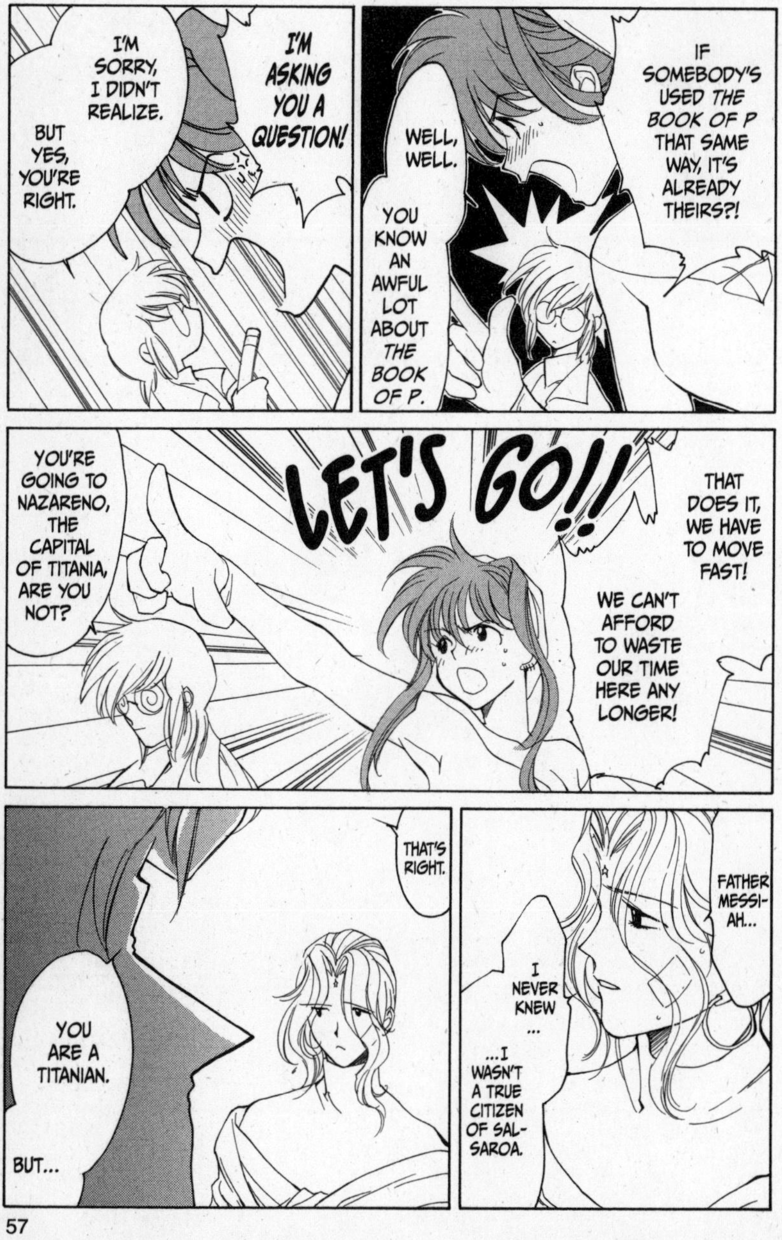
IF SOMEBODY'S USED *THE BOOK OF P* THAT SAME WAY, IT'S ALREADY THEIRS?!
WELL, WELL.
YOU KNOW AN AWFUL LOT ABOUT *THE BOOK OF P*.
I'M ASKING YOU A QUESTION!
I'M SORRY, I DIDN'T REALIZE.
BUT YES, YOU'RE RIGHT.
THAT DOES IT, WE HAVE TO MOVE FAST!
WE CAN'T AFFORD TO WASTE OUR TIME HERE ANY LONGER!
LET'S GO!!
YOU'RE GOING TO NAZARENO, THE CAPITAL OF TITANIA, ARE YOU NOT?
FATHER MESSI-AH...
I NEVER KNEW ...
...I WASN'T A TRUE CITIZEN OF SAL-SAROA.
THAT'S RIGHT.
YOU ARE A TITANIAN.
BUT...

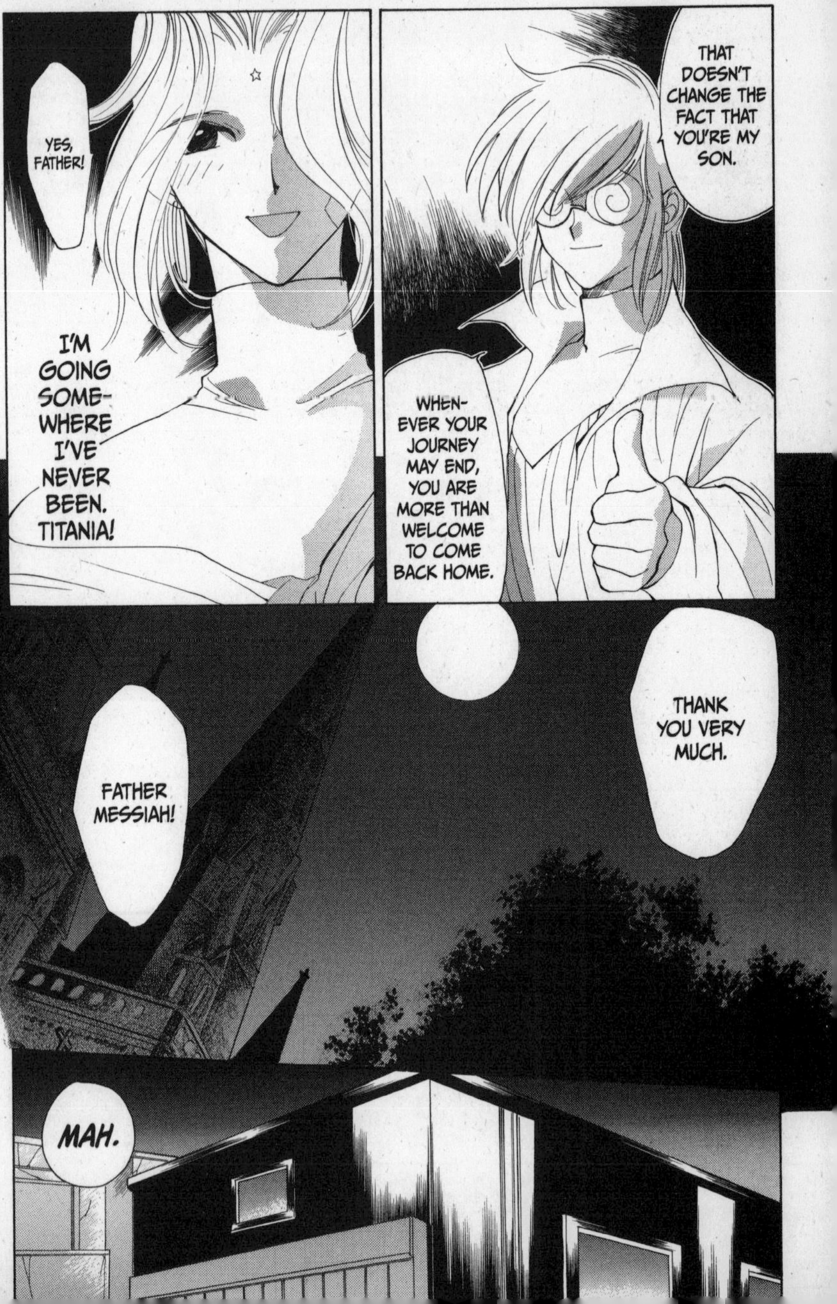
THAT DOESN'T CHANGE THE FACT THAT YOU'RE MY SON.
WHEN-EVER YOUR JOURNEY MAY END, YOU ARE MORE THAN WELCOME TO COME BACK HOME.
YES, FATHER!
I'M GOING SOME-WHERE I'VE NEVER BEEN. TITANIA!
THANK YOU VERY MUCH.
FATHER MESSIAH!
MAH.

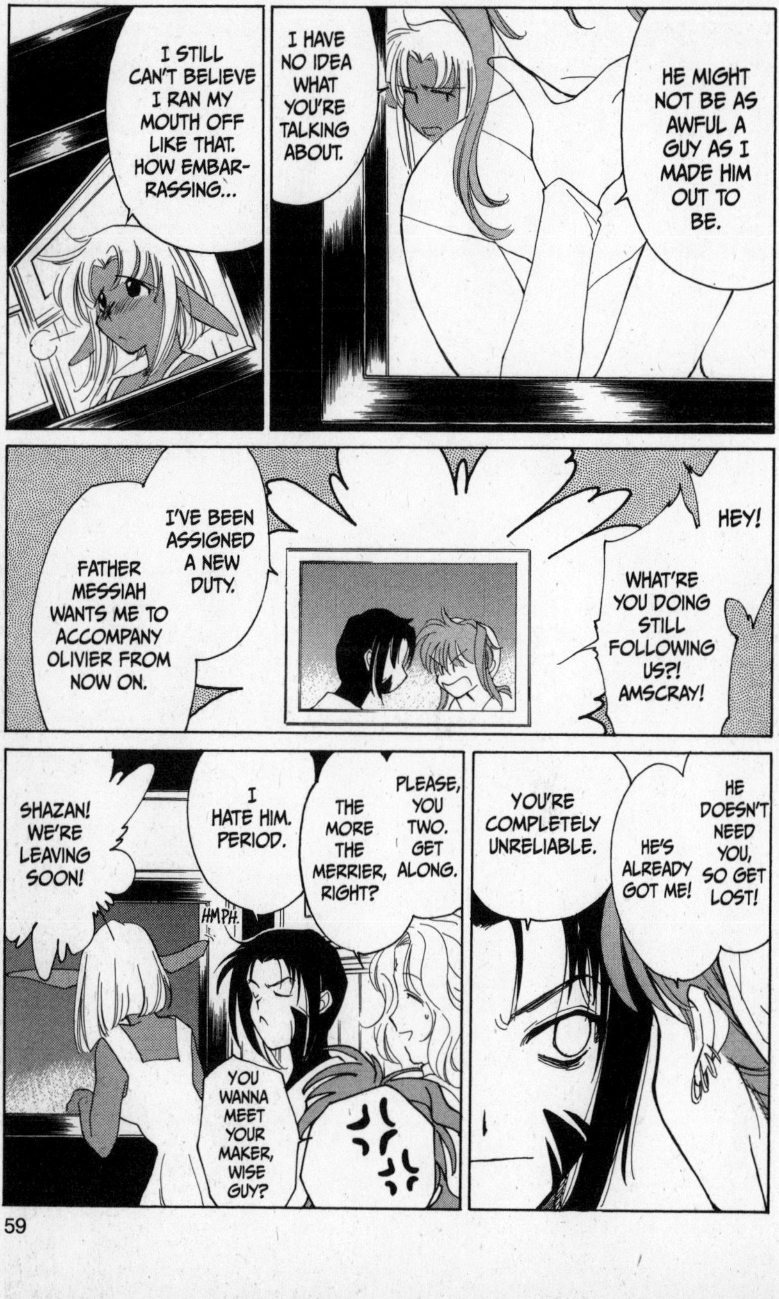
HE MIGHT NOT BE AS AWFUL A GUY AS I MADE HIM OUT TO BE.
I HAVE NO IDEA WHAT YOU'RE TALKING ABOUT.
I STILL CAN'T BELIEVE I RAN MY MOUTH OFF LIKE THAT. HOW EMBARRASSING...
HEY!
WHAT'RE YOU DOING STILL FOLLOWING US?! AMSCRAY!
I'VE BEEN ASSIGNED A NEW DUTY.
FATHER MESSIAH WANTS ME TO ACCOMPANY OLIVIER FROM NOW ON.
HE DOESN'T NEED YOU, SO GET LOST!
HE'S ALREADY GOT ME!
YOU'RE COMPLETELY UNRELIABLE.
PLEASE, YOU TWO. GET ALONG.
THE MORE THE MERRIER, RIGHT?
I HATE HIM. PERIOD.
SHAZAN! WE'RE LEAVING SOON!
HMPH.
YOU WANNA MEET YOUR MAKER, WISE GUY?

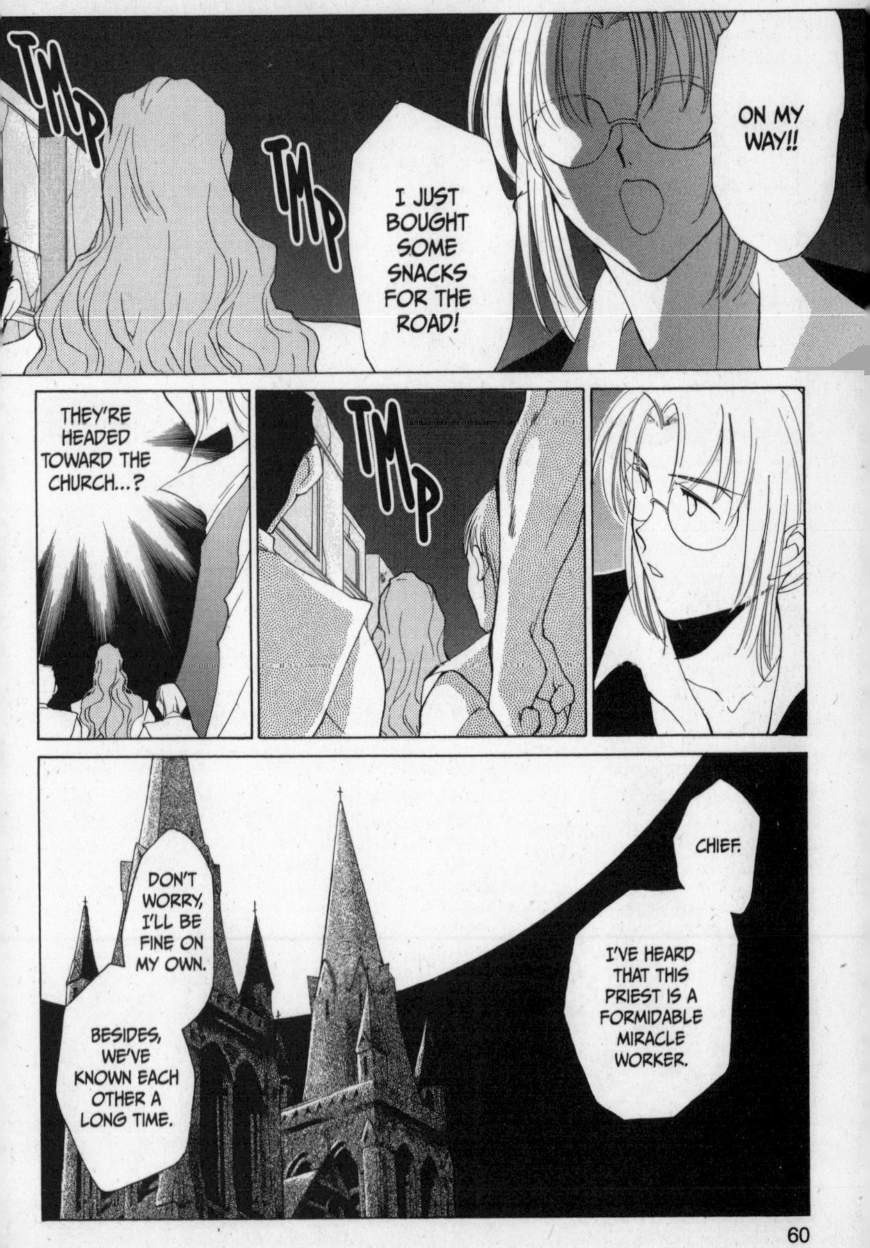
ON MY WAY!!
I JUST BOUGHT SOME SNACKS FOR THE ROAD!
TMP
TMP
TMP
THEY'RE HEADED TOWARD THE CHURCH...?
CHIEF.
I'VE HEARD THAT THIS PRIEST IS A FORMIDABLE MIRACLE WORKER.
DON'T WORRY, I'LL BE FINE ON MY OWN.
BESIDES, WE'VE KNOWN EACH OTHER A LONG TIME.

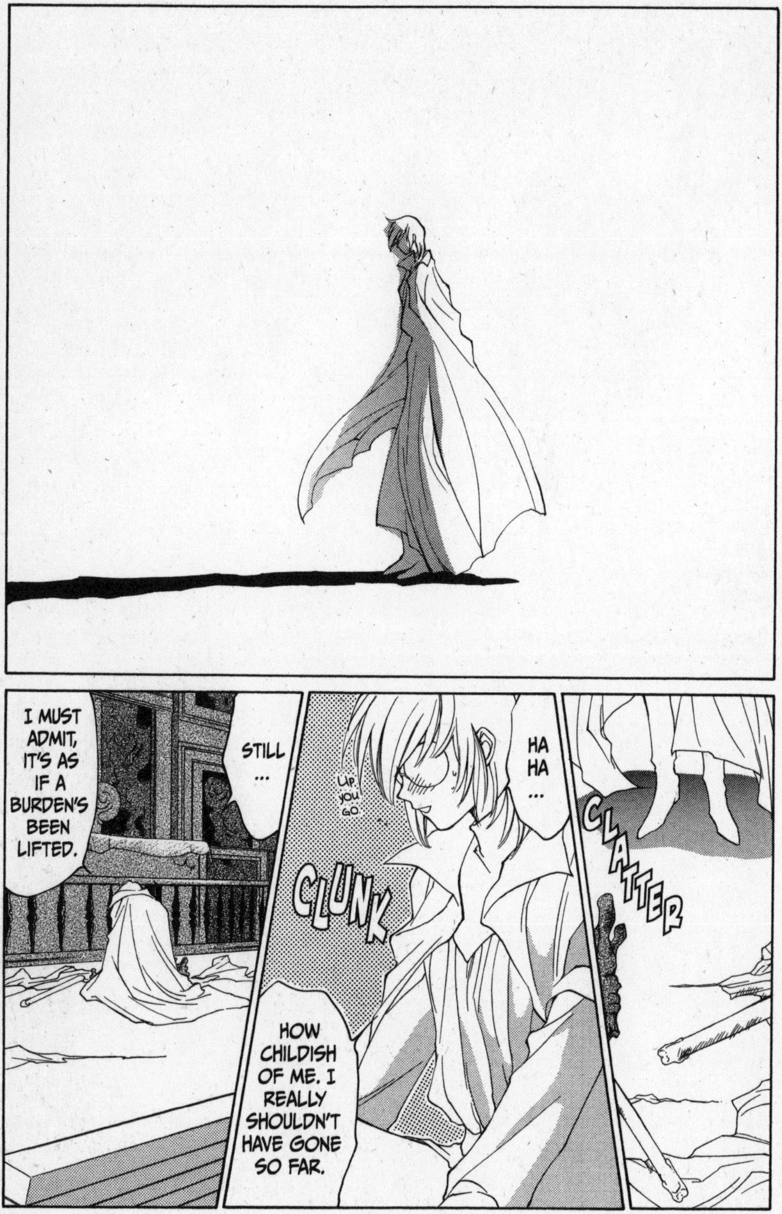
CLATTER
HA HA ...
Up, you go.
CLUNK
HOW CHILDISH OF ME. I REALLY SHOULDN'T HAVE GONE SO FAR.
STILL ...
I MUST ADMIT, IT'S AS IF A BURDEN'S BEEN LIFTED.

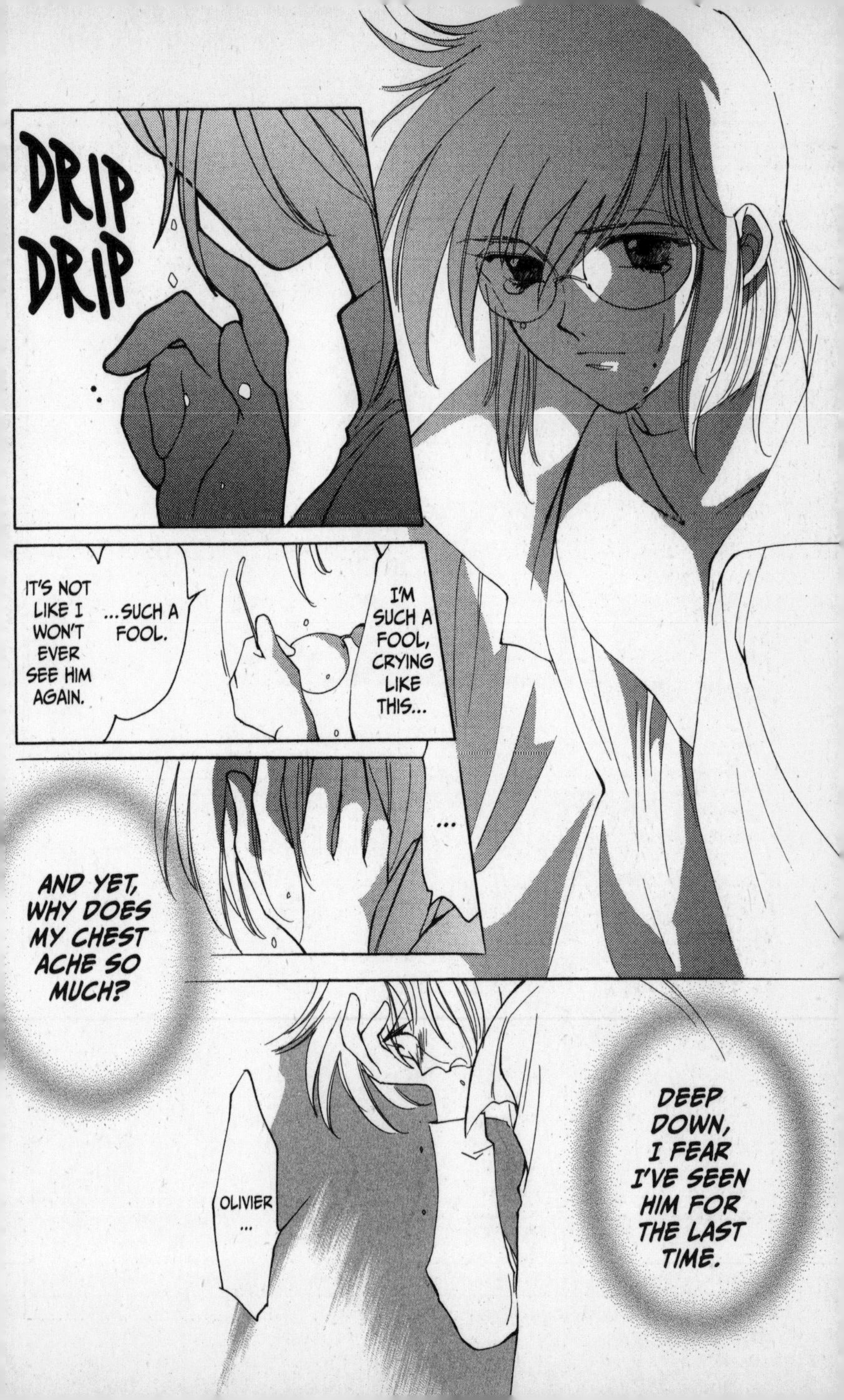
DRIP DRIP
I'M SUCH A FOOL, CRYING LIKE THIS...
...SUCH A FOOL.
IT'S NOT LIKE I WON'T EVER SEE HIM AGAIN.
...
AND YET, WHY DOES MY CHEST ACHE SO MUCH?
DEEP DOWN, I FEAR I'VE SEEN HIM FOR THE LAST TIME.
OLIVIER ...

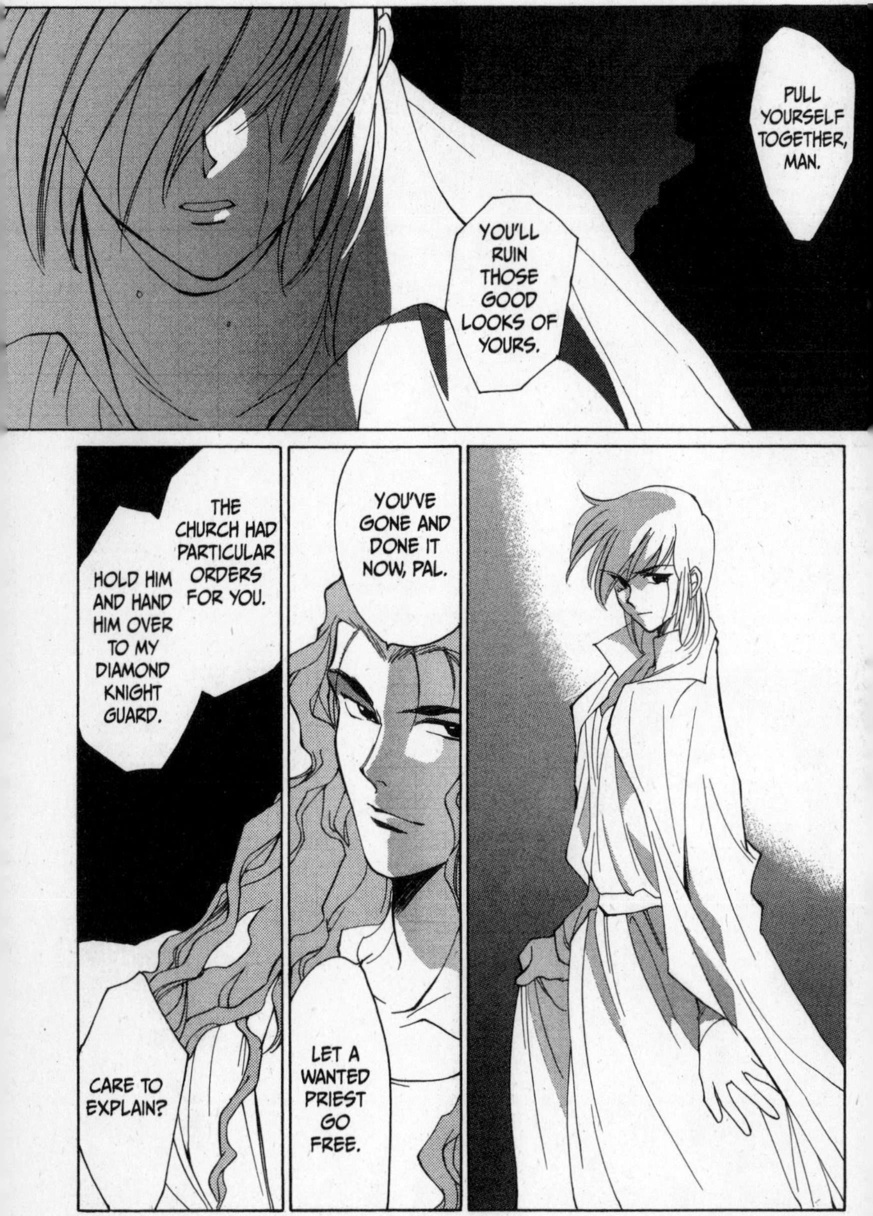
PULL YOURSELF TOGETHER, MAN.
YOU'LL RUIN THOSE GOOD LOOKS OF YOURS.
YOU'VE GONE AND DONE IT NOW, PAL.
LET A WANTED PRIEST GO FREE.
THE CHURCH HAD PARTICULAR ORDERS FOR YOU.
HOLD HIM AND HAND HIM OVER TO MY DIAMOND KNIGHT GUARD.
CARE TO EXPLAIN?

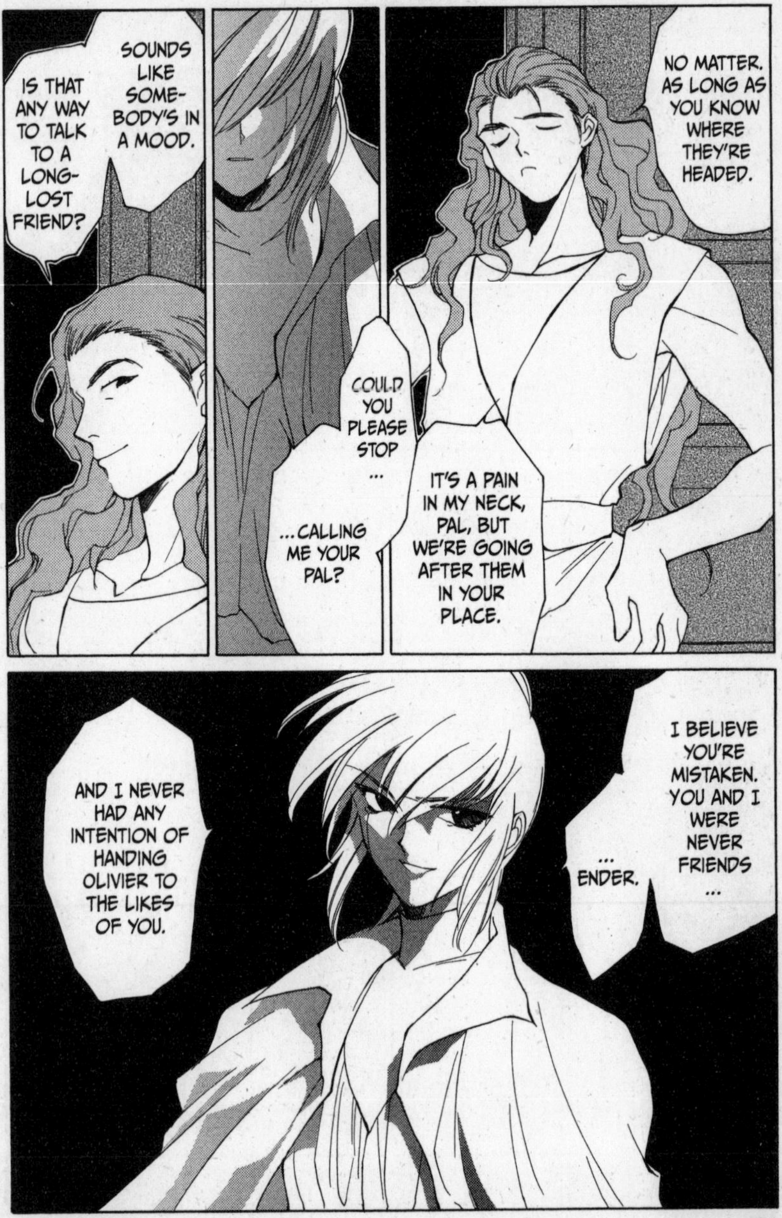
NO MATTER. AS LONG AS YOU KNOW WHERE THEY'RE HEADED.
IT'S A PAIN IN MY NECK, PAL, BUT WE'RE GOING AFTER THEM IN YOUR PLACE.
COULD YOU PLEASE STOP ...
...CALLING ME YOUR PAL?
SOUNDS LIKE SOME-BODY'S IN A MOOD.
IS THAT ANY WAY TO TALK TO A LONG-LOST FRIEND?
I BELIEVE YOU'RE MISTAKEN. YOU AND I WERE NEVER FRIENDS ...
... ENDER.
AND I NEVER HAD ANY INTENTION OF HANDING OLIVIER TO THE LIKES OF YOU.

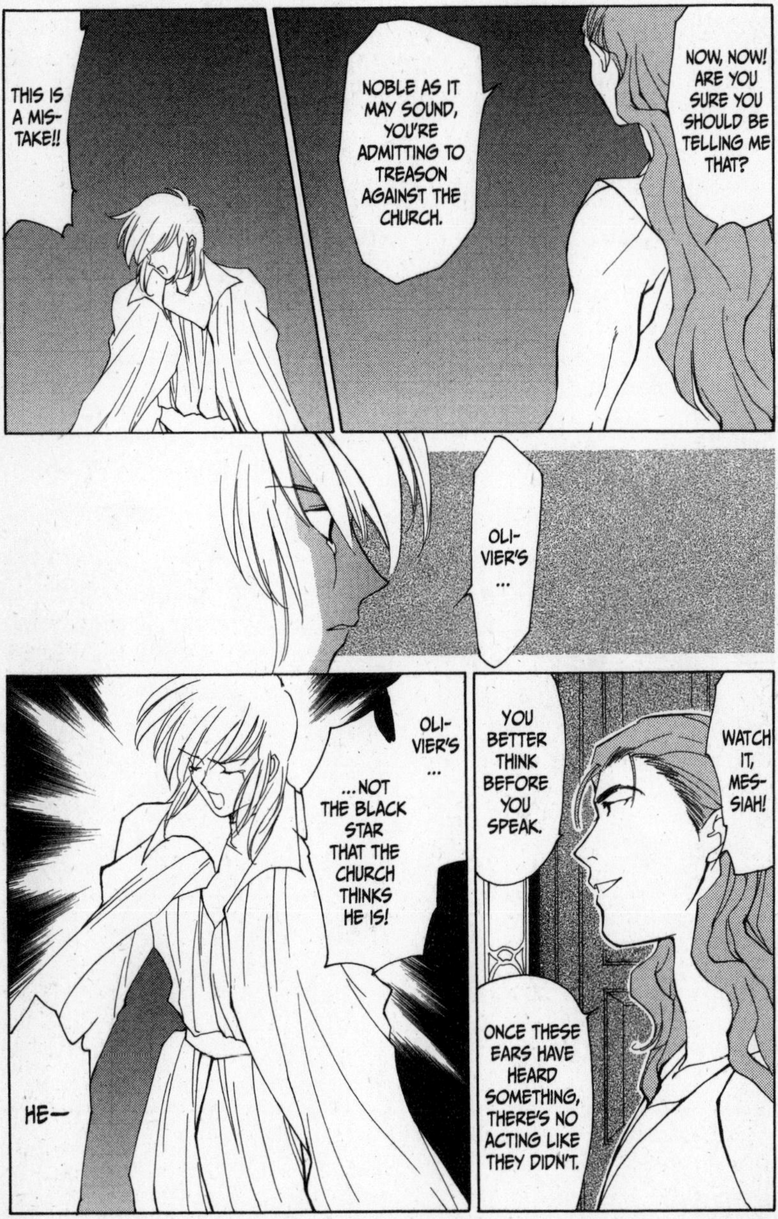
NOW, NOW! ARE YOU SURE YOU SHOULD BE TELLING ME THAT?
NOBLE AS IT MAY SOUND, YOU'RE ADMITTING TO TREASON AGAINST THE CHURCH.
THIS IS A MIS-TAKE!!
OLI-VIER'S ...
WATCH IT, MES-SIAH!
YOU BETTER THINK BEFORE YOU SPEAK.
ONCE THESE EARS HAVE HEARD SOMETHING, THERE'S NO ACTING LIKE THEY DIDN'T.
OLI-VIER'S ...
...NOT THE BLACK STAR THAT THE CHURCH THINKS HE IS!
HE—

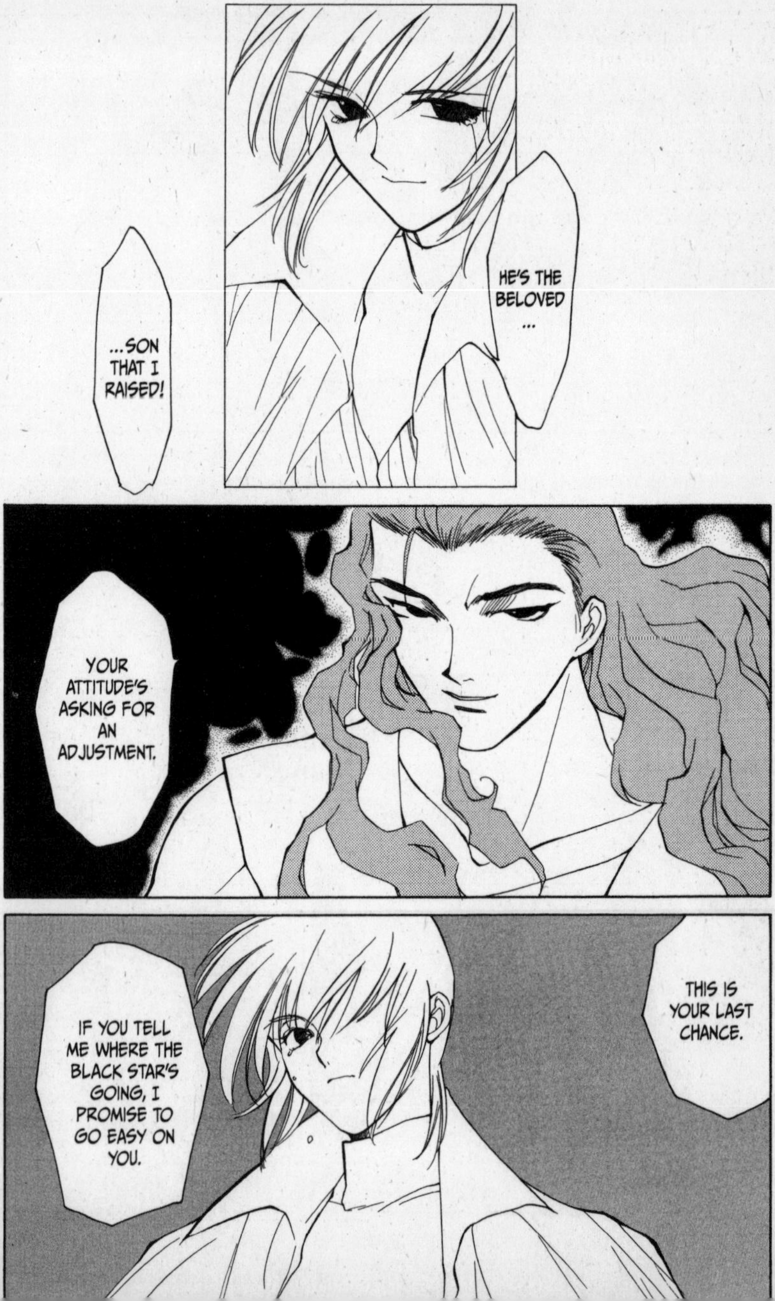
HE'S THE BELOVED ...
...SON THAT I RAISED!
YOUR ATTITUDE'S ASKING FOR AN ADJUSTMENT.
THIS IS YOUR LAST CHANCE.
IF YOU TELL ME WHERE THE BLACK STAR'S GOING, I PROMISE TO GO EASY ON YOU.

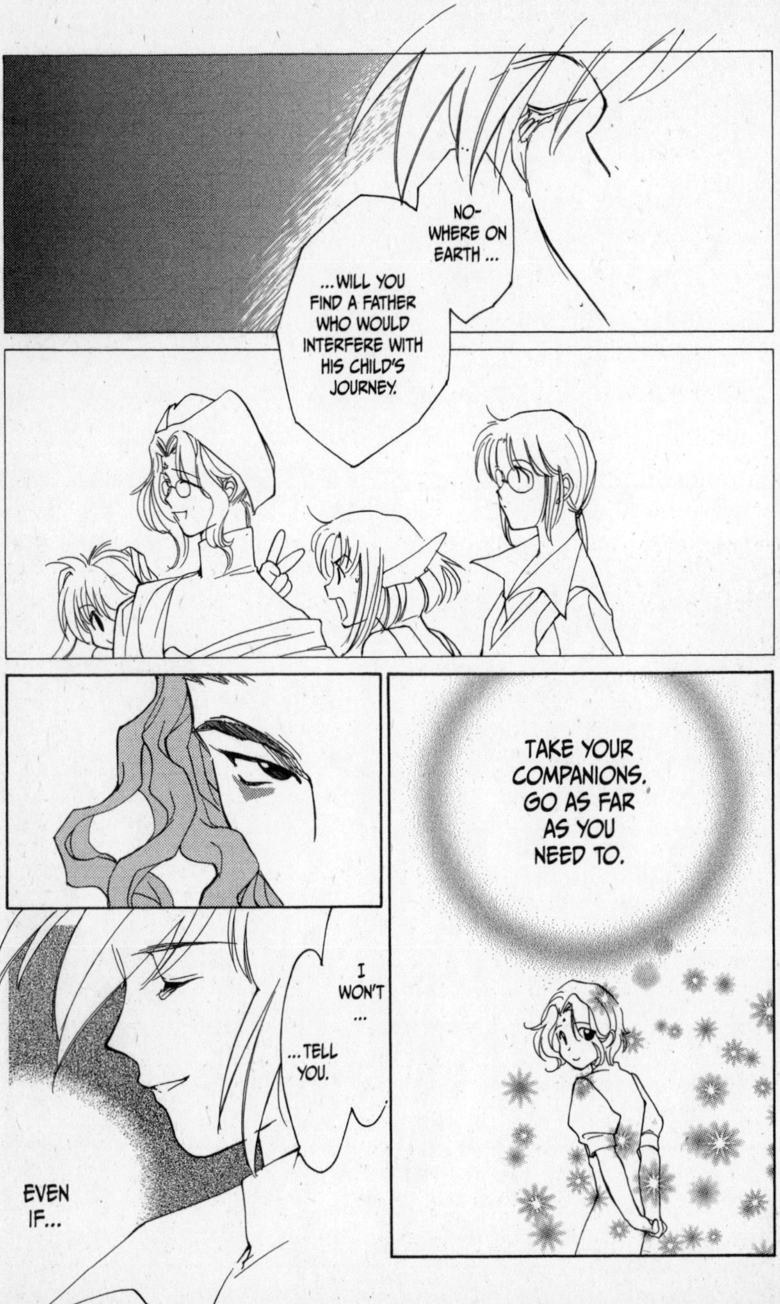
NO-WHERE ON EARTH ...
...WILL YOU FIND A FATHER WHO WOULD INTERFERE WITH HIS CHILD'S JOURNEY.
TAKE YOUR COMPANIONS. GO AS FAR AS YOU NEED TO.
I WON'T ...
...TELL YOU.
EVEN IF...

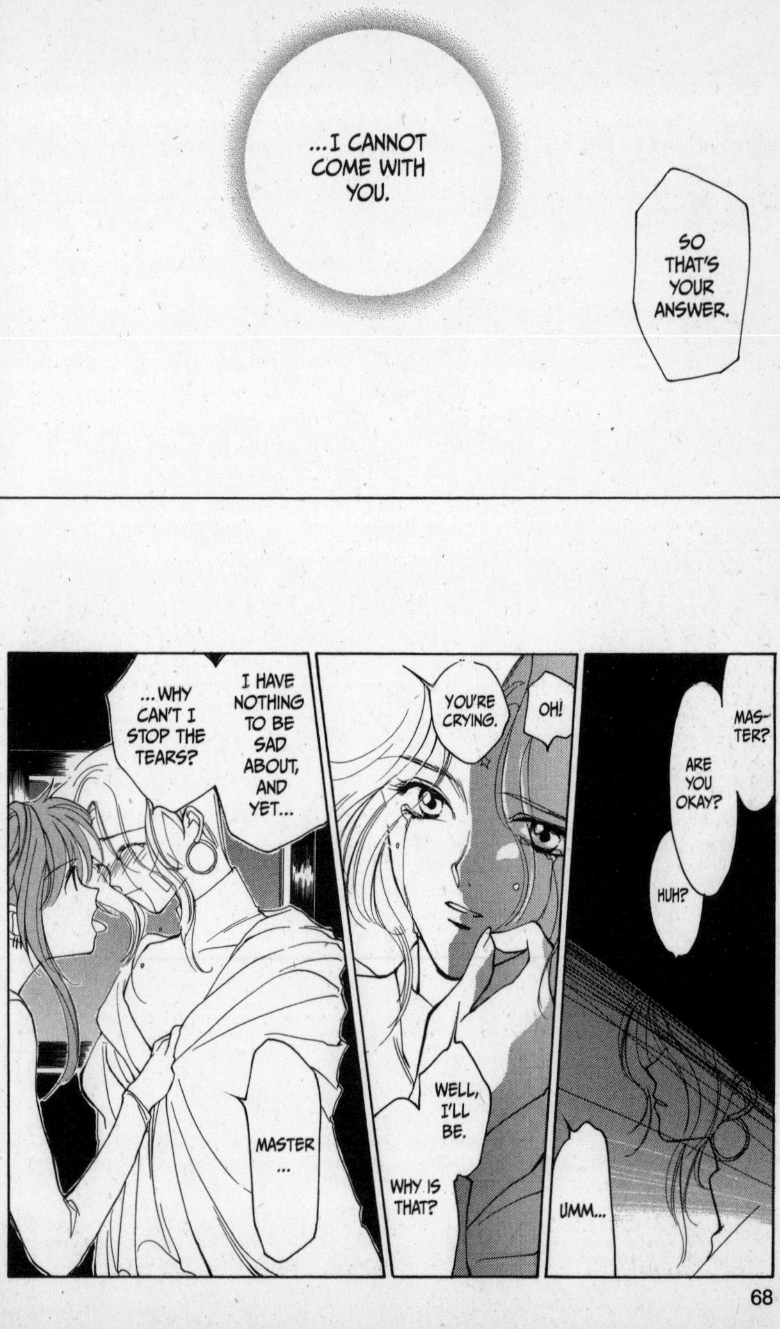
...I CANNOT COME WITH YOU.
SO THAT'S YOUR ANSWER.
MAS-TER?
ARE YOU OKAY?
HUH?
UMM...
OH!
YOU'RE CRYING.
WELL, I'LL BE.
WHY IS THAT?
I HAVE NOTHING TO BE SAD ABOUT, AND YET...
...WHY CAN'T I STOP THE TEARS?
MASTER ...

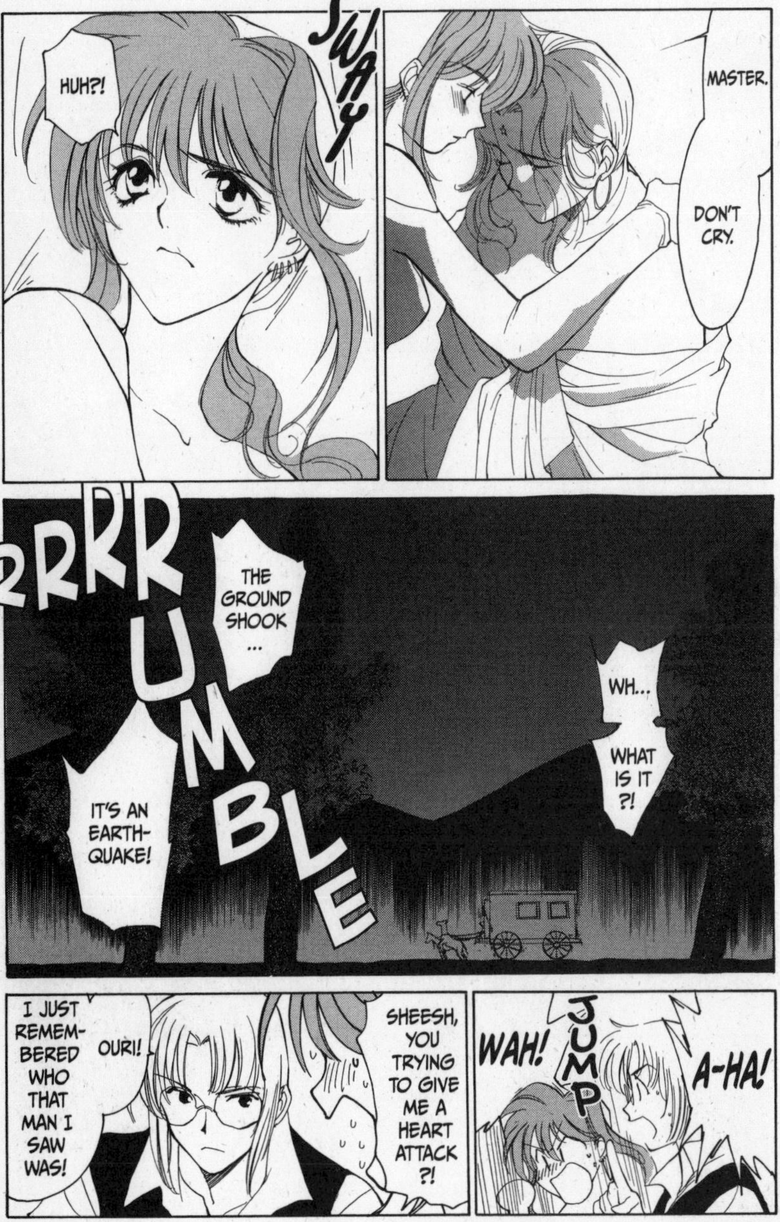
MASTER.
DON'T CRY.
SWAY
HUH?!
WH...
WHAT IS IT ?!
THE GROUND SHOOK ...
RRRRUMBLE
IT'S AN EARTH-QUAKE!
A-HA!
JUMP
WAH!
SHEESH, YOU TRYING TO GIVE ME A HEART ATTACK ?!
OURI!
I JUST REMEM-BERED WHO THAT MAN I SAW WAS!

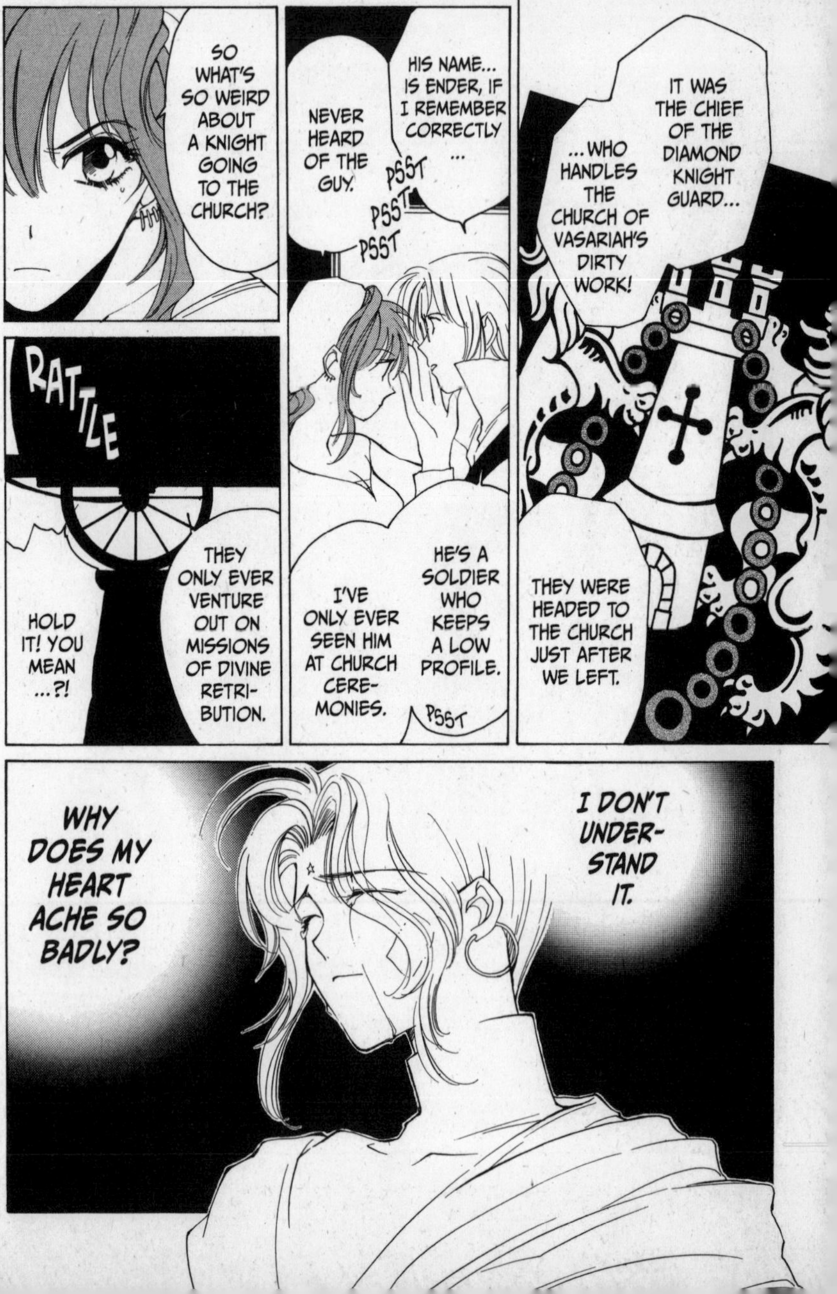
IT WAS THE CHIEF OF THE DIAMOND KNIGHT GUARD...
...WHO HANDLES THE CHURCH OF VASARIAH'S DIRTY WORK!
THEY WERE HEADED TO THE CHURCH JUST AFTER WE LEFT.
HIS NAME... IS ENDER, IF I REMEMBER CORRECTLY ...
NEVER HEARD OF THE GUY.
PSST
PSST
PSST
HE'S A SOLDIER WHO KEEPS A LOW PROFILE.
I'VE ONLY EVER SEEN HIM AT CHURCH CEREMONIES.
PSST
SO WHAT'S SO WEIRD ABOUT A KNIGHT GOING TO THE CHURCH?
RATTLE
THEY ONLY EVER VENTURE OUT ON MISSIONS OF DIVINE RETRIBUTION.
HOLD IT! YOU MEAN ...?!
I DON'T UNDERSTAND IT.
WHY DOES MY HEART ACHE SO BADLY?

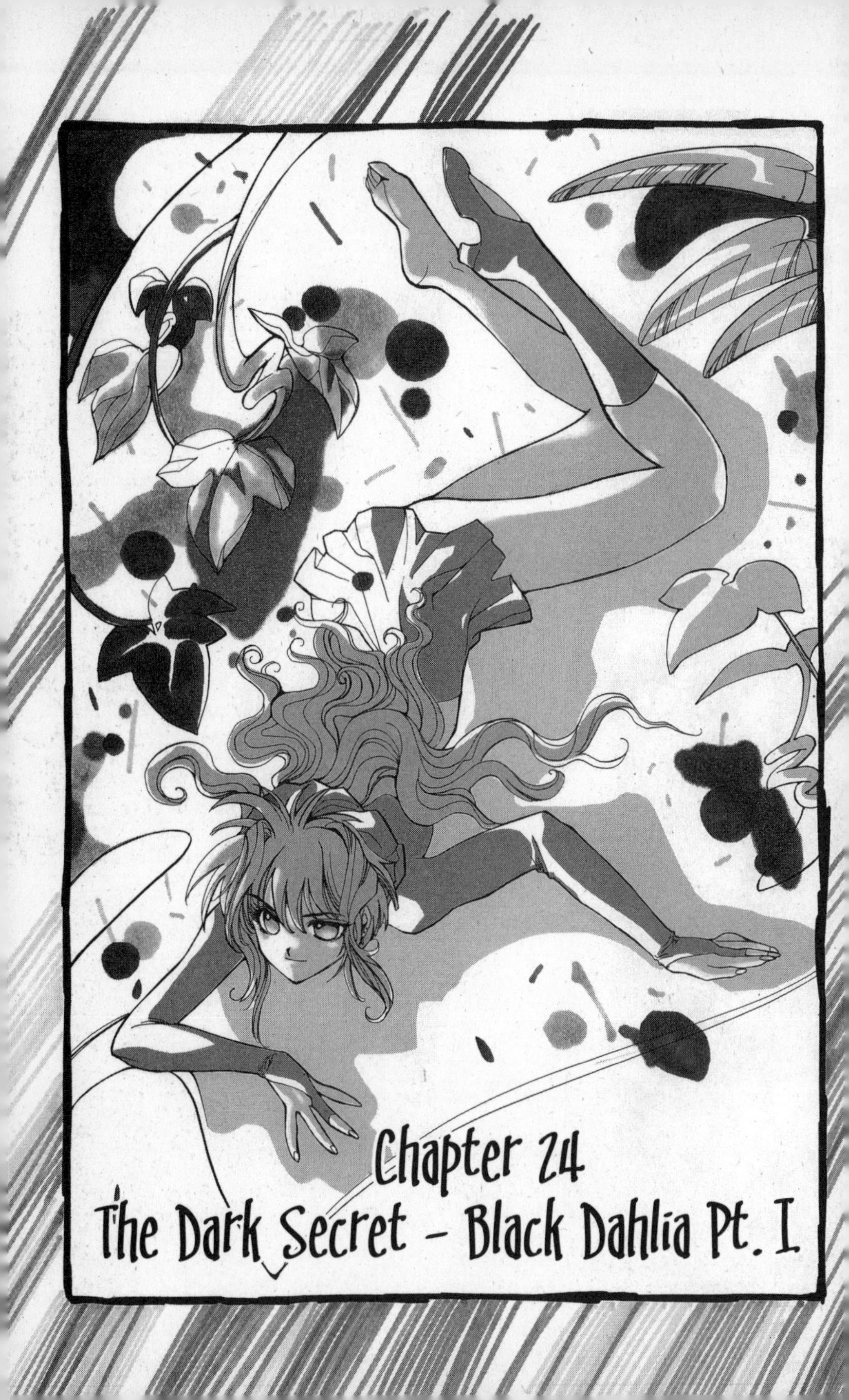
Chapter 24
The Dark Secret - Black Dahlia Pt. I.

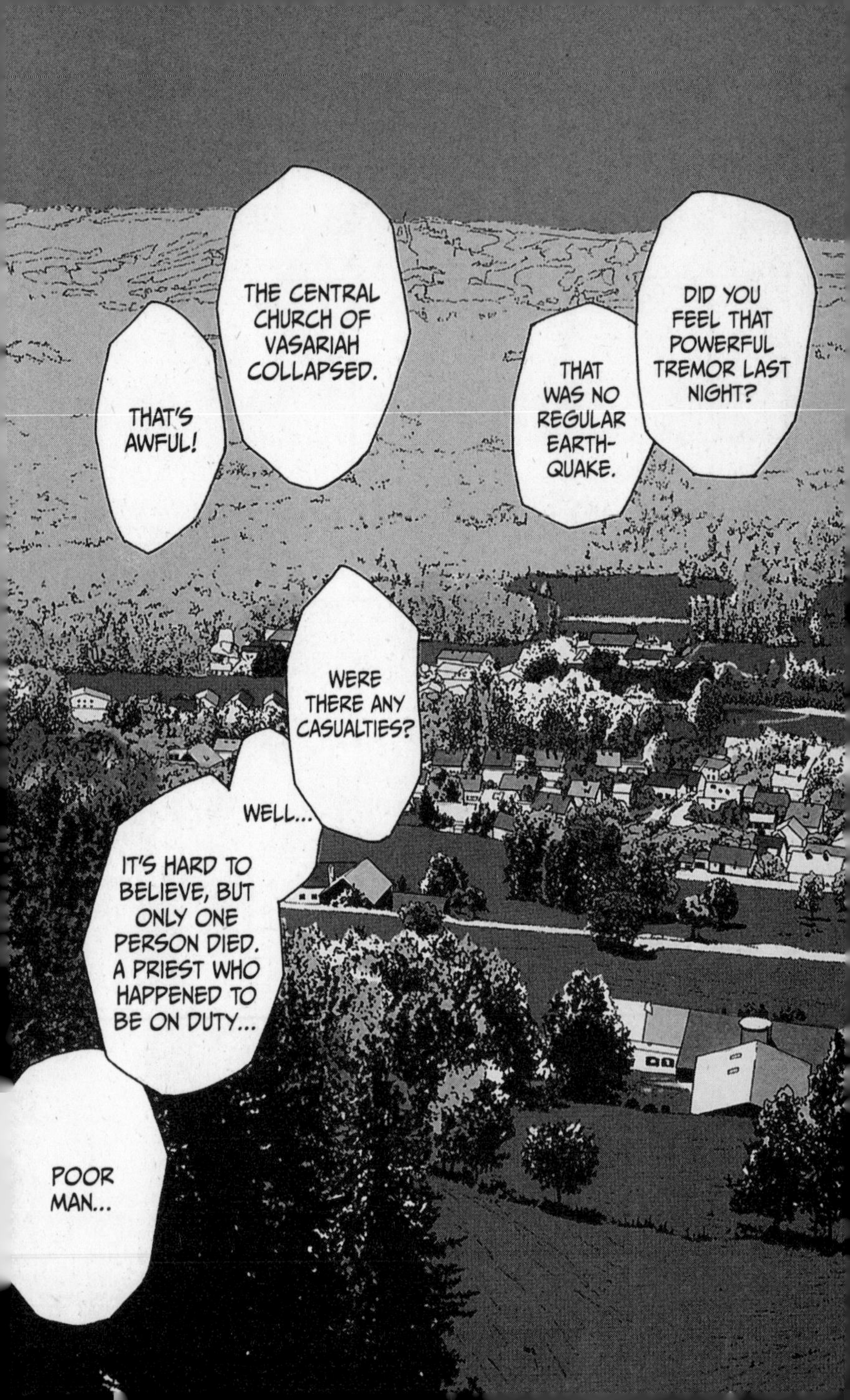
DID YOU FEEL THAT POWERFUL TREMOR LAST NIGHT?
THAT WAS NO REGULAR EARTH-QUAKE.
THE CENTRAL CHURCH OF VASARIAH COLLAPSED.
THAT'S AWFUL!
WERE THERE ANY CASUALTIES?
WELL...
IT'S HARD TO BELIEVE, BUT ONLY ONE PERSON DIED. A PRIEST WHO HAPPENED TO BE ON DUTY...
POOR MAN...

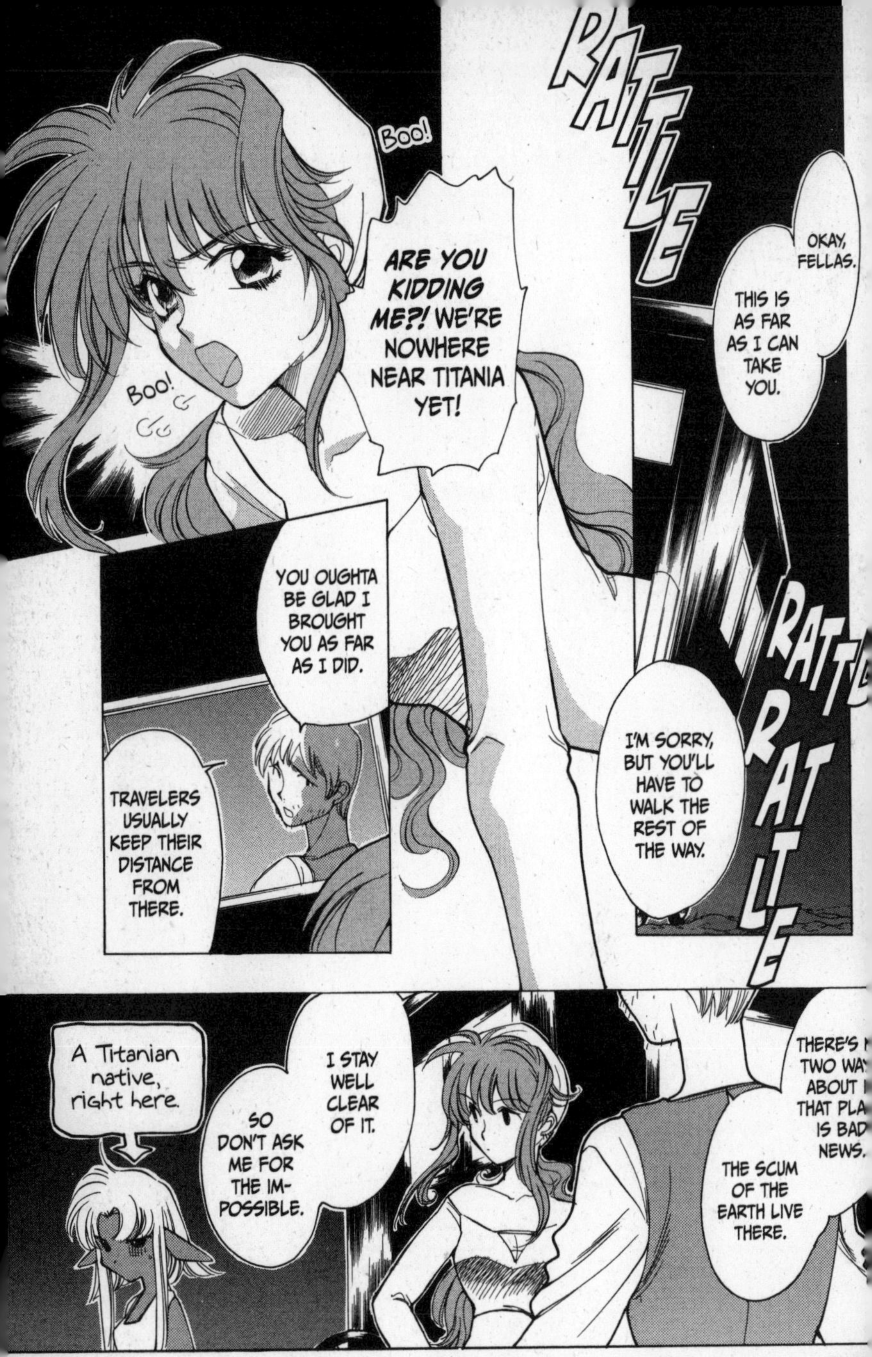
RATTLE
OKAY, FELLAS.
THIS IS AS FAR AS I CAN TAKE YOU.
RATTLE
RATTLE
I'M SORRY, BUT YOU'LL HAVE TO WALK THE REST OF THE WAY.
Boo!
ARE YOU KIDDING ME?! WE'RE NOWHERE NEAR TITANIA YET!
Boo!
YOU OUGHTA BE GLAD I BROUGHT YOU AS FAR AS I DID.
TRAVELERS USUALLY KEEP THEIR DISTANCE FROM THERE.
THERE'S TWO WA ABOUT THAT PLA IS BAD NEWS.
THE SCUM OF THE EARTH LIVE THERE.
I STAY WELL CLEAR OF IT.
SO DON'T ASK ME FOR THE IM-POSSIBLE.
A Titanian native, right here.

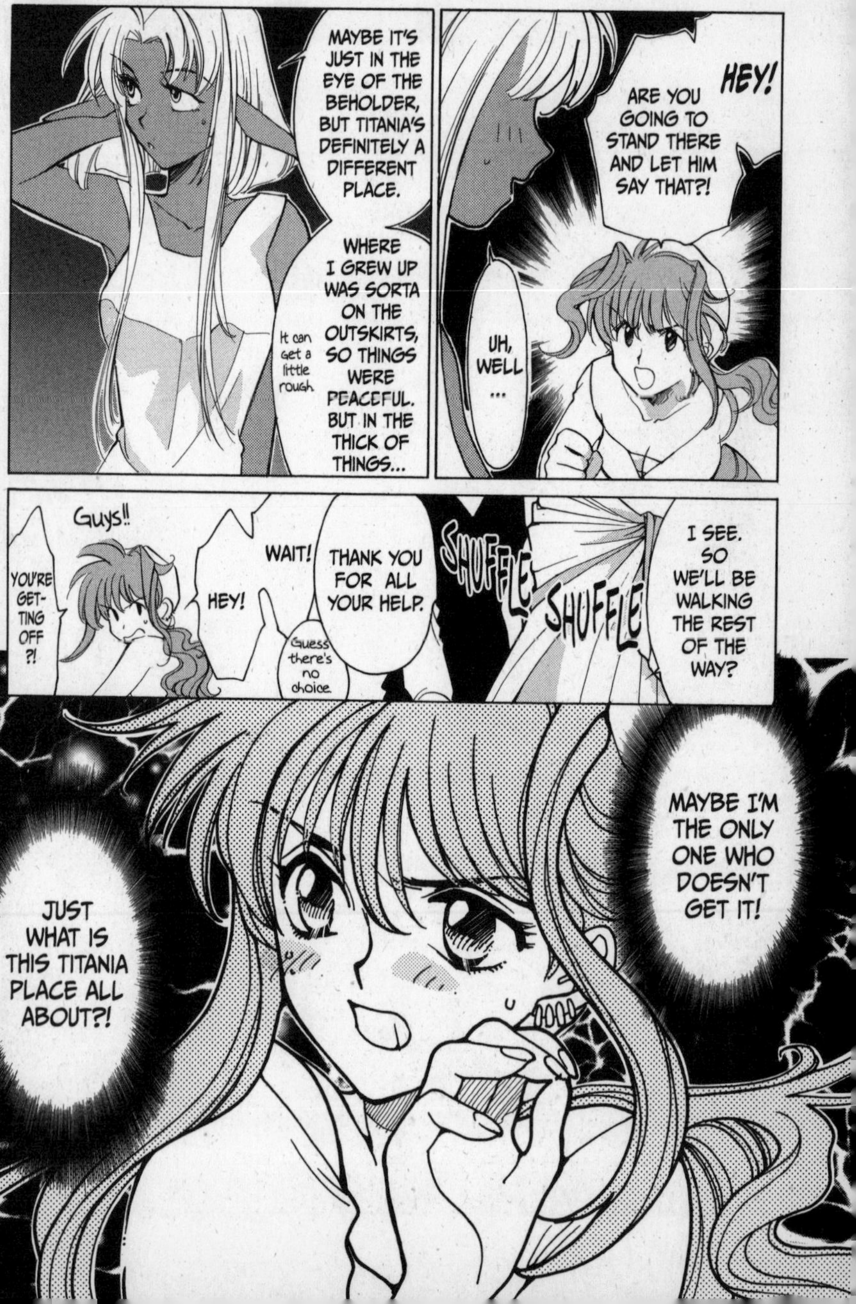
HEY!
ARE YOU GOING TO STAND THERE AND LET HIM SAY THAT?!
UH, WELL ...
MAYBE IT'S JUST IN THE EYE OF THE BEHOLDER, BUT TITANIA'S DEFINITELY A DIFFERENT PLACE.
WHERE I GREW UP WAS SORTA ON THE OUTSKIRTS, SO THINGS WERE PEACEFUL. BUT IN THE THICK OF THINGS...
It can get a little rough.
I SEE. SO WE'LL BE WALKING THE REST OF THE WAY?
SHUFFLE
SHUFFLE
THANK YOU FOR ALL YOUR HELP.
Guess there's no choice.
WAIT!
HEY!
Guys!!
YOU'RE GETTING OFF?!
MAYBE I'M THE ONLY ONE WHO DOESN'T GET IT!
JUST WHAT IS THIS TITANIA PLACE ALL ABOUT?!

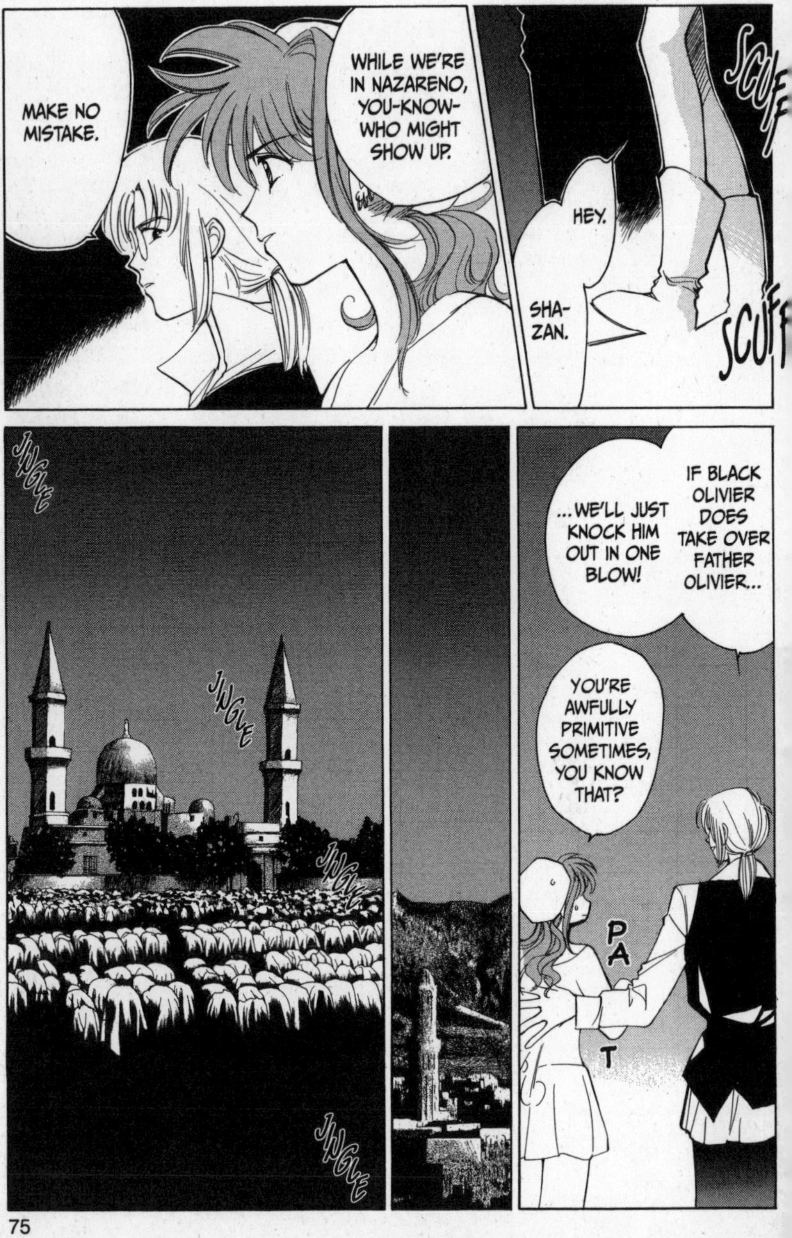
SCUFF
HEY.
SHA-ZAN.
SCUFF
WHILE WE'RE IN NAZARENO, YOU-KNOW-WHO MIGHT SHOW UP.
MAKE NO MISTAKE.
IF BLACK OLIVIER DOES TAKE OVER FATHER OLIVIER...
...WE'LL JUST KNOCK HIM OUT IN ONE BLOW!
YOU'RE AWFULLY PRIMITIVE SOMETIMES, YOU KNOW THAT?
PAT
JINGLE
JINGLE
JINGLE
JINGLE

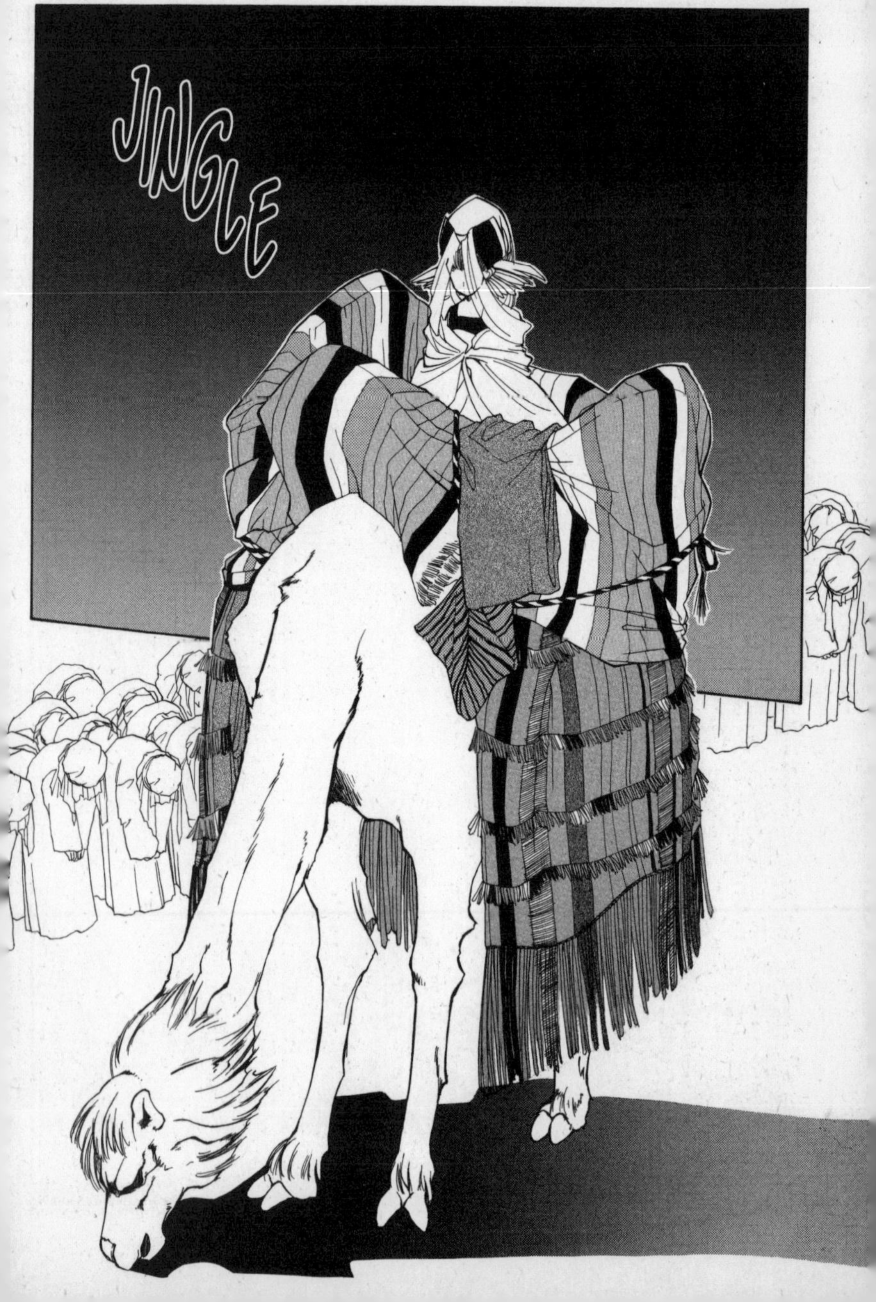
JINGLE

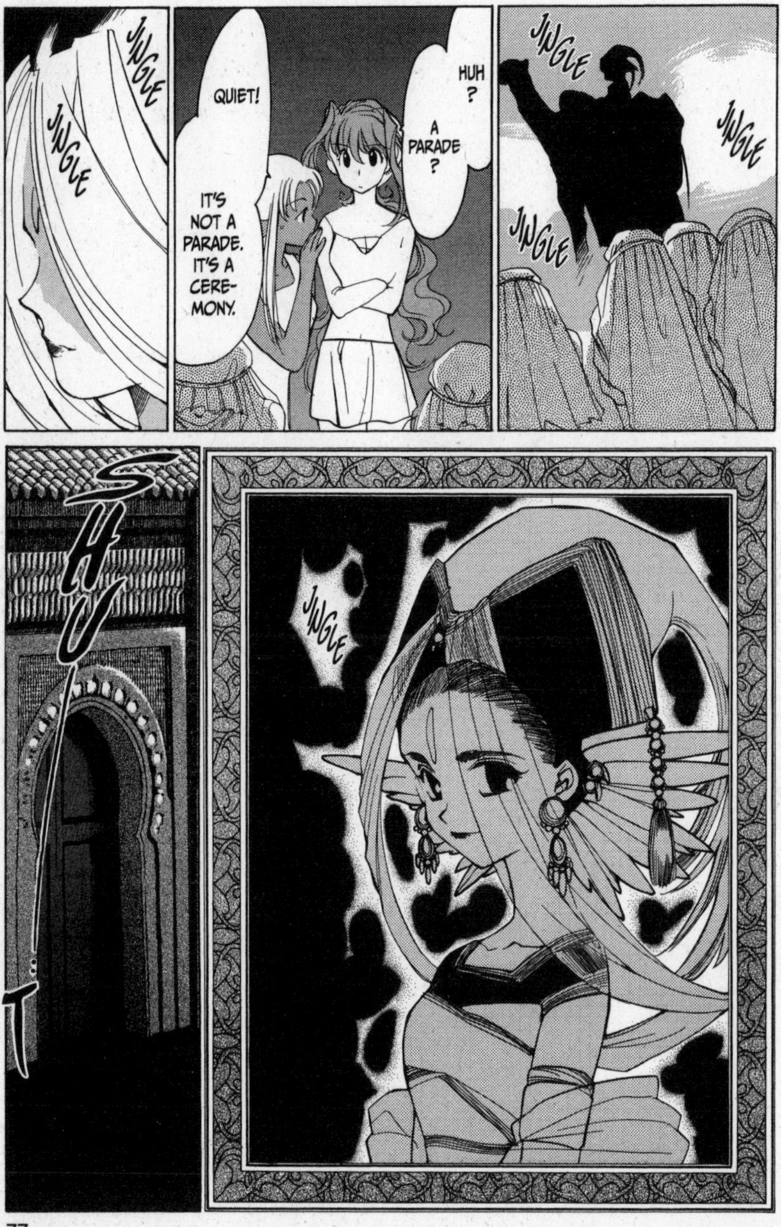
JINGLE
JINGLE
JINGLE
HUH?
A PARADE?
QUIET!
IT'S NOT A PARADE. IT'S A CEREMONY.
JINGLE
JINGLE
JINGLE
SHU...T

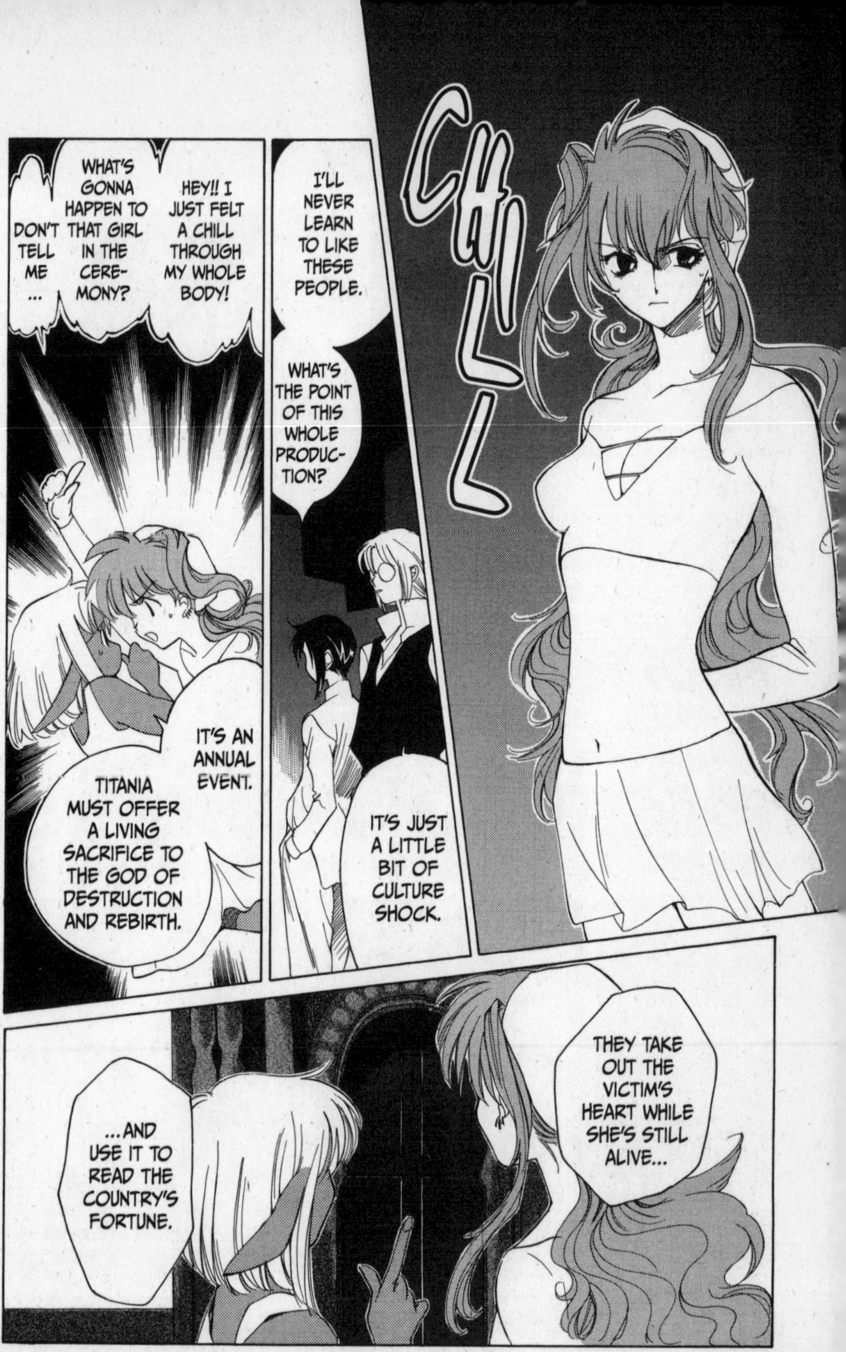
CHILL
I'LL NEVER LEARN TO LIKE THESE PEOPLE.
WHAT'S THE POINT OF THIS WHOLE PRODUC-TION?
IT'S JUST A LITTLE BIT OF CULTURE SHOCK.
HEY!! I JUST FELT A CHILL THROUGH MY WHOLE BODY!
WHAT'S GONNA HAPPEN TO THAT GIRL IN THE CERE-MONY?
DON'T TELL ME ...
IT'S AN ANNUAL EVENT.
TITANIA MUST OFFER A LIVING SACRIFICE TO THE GOD OF DESTRUCTION AND REBIRTH.
THEY TAKE OUT THE VICTIM'S HEART WHILE SHE'S STILL ALIVE...
...AND USE IT TO READ THE COUNTRY'S FORTUNE.

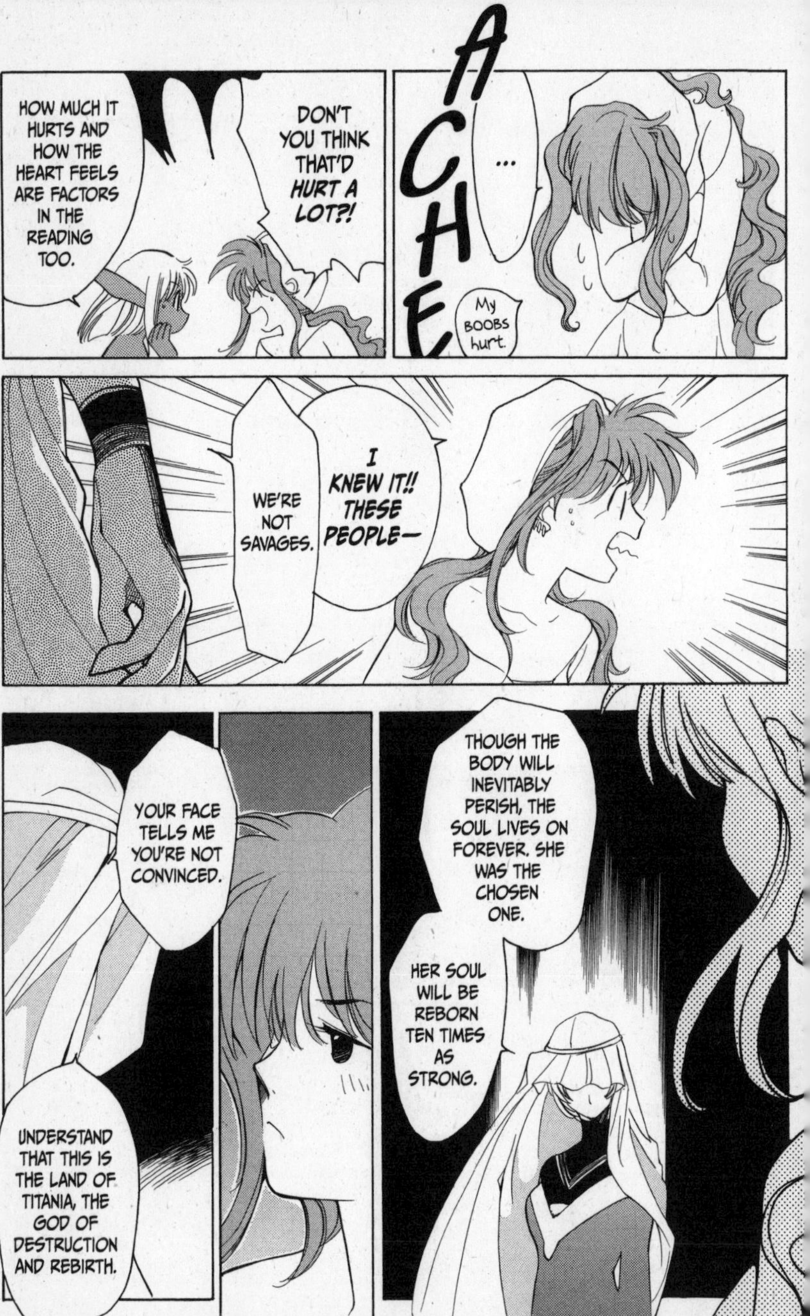
ACHE
...
My BOOBS hurt.
DON'T YOU THINK THAT'D *HURT A LOT?!*
HOW MUCH IT HURTS AND HOW THE HEART FEELS ARE FACTORS IN THE READING TOO.
I KNEW IT!! THESE PEOPLE—
WE'RE NOT SAVAGES.
THOUGH THE BODY WILL INEVITABLY PERISH, THE SOUL LIVES ON FOREVER. SHE WAS THE CHOSEN ONE.
HER SOUL WILL BE REBORN TEN TIMES AS STRONG.
YOUR FACE TELLS ME YOU'RE NOT CONVINCED.
UNDERSTAND THAT THIS IS THE LAND OF TITANIA, THE GOD OF DESTRUCTION AND REBIRTH.

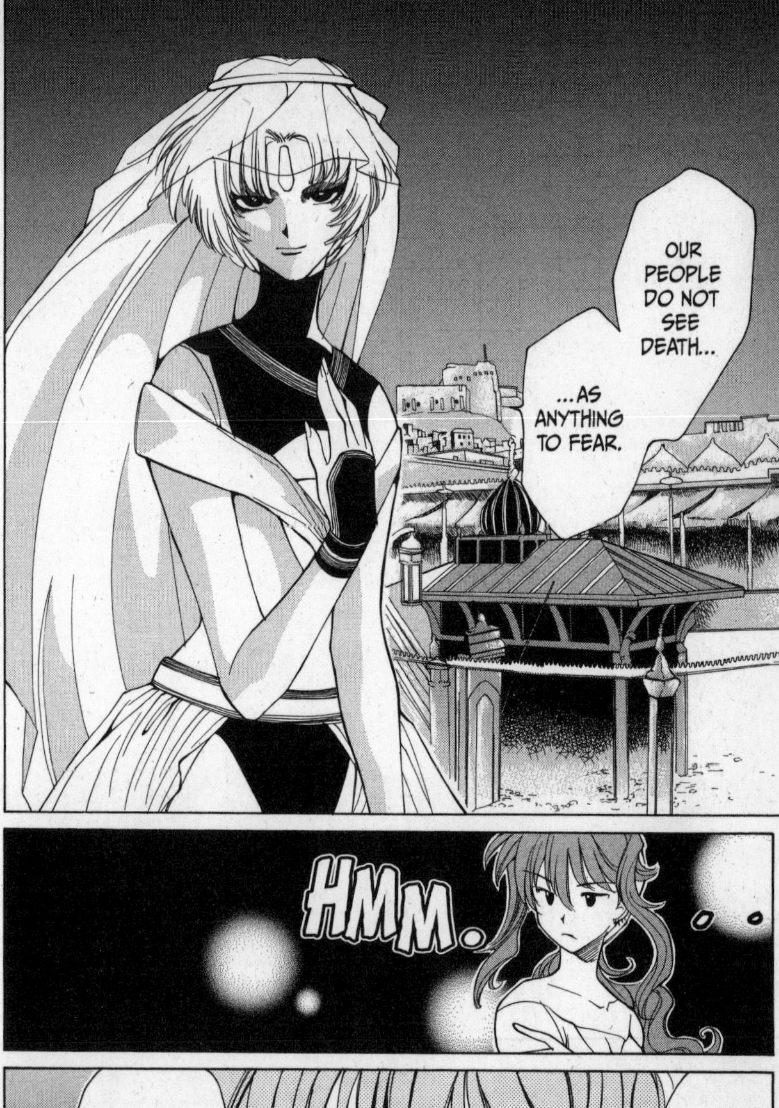
OUR PEOPLE DO NOT SEE DEATH...
...AS ANYTHING TO FEAR.
HMM.
FOR YOUR INFORMATION...
THE NOTION THAT YOU CAN ALWAYS JUST START OVER AGAIN, NO BIG DEAL...
...IS ONE THAT I *HATE*. JUST MY OPINION.

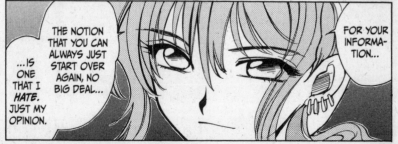

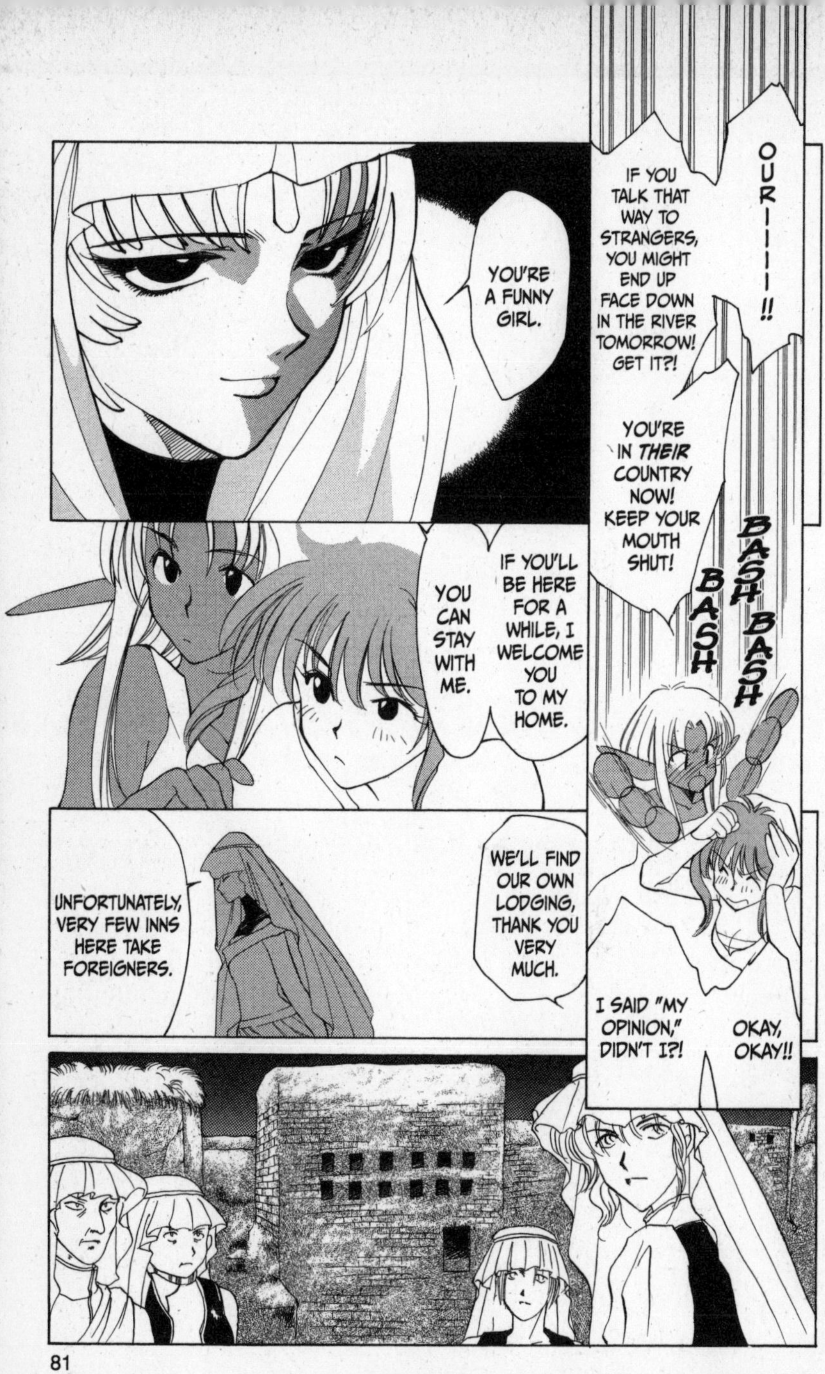
OUR-----!!
IF YOU TALK THAT WAY TO STRANGERS, YOU MIGHT END UP FACE DOWN IN THE RIVER TOMORROW! GET IT?!
YOU'RE IN *THEIR* COUNTRY NOW! KEEP YOUR MOUTH SHUT!
BASH BASH BASH
OKAY, OKAY!!
I SAID "MY OPINION," DIDN'T I?!
YOU'RE A FUNNY GIRL.
IF YOU'LL BE HERE FOR A WHILE, I WELCOME YOU TO MY HOME.
YOU CAN STAY WITH ME.
WE'LL FIND OUR OWN LODGING, THANK YOU VERY MUCH.
UNFORTUNATELY, VERY FEW INNS HERE TAKE FOREIGNERS.

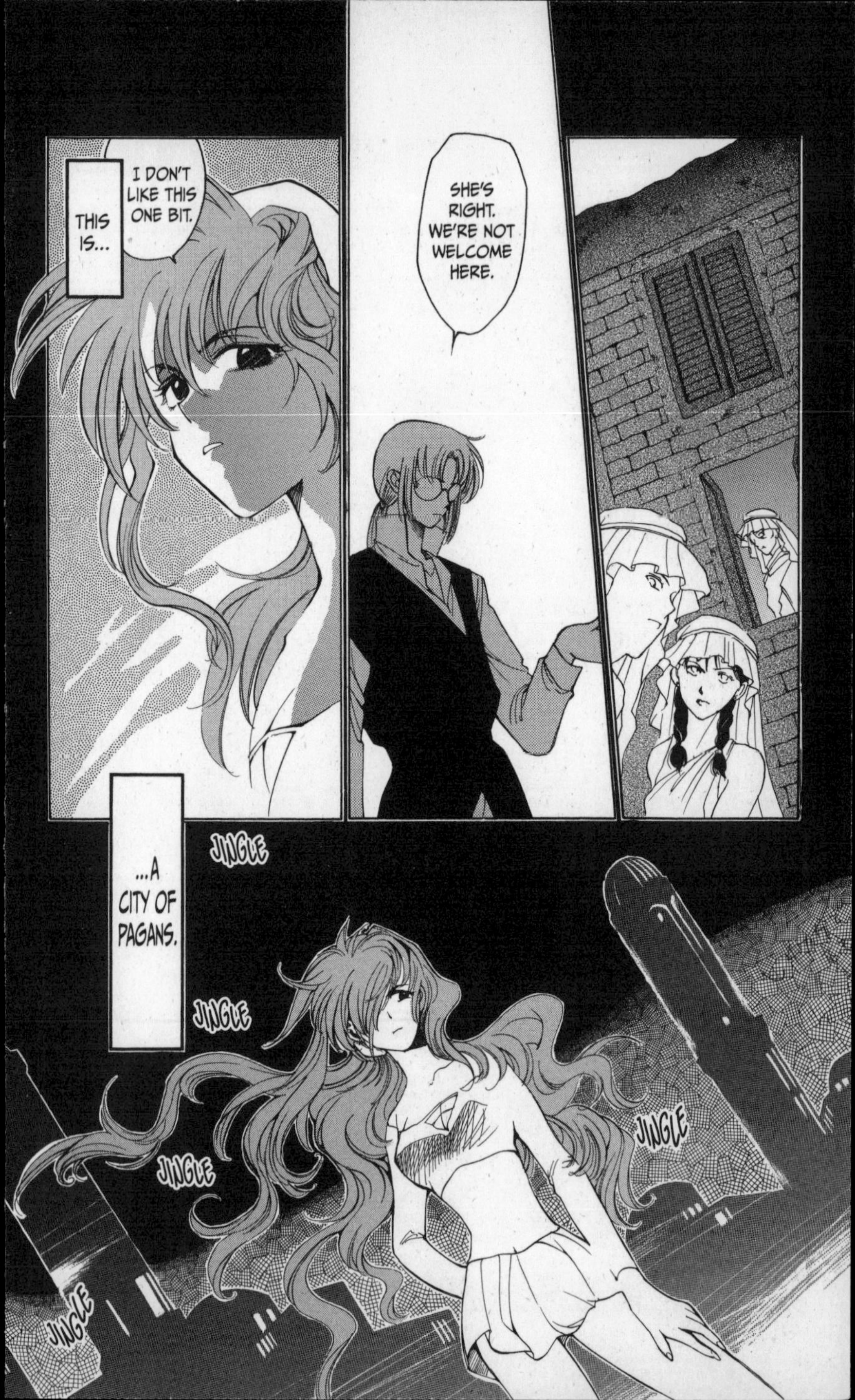
SHE'S RIGHT. WE'RE NOT WELCOME HERE.
I DON'T LIKE THIS ONE BIT.
THIS IS...
...A CITY OF PAGANS.
JINGLE
JINGLE
JINGLE
JINGLE
JINGLE

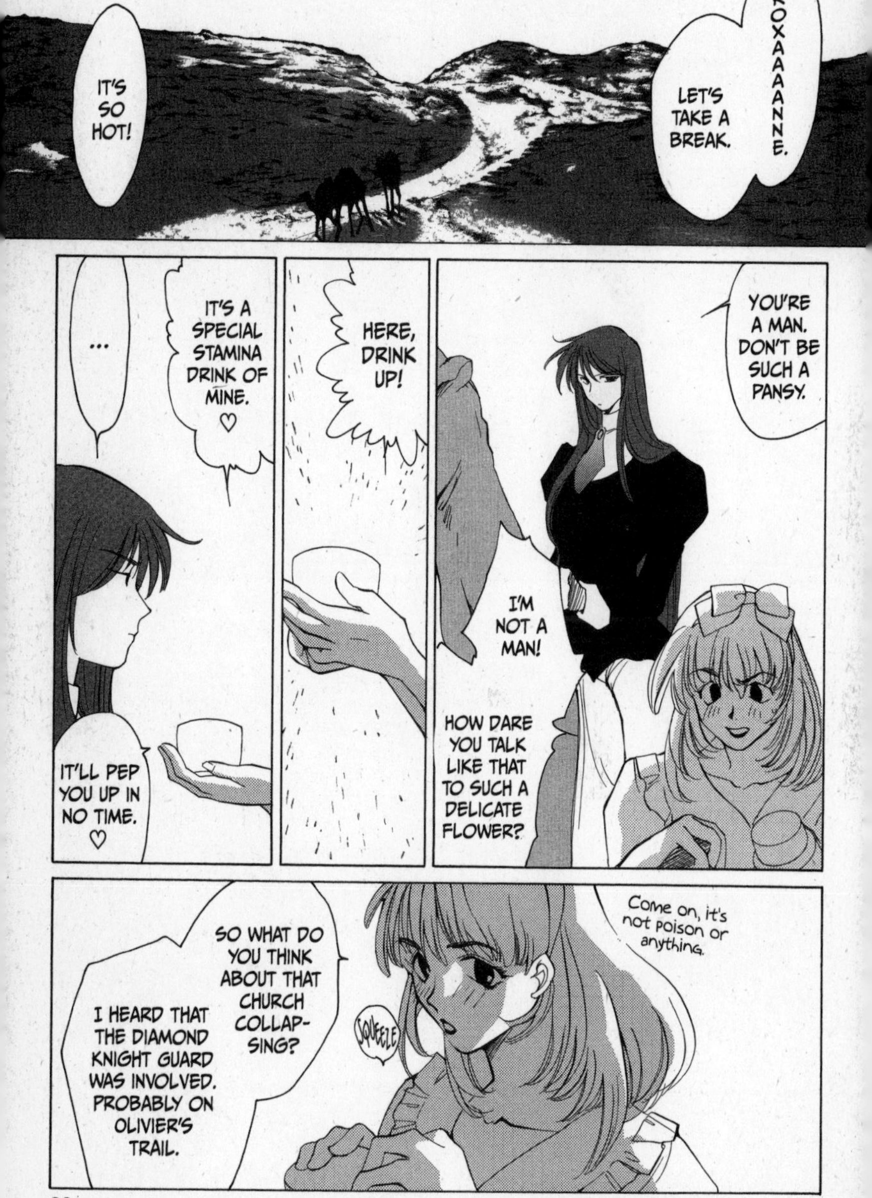
ROXAAAANNE.
LET'S TAKE A BREAK.
IT'S SO HOT!
YOU'RE A MAN. DON'T BE SUCH A PANSY.
I'M NOT A MAN!
HOW DARE YOU TALK LIKE THAT TO SUCH A DELICATE FLOWER?
HERE, DRINK UP!
IT'S A SPECIAL STAMINA DRINK OF MINE. ♡
...
IT'LL PEP YOU UP IN NO TIME. ♡
Come on, it's not poison or anything.
SQUEEZE
SO WHAT DO YOU THINK ABOUT THAT CHURCH COLLAPSING?
I HEARD THAT THE DIAMOND KNIGHT GUARD WAS INVOLVED. PROBABLY ON OLIVIER'S TRAIL.

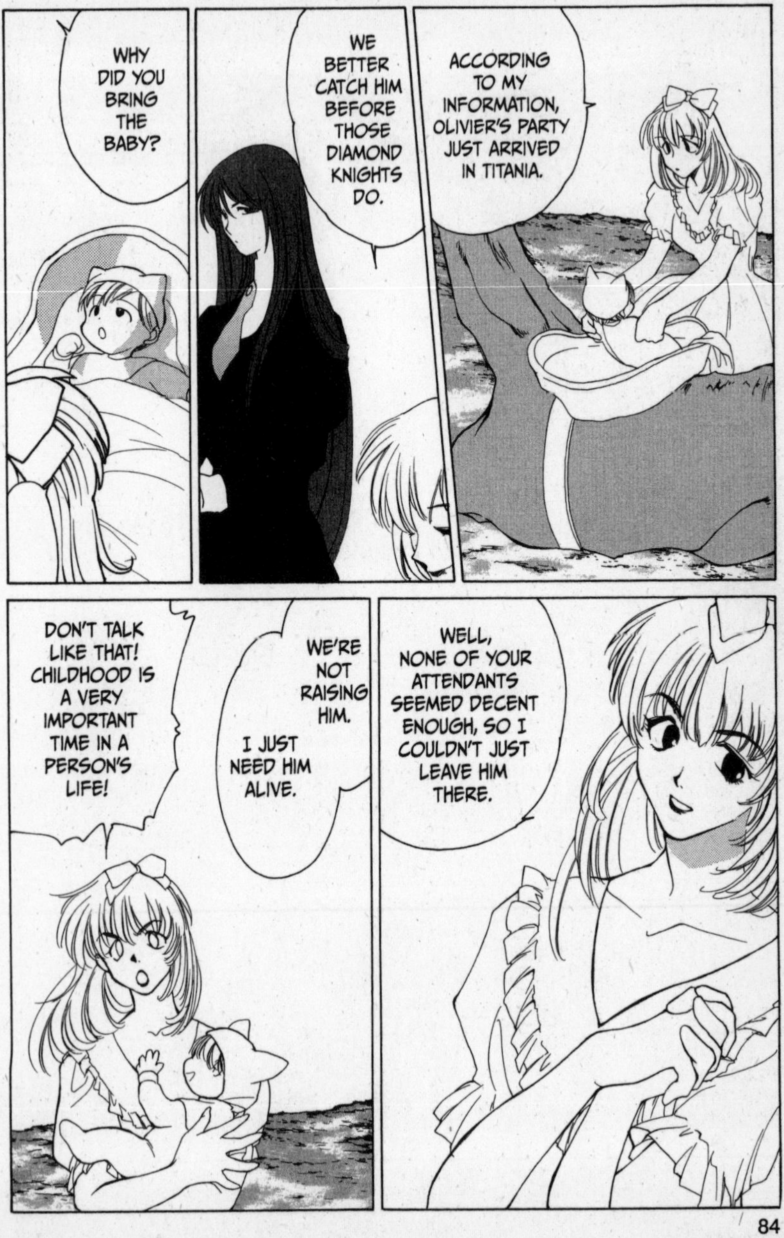
ACCORDING TO MY INFORMATION, OLIVIER'S PARTY JUST ARRIVED IN TITANIA.
WE BETTER CATCH HIM BEFORE THOSE DIAMOND KNIGHTS DO.
WHY DID YOU BRING THE BABY?
WELL, NONE OF YOUR ATTENDANTS SEEMED DECENT ENOUGH, SO I COULDN'T JUST LEAVE HIM THERE.
WE'RE NOT RAISING HIM.
I JUST NEED HIM ALIVE.
DON'T TALK LIKE THAT! CHILDHOOD IS A VERY IMPORTANT TIME IN A PERSON'S LIFE!

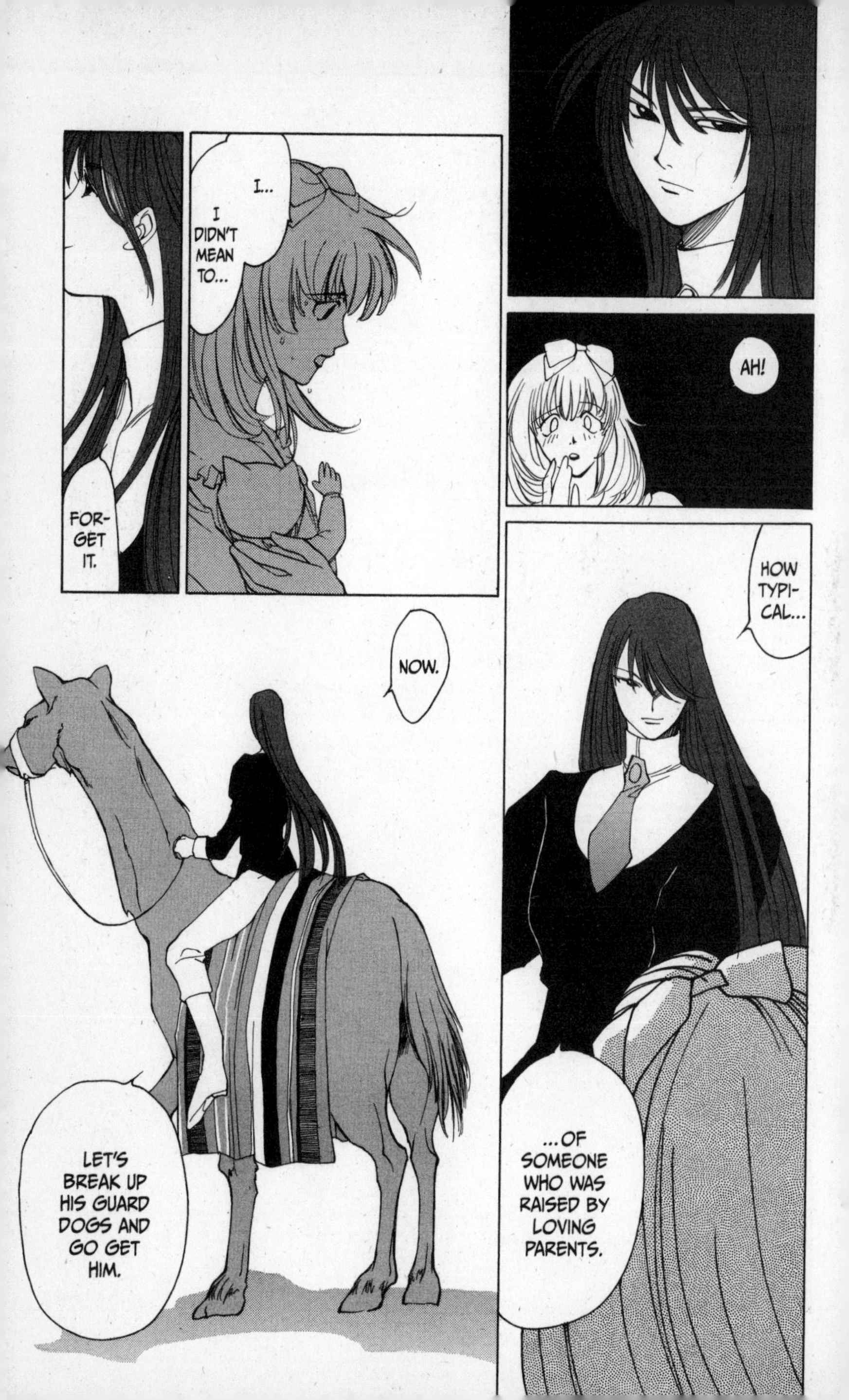
AH!
HOW TYPICAL...
...OF SOMEONE WHO WAS RAISED BY LOVING PARENTS.
I...
I DIDN'T MEAN TO...
FORGET IT.
NOW.
LET'S BREAK UP HIS GUARD DOGS AND GO GET HIM.

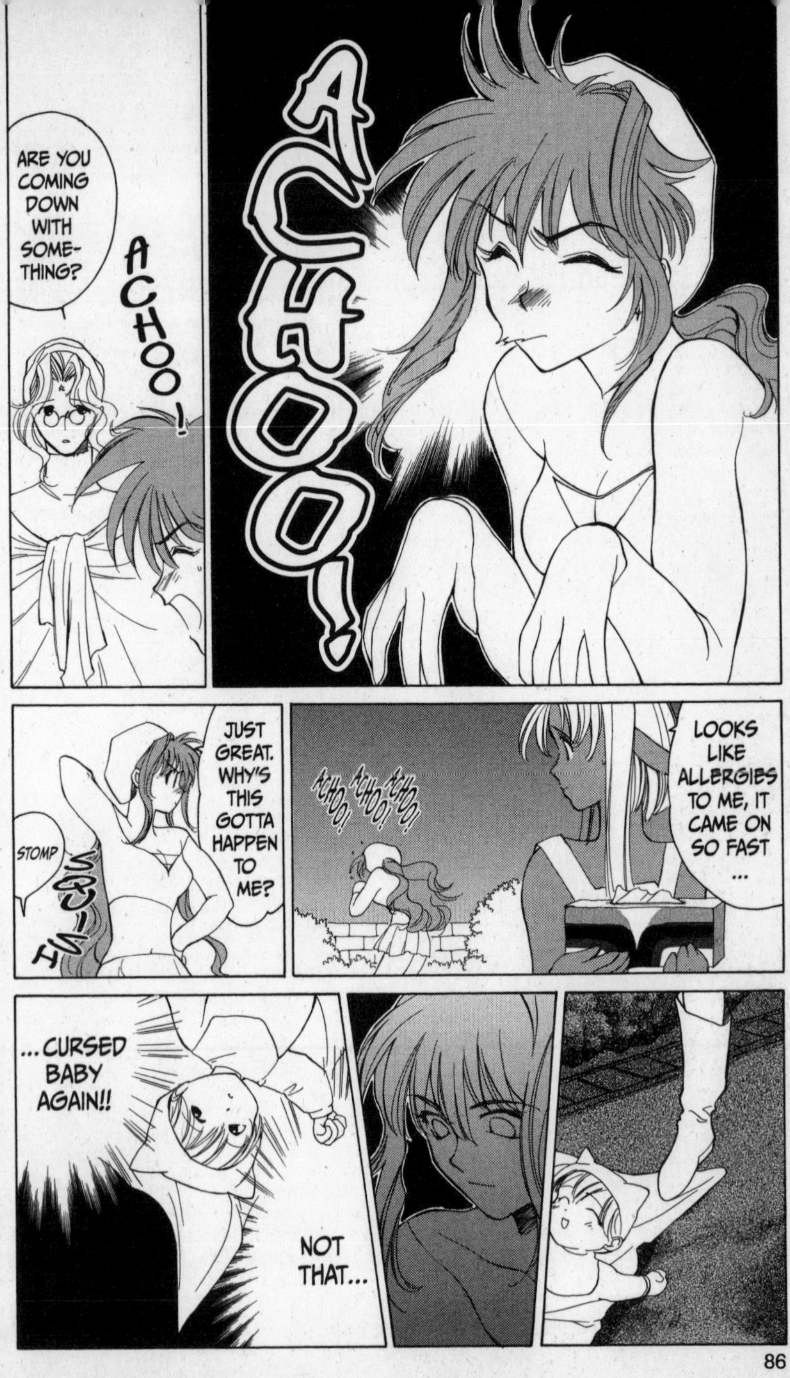
ACHOO!
ACHOO!
ARE YOU COMING DOWN WITH SOME-THING?
LOOKS LIKE ALLERGIES TO ME, IT CAME ON SO FAST ...
ACHOO! ACHOO! ACHOO!
JUST GREAT. WHY'S THIS GOTTA HAPPEN TO ME?
STOMP
SQUISH
NOT THAT...
...CURSED BABY AGAIN!!

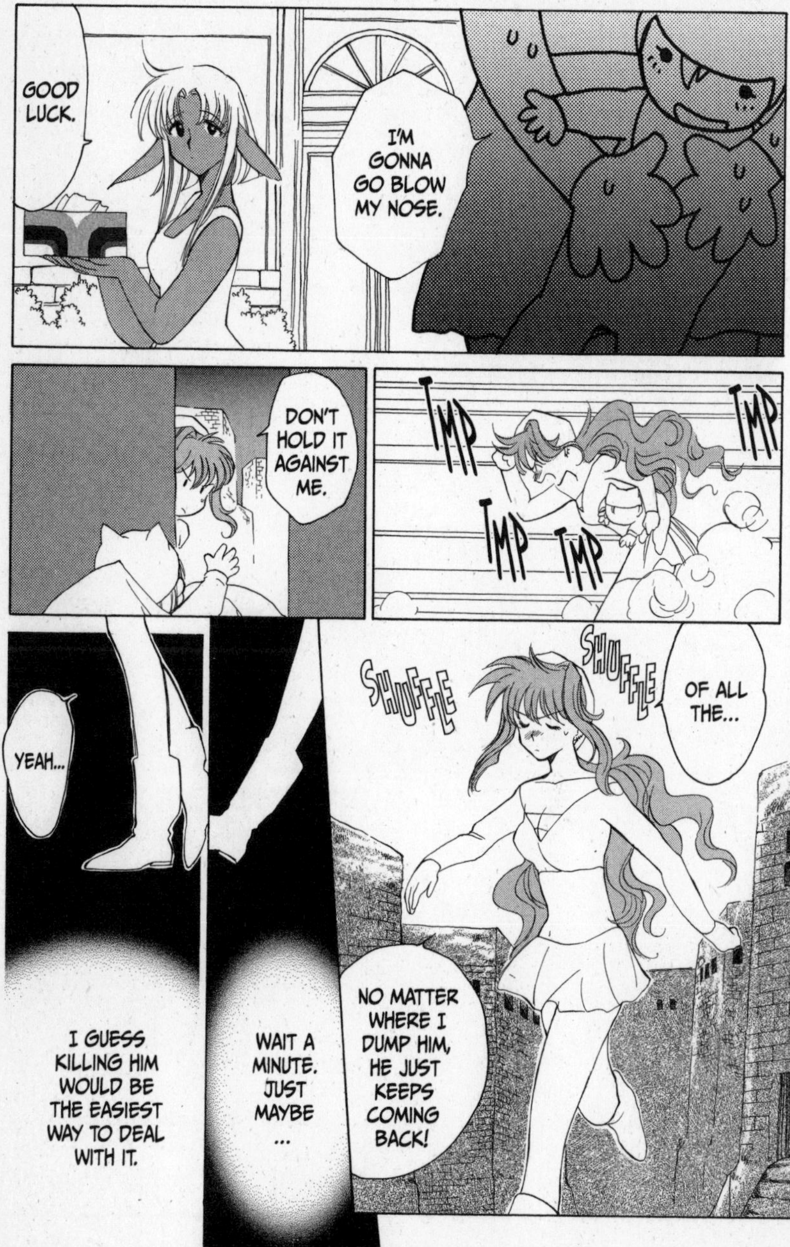
I'M GONNA GO BLOW MY NOSE.
GOOD LUCK.
TMP
TMP
TMP
TMP
DON'T HOLD IT AGAINST ME.
SHUFFLE
SHUFFLE
OF ALL THE...
NO MATTER WHERE I DUMP HIM, HE JUST KEEPS COMING BACK!
WAIT A MINUTE. JUST MAYBE ...
YEAH...
I GUESS KILLING HIM WOULD BE THE EASIEST WAY TO DEAL WITH IT.

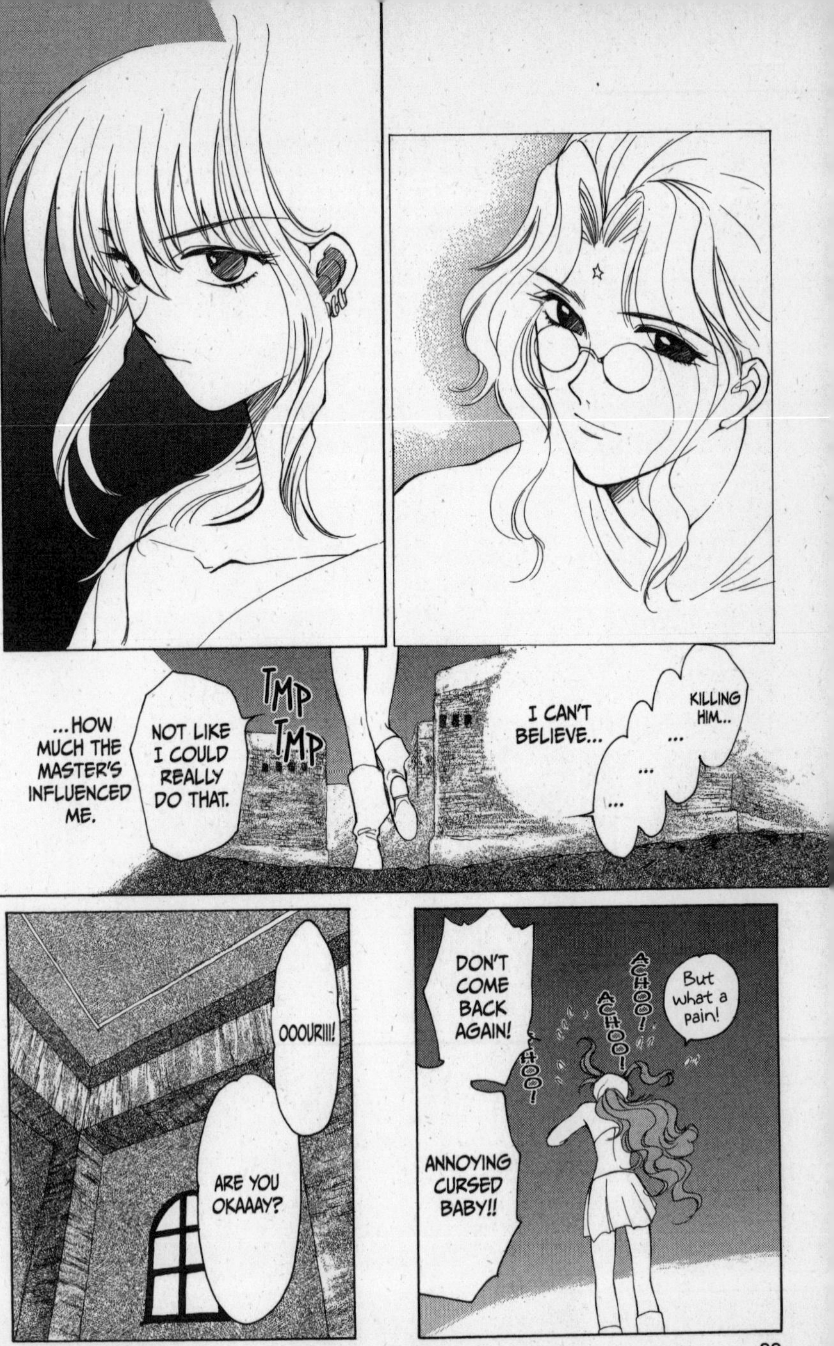
KILLING HIM...
...
...
...
I CAN'T BELIEVE...
TMP
TMP
NOT LIKE I COULD REALLY DO THAT.
...HOW MUCH THE MASTER'S INFLUENCED ME.
But what a pain!
ACHOO!
ACHOO!
CHOO!
DON'T COME BACK AGAIN!
ANNOYING CURSED BABY!!
OOOURIII!
ARE YOU OKAAAY?

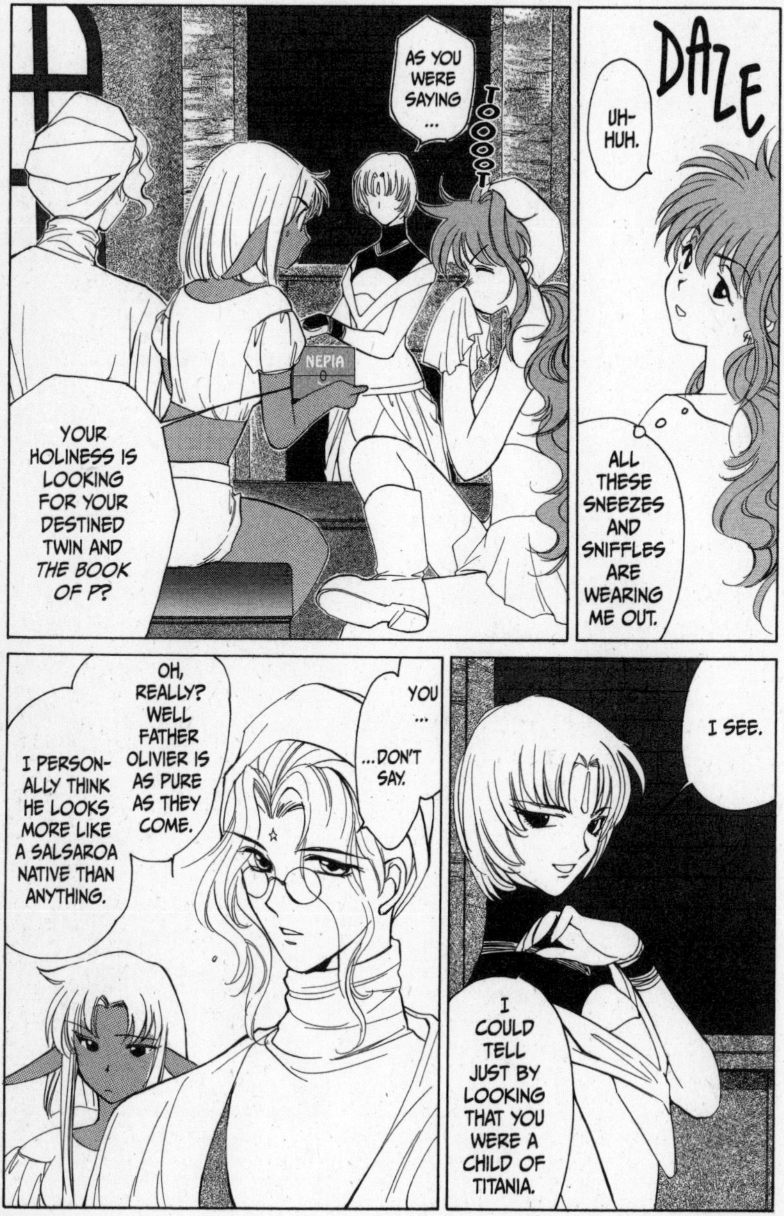
DAZE
UH-HUH.
ALL THESE SNEEZES AND SNIFFLES ARE WEARING ME OUT.
AS YOU WERE SAYING ...
TOOOOT
NEPIA
YOUR HOLINESS IS LOOKING FOR YOUR DESTINED TWIN AND *THE BOOK OF P*?
I SEE.
I COULD TELL JUST BY LOOKING THAT YOU WERE A CHILD OF TITANIA.
YOU ...
...DON'T SAY.
OH, REALLY? WELL FATHER OLIVIER IS AS PURE AS THEY COME.
I PERSON-ALLY THINK HE LOOKS MORE LIKE A SALSAROA NATIVE THAN ANYTHING.

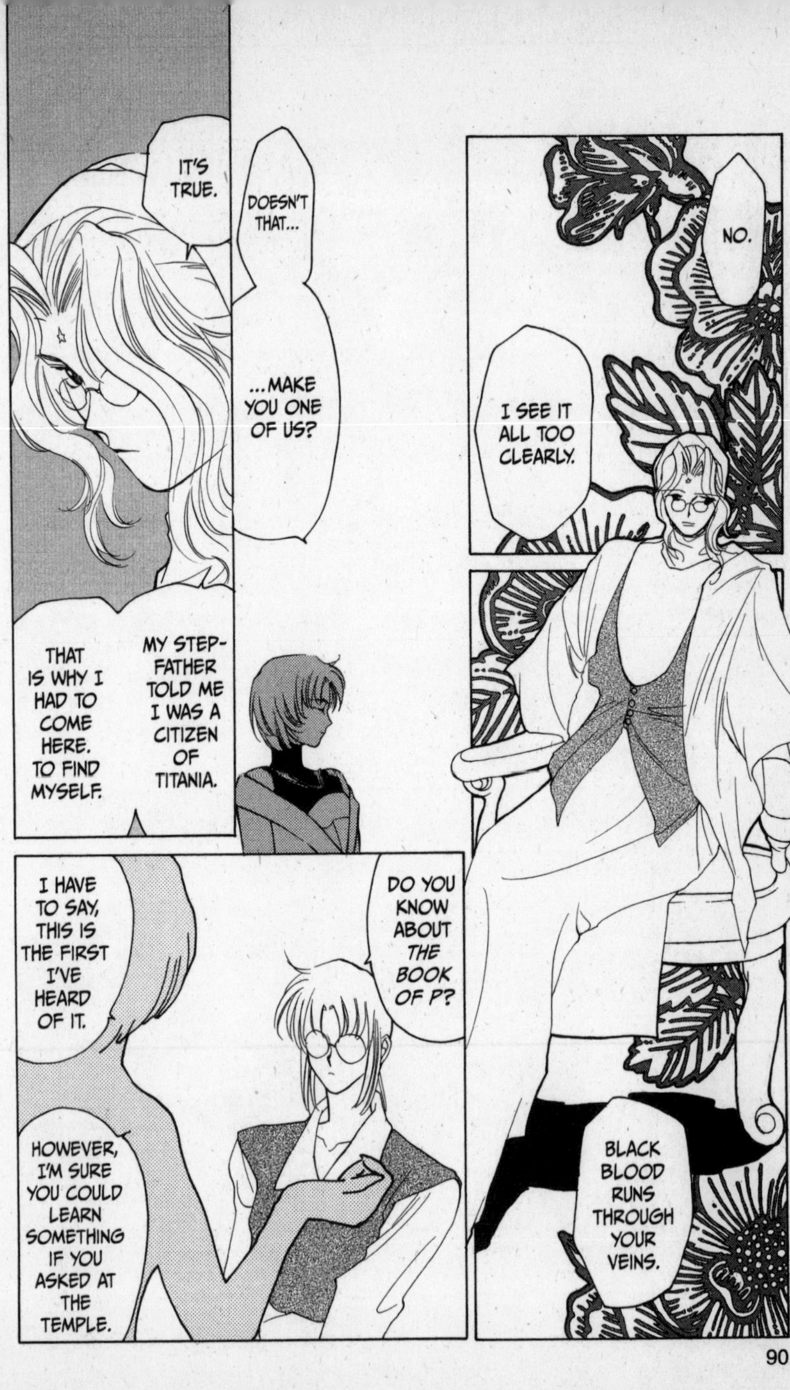
NO.
I SEE IT ALL TOO CLEARLY.
BLACK BLOOD RUNS THROUGH YOUR VEINS.
IT'S TRUE.
DOESN'T THAT...
...MAKE YOU ONE OF US?
MY STEP-FATHER TOLD ME I WAS A CITIZEN OF TITANIA.
THAT IS WHY I HAD TO COME HERE. TO FIND MYSELF.
DO YOU KNOW ABOUT *THE BOOK OF P*?
I HAVE TO SAY, THIS IS THE FIRST I'VE HEARD OF IT.
HOWEVER, I'M SURE YOU COULD LEARN SOMETHING IF YOU ASKED AT THE TEMPLE.

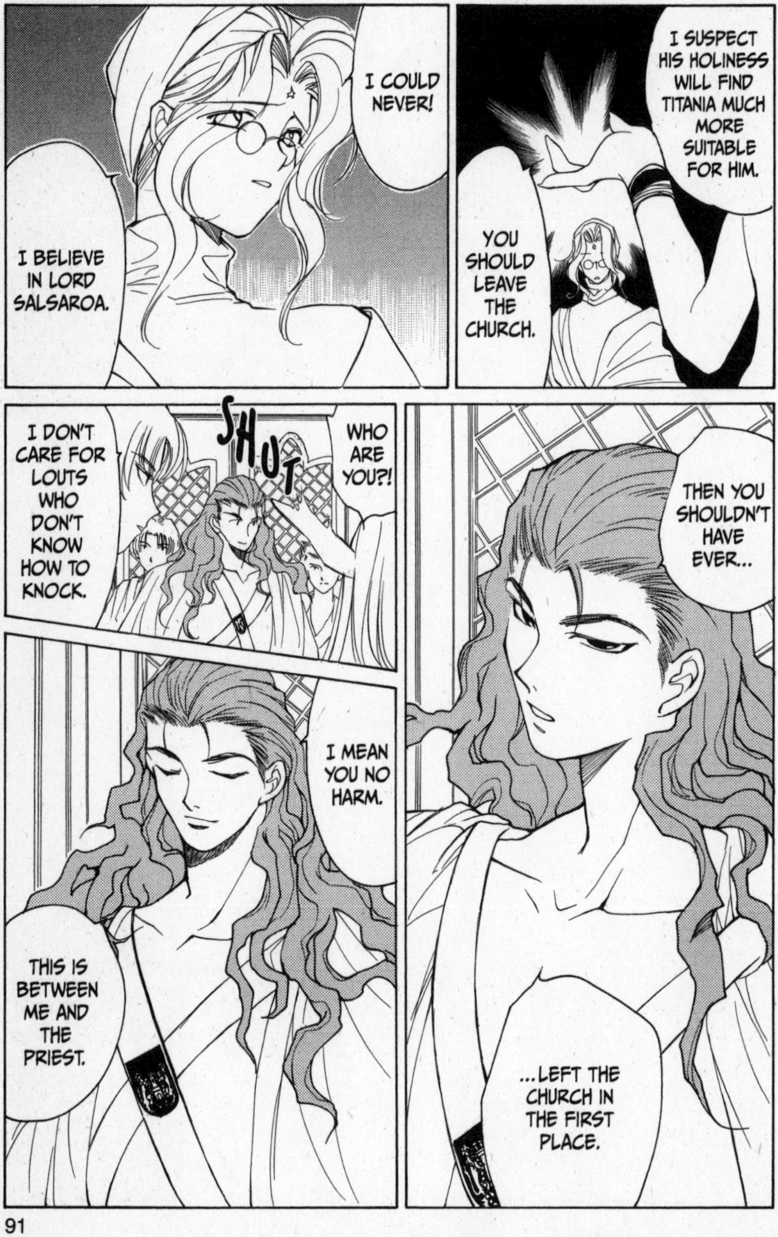
I SUSPECT HIS HOLINESS WILL FIND TITANIA MUCH MORE SUITABLE FOR HIM.
YOU SHOULD LEAVE THE CHURCH.
I COULD NEVER!
I BELIEVE IN LORD SALSAROA.
THEN YOU SHOULDN'T HAVE EVER...
...LEFT THE CHURCH IN THE FIRST PLACE.
WHO ARE YOU?!
SHUT
I DON'T CARE FOR LOUTS WHO DON'T KNOW HOW TO KNOCK.
I MEAN YOU NO HARM.
THIS IS BETWEEN ME AND THE PRIEST.

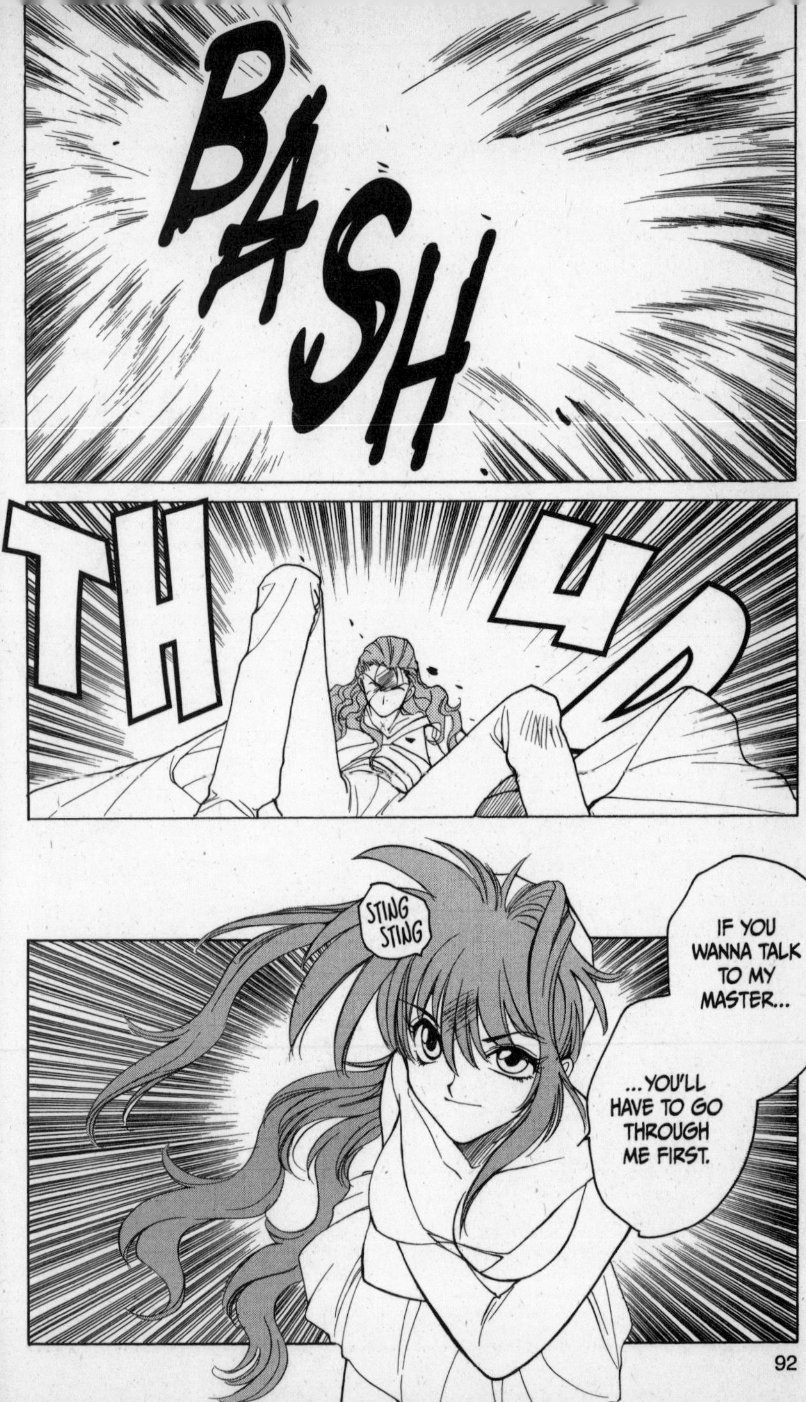
BASH
THUD
STING STING
IF YOU WANNA TALK TO MY MASTER...
...YOU'LL HAVE TO GO THROUGH ME FIRST.

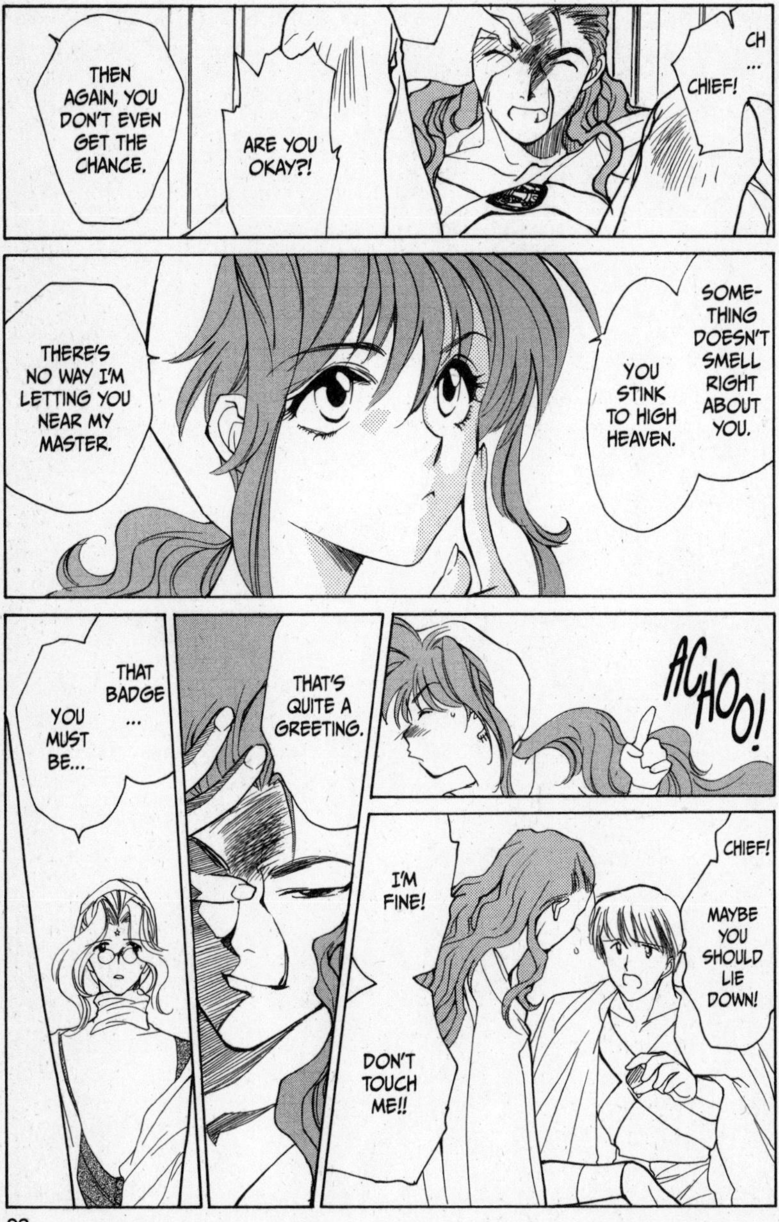
CH... CHIEF!
ARE YOU OKAY?!
THEN AGAIN, YOU DON'T EVEN GET THE CHANCE.
SOME-THING DOESN'T SMELL RIGHT ABOUT YOU.
YOU STINK TO HIGH HEAVEN.
THERE'S NO WAY I'M LETTING YOU NEAR MY MASTER.
ACHOO!
CHIEF!
MAYBE YOU SHOULD LIE DOWN!
I'M FINE!
DON'T TOUCH ME!!
THAT'S QUITE A GREETING.
THAT BADGE...
YOU MUST BE...

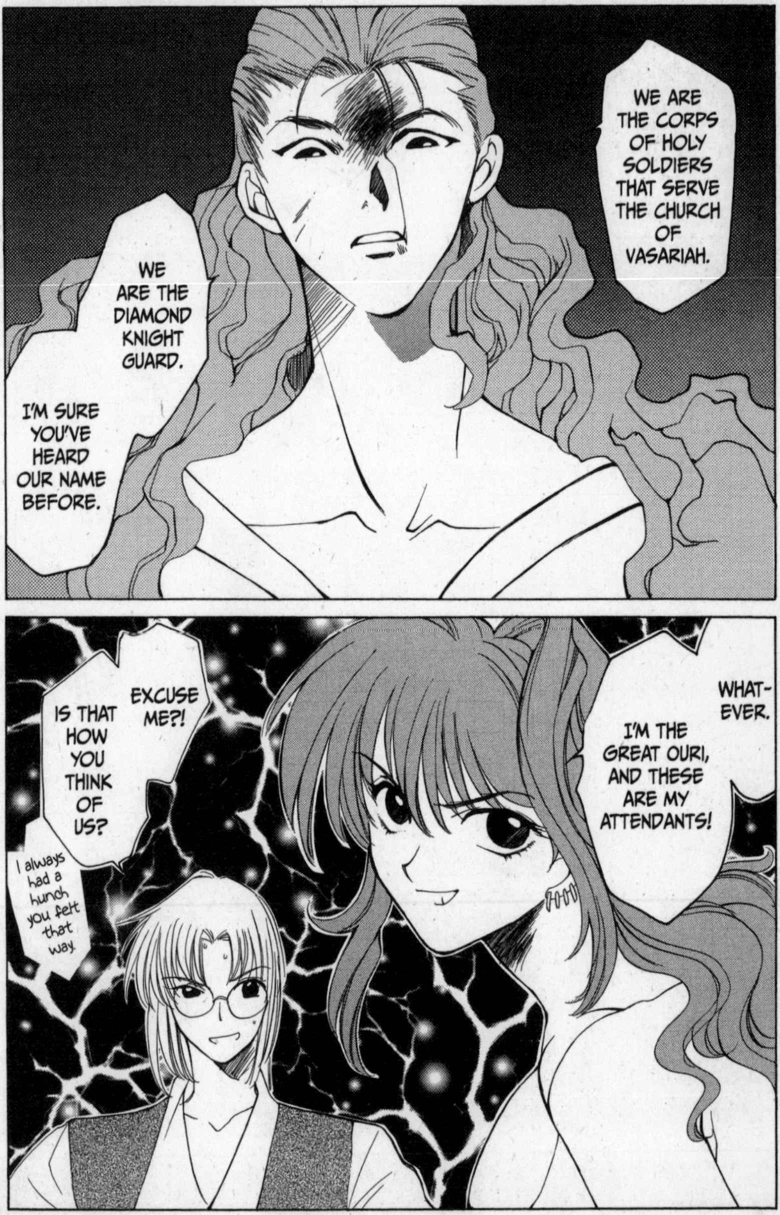
WE ARE THE CORPS OF HOLY SOLDIERS THAT SERVE THE CHURCH OF VASARIAH.
WE ARE THE DIAMOND KNIGHT GUARD.
I'M SURE YOU'VE HEARD OUR NAME BEFORE.
WHAT-EVER.
I'M THE GREAT OURI, AND THESE ARE MY ATTENDANTS!
EXCUSE ME?!
IS THAT HOW YOU THINK OF US?
I always had a hunch you felt that way.

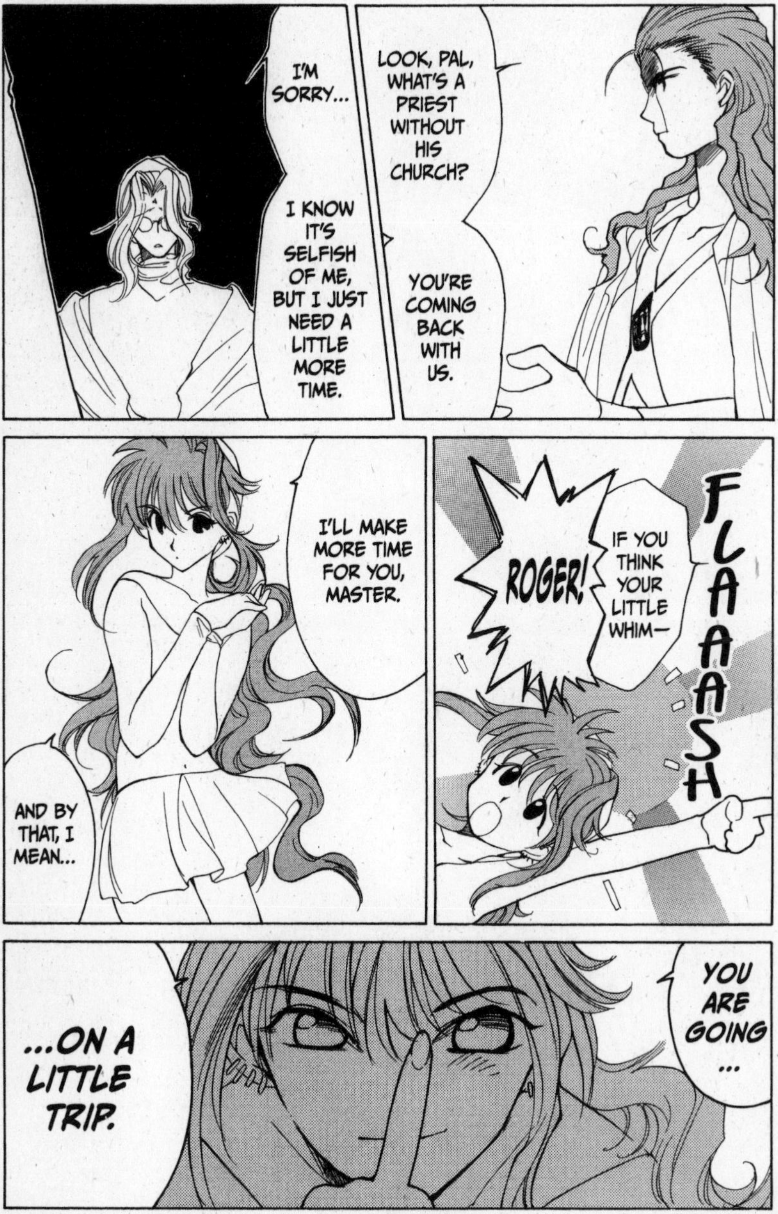
LOOK, PAL, WHAT'S A PRIEST WITHOUT HIS CHURCH?
YOU'RE COMING BACK WITH US.
I'M SORRY...
I KNOW IT'S SELFISH OF ME, BUT I JUST NEED A LITTLE MORE TIME.
IF YOU THINK YOUR LITTLE WHIM—
ROGER!
FLAAASH
I'LL MAKE MORE TIME FOR YOU, MASTER.
AND BY THAT, I MEAN...
YOU ARE GOING ...
...ON A LITTLE TRIP.

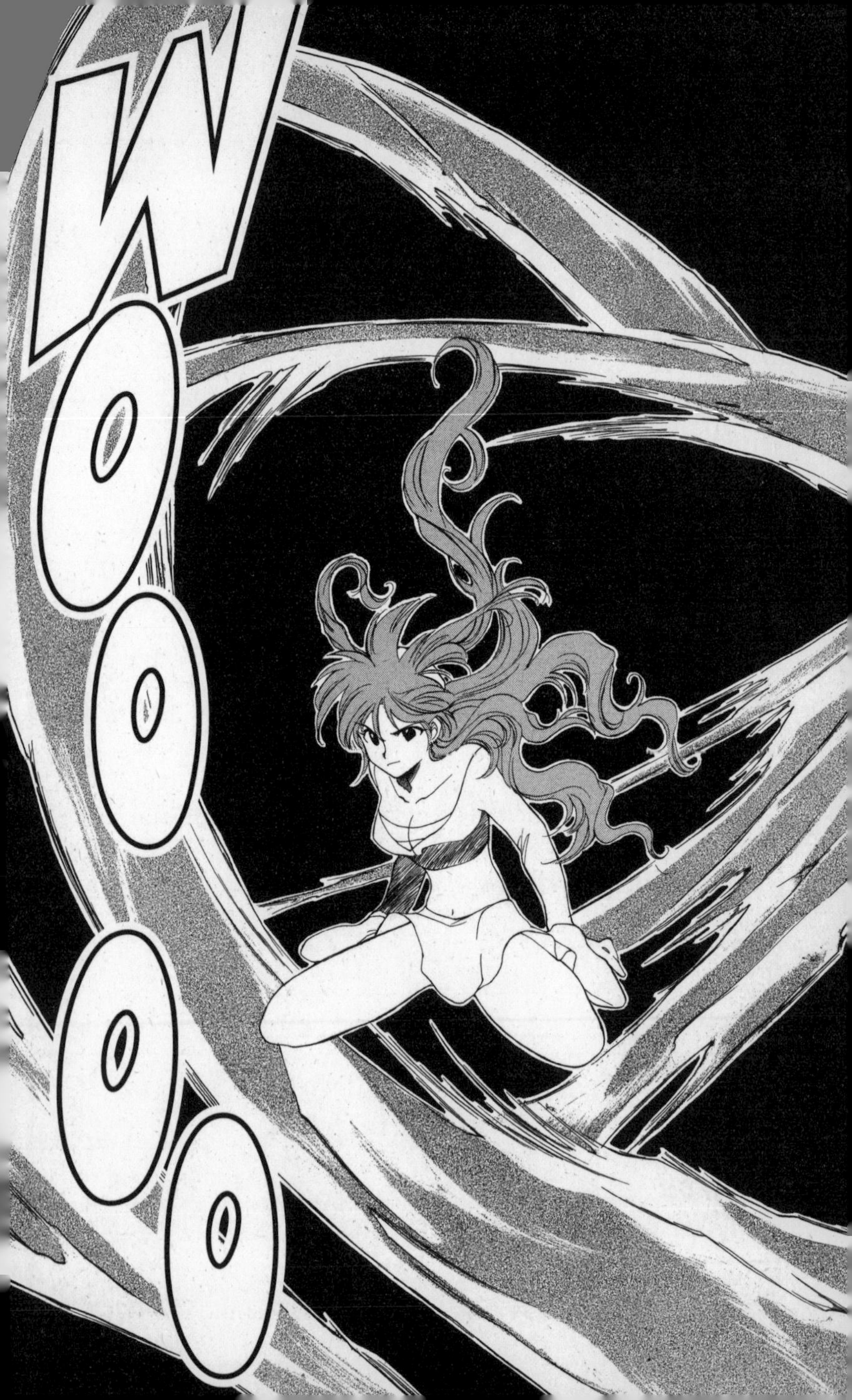
WOOOO

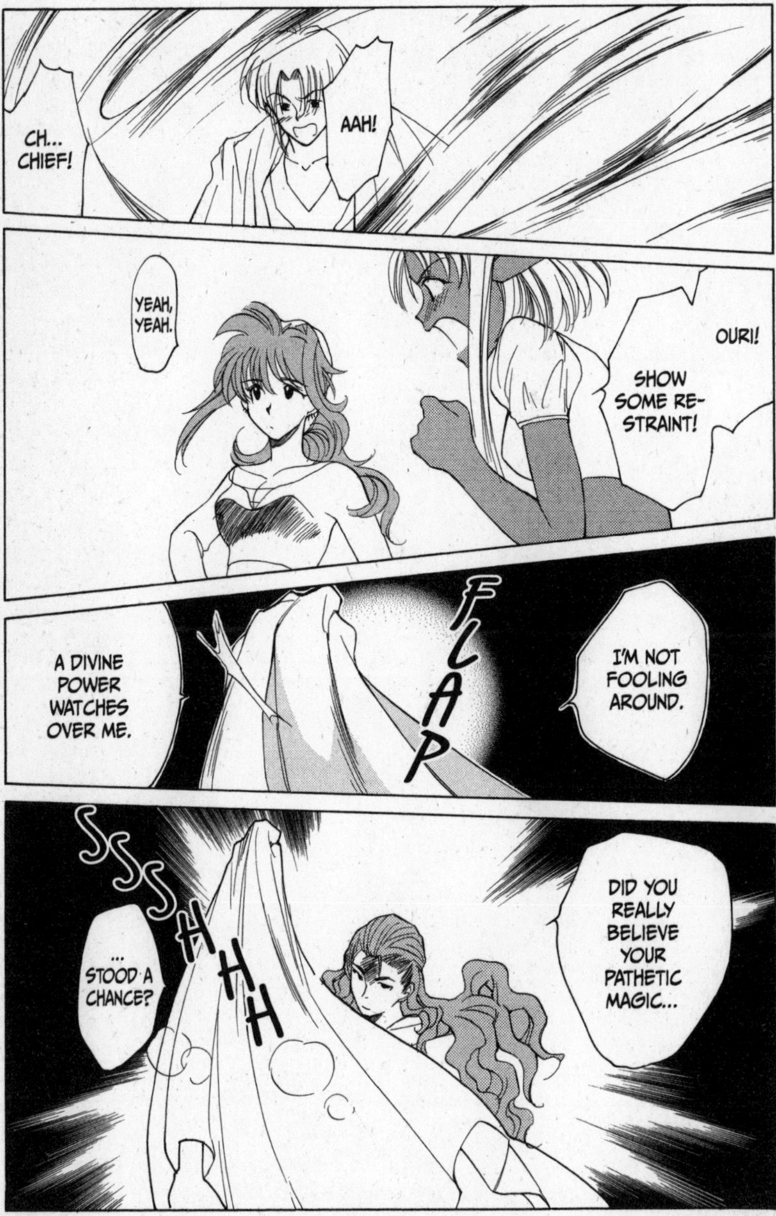
AAH!
CH... CHIEF!
OURI!
SHOW SOME RE-STRAINT!
YEAH, YEAH.
I'M NOT FOOLING AROUND.
FLAP
A DIVINE POWER WATCHES OVER ME.
DID YOU REALLY BELIEVE YOUR PATHETIC MAGIC...
SSSHHH
... STOOD A CHANCE?

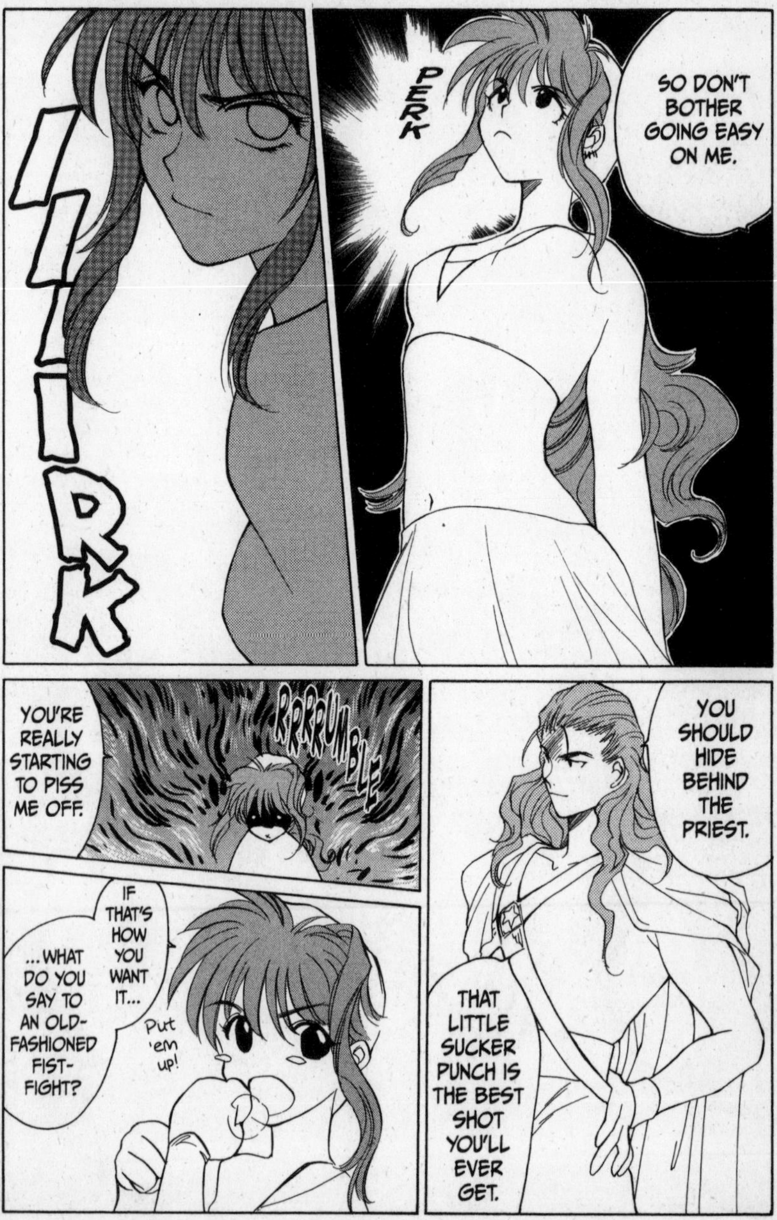
SO DON'T BOTHER GOING EASY ON ME.
PERK
I-I-I-IRK
YOU SHOULD HIDE BEHIND THE PRIEST.
THAT LITTLE SUCKER PUNCH IS THE BEST SHOT YOU'LL EVER GET.
YOU'RE REALLY STARTING TO PISS ME OFF.
RRRRUMBLE
IF THAT'S HOW YOU WANT IT...
...WHAT DO YOU SAY TO AN OLD-FASHIONED FIST-FIGHT?
Put 'em up!

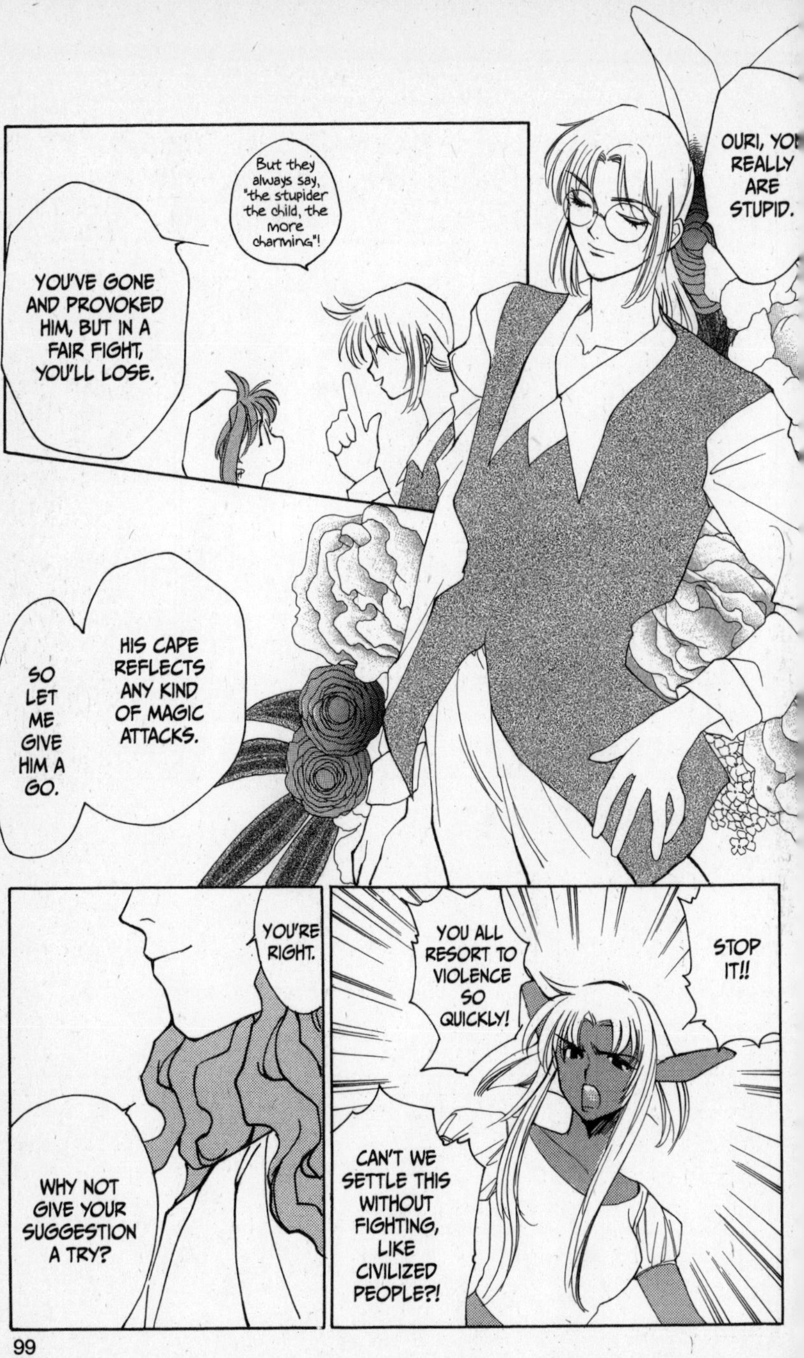
OURI, YOU REALLY ARE STUPID.
But they always say, "the stupider the child, the more charming"!
YOU'VE GONE AND PROVOKED HIM, BUT IN A FAIR FIGHT, YOU'LL LOSE.
HIS CAPE REFLECTS ANY KIND OF MAGIC ATTACKS.
SO LET ME GIVE HIM A GO.
STOP IT!!
YOU ALL RESORT TO VIOLENCE SO QUICKLY!
CAN'T WE SETTLE THIS WITHOUT FIGHTING, LIKE CIVILIZED PEOPLE?!
YOU'RE RIGHT.
WHY NOT GIVE YOUR SUGGESTION A TRY?

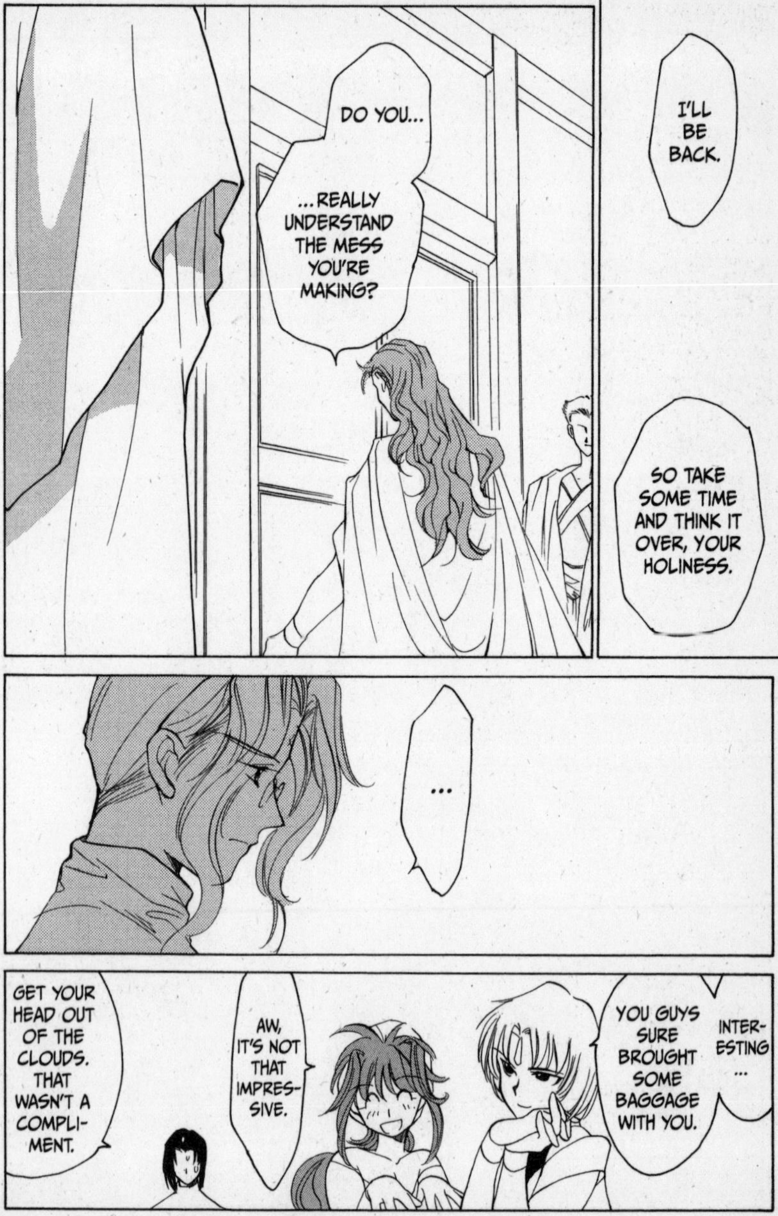
I'LL BE BACK.
SO TAKE SOME TIME AND THINK IT OVER, YOUR HOLINESS.
DO YOU...
...REALLY UNDERSTAND THE MESS YOU'RE MAKING?
...
INTER-ESTING...
YOU GUYS SURE BROUGHT SOME BAGGAGE WITH YOU.
AW, IT'S NOT THAT IMPRES-SIVE.
GET YOUR HEAD OUT OF THE CLOUDS. THAT WASN'T A COMPLI-MENT.

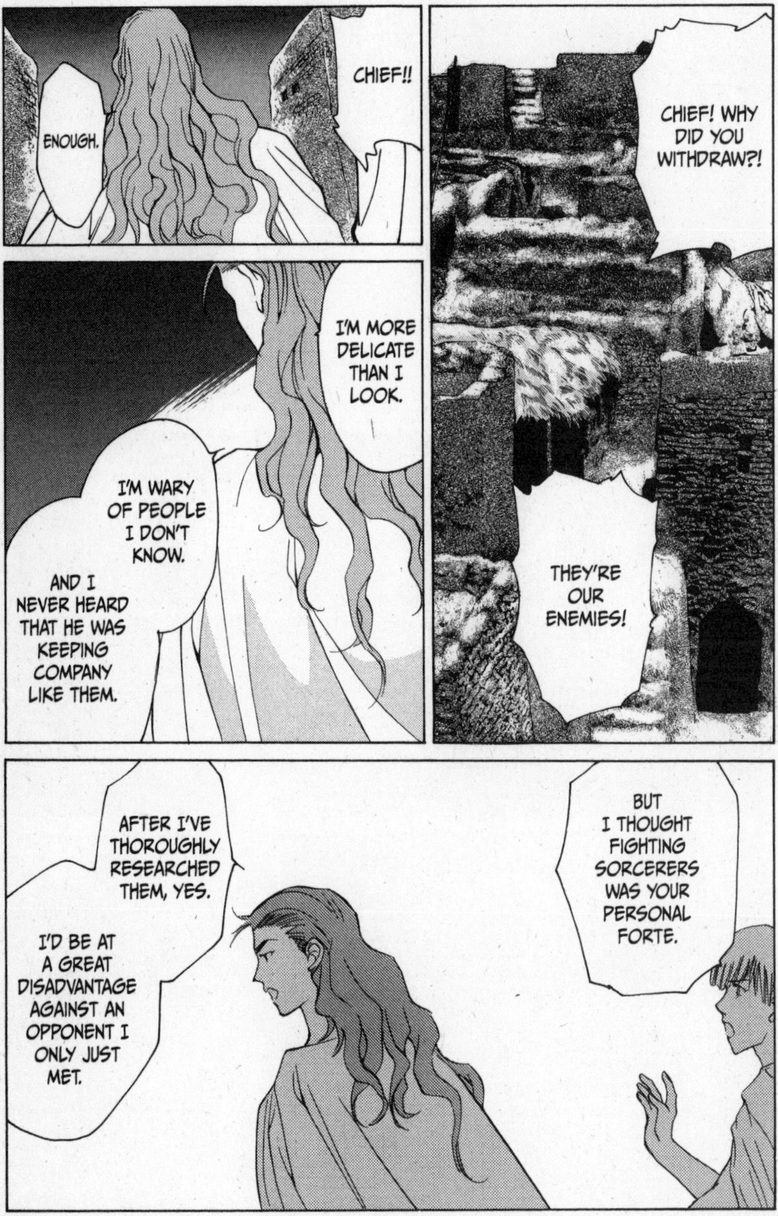
CHIEF! WHY DID YOU WITHDRAW?!
THEY'RE OUR ENEMIES!
CHIEF!!
ENOUGH.
I'M MORE DELICATE THAN I LOOK.
I'M WARY OF PEOPLE I DON'T KNOW.
AND I NEVER HEARD THAT HE WAS KEEPING COMPANY LIKE THEM.
BUT I THOUGHT FIGHTING SORCERERS WAS YOUR PERSONAL FORTE.
AFTER I'VE THOROUGHLY RESEARCHED THEM, YES.
I'D BE AT A GREAT DISADVANTAGE AGAINST AN OPPONENT I ONLY JUST MET.

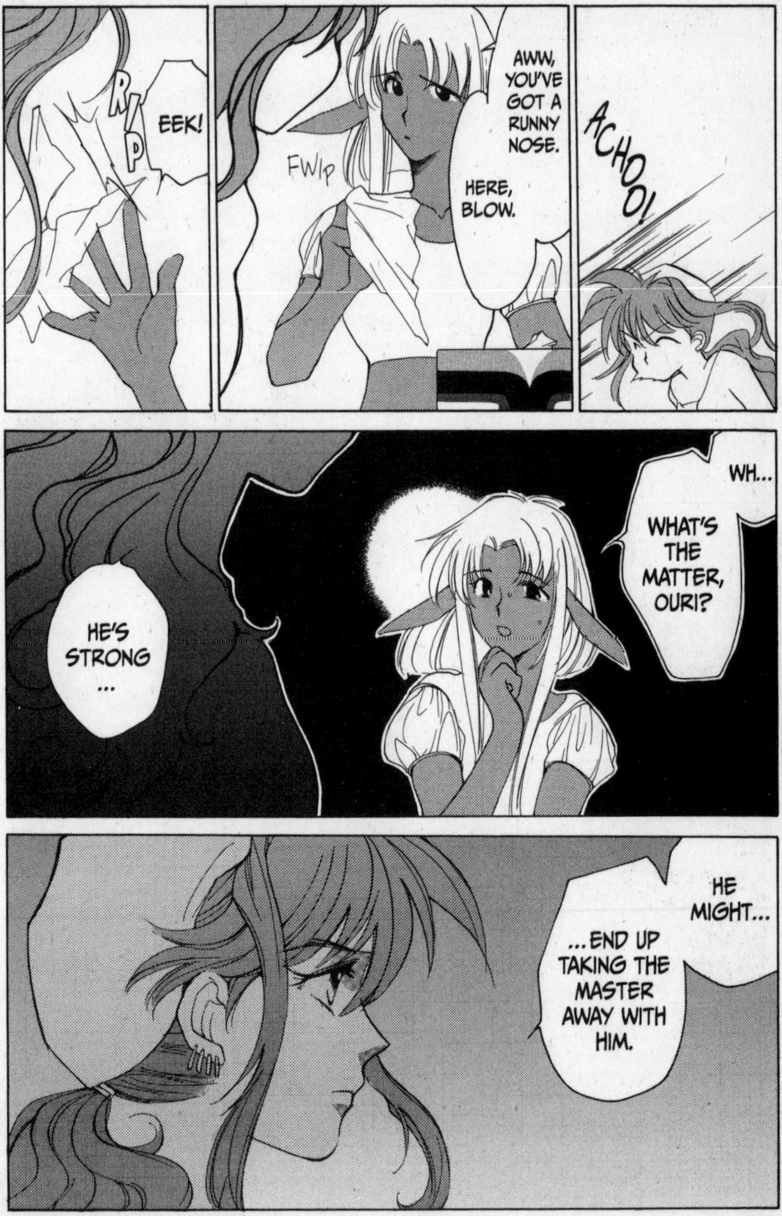
ACHOO!
AWW, YOU'VE GOT A RUNNY NOSE.
HERE, BLOW.
FWIP
RIP
EEK!
WH...
WHAT'S THE MATTER, OURI?
HE'S STRONG ...
HE MIGHT...
...END UP TAKING THE MASTER AWAY WITH HIM.

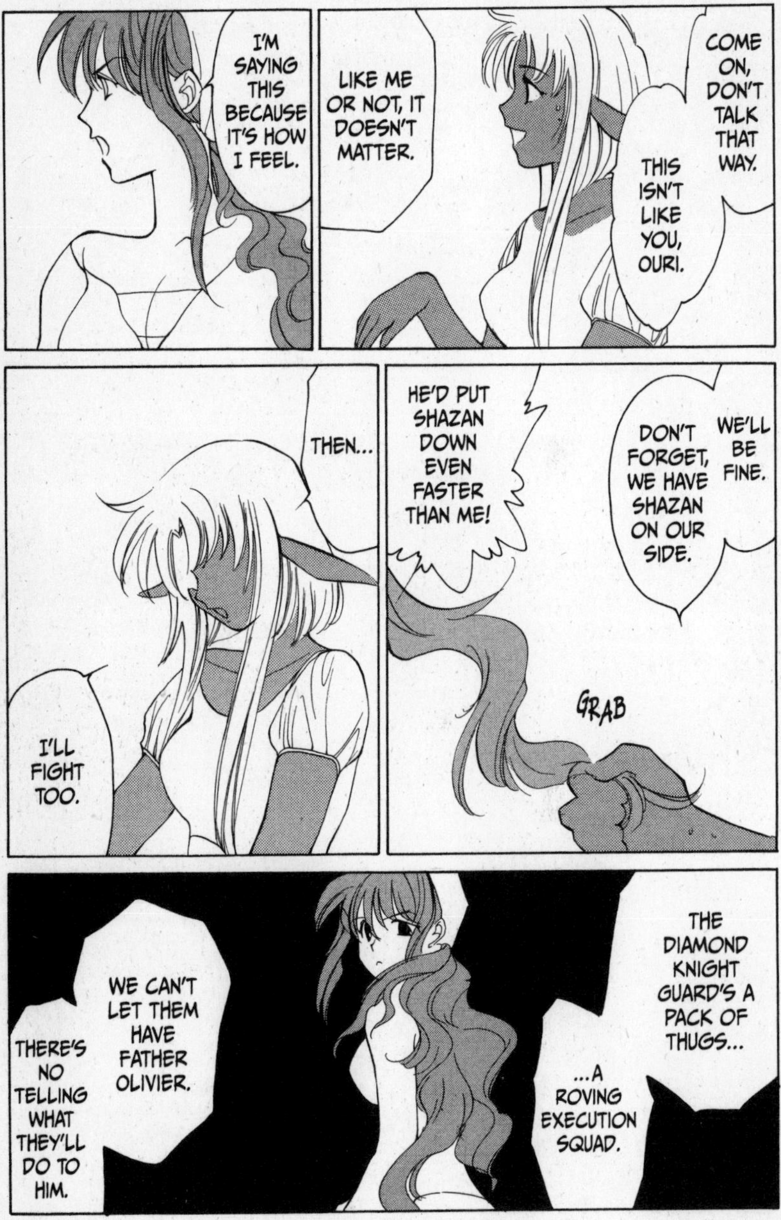
COME ON, DON'T TALK THAT WAY.
THIS ISN'T LIKE YOU, OURI.
LIKE ME OR NOT, IT DOESN'T MATTER.
I'M SAYING THIS BECAUSE IT'S HOW I FEEL.
WE'LL BE FINE.
DON'T FORGET, WE HAVE SHAZAN ON OUR SIDE.
HE'D PUT SHAZAN DOWN EVEN FASTER THAN ME!
GRAB
THEN...
I'LL FIGHT TOO.
THE DIAMOND KNIGHT GUARD'S A PACK OF THUGS...
...A ROVING EXECUTION SQUAD.
WE CAN'T LET THEM HAVE FATHER OLIVIER.
THERE'S NO TELLING WHAT THEY'LL DO TO HIM.

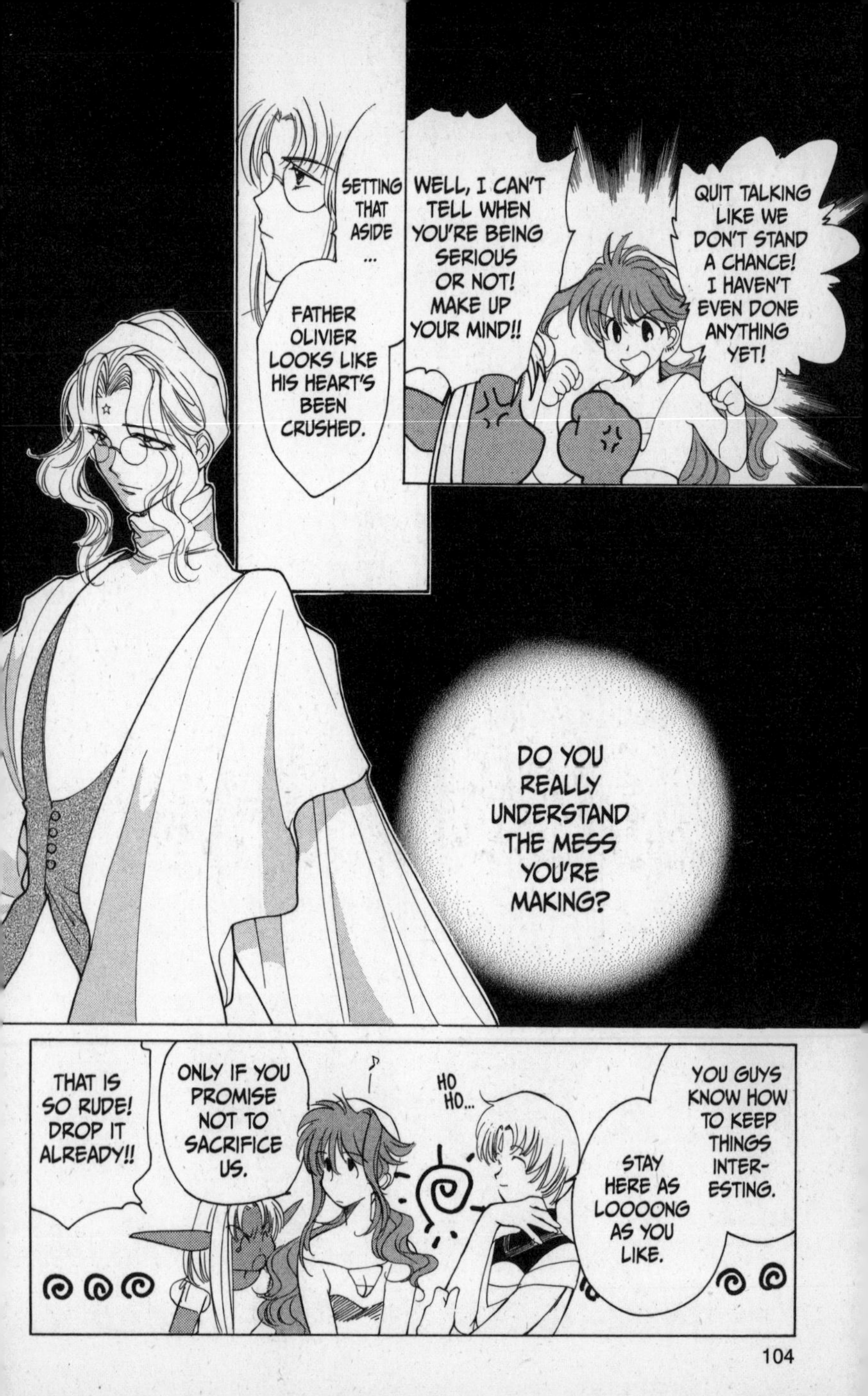
QUIT TALKING LIKE WE DON'T STAND A CHANCE! I HAVEN'T EVEN DONE ANYTHING YET!
WELL, I CAN'T TELL WHEN YOU'RE BEING SERIOUS OR NOT! MAKE UP YOUR MIND!!
SETTING THAT ASIDE ...
FATHER OLIVIER LOOKS LIKE HIS HEART'S BEEN CRUSHED.
DO YOU REALLY UNDERSTAND THE MESS YOU'RE MAKING?
YOU GUYS KNOW HOW TO KEEP THINGS INTER-ESTING.
STAY HERE AS LOOOONG AS YOU LIKE.
HO HO...
ONLY IF YOU PROMISE NOT TO SACRIFICE US.
THAT IS SO RUDE! DROP IT ALREADY!!

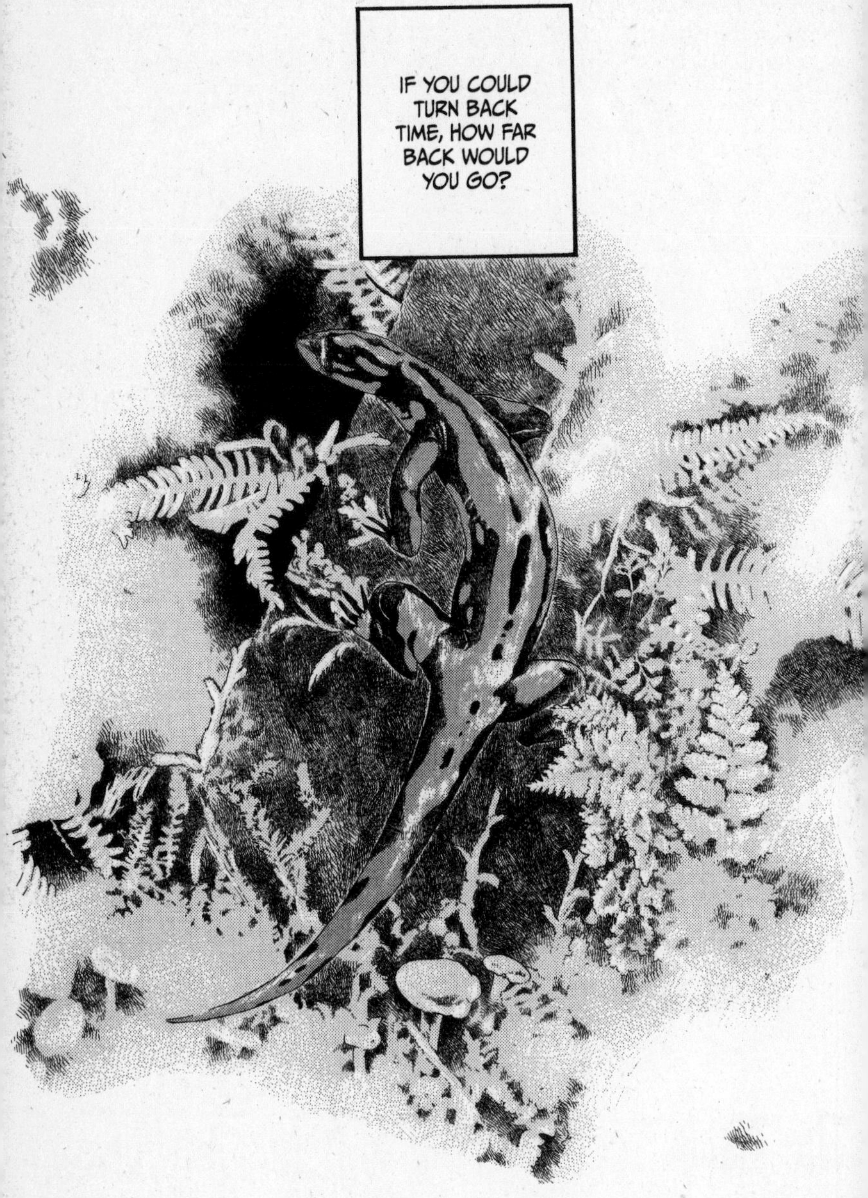
IF YOU COULD TURN BACK TIME, HOW FAR BACK WOULD YOU GO?

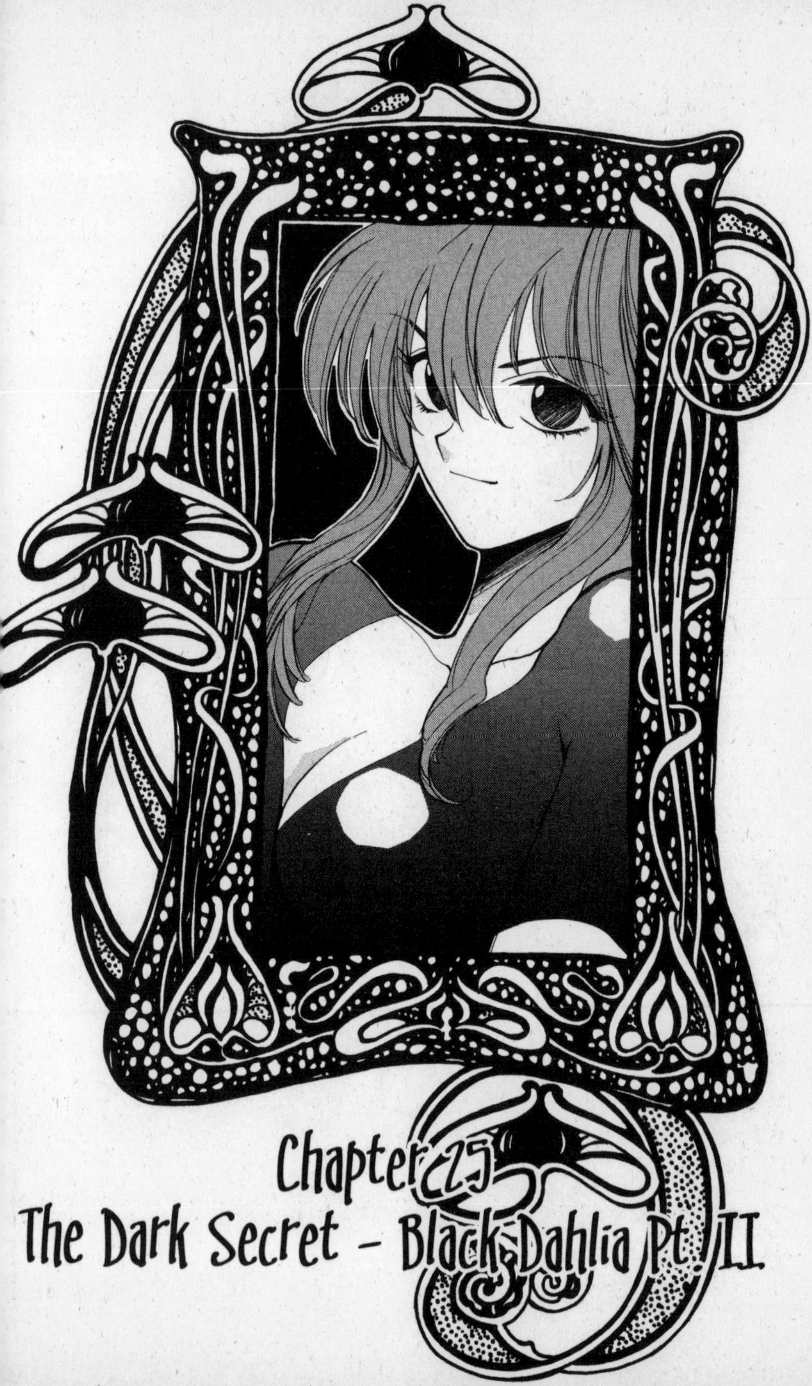

Chapter 25
The Dark Secret – Black Dahlia Pt. II

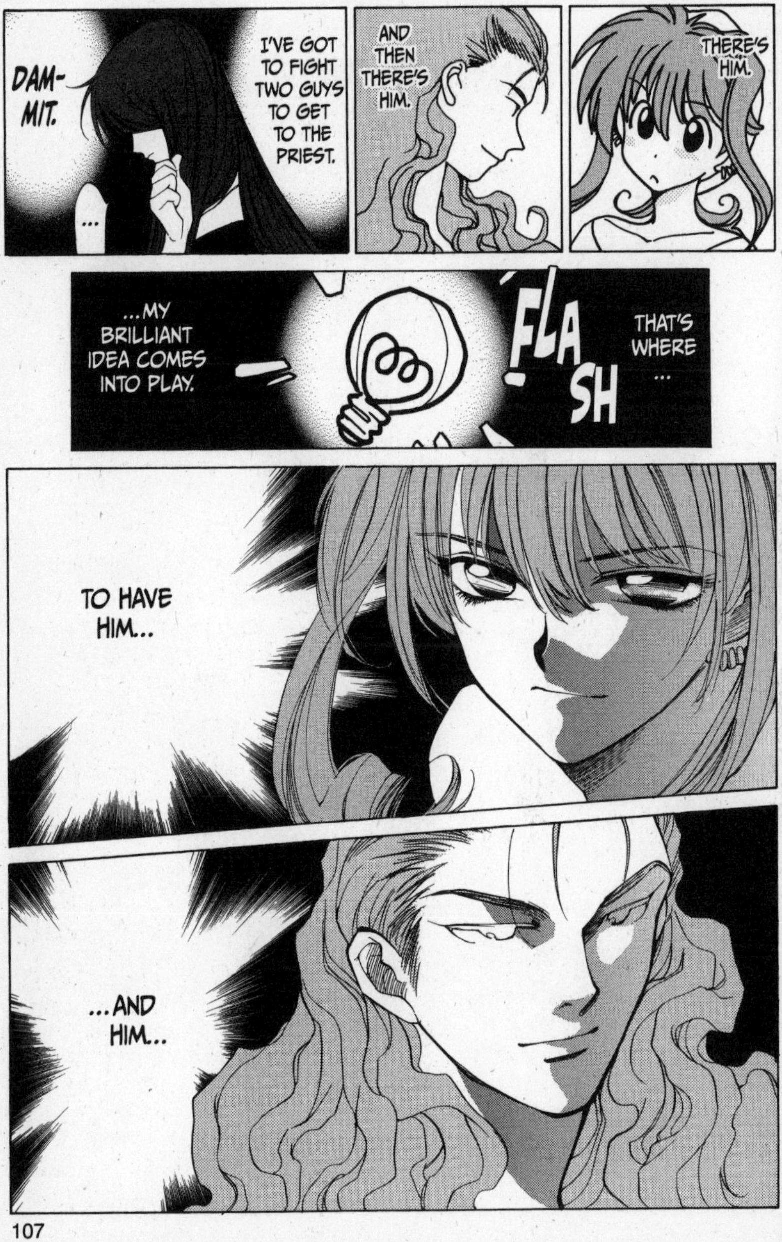
THERE'S HIM.
AND THEN THERE'S HIM.
I'VE GOT TO FIGHT TWO GUYS TO GET TO THE PRIEST.
DAM-MIT.
...
THAT'S WHERE ...
FLASH
...MY BRILLIANT IDEA COMES INTO PLAY.
TO HAVE HIM...
...AND HIM...

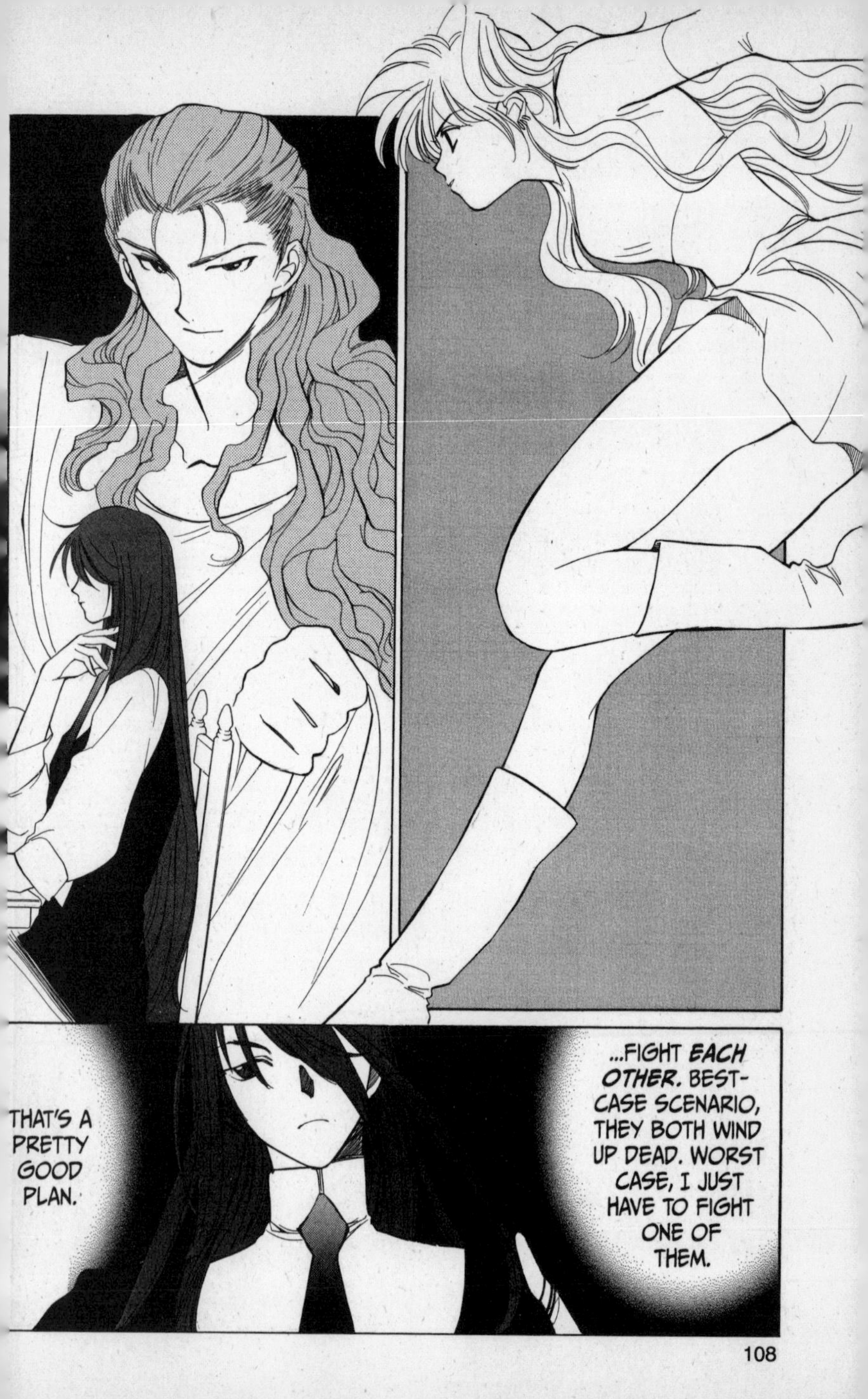
...FIGHT EACH OTHER. BEST-CASE SCENARIO, THEY BOTH WIND UP DEAD. WORST CASE, I JUST HAVE TO FIGHT ONE OF THEM.
THAT'S A PRETTY GOOD PLAN.

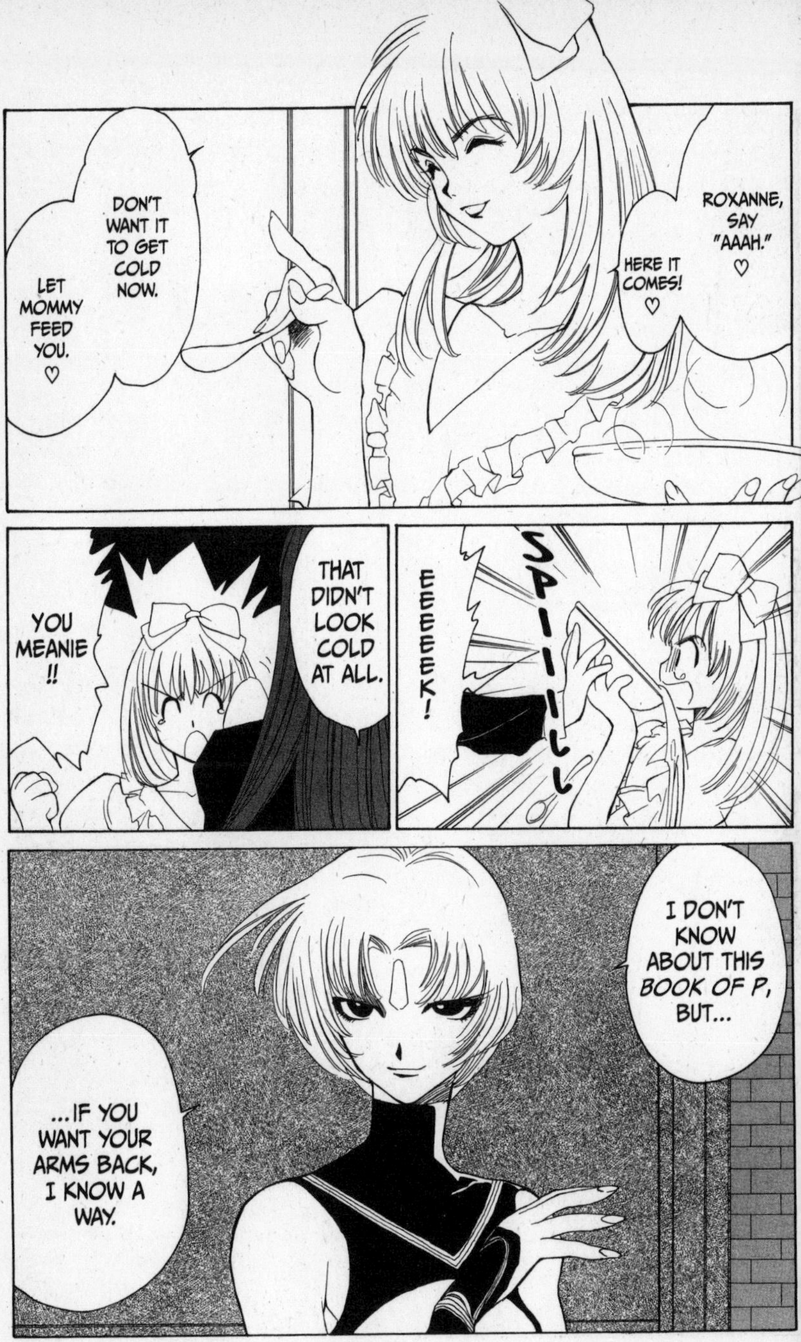
ROXANNE, SAY "AAAH." ♡
HERE IT COMES! ♡
DON'T WANT IT TO GET COLD NOW.
LET MOMMY FEED YOU. ♡
SPIIIILL
EEEEEK!
THAT DIDN'T LOOK COLD AT ALL.
YOU MEANIE!!
I DON'T KNOW ABOUT THIS *BOOK OF P*, BUT...
...IF YOU WANT YOUR ARMS BACK, I KNOW A WAY.

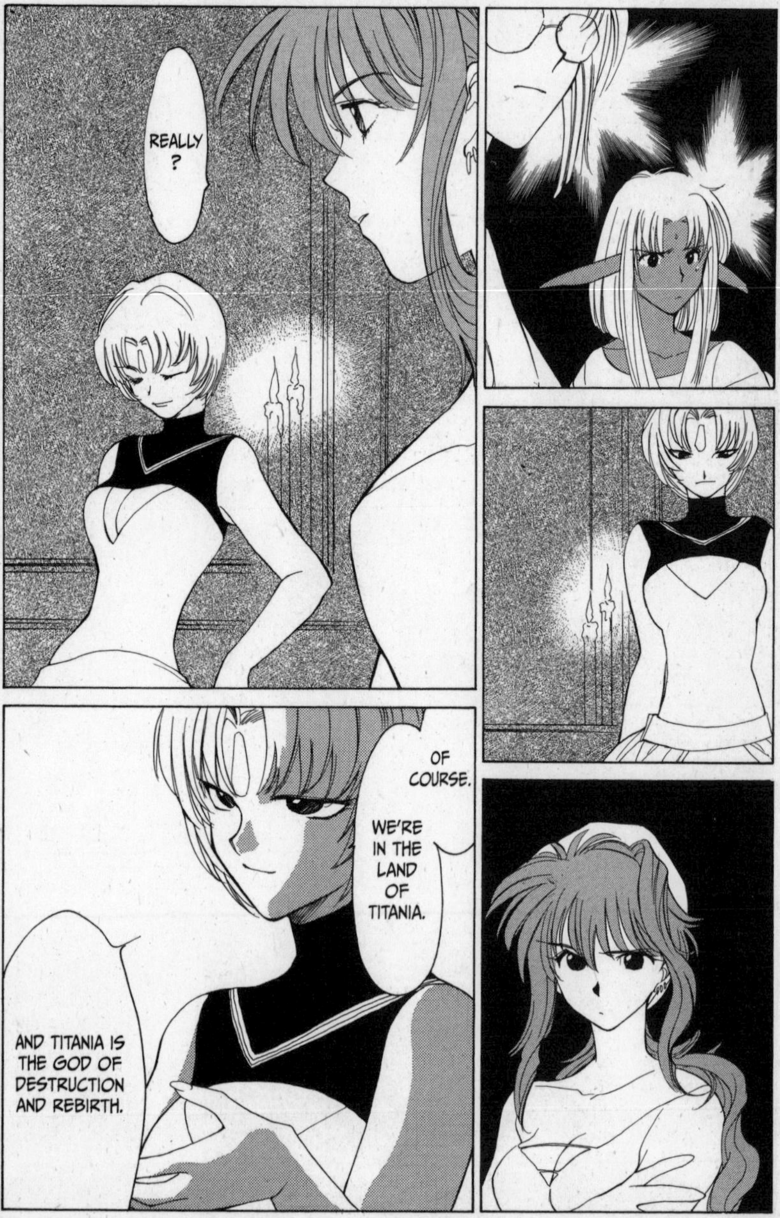
REALLY?
OF COURSE.
WE'RE IN THE LAND OF TITANIA.
AND TITANIA IS THE GOD OF DESTRUCTION AND REBIRTH.

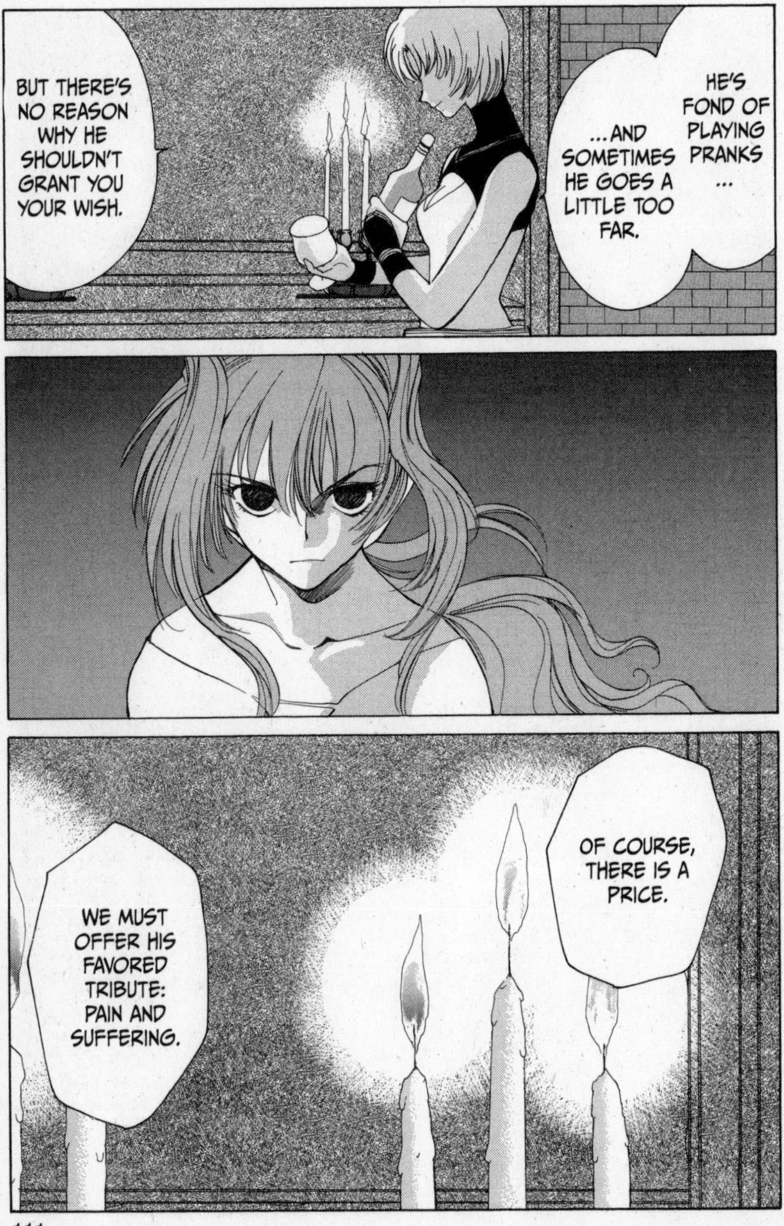
HE'S FOND OF PLAYING PRANKS ...
...AND SOMETIMES HE GOES A LITTLE TOO FAR.
BUT THERE'S NO REASON WHY HE SHOULDN'T GRANT YOU YOUR WISH.
OF COURSE, THERE IS A PRICE.
WE MUST OFFER HIS FAVORED TRIBUTE: PAIN AND SUFFERING.

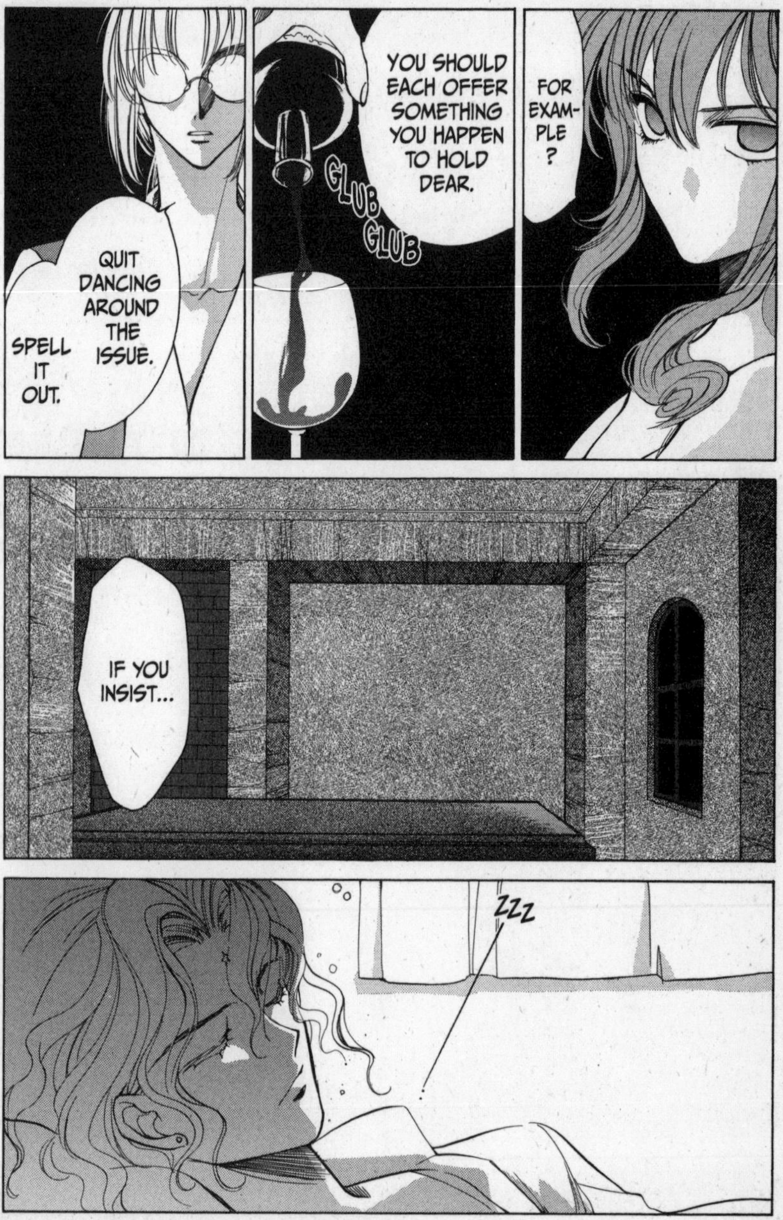
FOR EXAMPLE?
YOU SHOULD EACH OFFER SOMETHING YOU HAPPEN TO HOLD DEAR.
GLUB GLUB
QUIT DANCING AROUND THE ISSUE.
SPELL IT OUT.
IF YOU INSIST...
ZZZ

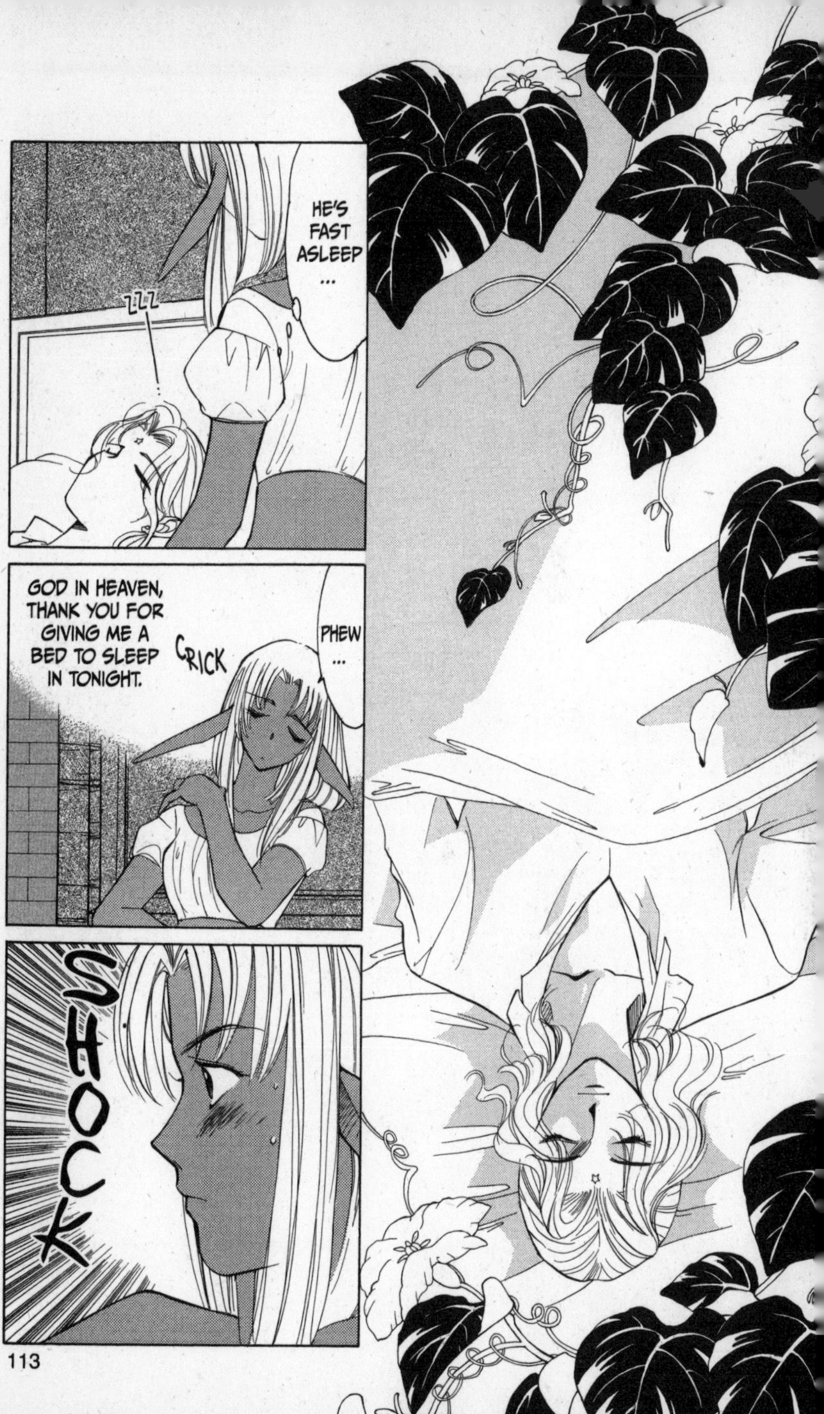
HE'S FAST ASLEEP ...
ZZZ
PHEW ...
CRICK
GOD IN HEAVEN, THANK YOU FOR GIVING ME A BED TO SLEEP IN TONIGHT.
SHOCK

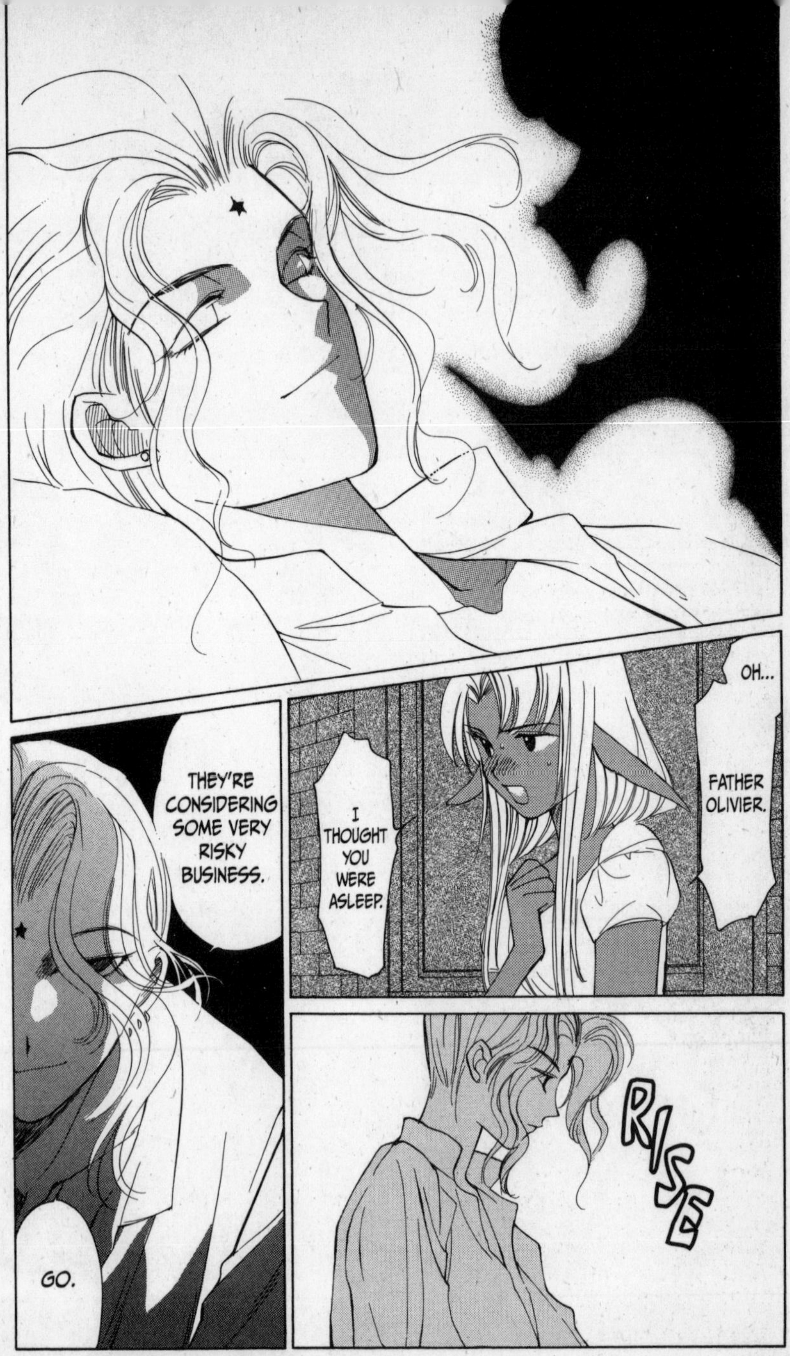
OH...
FATHER OLIVIER.
I THOUGHT YOU WERE ASLEEP.
RISE
THEY'RE CONSIDERING SOME VERY RISKY BUSINESS.
GO.

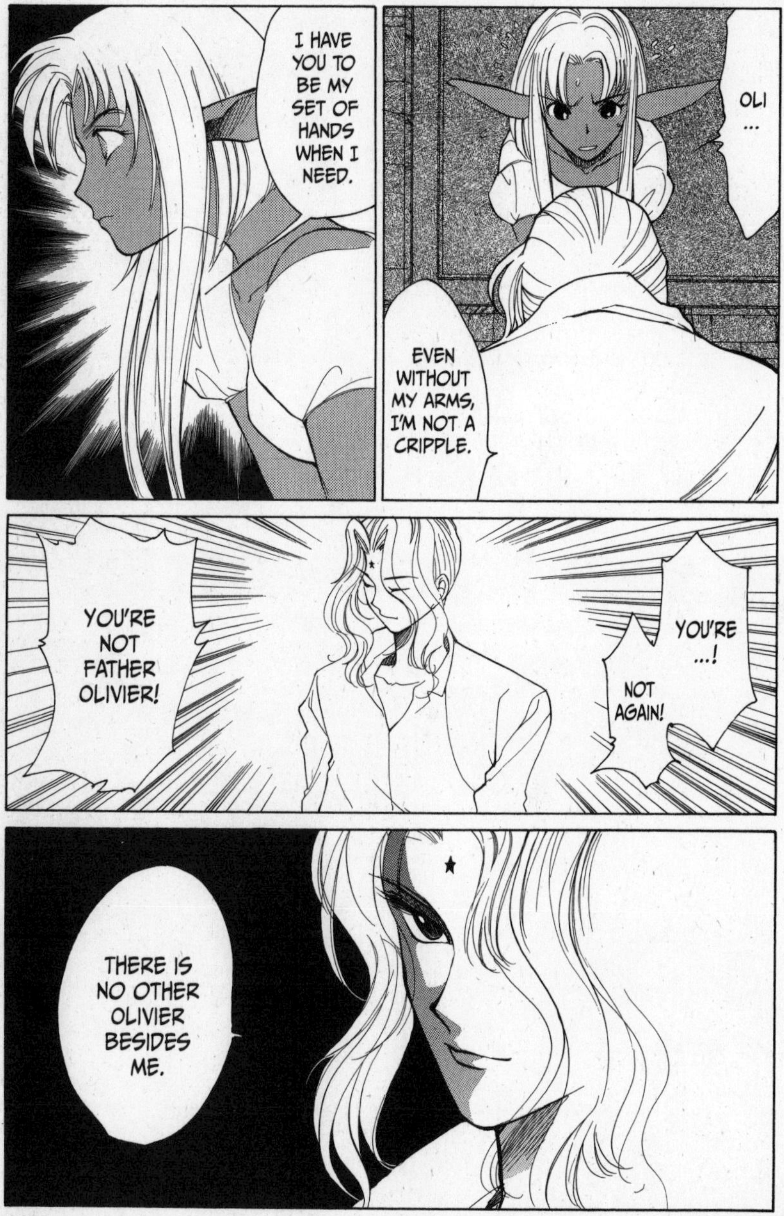
OLI ...
EVEN WITHOUT MY ARMS, I'M NOT A CRIPPLE.
I HAVE YOU TO BE MY SET OF HANDS WHEN I NEED.
YOU'RE ...!
NOT AGAIN!
YOU'RE NOT FATHER OLIVIER!
THERE IS NO OTHER OLIVIER BESIDES ME.

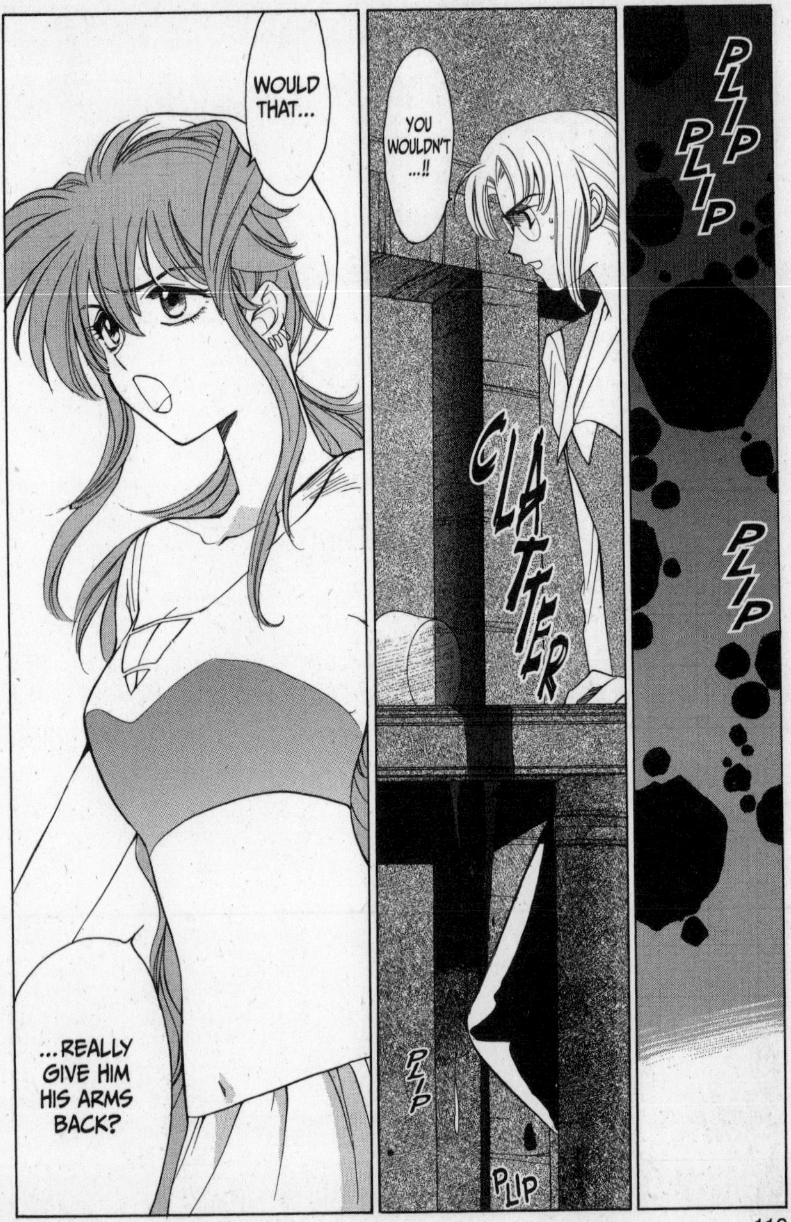
PLIP
PLIP
PLIP
YOU WOULDN'T ...!!
CLATTER
PLIP
PLIP
WOULD THAT...
...REALLY GIVE HIM HIS ARMS BACK?

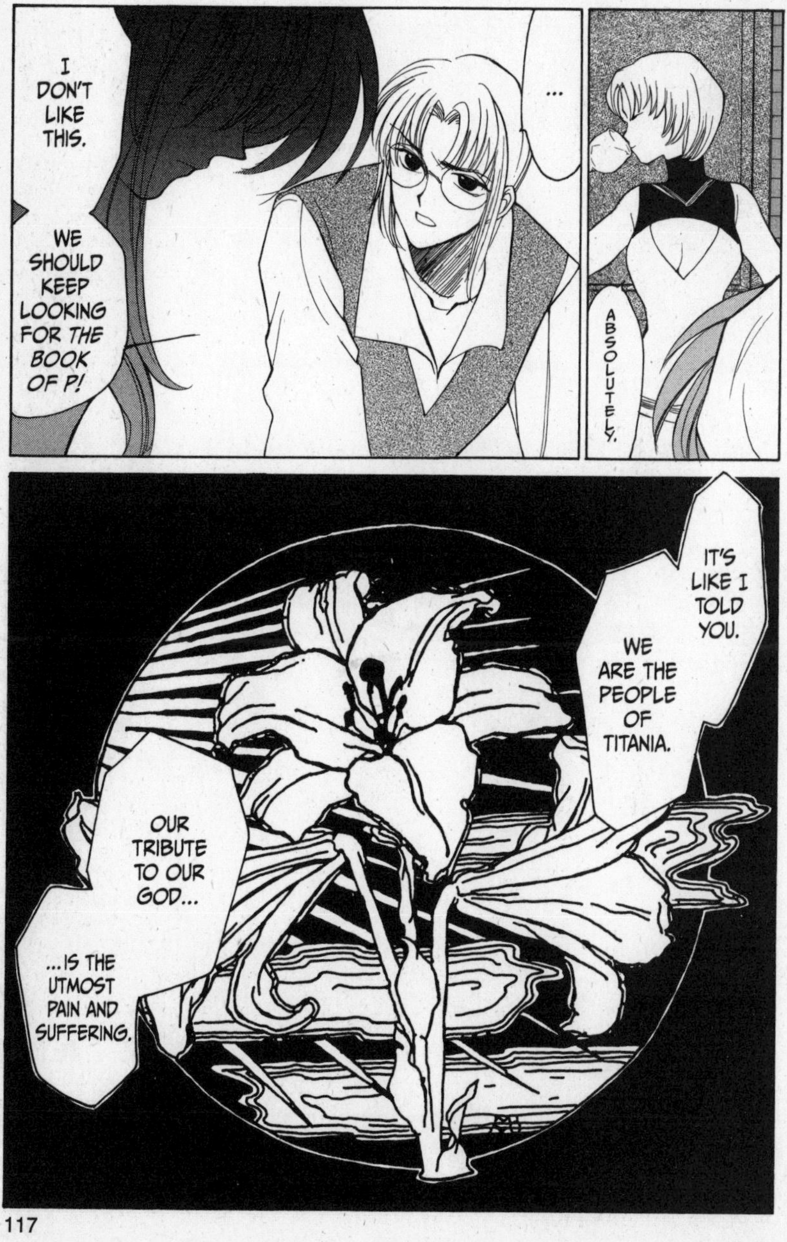
ABSOLUTELY.
...
I DON'T LIKE THIS.
WE SHOULD KEEP LOOKING FOR *THE BOOK OF P*!
IT'S LIKE I TOLD YOU.
WE ARE THE PEOPLE OF TITANIA.
OUR TRIBUTE TO OUR GOD...
...IS THE UTMOST PAIN AND SUFFERING.

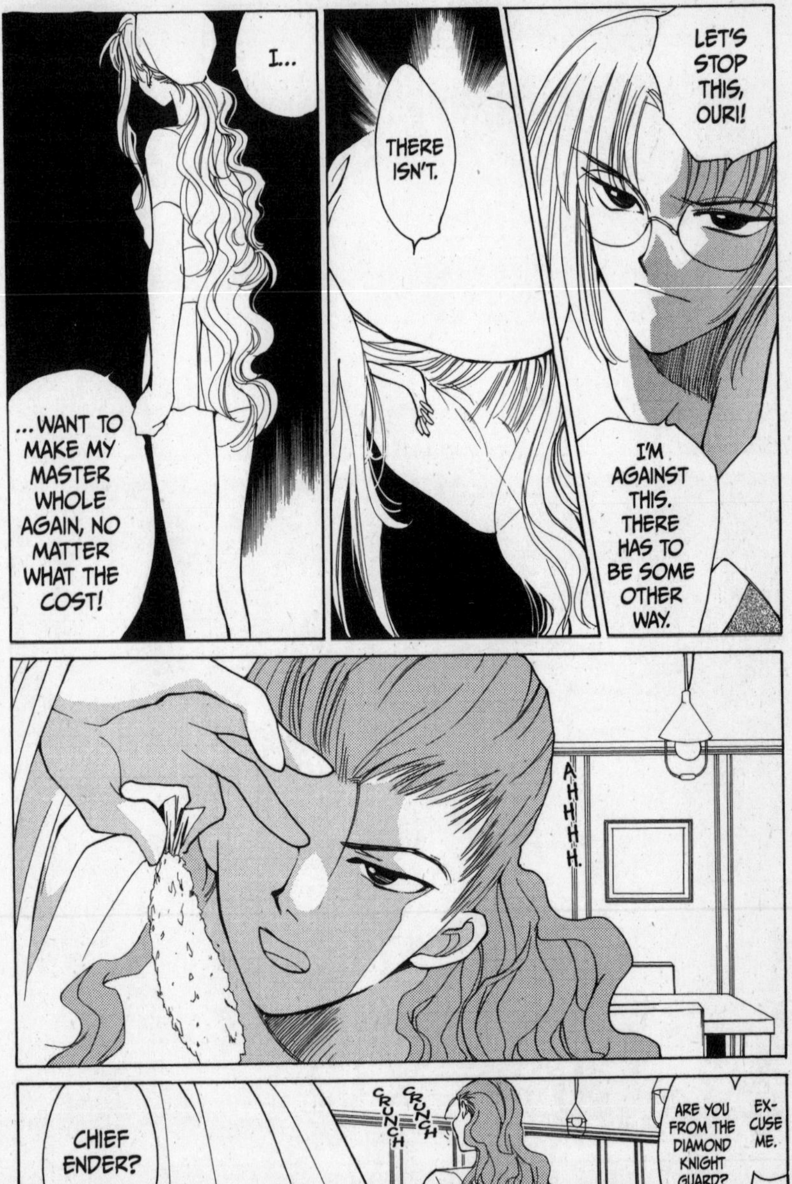
LET'S STOP THIS, OURI!
I'M AGAINST THIS. THERE HAS TO BE SOME OTHER WAY.
THERE ISN'T.
I...
...WANT TO MAKE MY MASTER WHOLE AGAIN, NO MATTER WHAT THE COST!
AHHHHH.
EX-CUSE ME.
ARE YOU FROM THE DIAMOND KNIGHT GUARD?
CRUNCH CRUNCH
CHIEF ENDER?

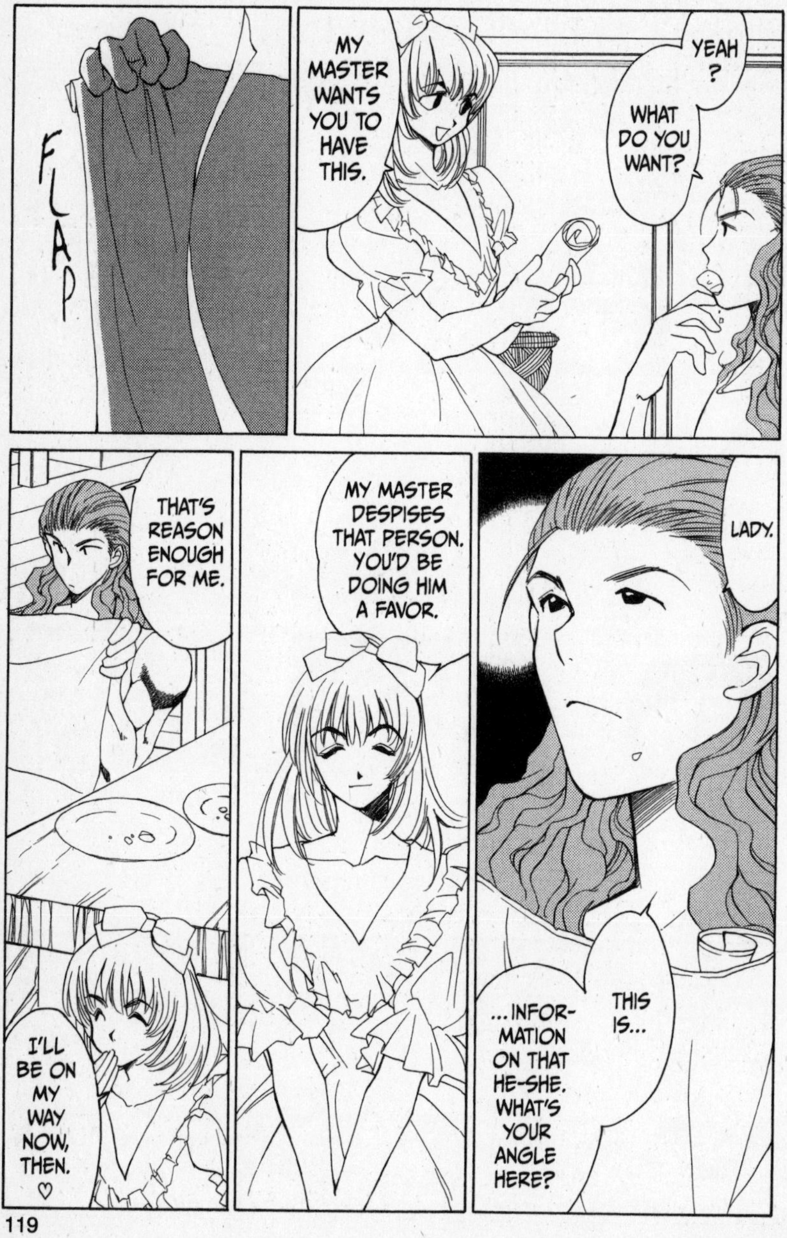
YEAH?
WHAT DO YOU WANT?
MY MASTER WANTS YOU TO HAVE THIS.
FLAP
LADY.
THIS IS...
...INFORMATION ON THAT HE-SHE. WHAT'S YOUR ANGLE HERE?
MY MASTER DESPISES THAT PERSON. YOU'D BE DOING HIM A FAVOR.
THAT'S REASON ENOUGH FOR ME.
I'LL BE ON MY WAY NOW, THEN. ♡

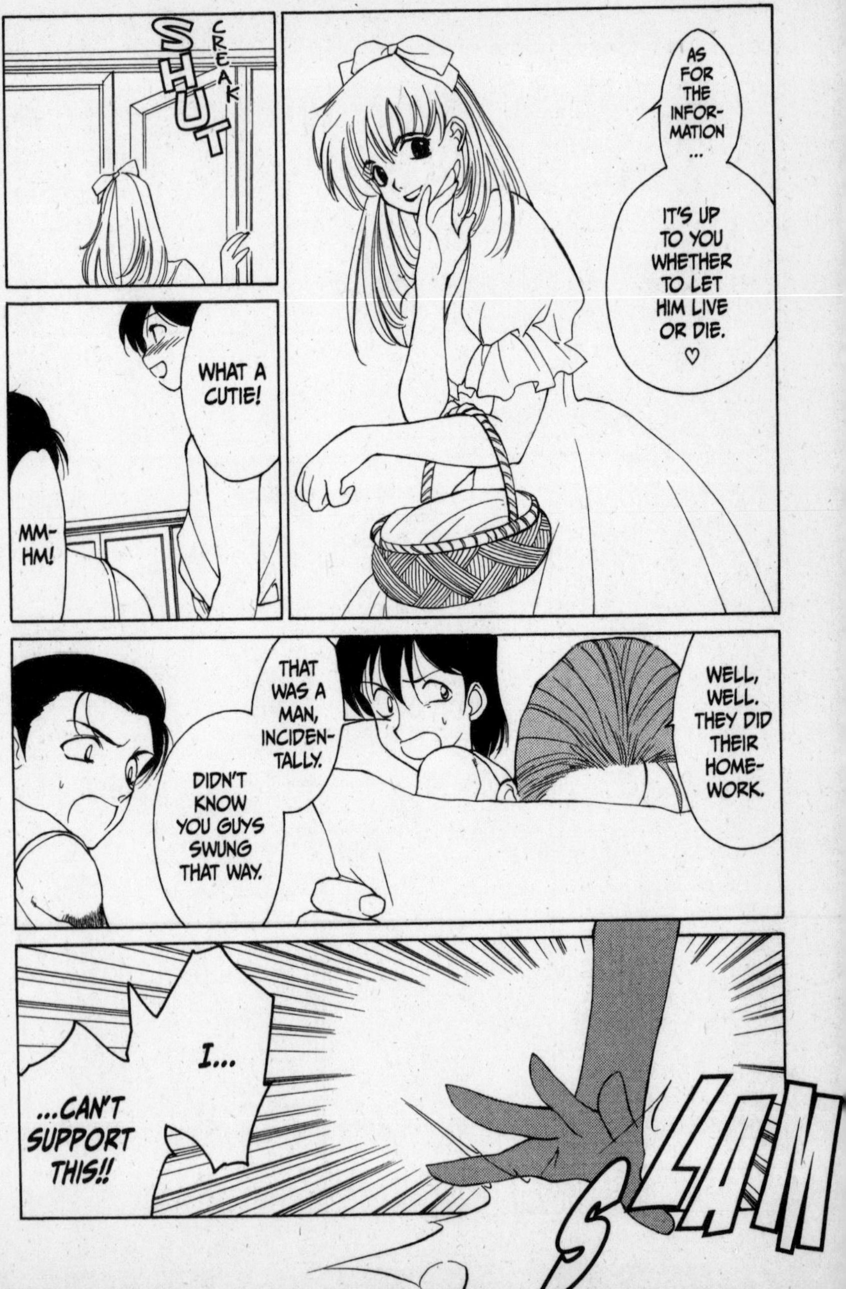
AS FOR THE INFORMATION...
IT'S UP TO YOU WHETHER TO LET HIM LIVE OR DIE. ♡
CREAK
SHUT
WHAT A CUTIE!
MM-HM!
WELL, WELL. THEY DID THEIR HOMEWORK.
THAT WAS A MAN, INCIDENTALLY.
DIDN'T KNOW YOU GUYS SWUNG THAT WAY.
SLAM
I...
...CAN'T SUPPORT THIS!!

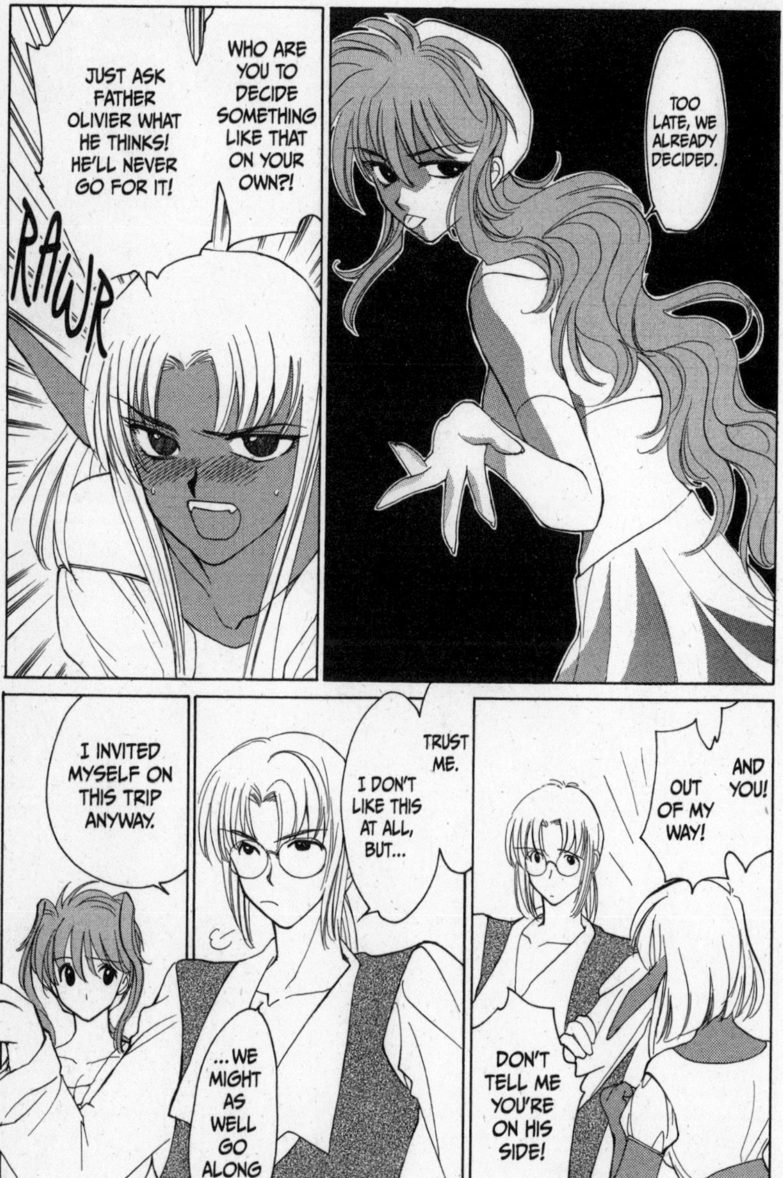
TOO LATE, WE ALREADY DECIDED.
WHO ARE YOU TO DECIDE SOMETHING LIKE THAT ON YOUR OWN?!
JUST ASK FATHER OLIVIER WHAT HE THINKS! HE'LL NEVER GO FOR IT!
RAWR
AND YOU!
OUT OF MY WAY!
DON'T TELL ME YOU'RE ON HIS SIDE!
TRUST ME.
I DON'T LIKE THIS AT ALL, BUT...
...WE MIGHT AS WELL GO ALONG WITH IT.
I INVITED MYSELF ON THIS TRIP ANYWAY.

WELL, I'M NOT HAVING IT!

DON'T YOU SEE HOW HORRIBLE IT'LL BE?!

FATHER OLIVIER WOULD NEVER ALLOW THIS!

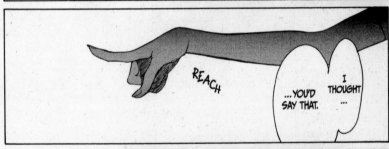

REACH

...YOU'D SAY THAT.

I THOUGHT...

BUT...

IT'S TOO LATE TO TAKE IT BACK.

TAP

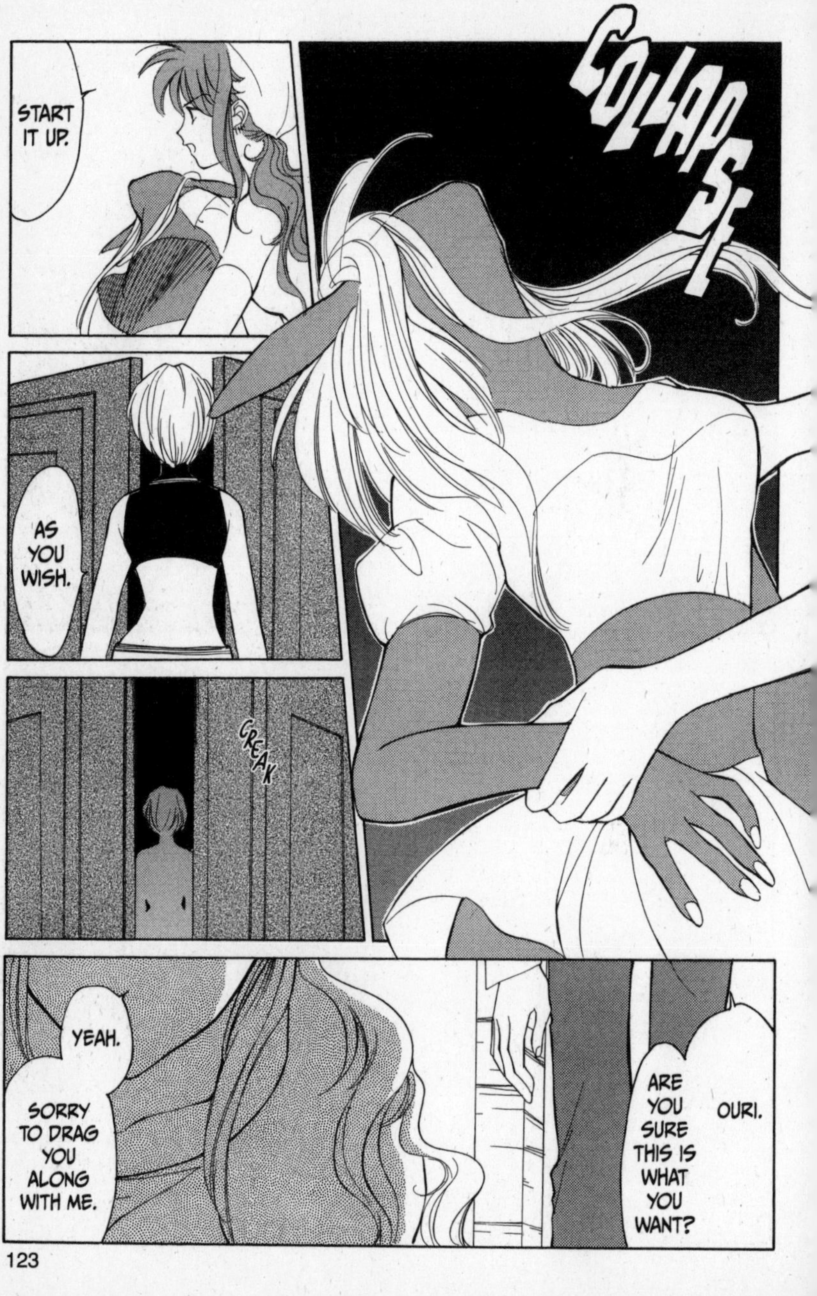
COLLAPSE
START IT UP.
AS YOU WISH.
CREAK
OURI.
ARE YOU SURE THIS IS WHAT YOU WANT?
YEAH.
SORRY TO DRAG YOU ALONG WITH ME.

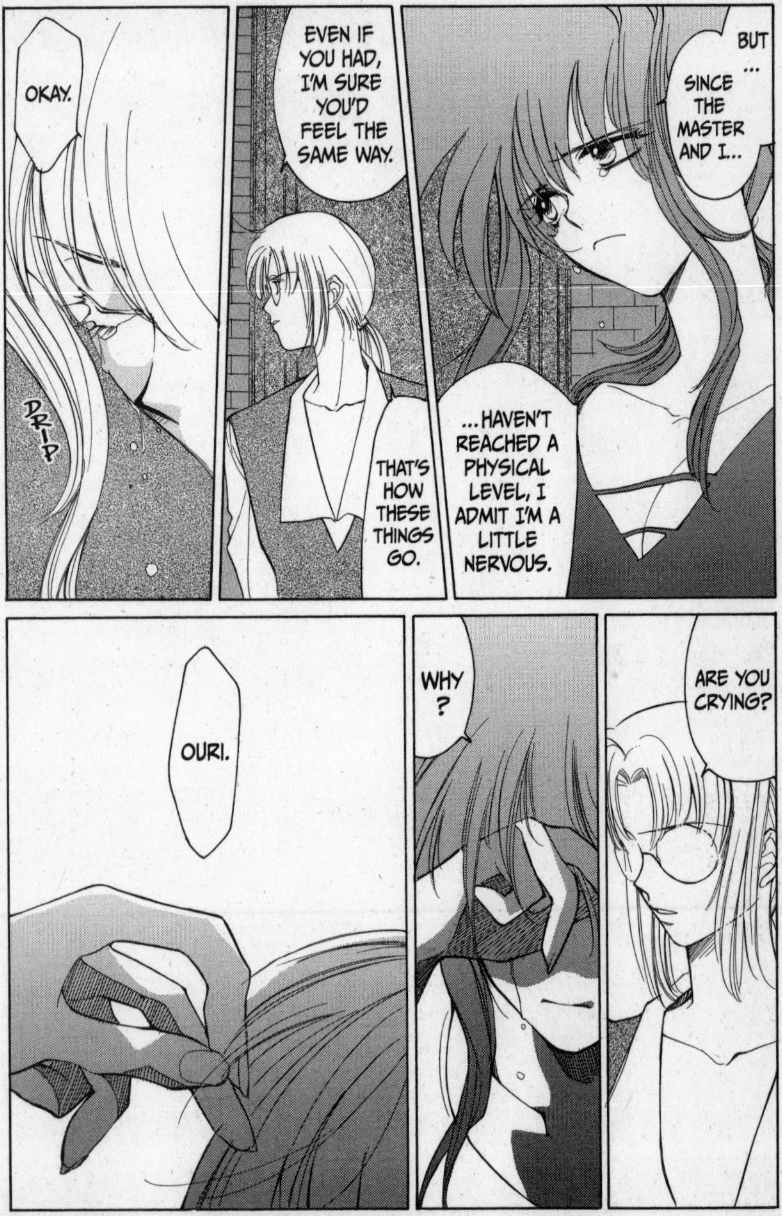
BUT ... SINCE THE MASTER AND I...
...HAVEN'T REACHED A PHYSICAL LEVEL, I ADMIT I'M A LITTLE NERVOUS.
EVEN IF YOU HAD, I'M SURE YOU'D FEEL THE SAME WAY.
THAT'S HOW THESE THINGS GO.
OKAY.
DRIP
ARE YOU CRYING?
WHY?
OURI.

YOU HAVE NO IDEA...

...HOW CUTE YOU CAN BE SOMETIMES.

I thought I always was.

CREEEAK

SHOT

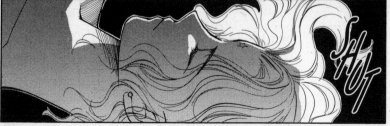

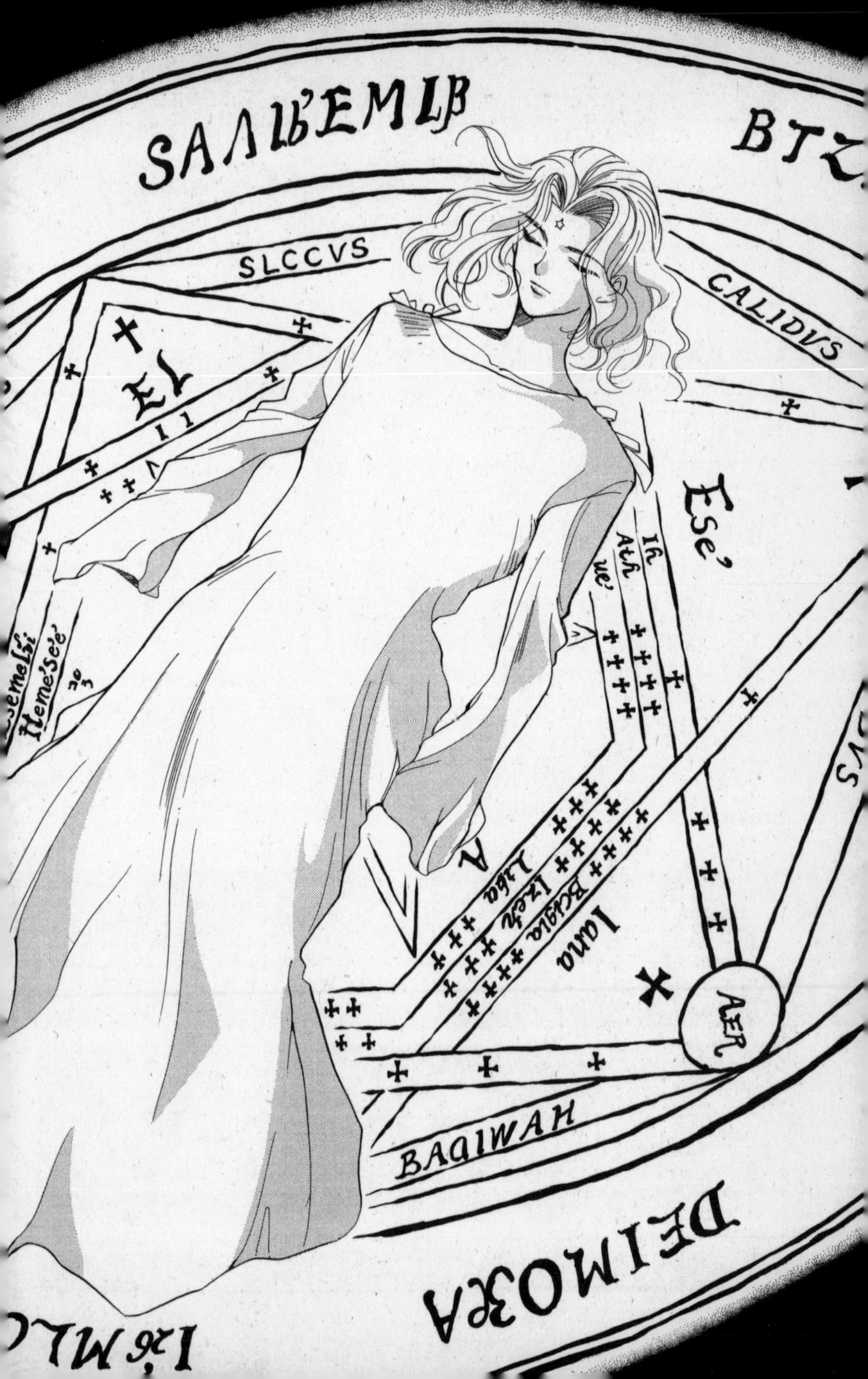
SLCCVS
CALIDVS
Ese'
Iana
AER
BAGIWAH

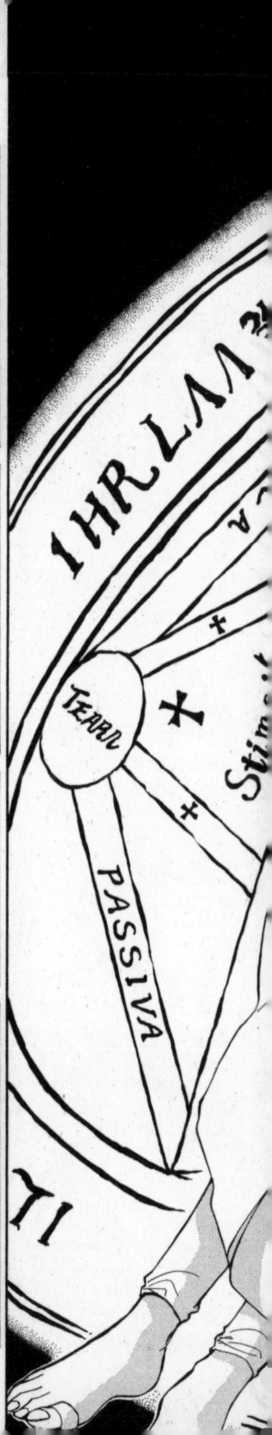
TEARR
PASSIVA

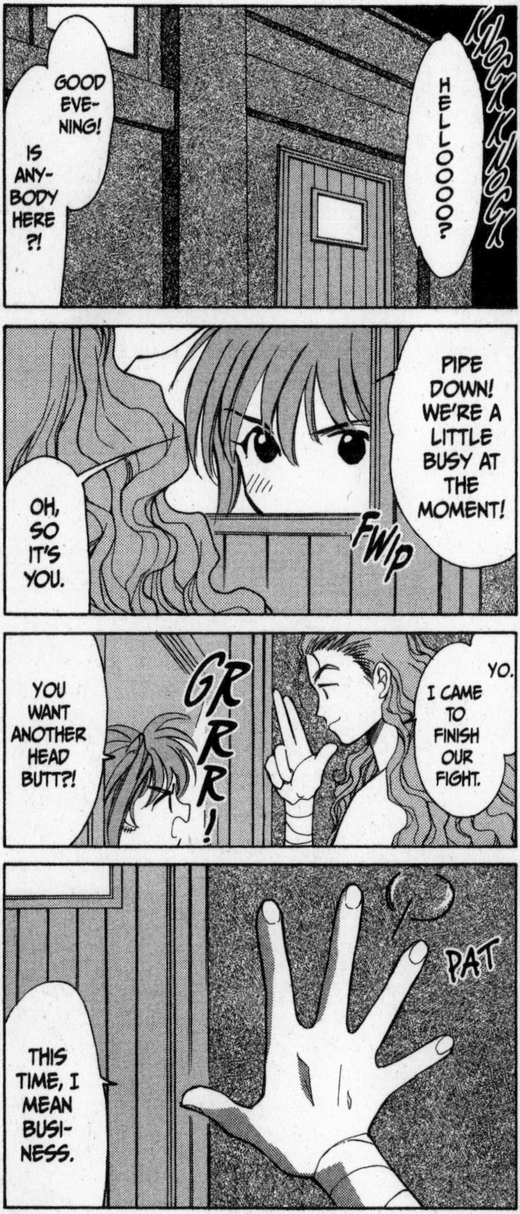
KNOCK KNOCK
HELLOOOO?
GOOD EVENING! IS ANYBODY HERE?!
PIPE DOWN! WE'RE A LITTLE BUSY AT THE MOMENT!
FWIP
OH, SO IT'S YOU.
YO. I CAME TO FINISH OUR FIGHT.
GRRR!
YOU WANT ANOTHER HEAD BUTT?!
PAT
THIS TIME, I MEAN BUSINESS.

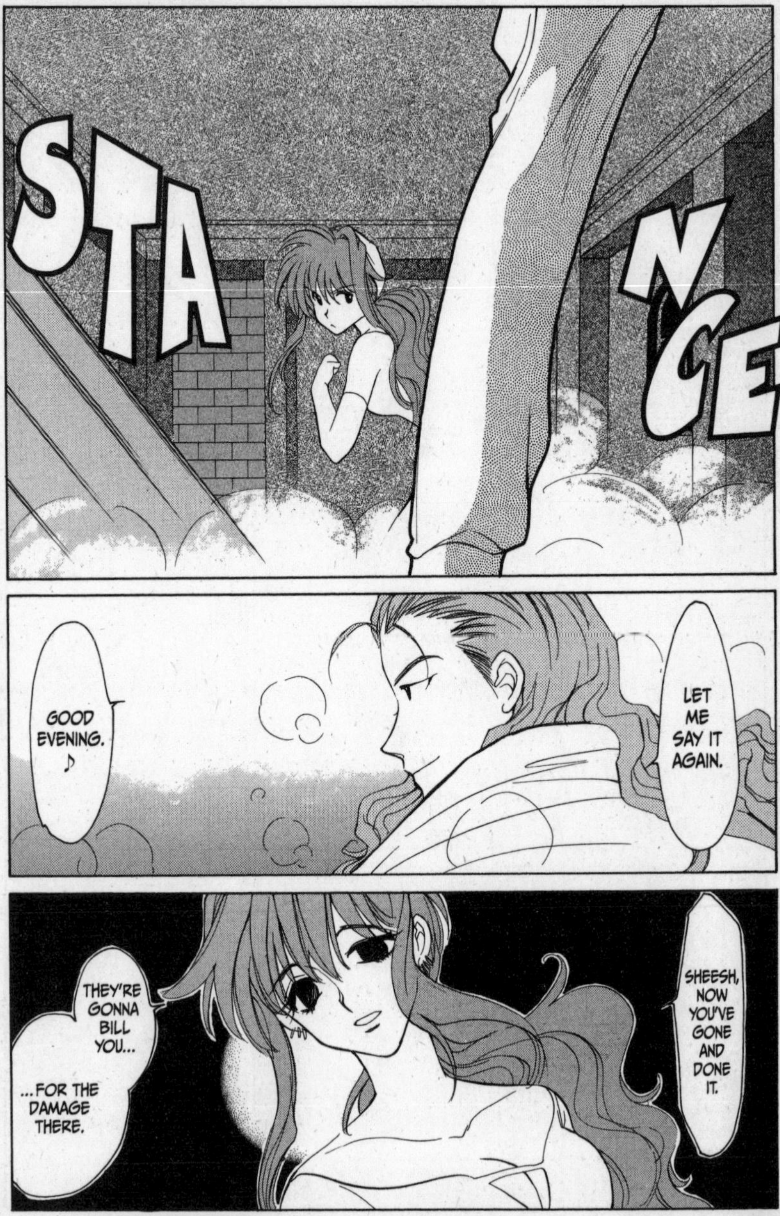
STA
NCE
LET ME SAY IT AGAIN.
GOOD EVENING. ♪
SHEESH, NOW YOU'VE GONE AND DONE IT.
THEY'RE GONNA BILL YOU...
...FOR THE DAMAGE THERE.

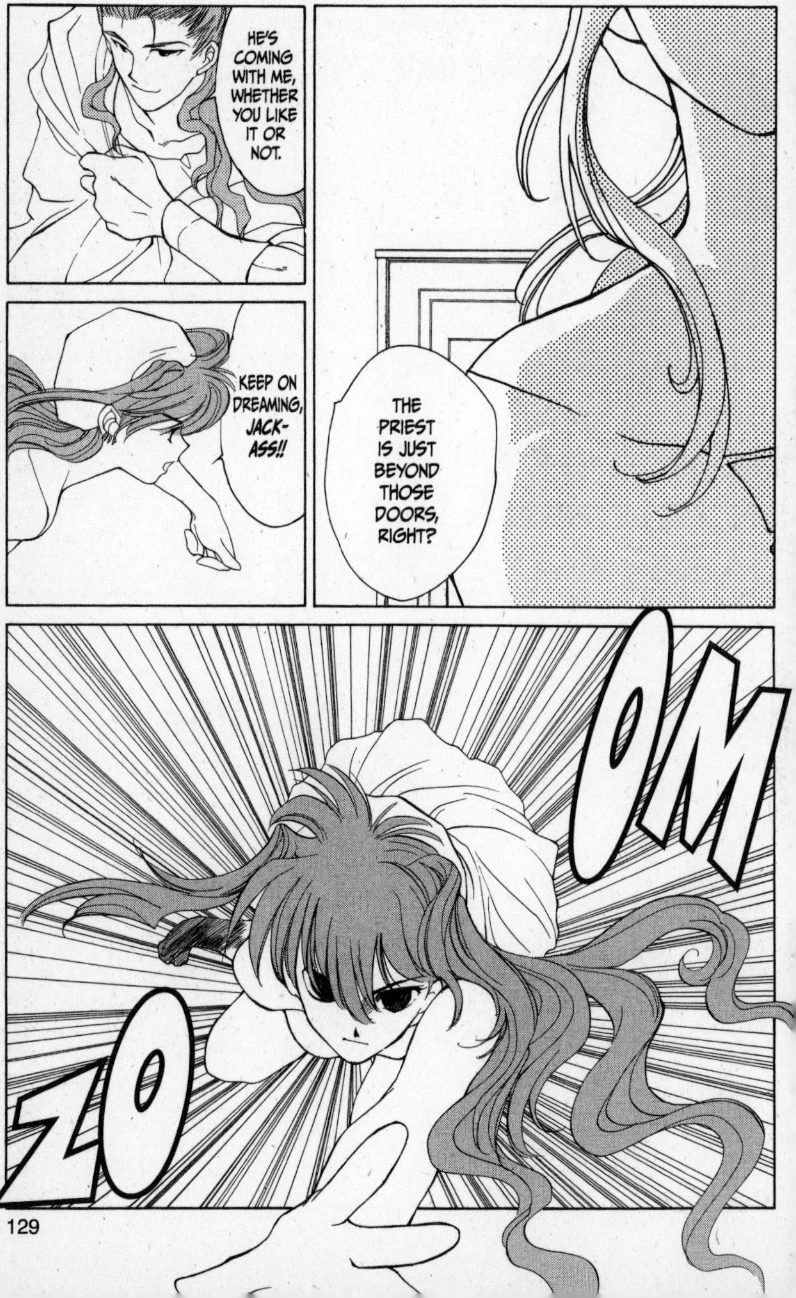
THE PRIEST IS JUST BEYOND THOSE DOORS, RIGHT?
HE'S COMING WITH ME, WHETHER YOU LIKE IT OR NOT.
KEEP ON DREAMING, JACK-ASS!!
ZO
OM

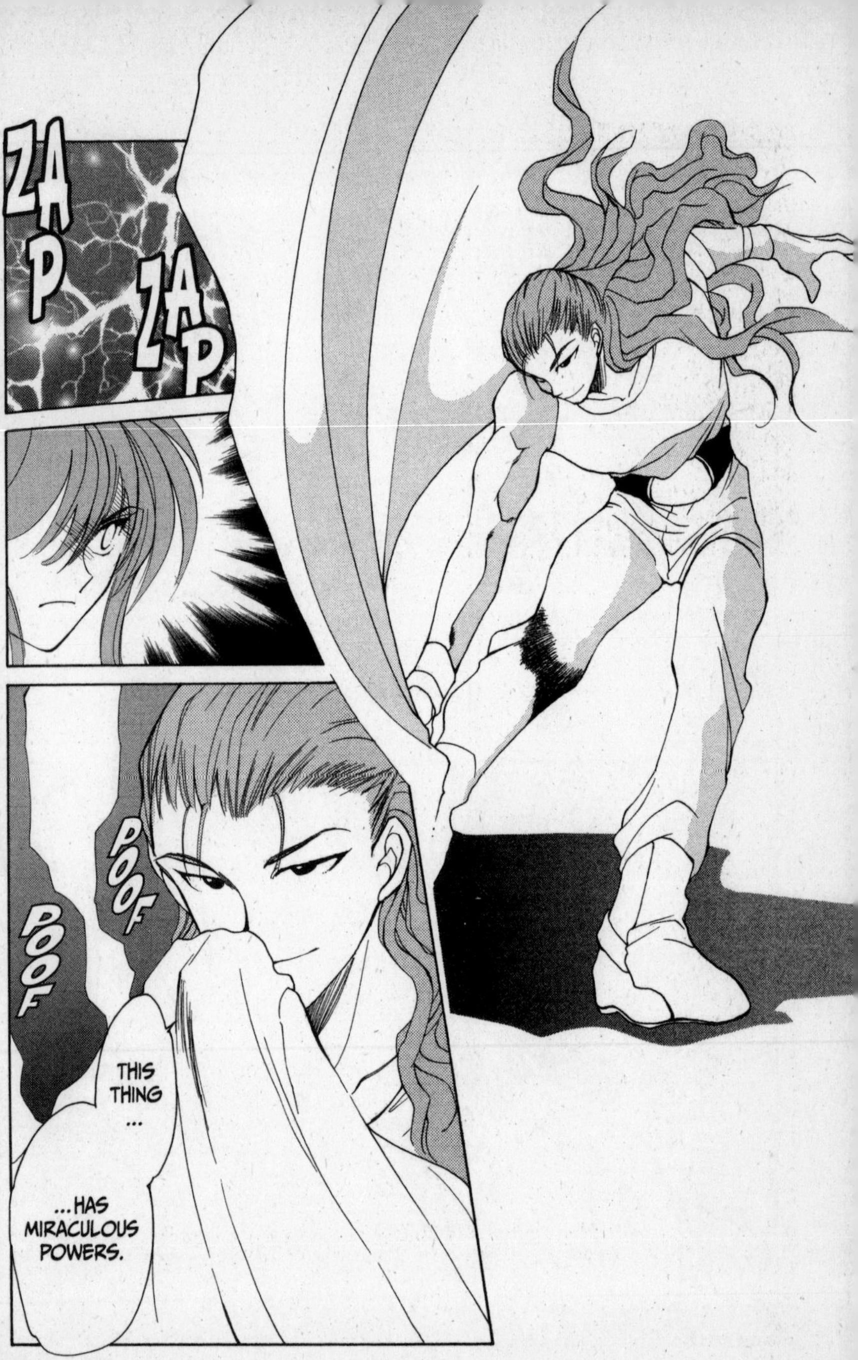
ZAP
ZAP
POOF
POOF
THIS THING ...
...HAS MIRACULOUS POWERS.

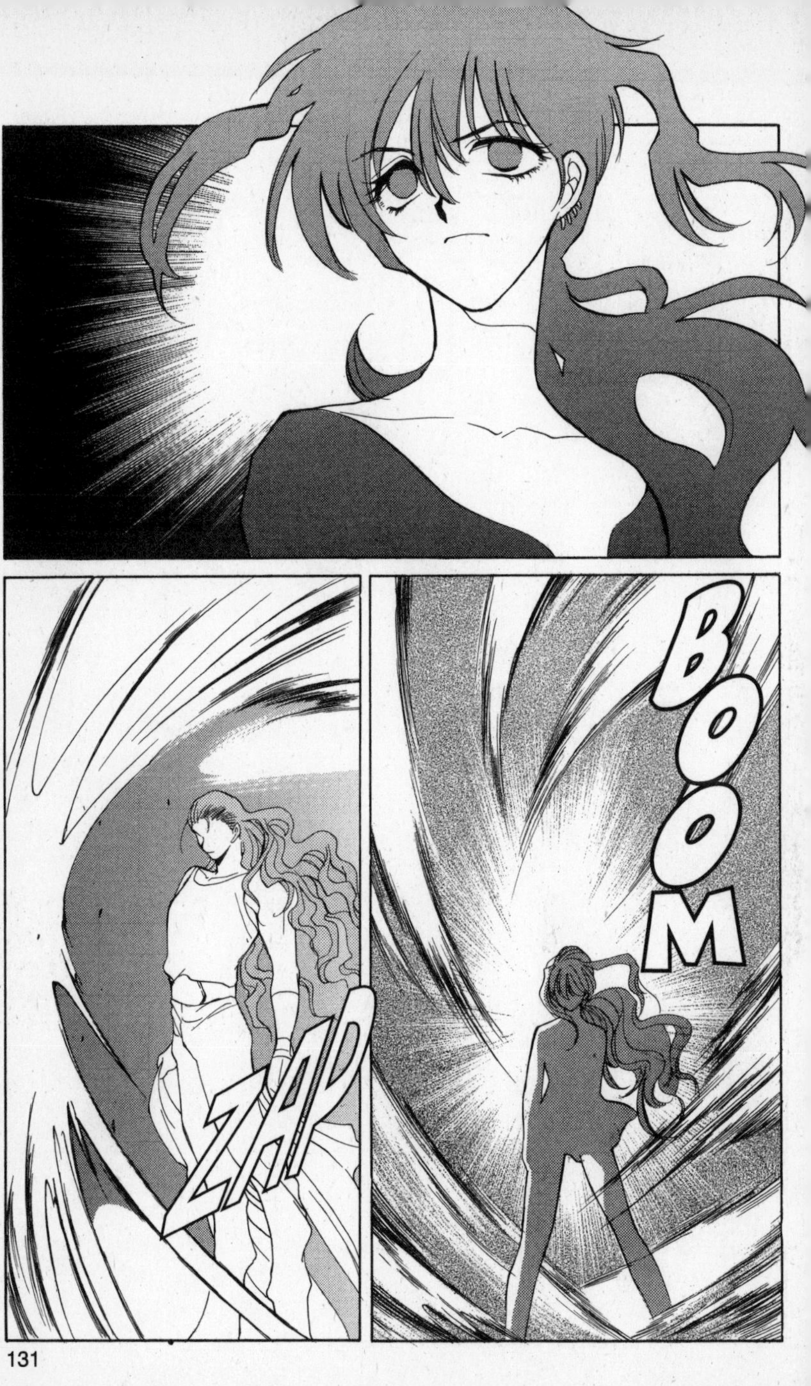
BOOOM
ZAP

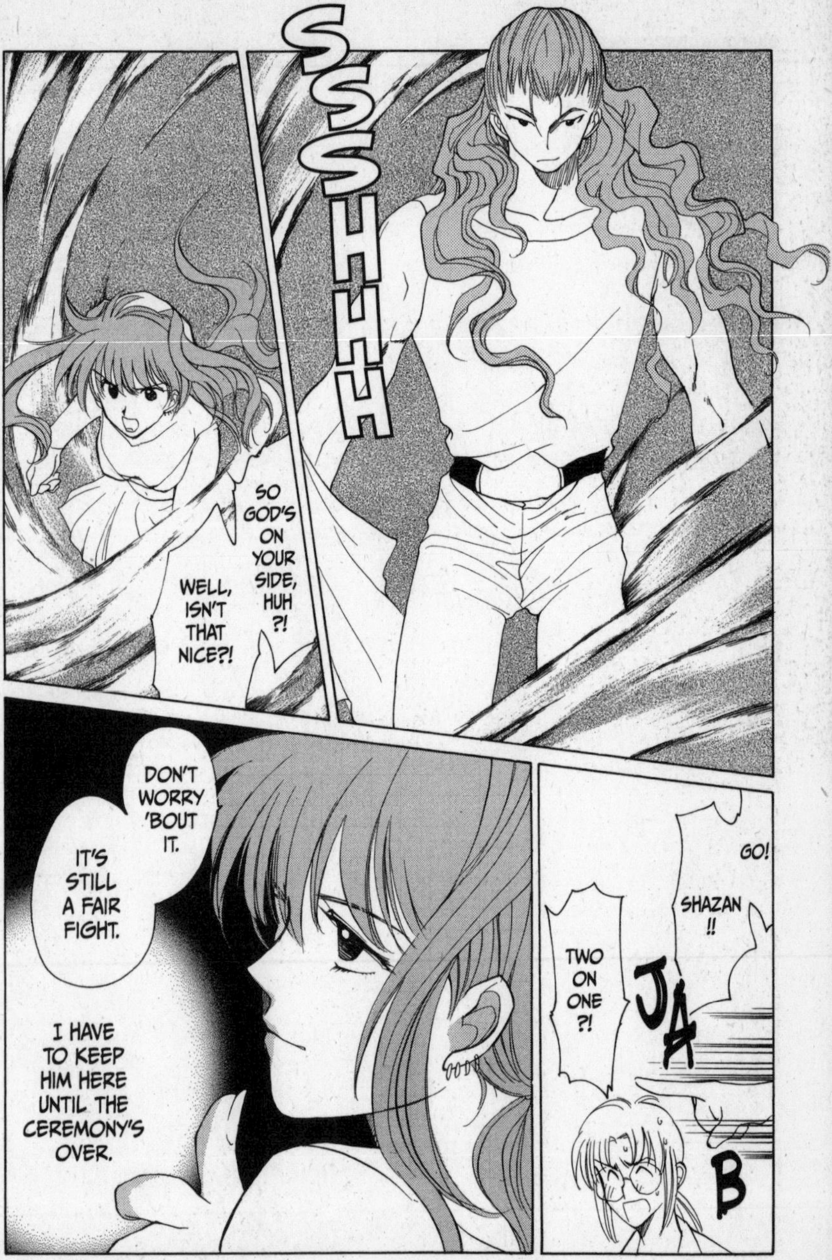
SSSHHHH
SO GOD'S ON YOUR SIDE, HUH?!
WELL, ISN'T THAT NICE?!
GO! SHAZAN!!
TWO ON ONE?!
JAB
DON'T WORRY 'BOUT IT.
IT'S STILL A FAIR FIGHT.
I HAVE TO KEEP HIM HERE UNTIL THE CEREMONY'S OVER.

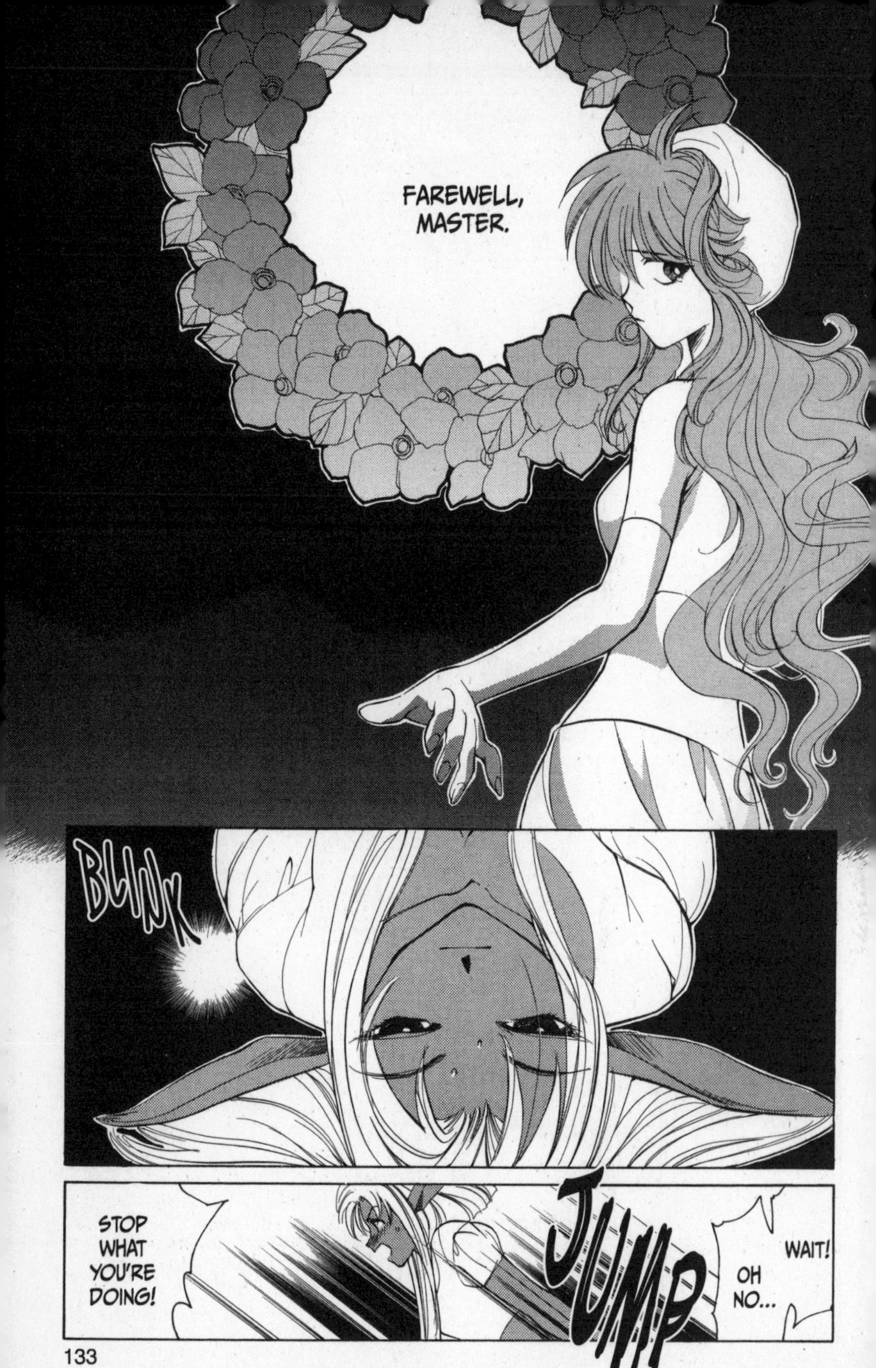
FAREWELL, MASTER.
BLINK
WAIT!
OH NO...
JUMP
STOP WHAT YOU'RE DOING!

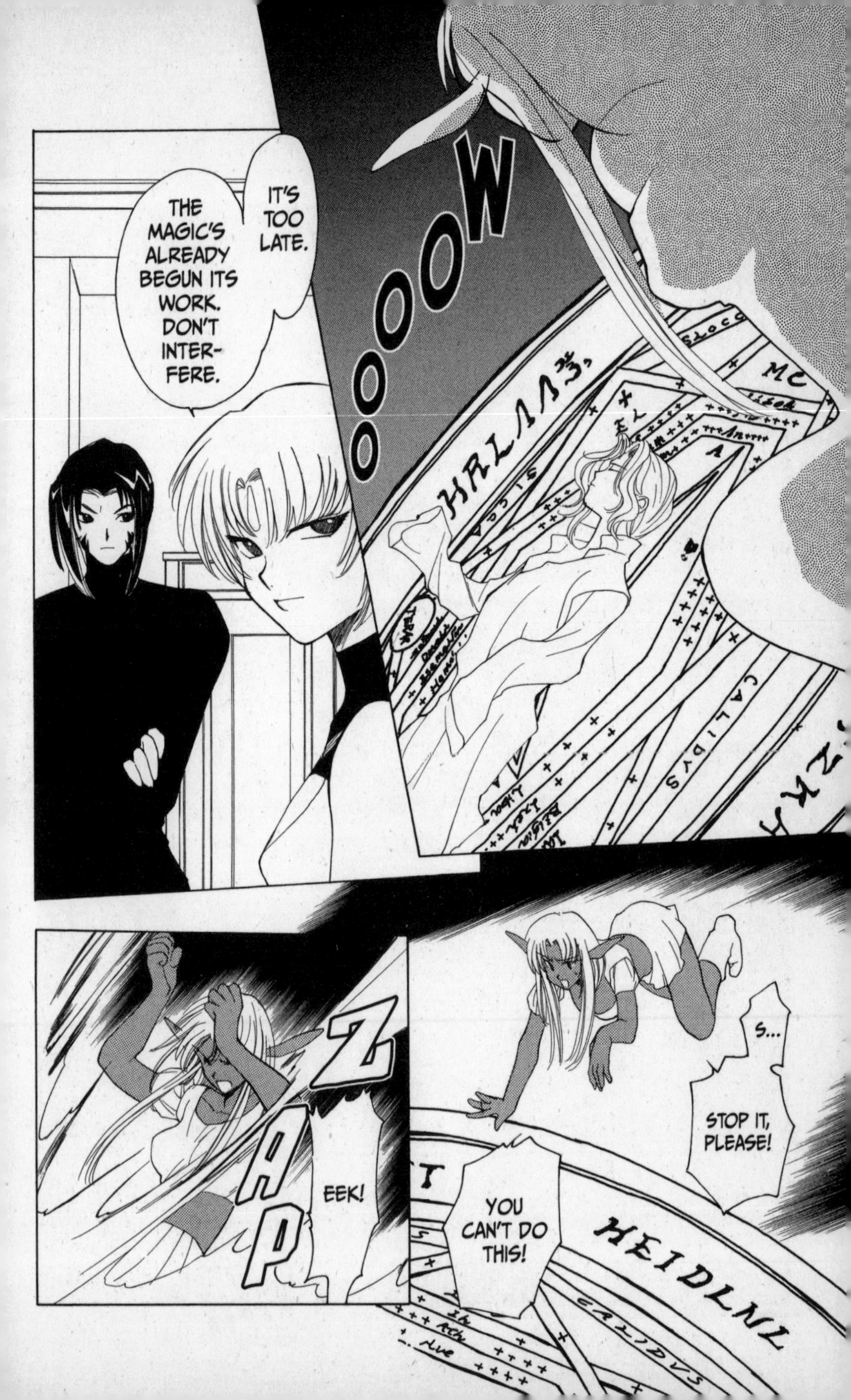
WOOOOO
IT'S TOO LATE.
THE MAGIC'S ALREADY BEGUN ITS WORK. DON'T INTER-FERE.
S...
STOP IT, PLEASE!
YOU CAN'T DO THIS!
ZAP
EEK!

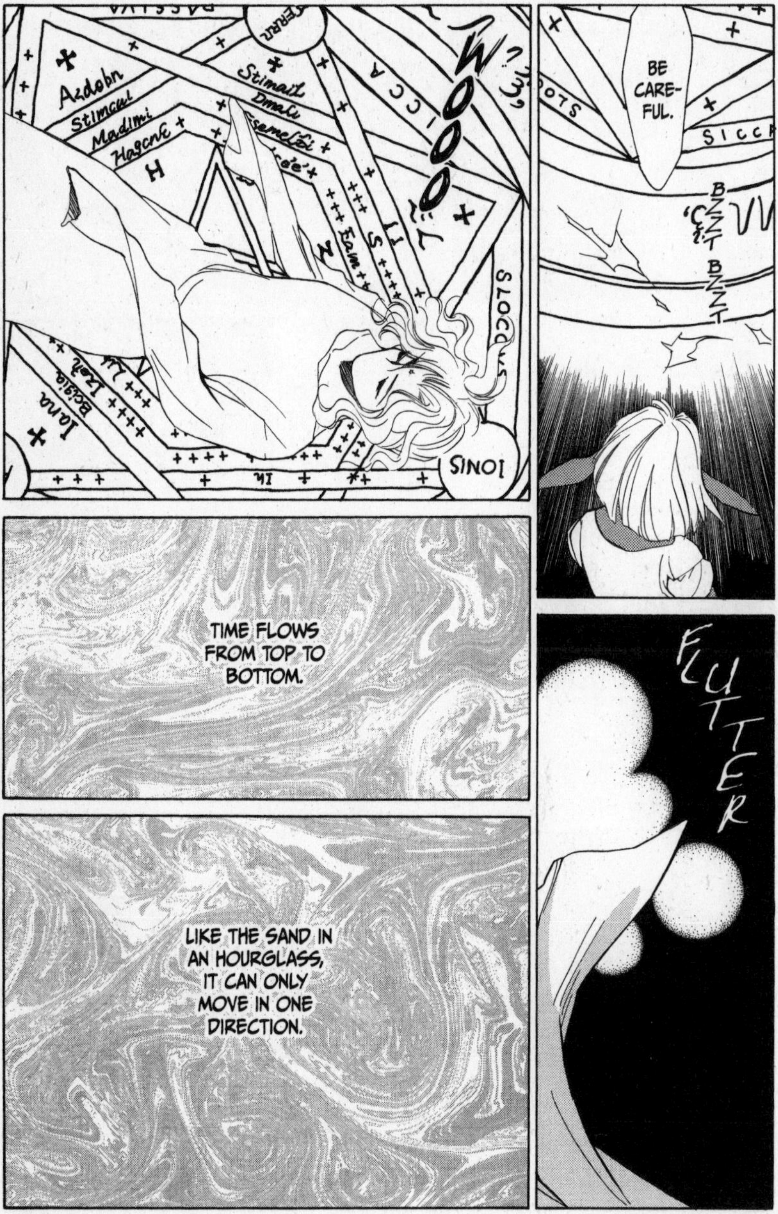
BE CAREFUL.
BZZZT BZZZT
WOOOO
FLUTTER
TIME FLOWS FROM TOP TO BOTTOM.
LIKE THE SAND IN AN HOURGLASS, IT CAN ONLY MOVE IN ONE DIRECTION.

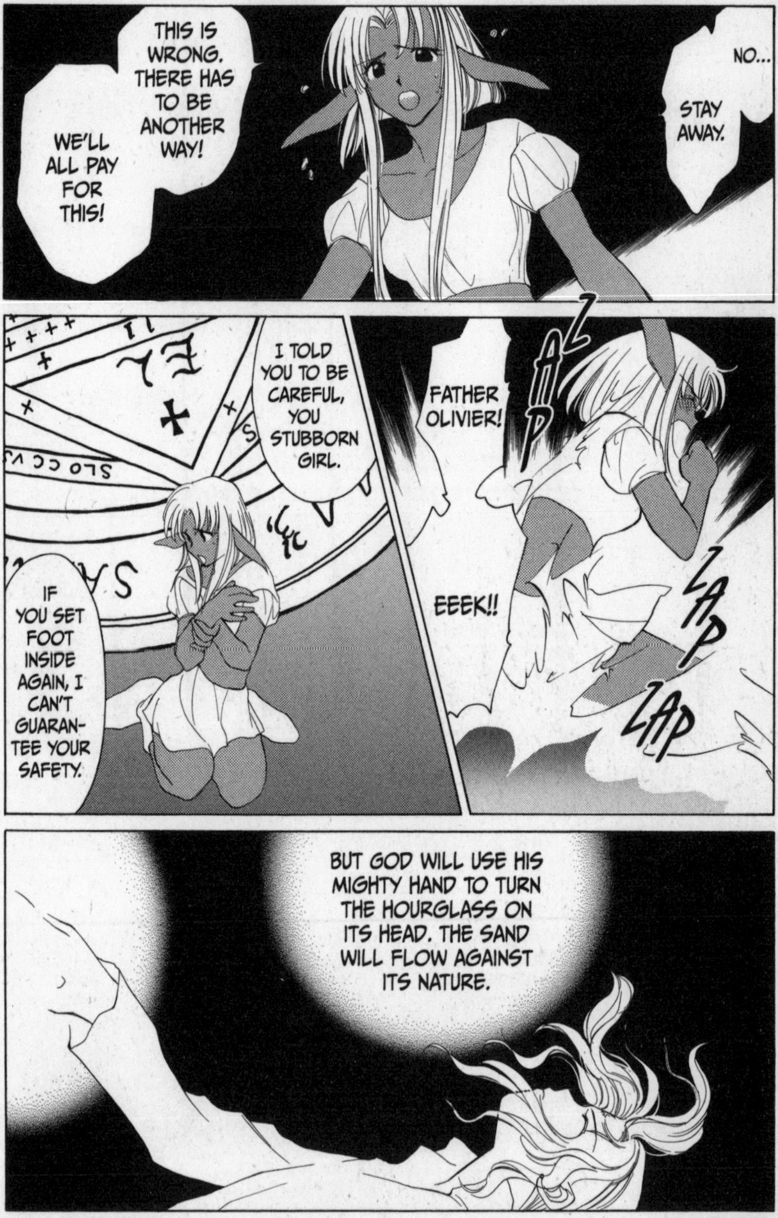
NO...
STAY AWAY.
THIS IS WRONG. THERE HAS TO BE ANOTHER WAY!
WE'LL ALL PAY FOR THIS!
ZAP
FATHER OLIVIER!
EEEK!!
ZAP ZAP
I TOLD YOU TO BE CAREFUL, YOU STUBBORN GIRL.
IF YOU SET FOOT INSIDE AGAIN, I CAN'T GUARANTEE YOUR SAFETY.
BUT GOD WILL USE HIS MIGHTY HAND TO TURN THE HOURGLASS ON ITS HEAD. THE SAND WILL FLOW AGAINST ITS NATURE.

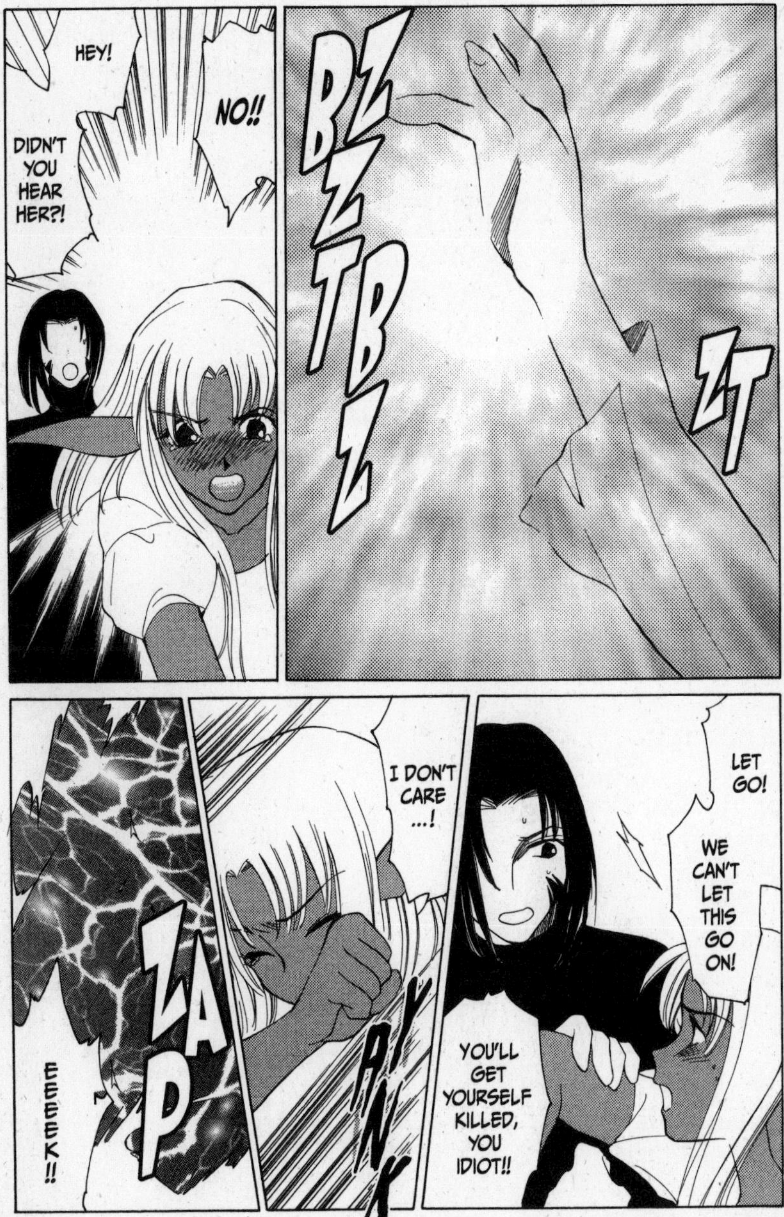
BZZTBZZ
ZT
HEY!
NO!!
DIDN'T YOU HEAR HER?!
LET GO!
WE CAN'T LET THIS GO ON!
YOU'LL GET YOURSELF KILLED, YOU IDIOT!!
I DON'T CARE ...!
YANK
ZAP
EEEEEK!!

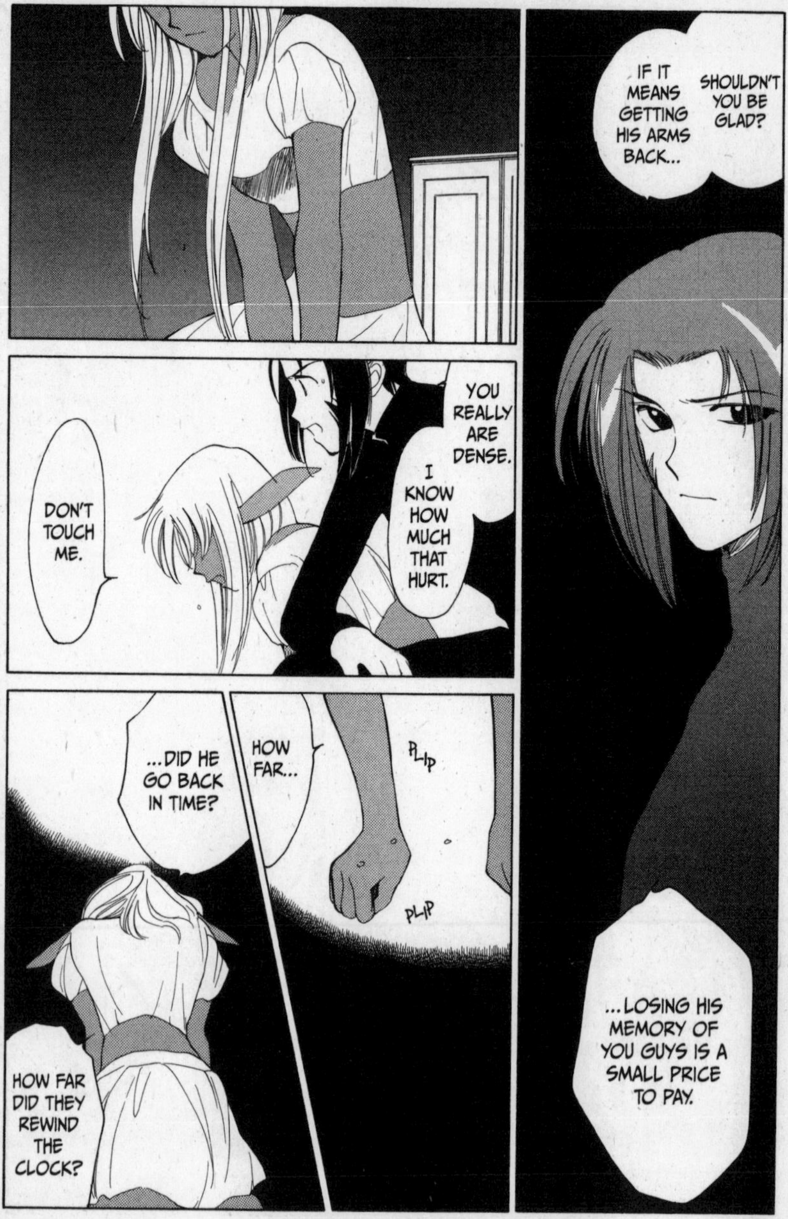
SHOULDN'T YOU BE GLAD?
IF IT MEANS GETTING HIS ARMS BACK...
...LOSING HIS MEMORY OF YOU GUYS IS A SMALL PRICE TO PAY.
YOU REALLY ARE DENSE.
I KNOW HOW MUCH THAT HURT.
DON'T TOUCH ME.
HOW FAR...
PLIP
PLIP
...DID HE GO BACK IN TIME?
HOW FAR DID THEY REWIND THE CLOCK?

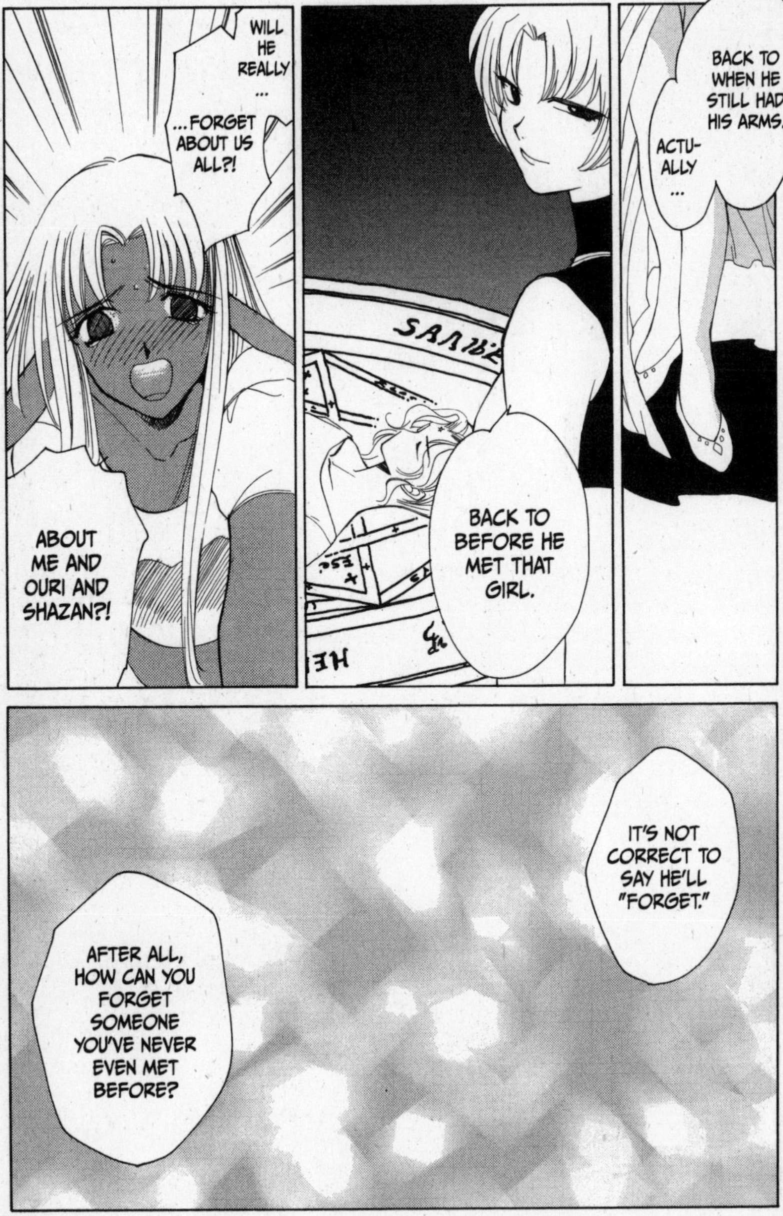
BACK TO WHEN HE STILL HAD HIS ARMS.
ACTU-ALLY ...
BACK TO BEFORE HE MET THAT GIRL.
WILL HE REALLY ...
...FORGET ABOUT US ALL?!
ABOUT ME AND OURI AND SHAZAN?!
IT'S NOT CORRECT TO SAY HE'LL "FORGET."
AFTER ALL, HOW CAN YOU FORGET SOMEONE YOU'VE NEVER EVEN MET BEFORE?

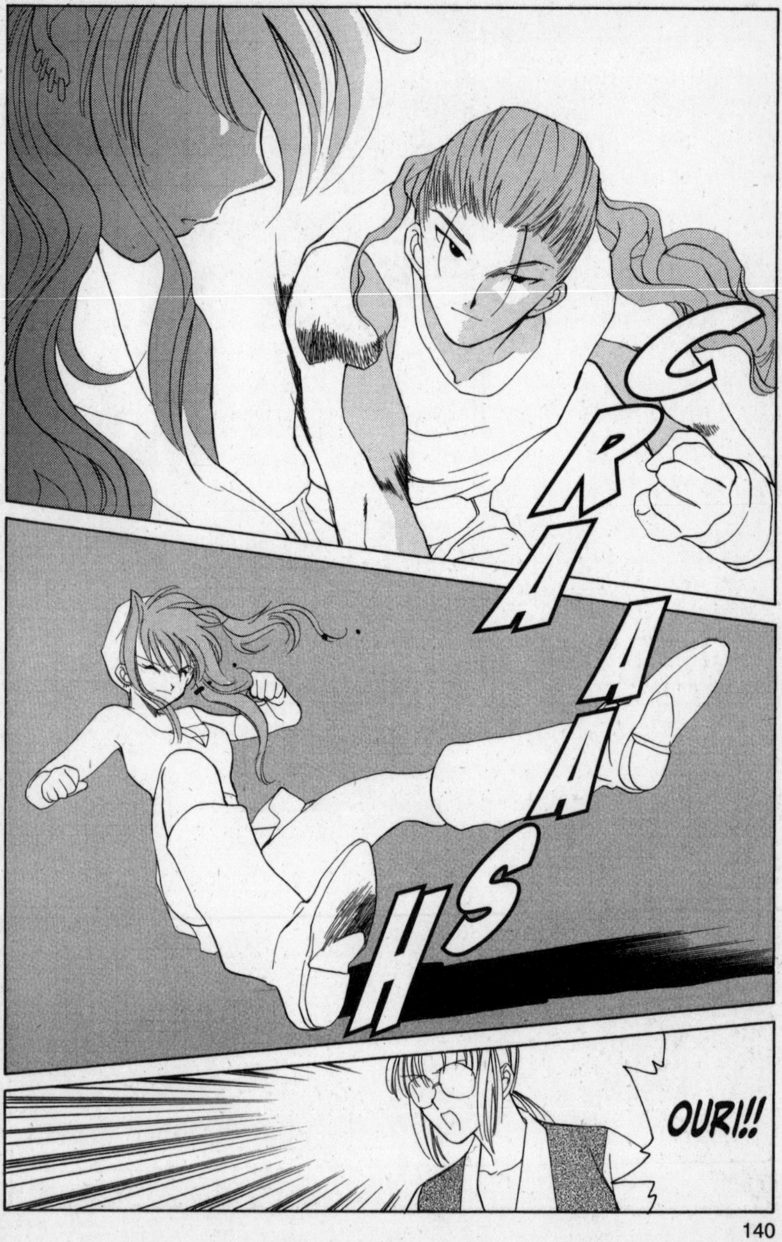
CRAAAASH
OURI!!

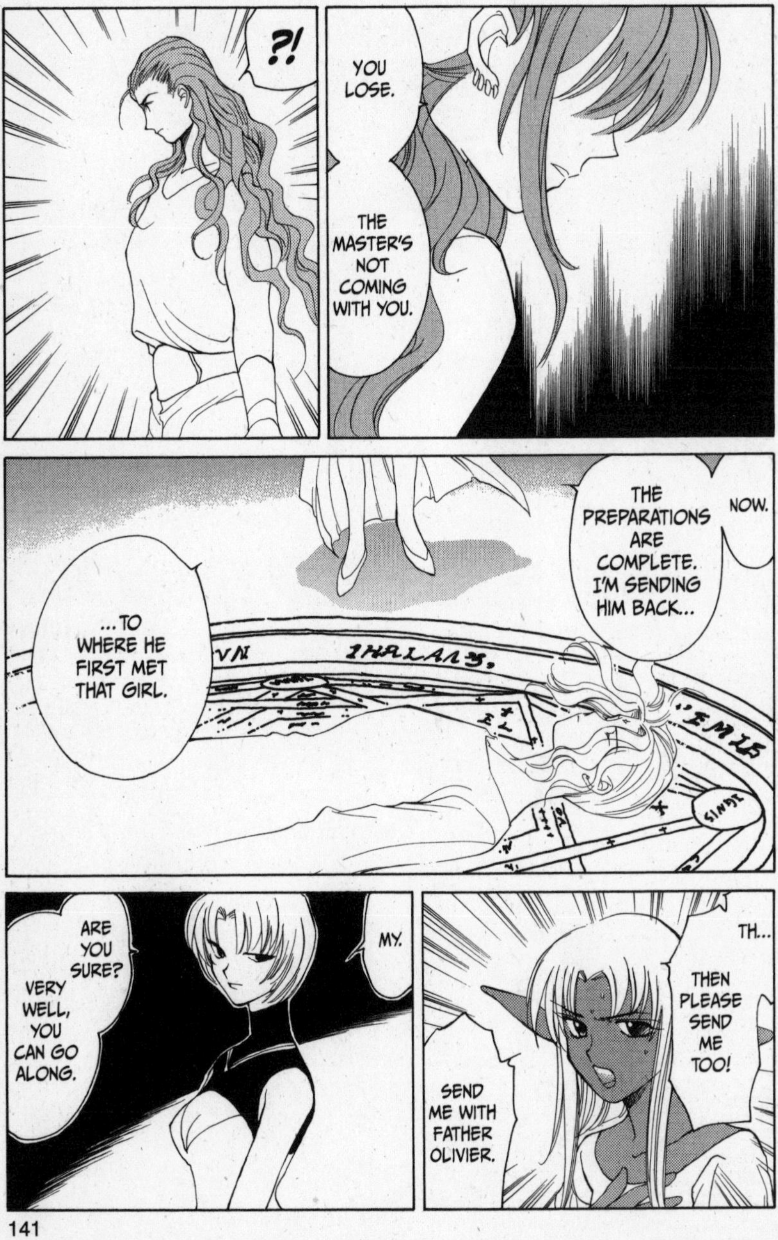
YOU LOSE.
THE MASTER'S NOT COMING WITH YOU.
?!
NOW.
THE PREPARATIONS ARE COMPLETE. I'M SENDING HIM BACK...
...TO WHERE HE FIRST MET THAT GIRL.
TH...
THEN PLEASE SEND ME TOO!
SEND ME WITH FATHER OLIVIER.
MY.
ARE YOU SURE?
VERY WELL, YOU CAN GO ALONG.

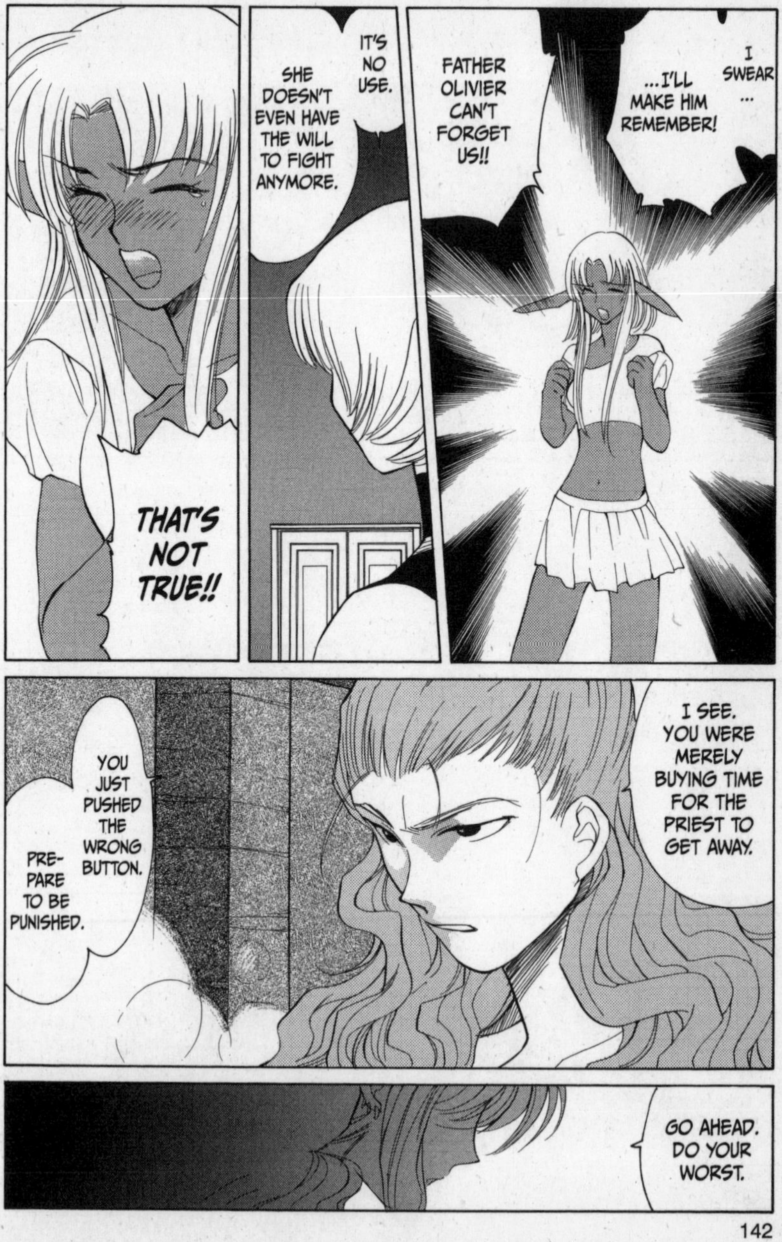
I SWEAR...
...I'LL MAKE HIM REMEMBER!
FATHER OLIVIER CAN'T FORGET US!!
IT'S NO USE.
SHE DOESN'T EVEN HAVE THE WILL TO FIGHT ANYMORE.
THAT'S NOT TRUE!!
I SEE. YOU WERE MERELY BUYING TIME FOR THE PRIEST TO GET AWAY.
YOU JUST PUSHED THE WRONG BUTTON.
PRE-PARE TO BE PUNISHED.
GO AHEAD. DO YOUR WORST.

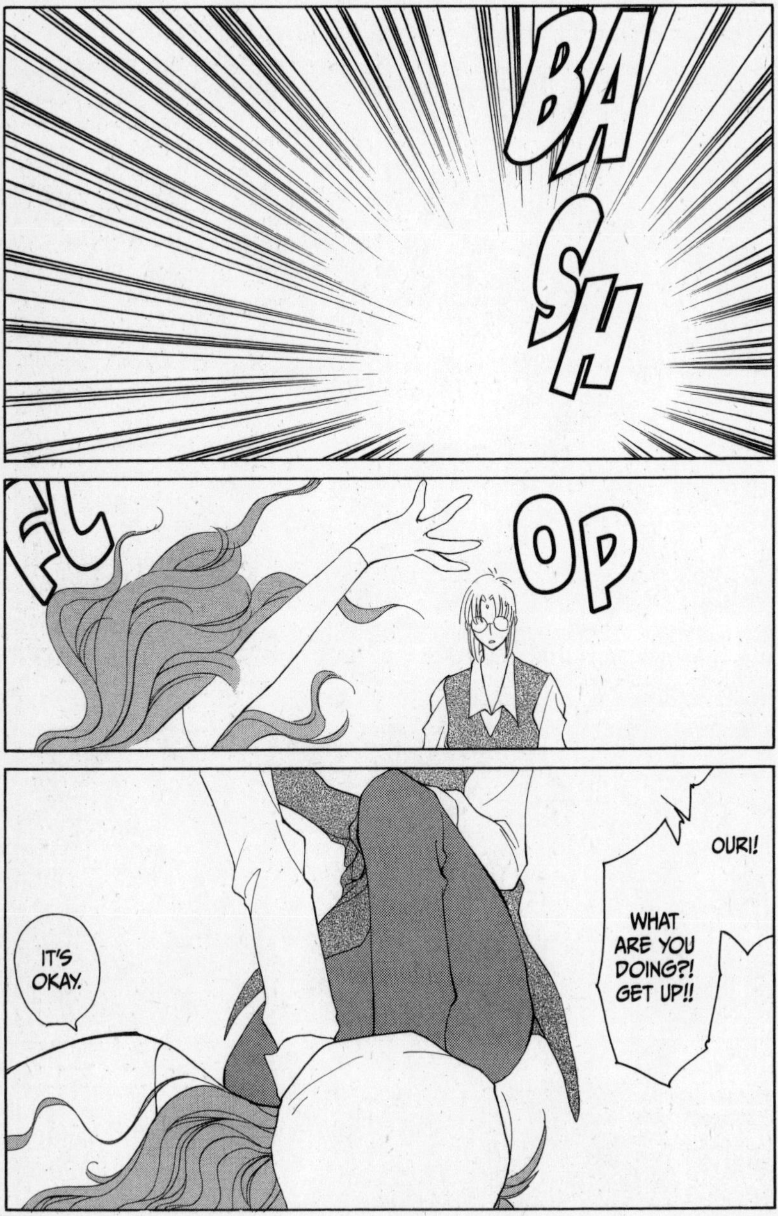
BASH
FLOP
OURI!
WHAT ARE YOU DOING?! GET UP!!
IT'S OKAY.

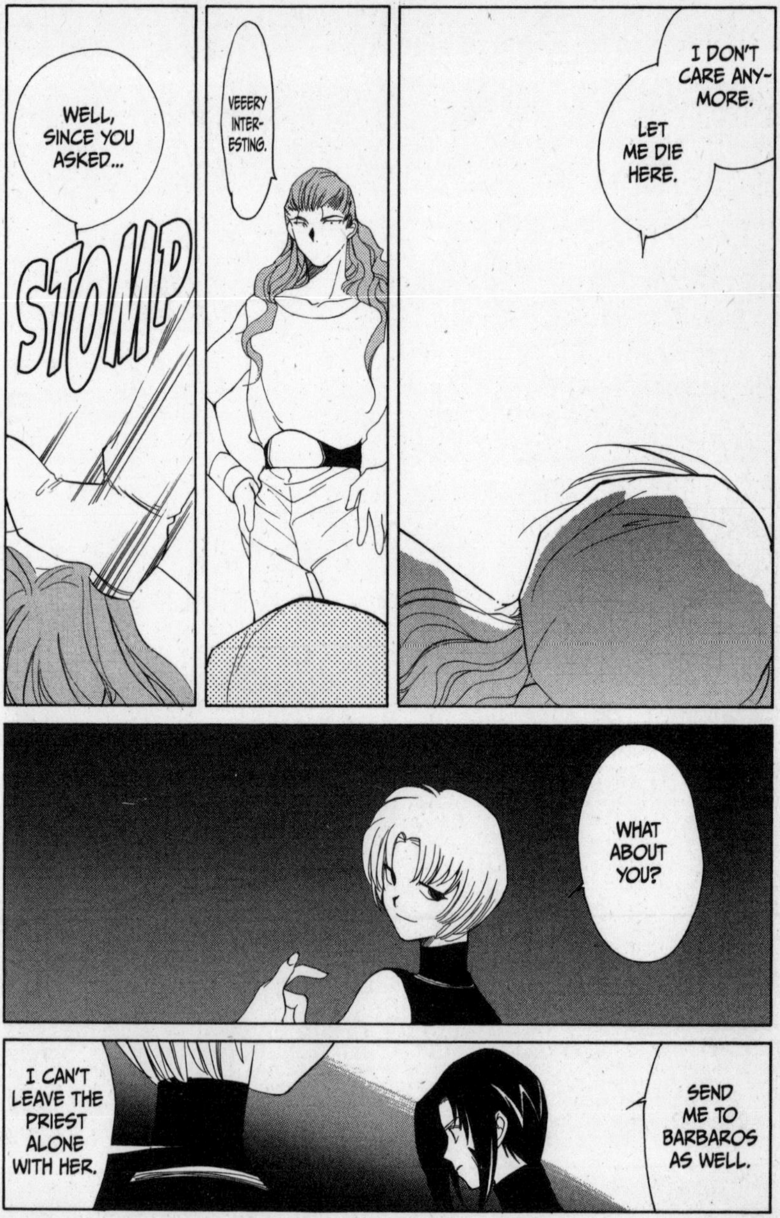
I DON'T CARE ANY-MORE.
LET ME DIE HERE.
VEEERY INTER-ESTING.
WELL, SINCE YOU ASKED...
STOMP
WHAT ABOUT YOU?
SEND ME TO BARBAROS AS WELL.
I CAN'T LEAVE THE PRIEST ALONE WITH HER.

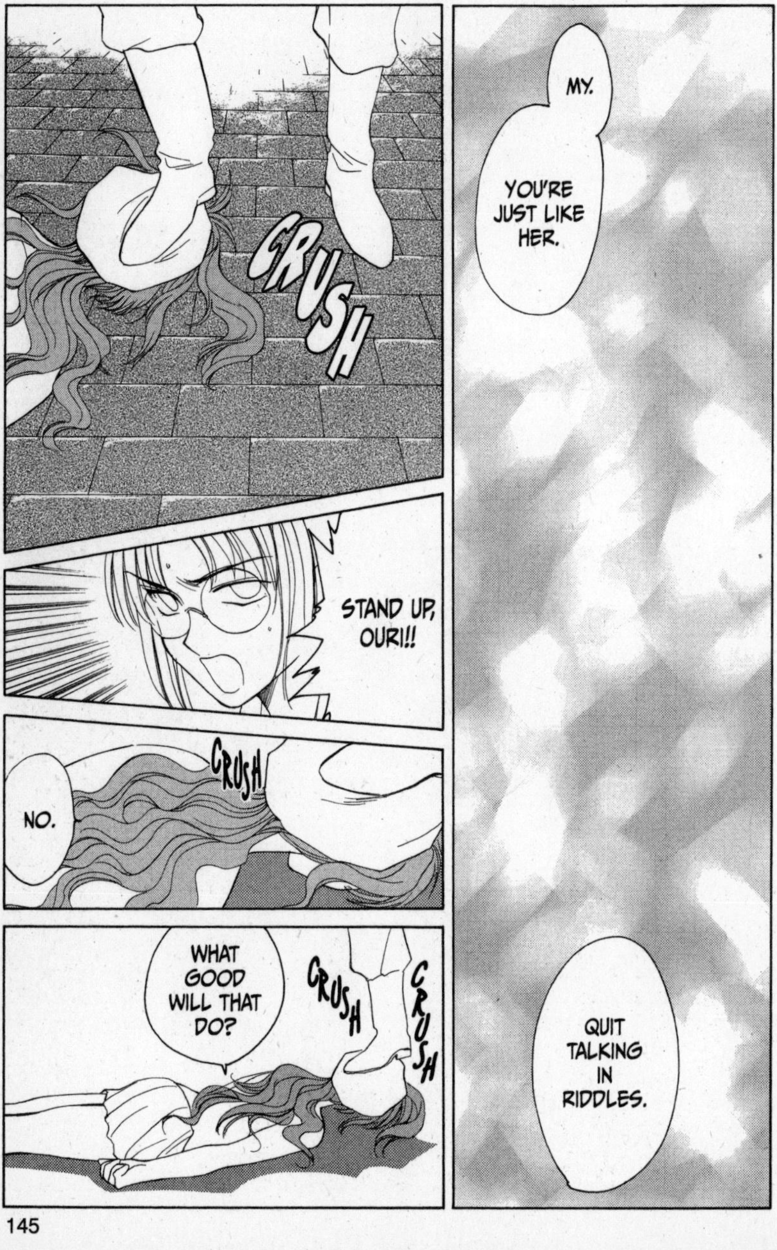
MY.
YOU'RE JUST LIKE HER.
QUIT TALKING IN RIDDLES.
CRUSH
STAND UP, OURI!!
CRUSH
NO.
CRUSH
CRUSH
WHAT GOOD WILL THAT DO?

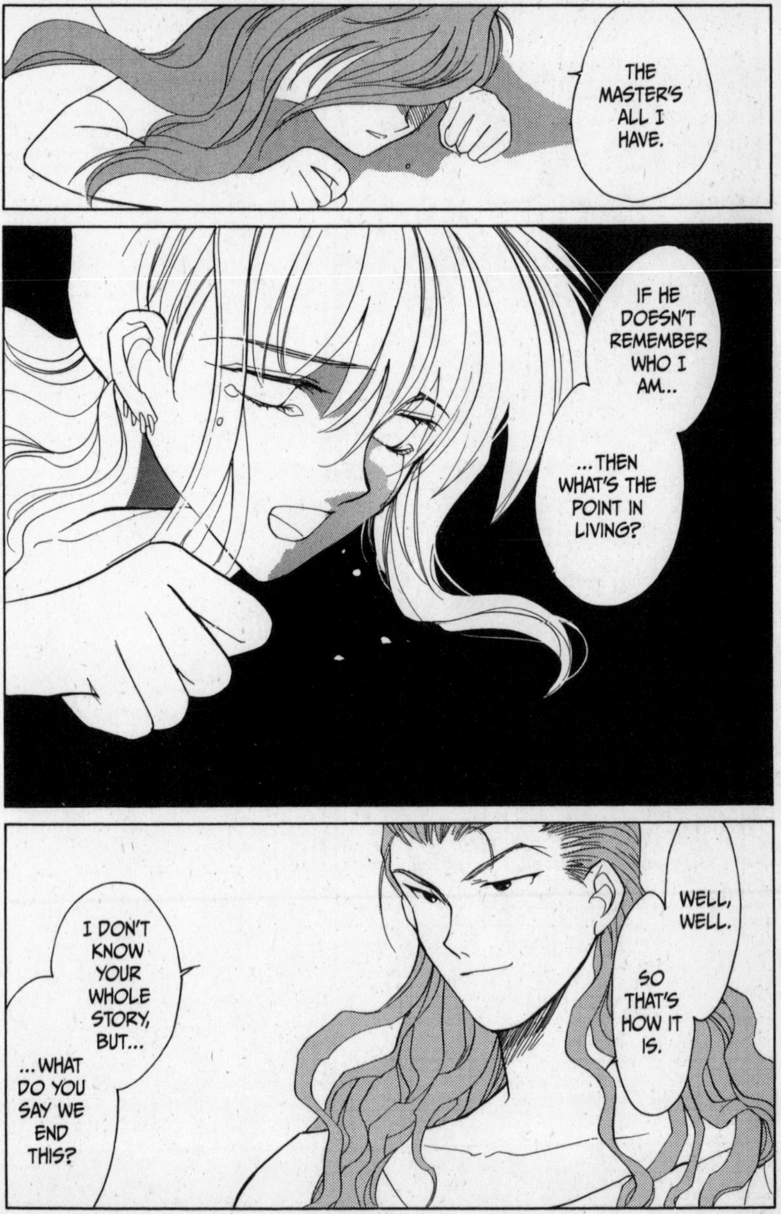
THE MASTER'S ALL I HAVE.
IF HE DOESN'T REMEMBER WHO I AM...
...THEN WHAT'S THE POINT IN LIVING?
WELL, WELL.
SO THAT'S HOW IT IS.
I DON'T KNOW YOUR WHOLE STORY, BUT...
...WHAT DO YOU SAY WE END THIS?

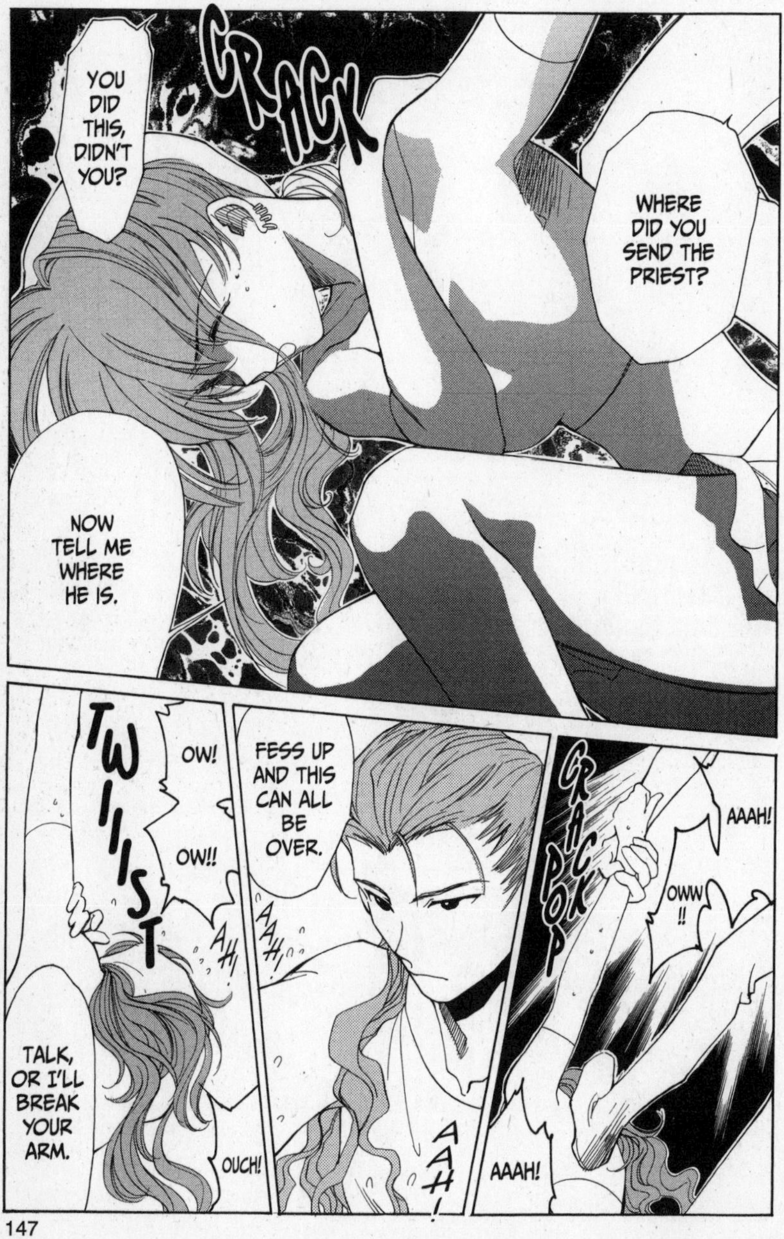
CRACK
WHERE DID YOU SEND THE PRIEST?
YOU DID THIS, DIDN'T YOU?
NOW TELL ME WHERE HE IS.
AAAH!
CRACK
POP
OWW !!
AAAH!
FESS UP AND THIS CAN ALL BE OVER.
AAAH!
AAH!
OW!
TWIIIST
OW!!
AH!
TALK, OR I'LL BREAK YOUR ARM.
OUCH!

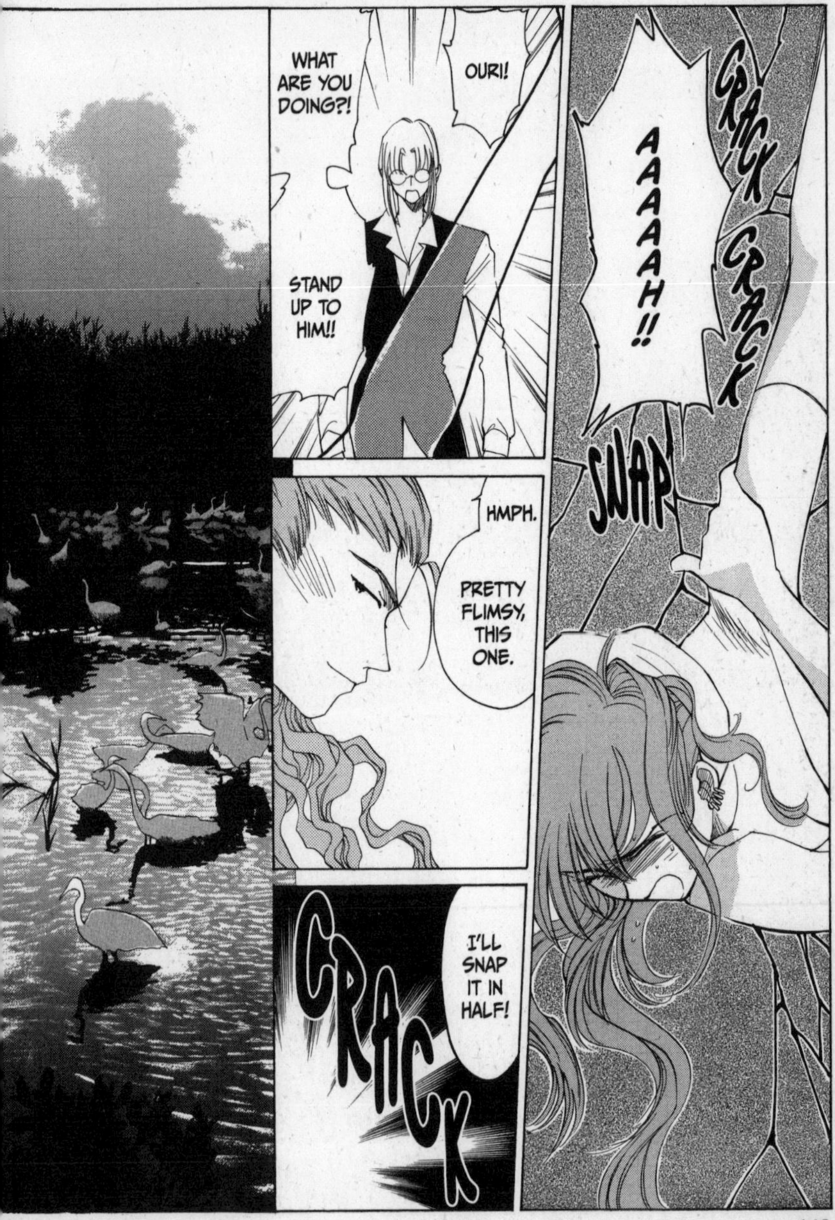
CRACK CRACK CRACK
AAAAAH!!
SNAP
OURI!
WHAT ARE YOU DOING?!
STAND UP TO HIM!!
HMPH.
PRETTY FLIMSY, THIS ONE.
I'LL SNAP IT IN HALF!
CRACK

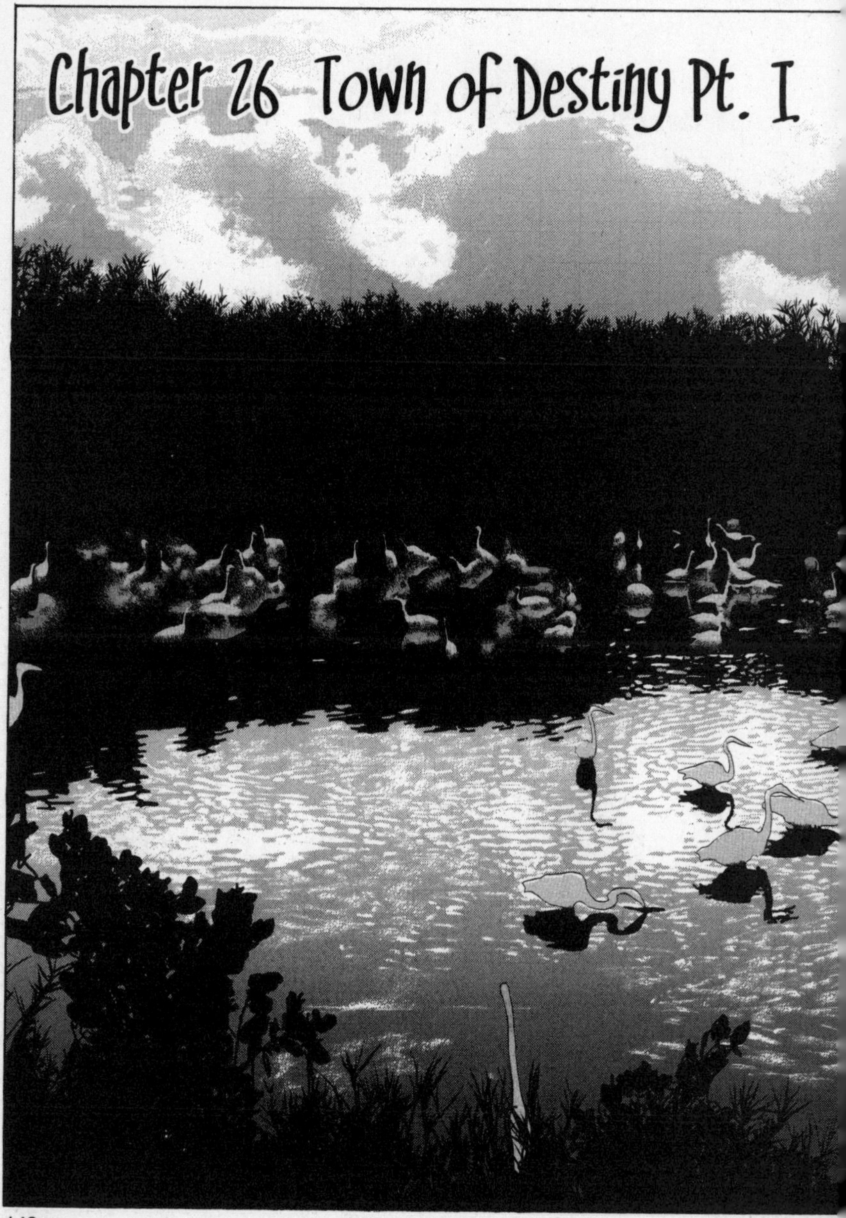
Chapter 26 Town of Destiny Pt. I

Summary Space ③

It feels like Shazan's popularity really shot up starting with this volume.

This chapter in particular displays both his good and bad sides, which I'm personally very fond of.

Either way, I'm a devoted fan of the honorable types. Like Olivier, for example.

At the same time, I also like characters like Suzu who are stingy, timid, compassionate, and sometimes lose their tempers.

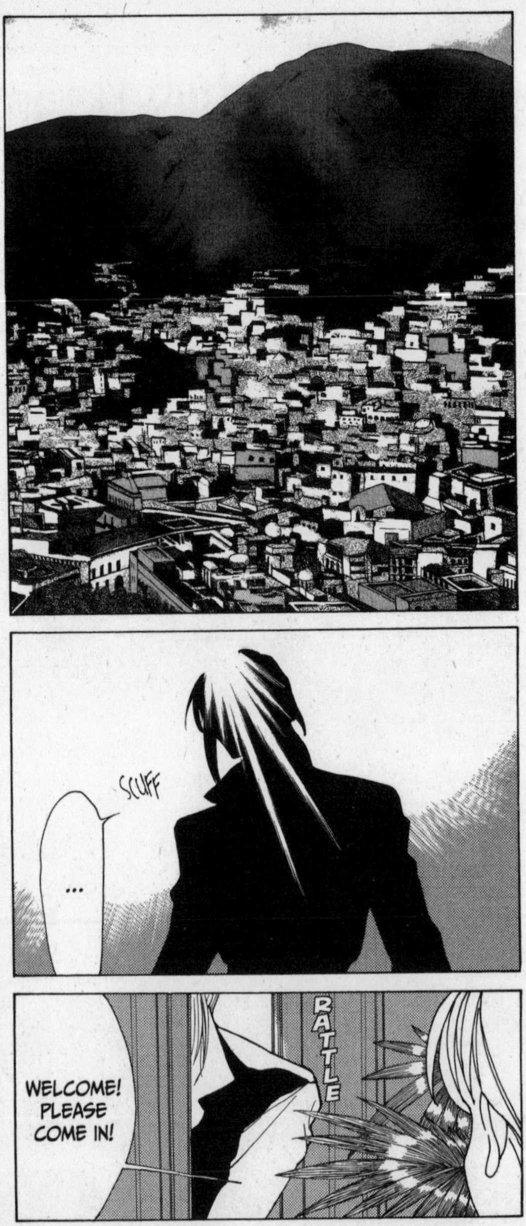
SCUFF
...
RATTLE
WELCOME! PLEASE COME IN!

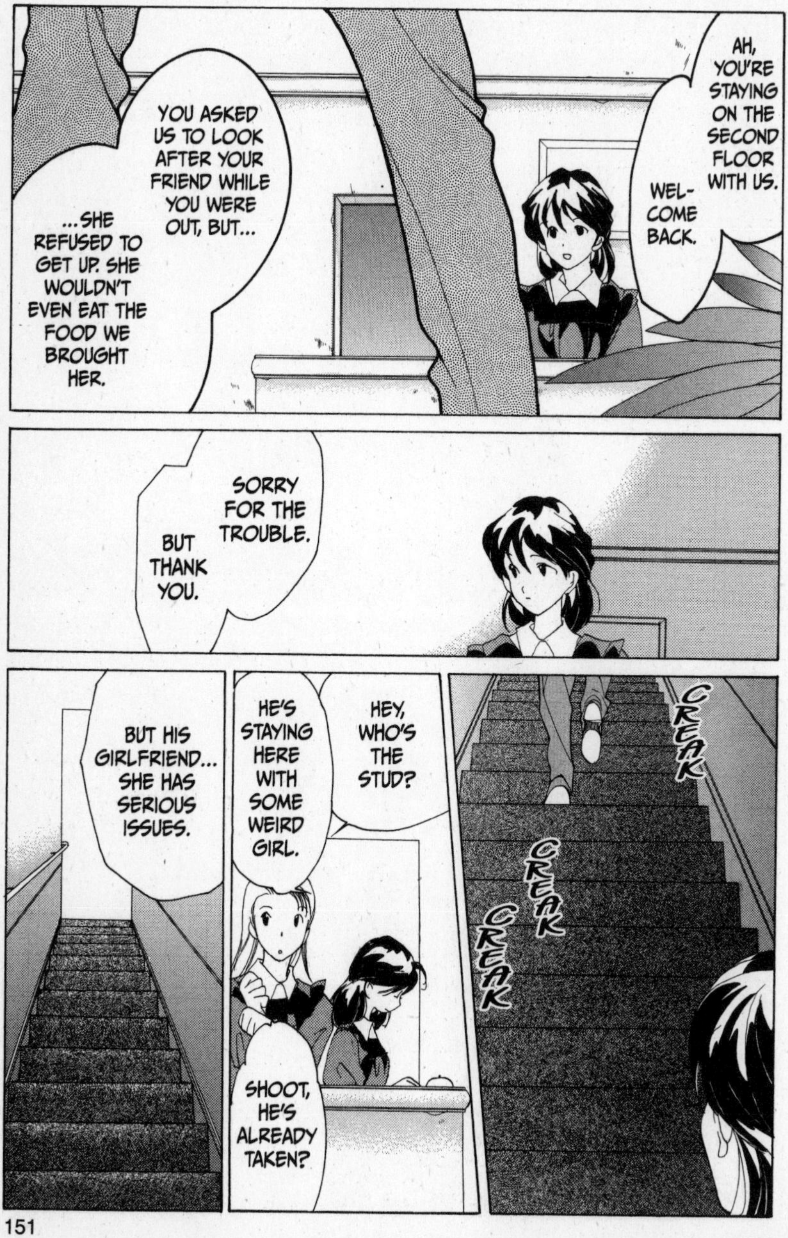
AH, YOU'RE STAYING ON THE SECOND FLOOR WITH US.
WEL-COME BACK.
YOU ASKED US TO LOOK AFTER YOUR FRIEND WHILE YOU WERE OUT, BUT...
...SHE REFUSED TO GET UP. SHE WOULDN'T EVEN EAT THE FOOD WE BROUGHT HER.
SORRY FOR THE TROUBLE.
BUT THANK YOU.
CREAK
CREAK
CREAK
HEY, WHO'S THE STUD?
HE'S STAYING HERE WITH SOME WEIRD GIRL.
SHOOT, HE'S ALREADY TAKEN?
BUT HIS GIRLFRIEND... SHE HAS SERIOUS ISSUES.

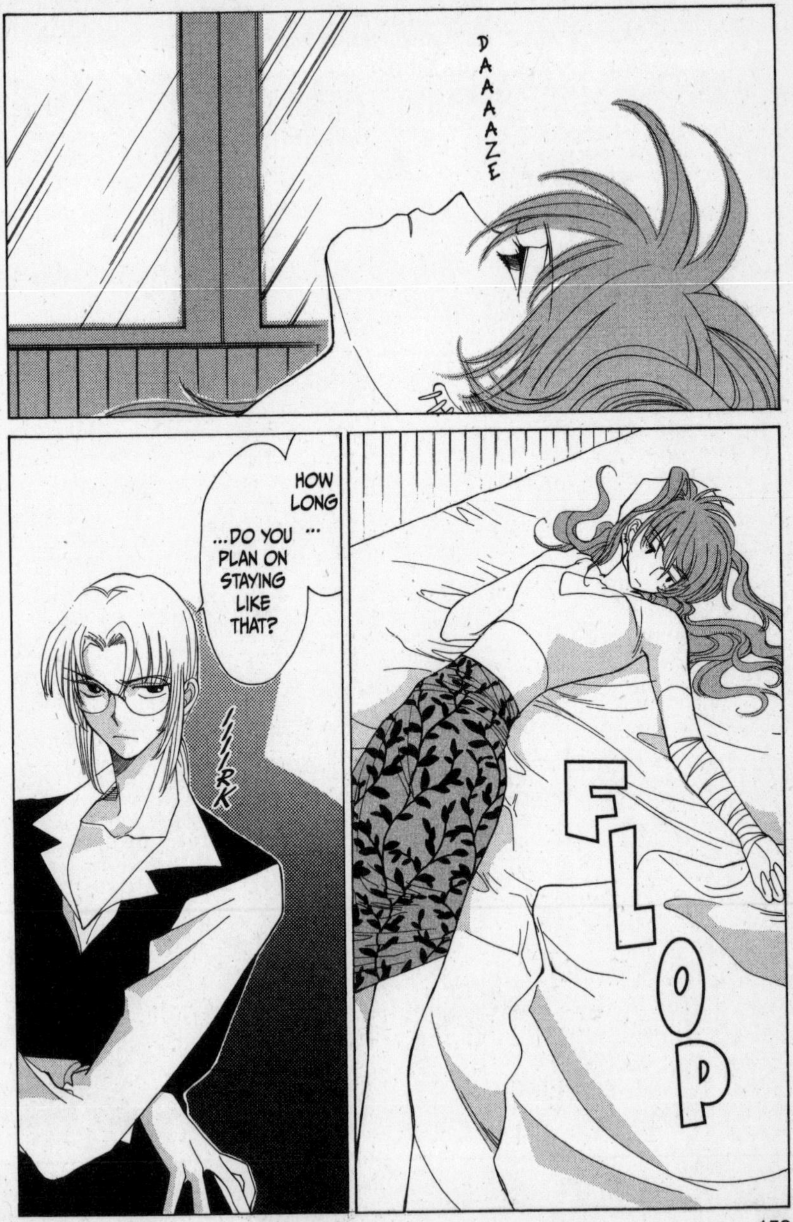
DAAAAAZE
FLOP
HOW LONG ...
...DO YOU PLAN ON STAYING LIKE THAT?
SIIIRK

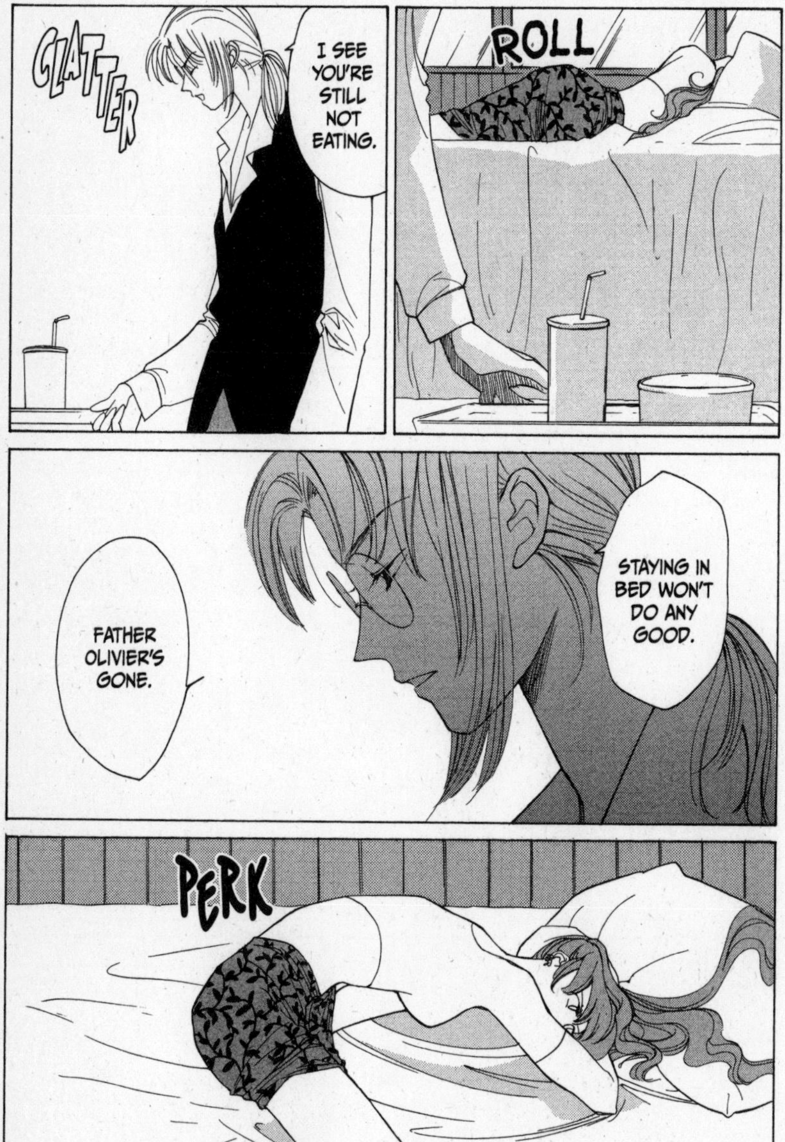
ROLL
CLATTER
I SEE YOU'RE STILL NOT EATING.
STAYING IN BED WON'T DO ANY GOOD.
FATHER OLIVIER'S GONE.
PERK

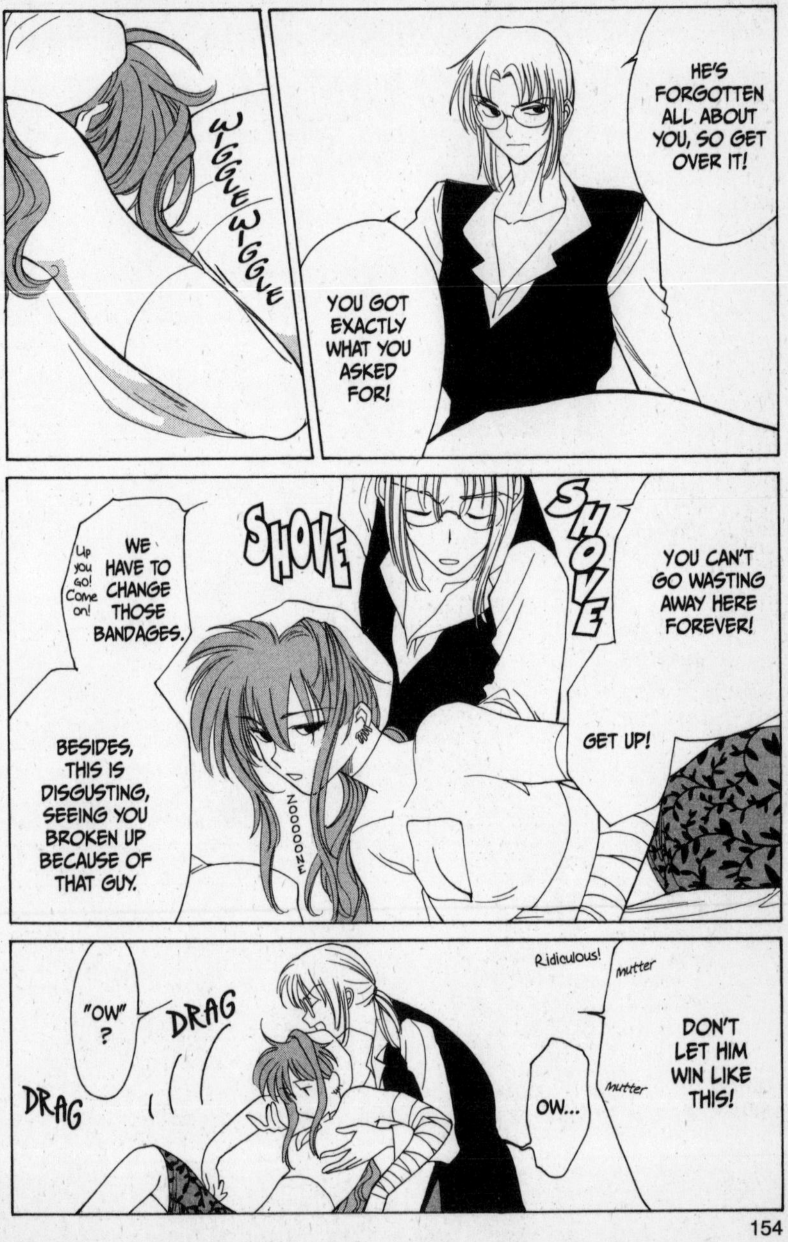
HE'S FORGOTTEN ALL ABOUT YOU, SO GET OVER IT!
YOU GOT EXACTLY WHAT YOU ASKED FOR!
WIGGLE WIGGLE
SHOVE
YOU CAN'T GO WASTING AWAY HERE FOREVER!
GET UP!
SHOVE
WE HAVE TO CHANGE THOSE BANDAGES.
Up you go! Come on!
BESIDES, THIS IS DISGUSTING, SEEING YOU BROKEN UP BECAUSE OF THAT GUY.
ZOOOOOONE
Ridiculous!
Mutter
DON'T LET HIM WIN LIKE THIS!
Mutter
OW...
DRAG
"OW"?
DRAG

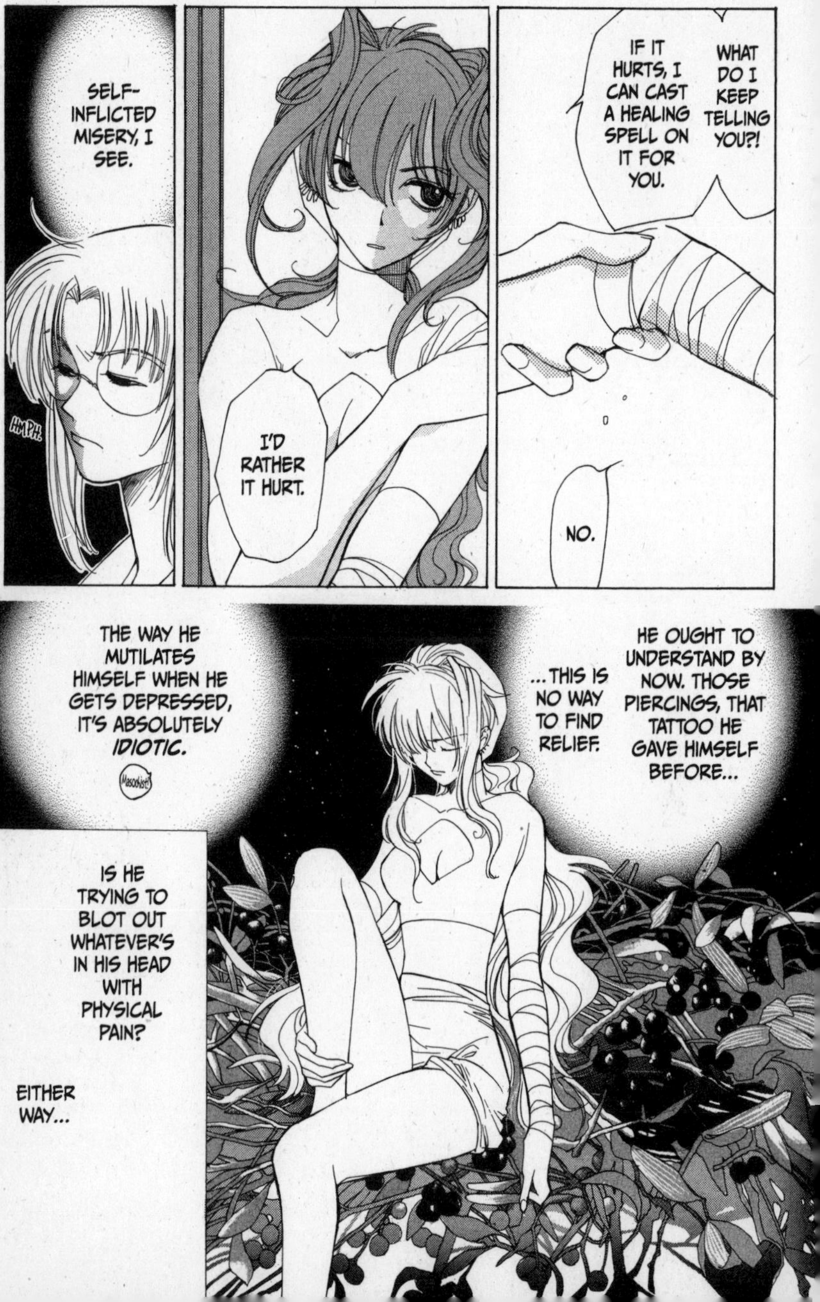
WHAT DO I KEEP TELLING YOU?!
IF IT HURTS, I CAN CAST A HEALING SPELL ON IT FOR YOU.
NO.
I'D RATHER IT HURT.
SELF-INFLICTED MISERY, I SEE.
HMPH.
HE OUGHT TO UNDERSTAND BY NOW. THOSE PIERCINGS, THAT TATTOO HE GAVE HIMSELF BEFORE...
...THIS IS NO WAY TO FIND RELIEF.
THE WAY HE MUTILATES HIMSELF WHEN HE GETS DEPRESSED, IT'S ABSOLUTELY *IDIOTIC.*
Masochist?
IS HE TRYING TO BLOT OUT WHATEVER'S IN HIS HEAD WITH PHYSICAL PAIN?
EITHER WAY...

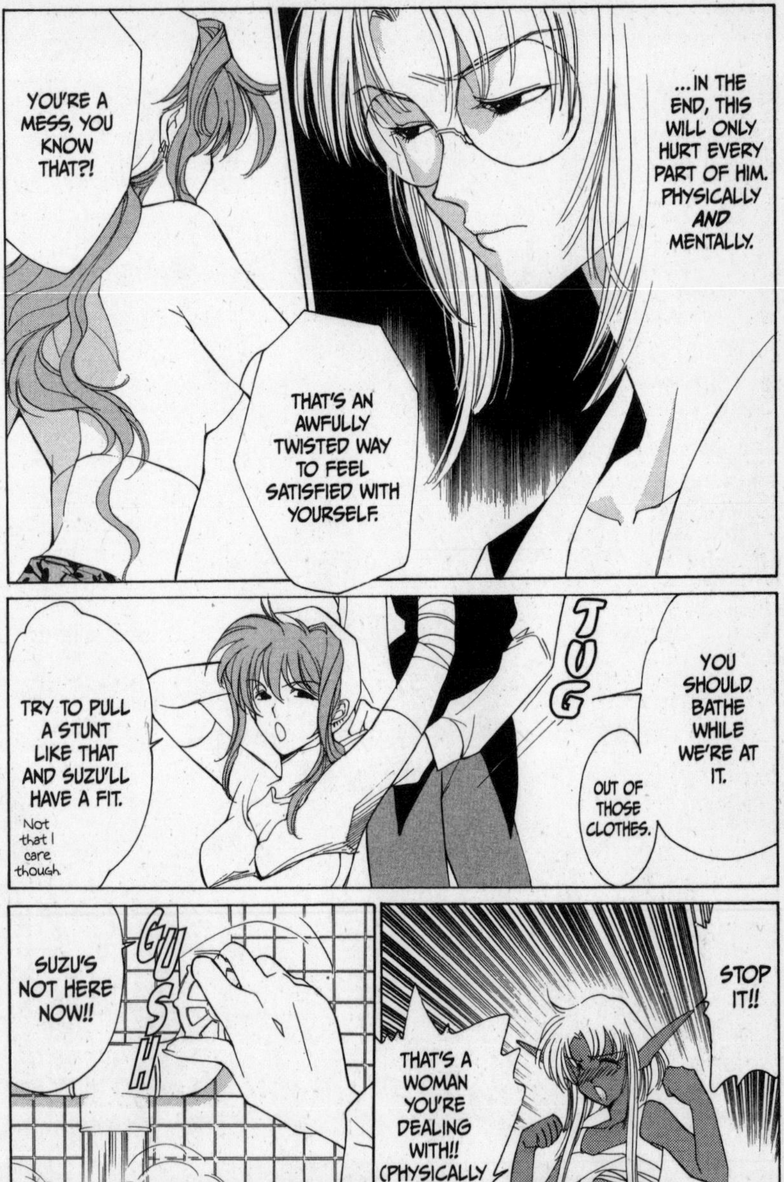
...IN THE END, THIS WILL ONLY HURT EVERY PART OF HIM. PHYSICALLY AND MENTALLY.
THAT'S AN AWFULLY TWISTED WAY TO FEEL SATISFIED WITH YOURSELF.
YOU'RE A MESS, YOU KNOW THAT?!
YOU SHOULD BATHE WHILE WE'RE AT IT.
OUT OF THOSE CLOTHES.
TUG
TRY TO PULL A STUNT LIKE THAT AND SUZU'LL HAVE A FIT.
Not that I care though.
STOP IT!!
THAT'S A WOMAN YOU'RE DEALING WITH!! (PHYSICALLY ANYWAY.)
GUSH
SUZU'S NOT HERE NOW!!

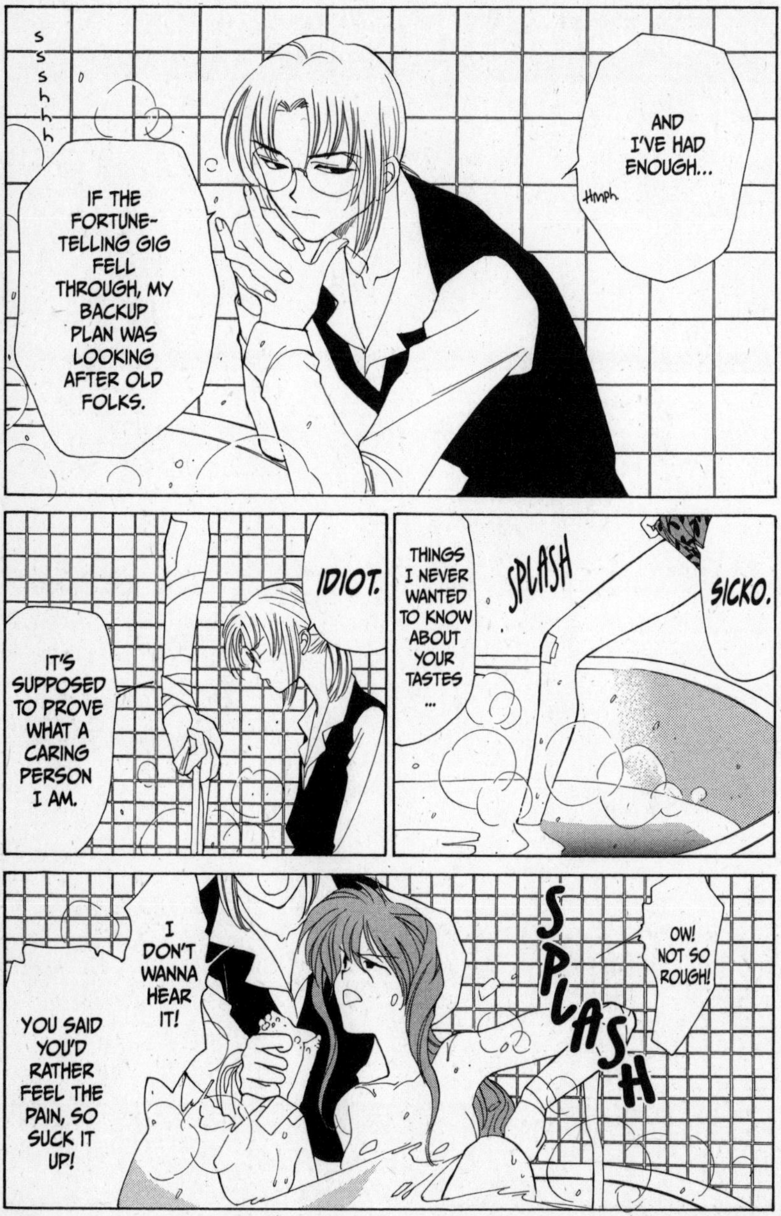
AND I'VE HAD ENOUGH...
Hmph.
ssshhh
IF THE FORTUNE-TELLING GIG FELL THROUGH, MY BACKUP PLAN WAS LOOKING AFTER OLD FOLKS.
SICKO.
SPLASH
THINGS I NEVER WANTED TO KNOW ABOUT YOUR TASTES...
IDIOT.
IT'S SUPPOSED TO PROVE WHAT A CARING PERSON I AM.
OW! NOT SO ROUGH!
SPLASH
I DON'T WANNA HEAR IT!
YOU SAID YOU'D RATHER FEEL THE PAIN, SO SUCK IT UP!

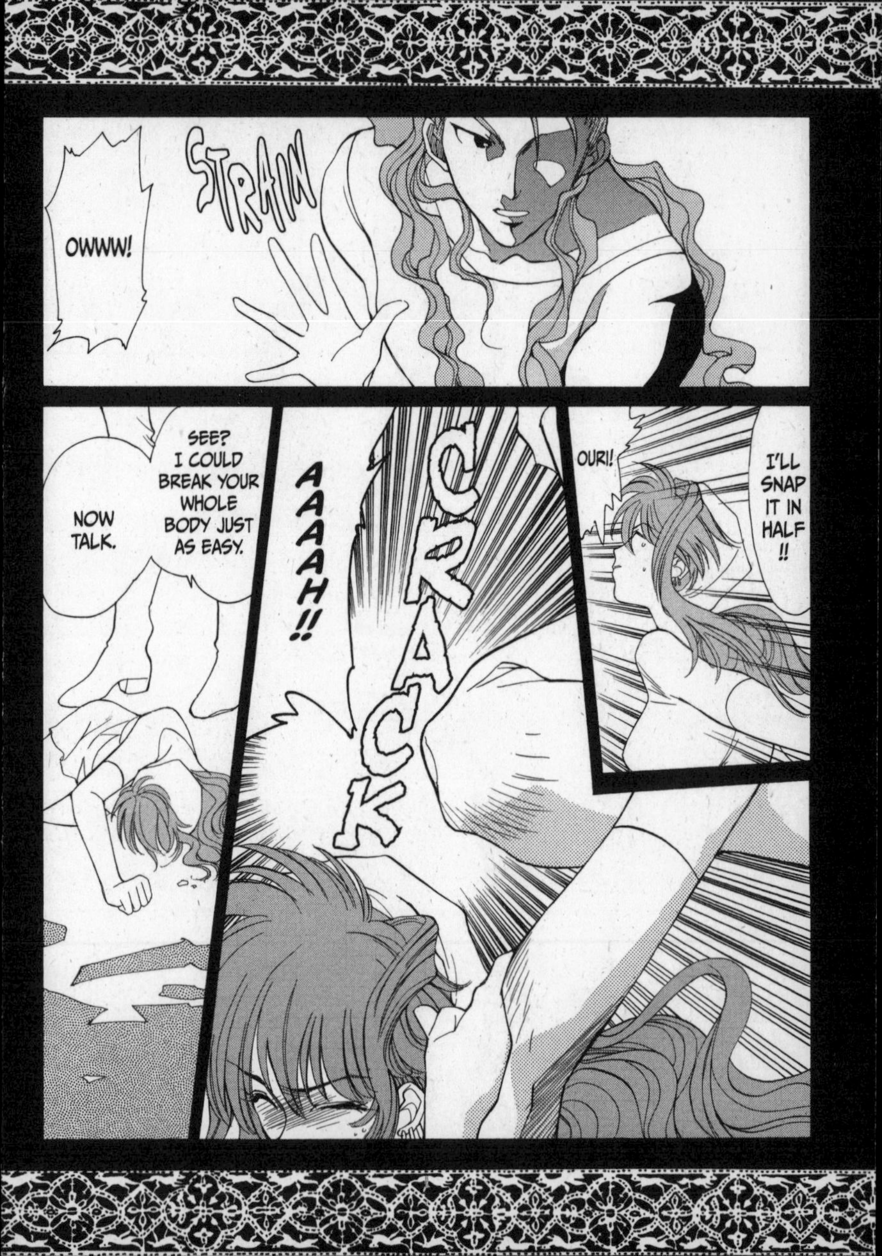
STRAIN
OWWW!
I'LL SNAP IT IN HALF !!
OURI!
CRACK
AAAAAH!!
SEE? I COULD BREAK YOUR WHOLE BODY JUST AS EASY.
NOW TALK.

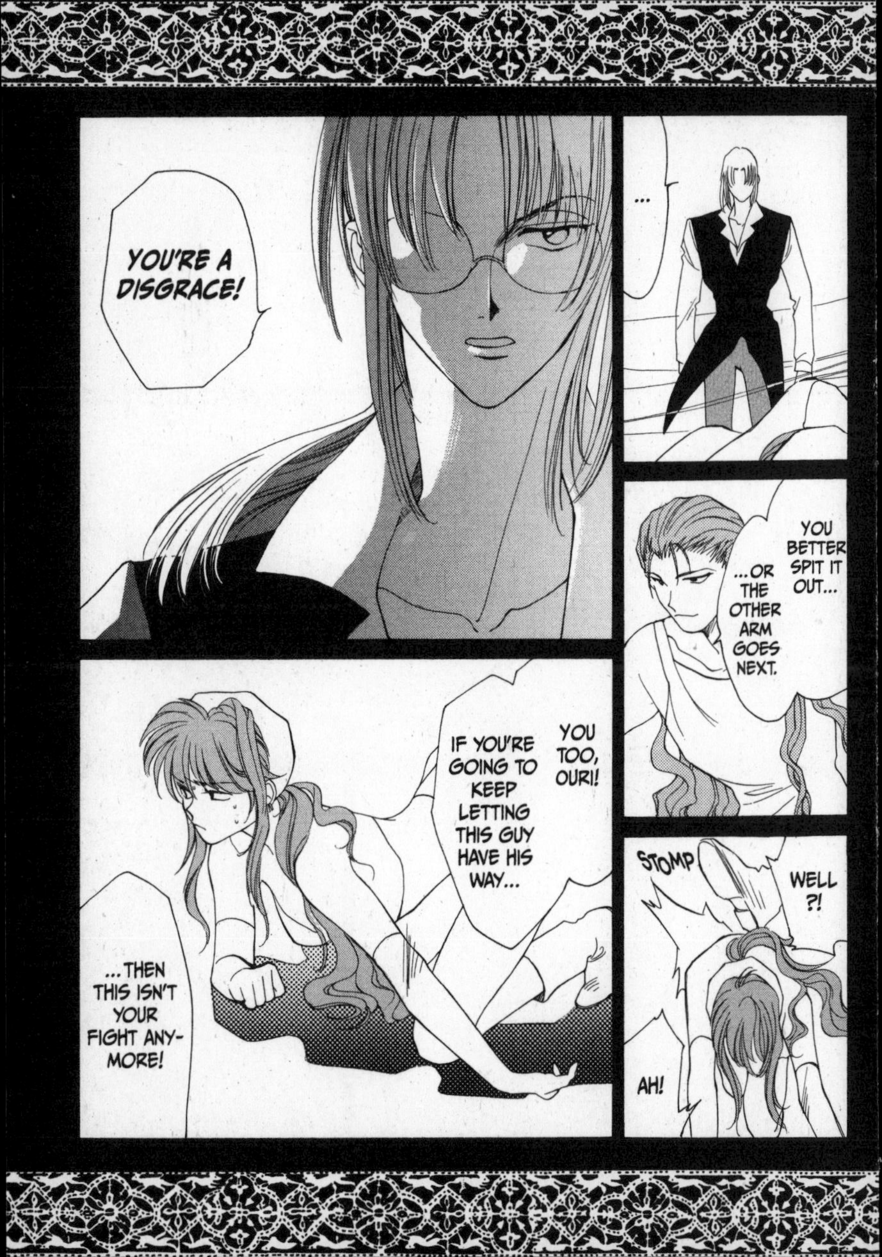
...
YOU'RE A DISGRACE!
YOU BETTER SPIT IT OUT...
...OR THE OTHER ARM GOES NEXT.
STOMP
WELL ?!
AH!
YOU TOO, OURI!
IF YOU'RE GOING TO KEEP LETTING THIS GUY HAVE HIS WAY...
...THEN THIS ISN'T YOUR FIGHT ANY-MORE!

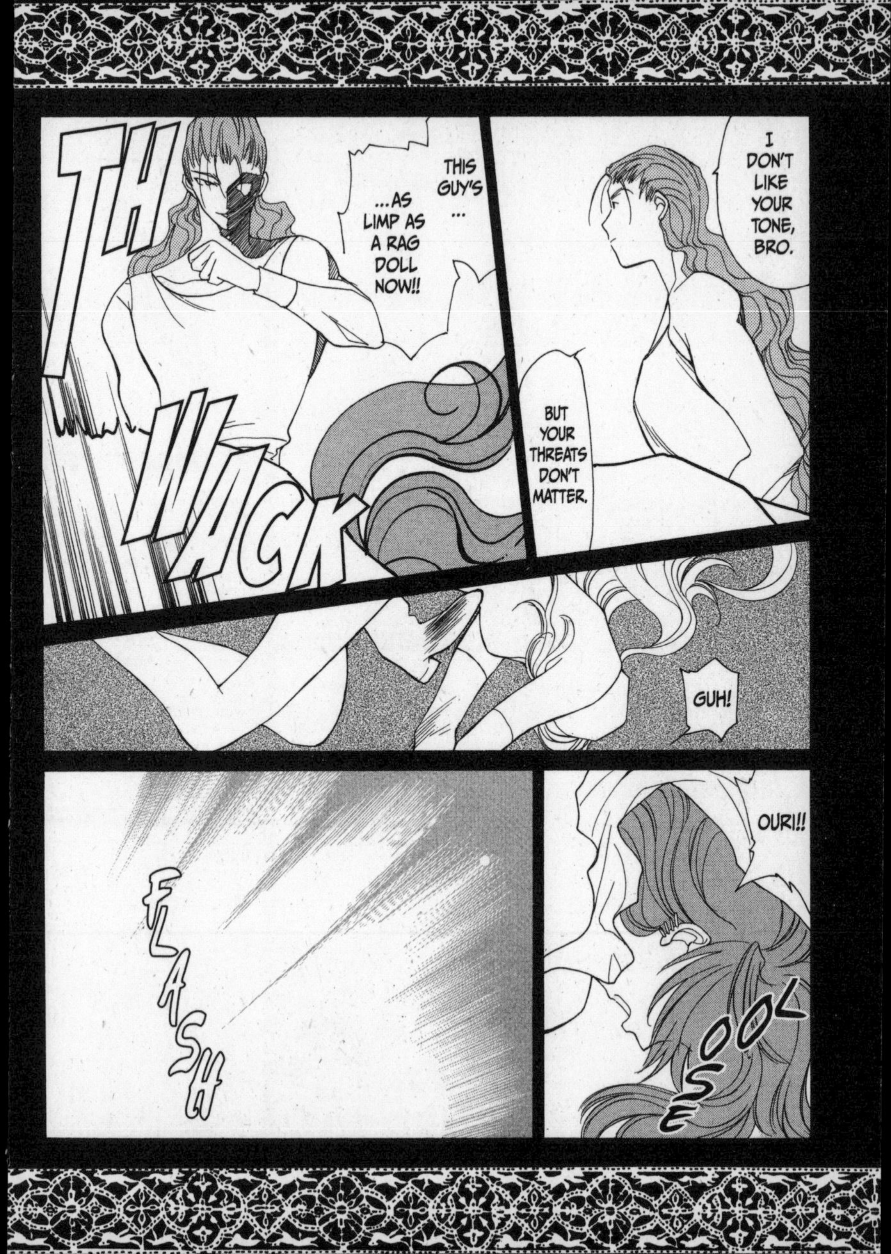
I DON'T LIKE YOUR TONE, BRO.
BUT YOUR THREATS DON'T MATTER.
THIS GUY'S ...
...AS LIMP AS A RAG DOLL NOW!!
THWACK
GUH!
OURI!!
LOOSE
FLASH

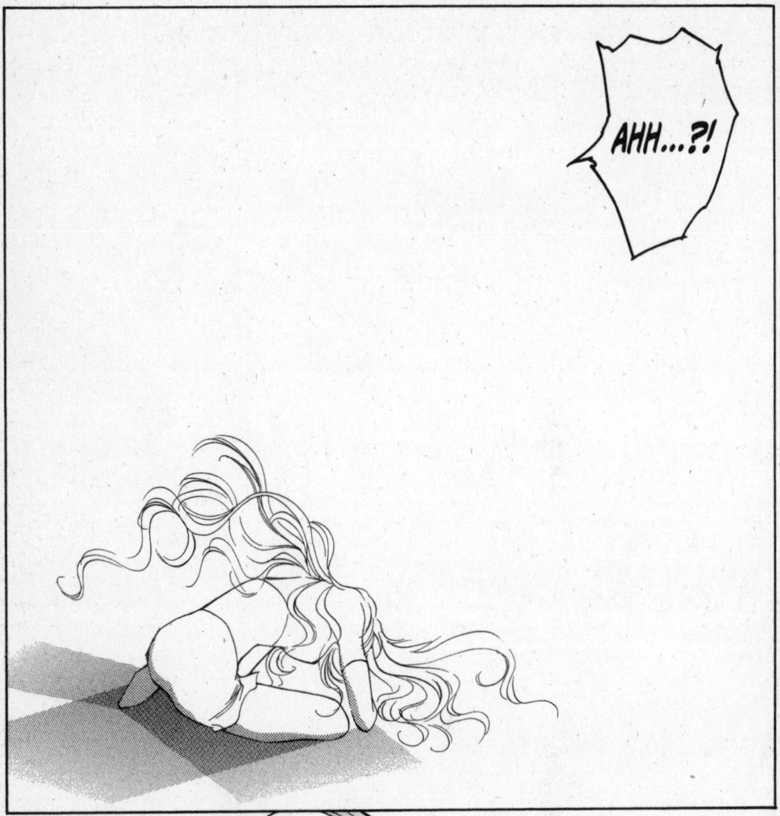
AHH...?!

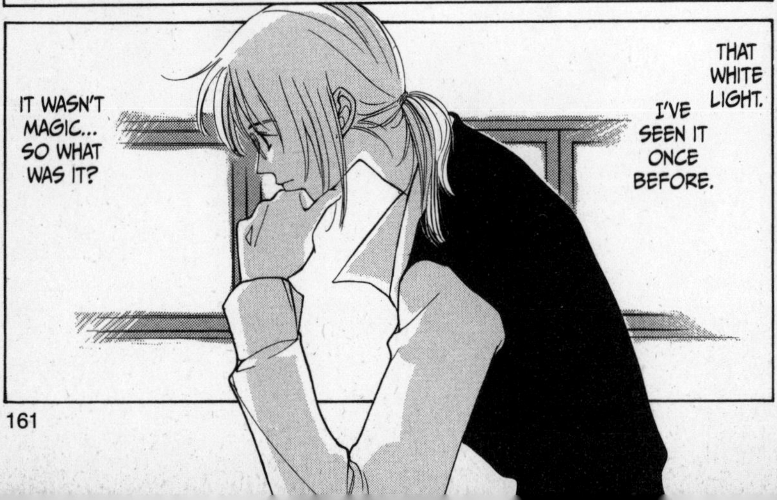
THAT WHITE LIGHT.
I'VE SEEN IT ONCE BEFORE.
IT WASN'T MAGIC... SO WHAT WAS IT?

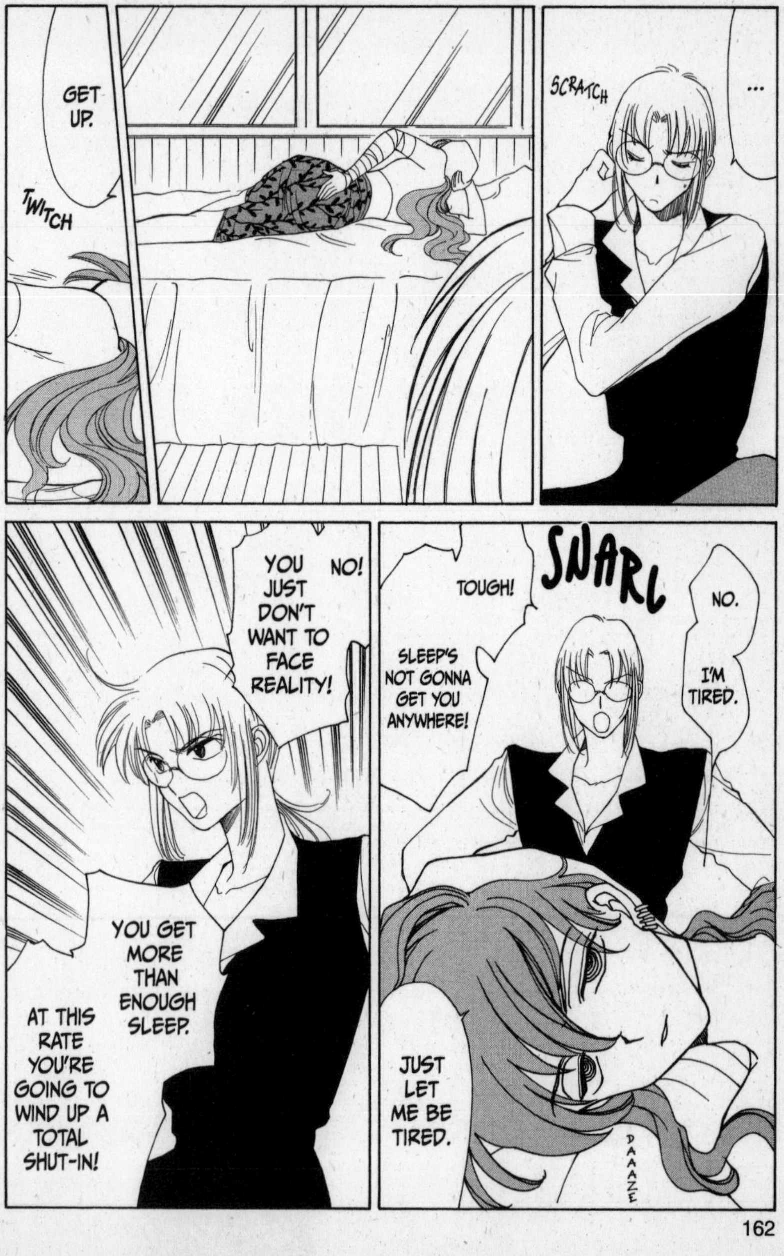
...
SCRATCH
GET UP.
TWITCH
NO.
I'M TIRED.
SNARL
TOUGH!
SLEEP'S NOT GONNA GET YOU ANYWHERE!
DAAAZE
JUST LET ME BE TIRED.
NO!
YOU JUST DON'T WANT TO FACE REALITY!
YOU GET MORE THAN ENOUGH SLEEP.
AT THIS RATE YOU'RE GOING TO WIND UP A TOTAL SHUT-IN!

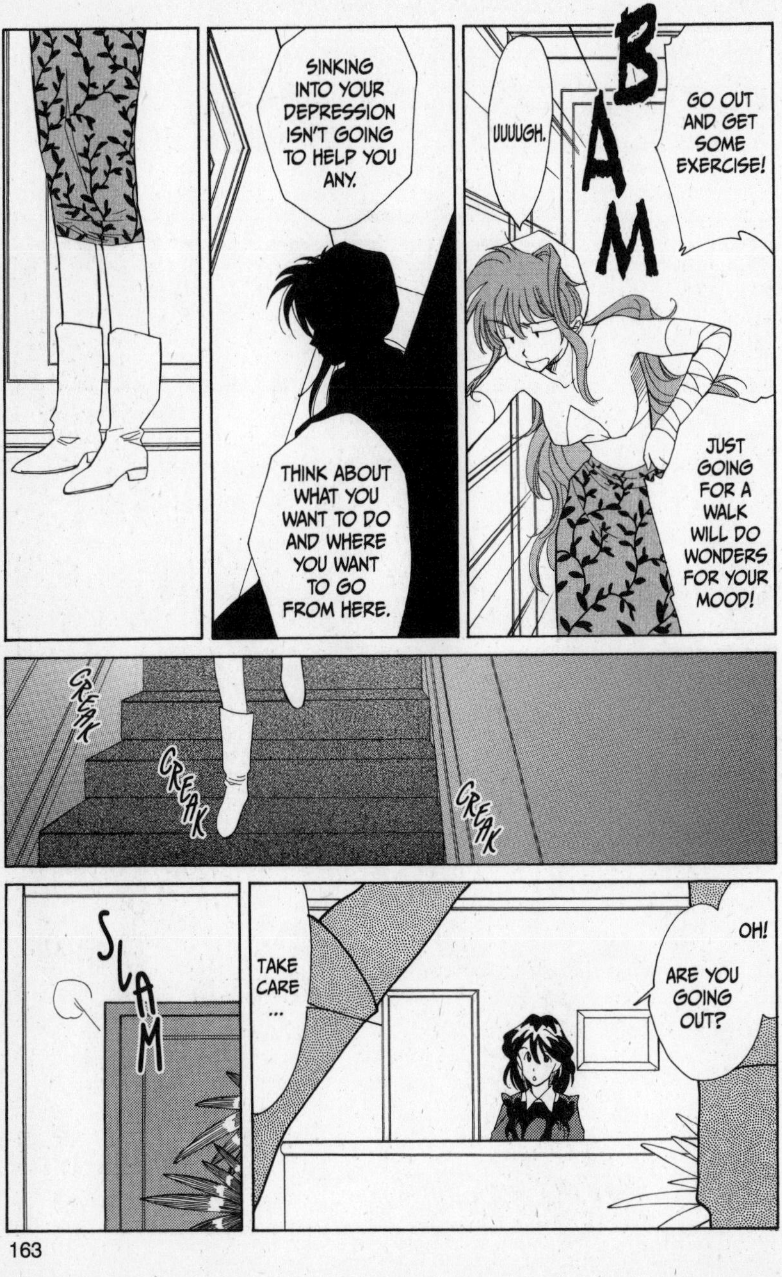
BAM
GO OUT AND GET SOME EXERCISE!
UUUUGH.
JUST GOING FOR A WALK WILL DO WONDERS FOR YOUR MOOD!
SINKING INTO YOUR DEPRESSION ISN'T GOING TO HELP YOU ANY.
THINK ABOUT WHAT YOU WANT TO DO AND WHERE YOU WANT TO GO FROM HERE.
CREAK
CREAK
CREAK
OH!
ARE YOU GOING OUT?
TAKE CARE ...
SLAM

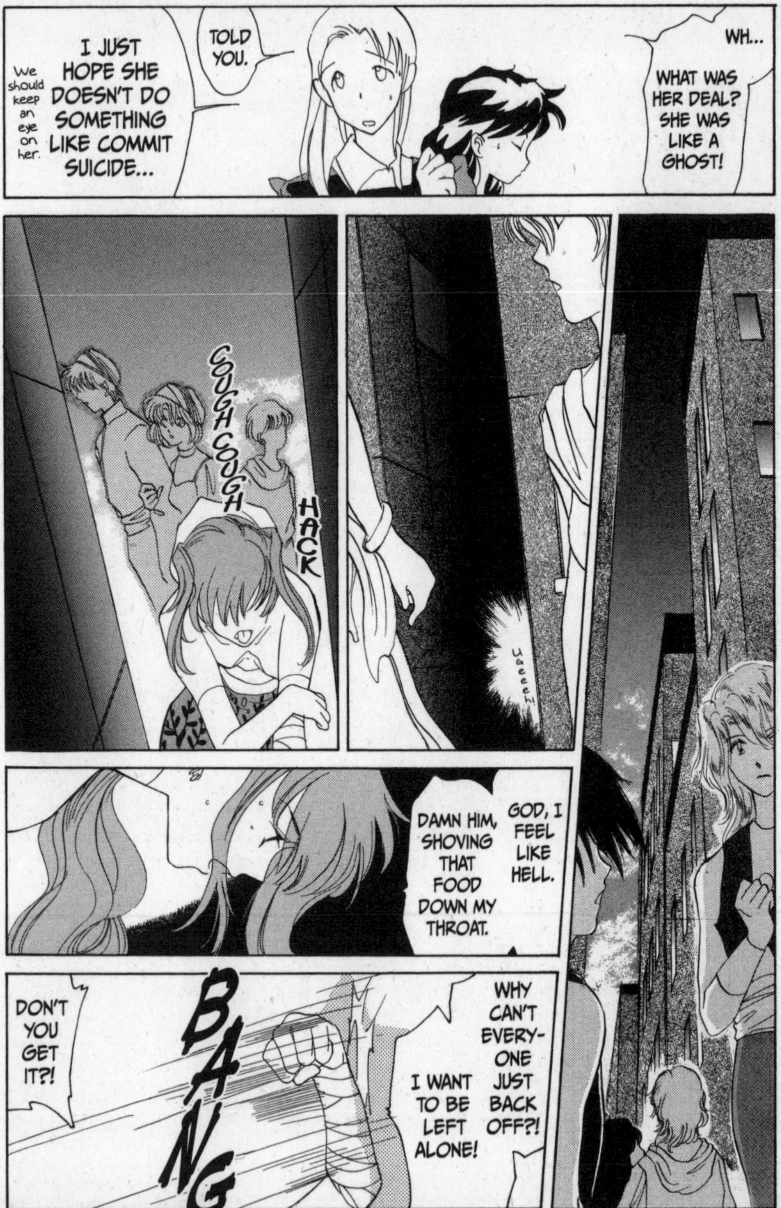
WH...
WHAT WAS HER DEAL? SHE WAS LIKE A GHOST!
TOLD YOU.
I JUST HOPE SHE DOESN'T DO SOMETHING LIKE COMMIT SUICIDE...
We should keep an eye on her.
Ugeeeh!
COUGH COUGH
HACK
GOD, I FEEL LIKE HELL.
DAMN HIM, SHOVING THAT FOOD DOWN MY THROAT.
WHY CAN'T EVERY-ONE JUST BACK OFF?!
I WANT TO BE LEFT ALONE!
BANG
DON'T YOU GET IT?!

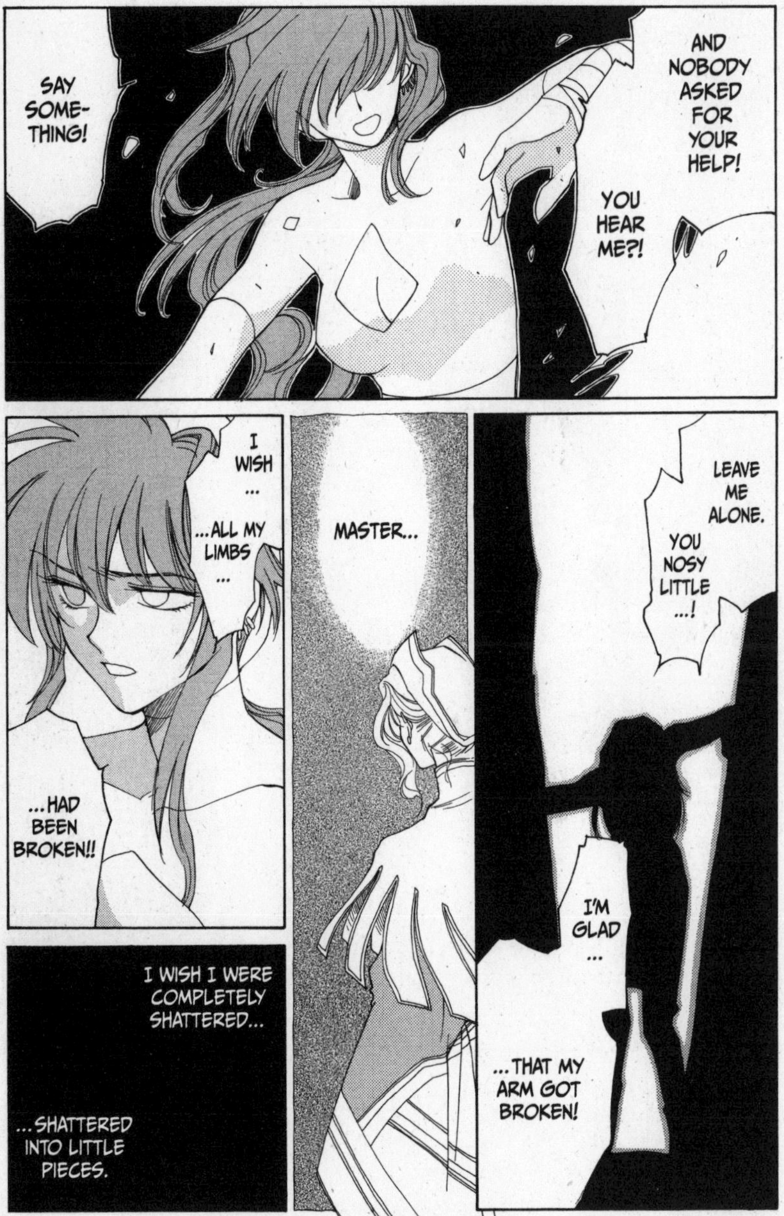
AND NOBODY ASKED FOR YOUR HELP!
YOU HEAR ME?!
SAY SOME-THING!
LEAVE ME ALONE.
YOU NOSY LITTLE ...!
I'M GLAD ...
...THAT MY ARM GOT BROKEN!
MASTER...
I WISH ...
...ALL MY LIMBS ...
...HAD BEEN BROKEN!!
I WISH I WERE COMPLETELY SHATTERED...
...SHATTERED INTO LITTLE PIECES.

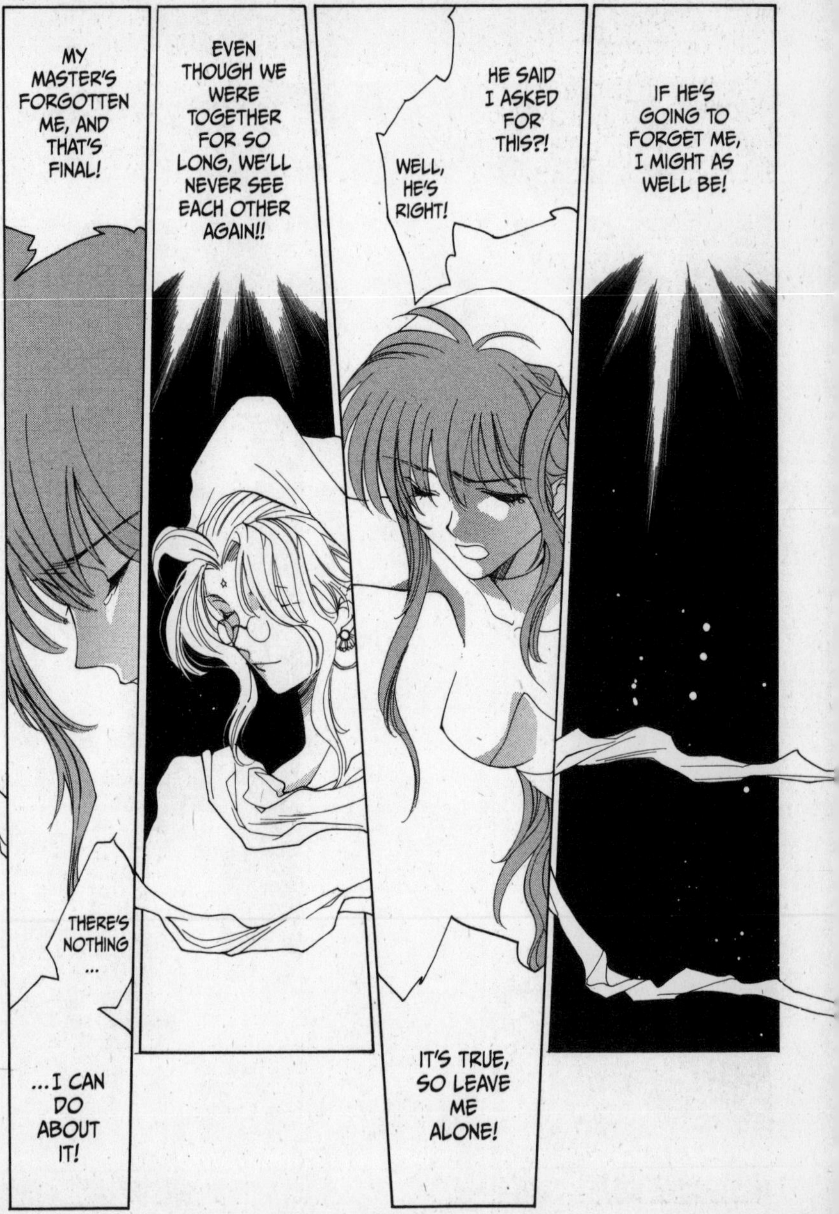
IF HE'S GOING TO FORGET ME, I MIGHT AS WELL BE!
HE SAID I ASKED FOR THIS?!
WELL, HE'S RIGHT!
IT'S TRUE, SO LEAVE ME ALONE!
EVEN THOUGH WE WERE TOGETHER FOR SO LONG, WE'LL NEVER SEE EACH OTHER AGAIN!!
MY MASTER'S FORGOTTEN ME, AND THAT'S FINAL!
THERE'S NOTHING ...
...I CAN DO ABOUT IT!

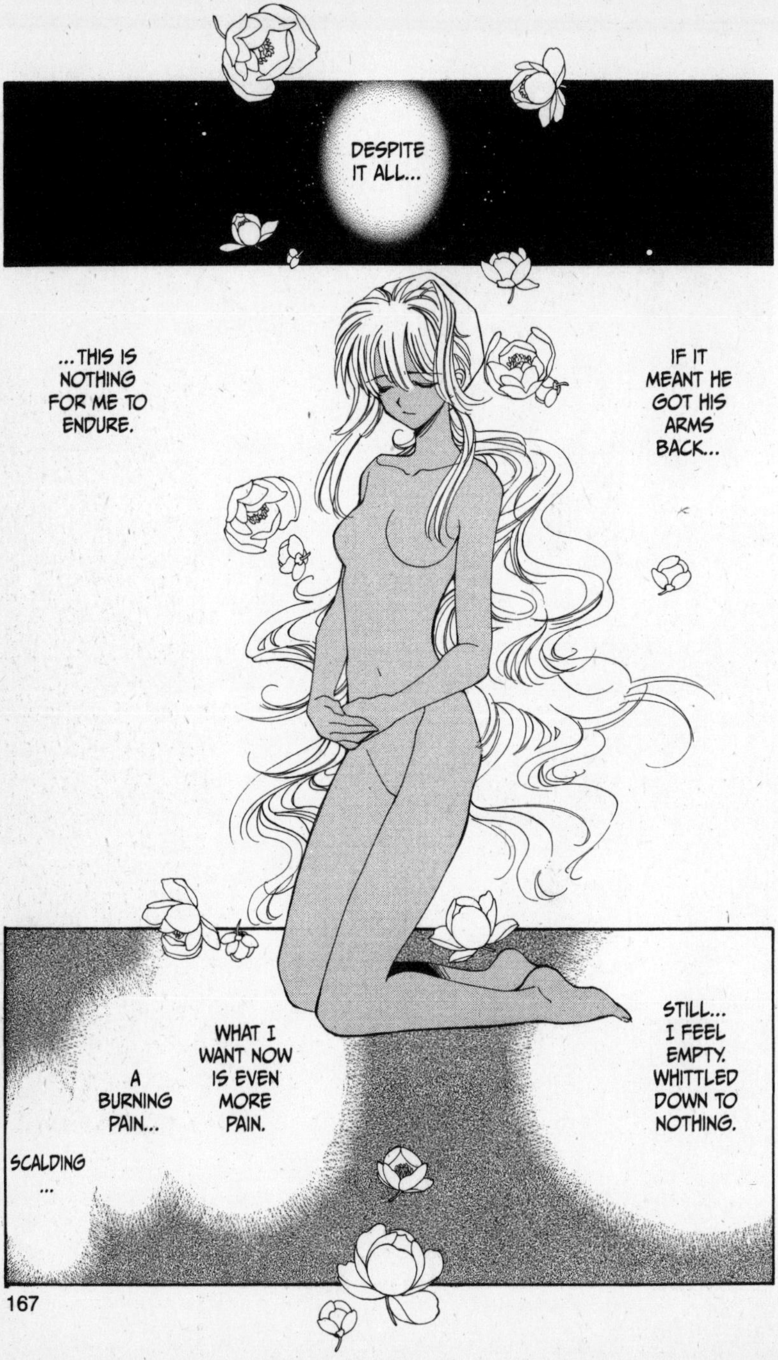
DESPITE IT ALL...
IF IT MEANT HE GOT HIS ARMS BACK...
...THIS IS NOTHING FOR ME TO ENDURE.
STILL... I FEEL EMPTY. WHITTLED DOWN TO NOTHING.
WHAT I WANT NOW IS EVEN MORE PAIN.
A BURNING PAIN...
SCALDING ...

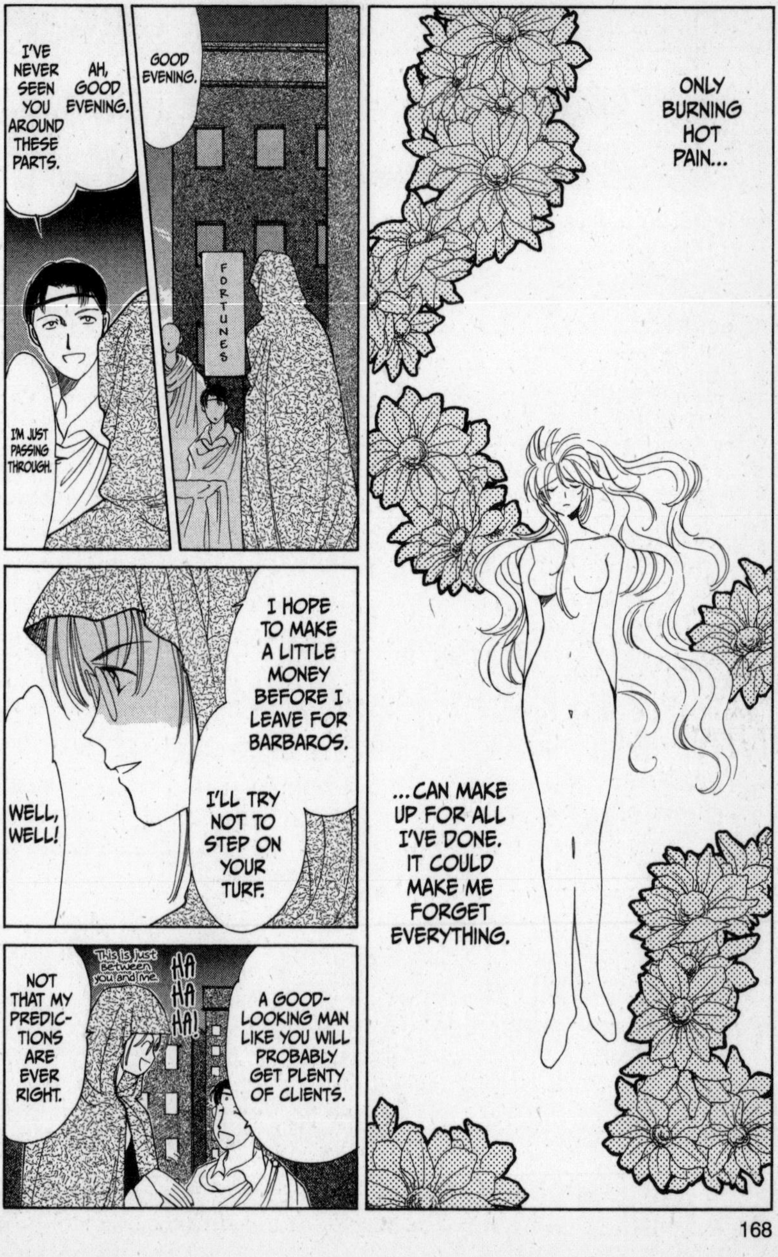
ONLY BURNING HOT PAIN...
...CAN MAKE UP FOR ALL I'VE DONE. IT COULD MAKE ME FORGET EVERYTHING.
GOOD EVENING.
FORTUNES
AH, GOOD EVENING.
I'VE NEVER SEEN YOU AROUND THESE PARTS.
I'M JUST PASSING THROUGH.
I HOPE TO MAKE A LITTLE MONEY BEFORE I LEAVE FOR BARBAROS.
I'LL TRY NOT TO STEP ON YOUR TURF.
WELL, WELL!
A GOOD-LOOKING MAN LIKE YOU WILL PROBABLY GET PLENTY OF CLIENTS.
HA HA HA!
This is just between you and me.
NOT THAT MY PREDICTIONS ARE EVER RIGHT.

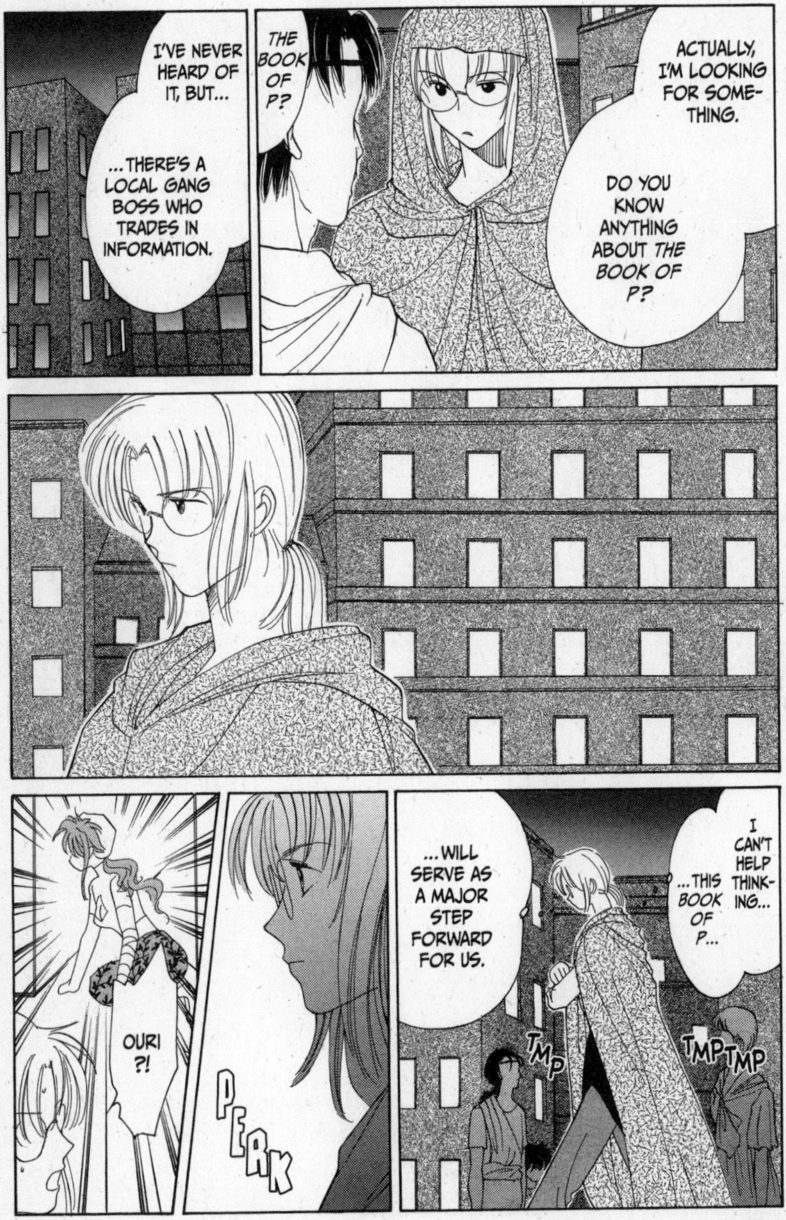
ACTUALLY, I'M LOOKING FOR SOME-THING.
DO YOU KNOW ANYTHING ABOUT *THE BOOK OF P?*
THE BOOK OF P?
I'VE NEVER HEARD OF IT, BUT...
...THERE'S A LOCAL GANG BOSS WHO TRADES IN INFORMATION.
I CAN'T HELP THINKING...
...THIS *BOOK OF P...*
...WILL SERVE AS A MAJOR STEP FORWARD FOR US.
TMP
TMPTMP
PERK
OURI ?!

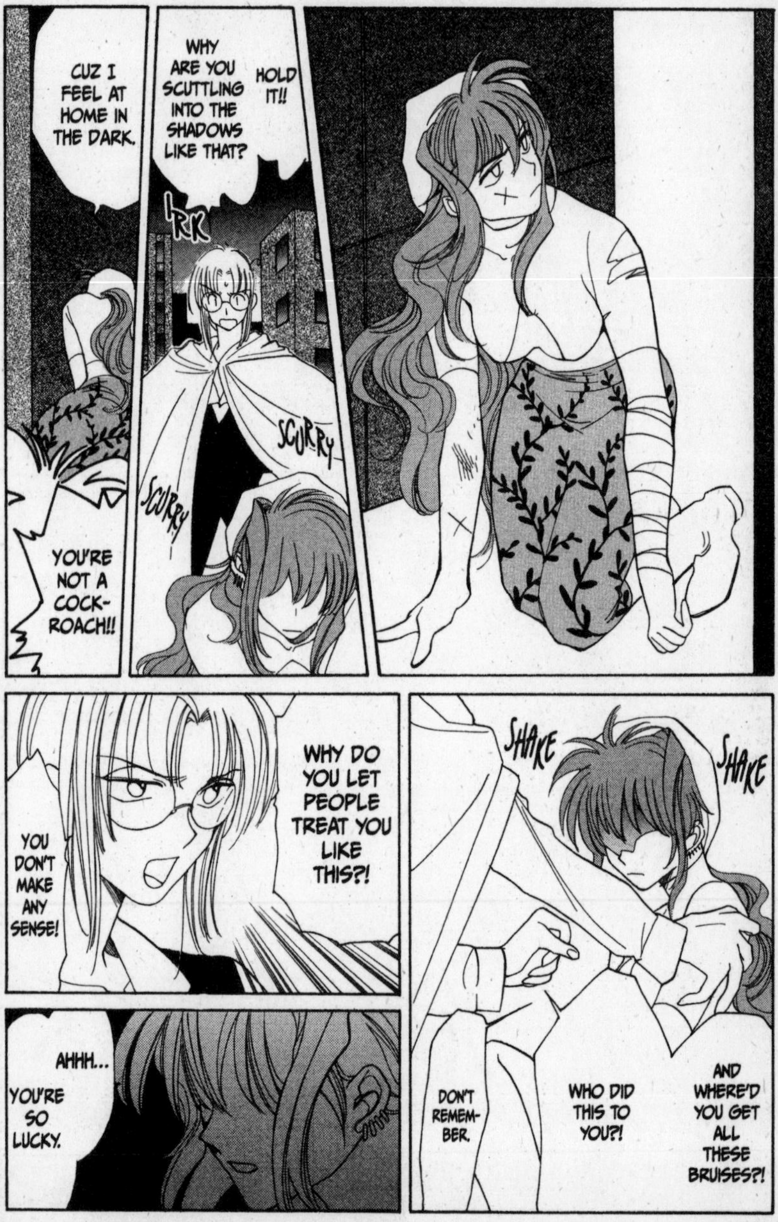
HOLD IT!!
WHY ARE YOU SCUTTLING INTO THE SHADOWS LIKE THAT?
IRK
SCURRY
SCURRY
CUZ I FEEL AT HOME IN THE DARK.
YOU'RE NOT A COCK-ROACH!!
SHAKE
SHAKE
AND WHERE'D YOU GET ALL THESE BRUISES?!
WHO DID THIS TO YOU?!
DON'T REMEM-BER.
WHY DO YOU LET PEOPLE TREAT YOU LIKE THIS?!
YOU DON'T MAKE ANY SENSE!
AHHH...
YOU'RE SO LUCKY.

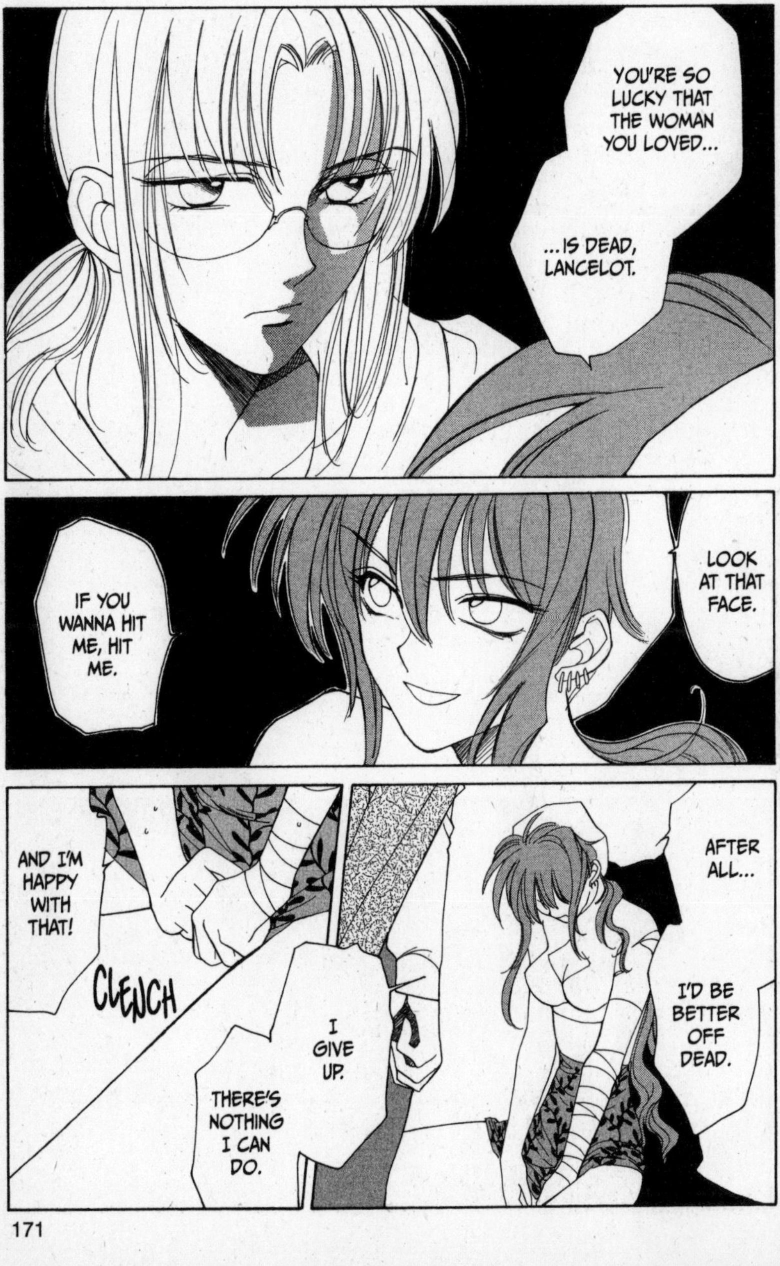
YOU'RE SO LUCKY THAT THE WOMAN YOU LOVED...
...IS DEAD, LANCELOT.
LOOK AT THAT FACE.
IF YOU WANNA HIT ME, HIT ME.
AFTER ALL...
I'D BE BETTER OFF DEAD.
I GIVE UP.
THERE'S NOTHING I CAN DO.
AND I'M HAPPY WITH THAT!
CLENCH

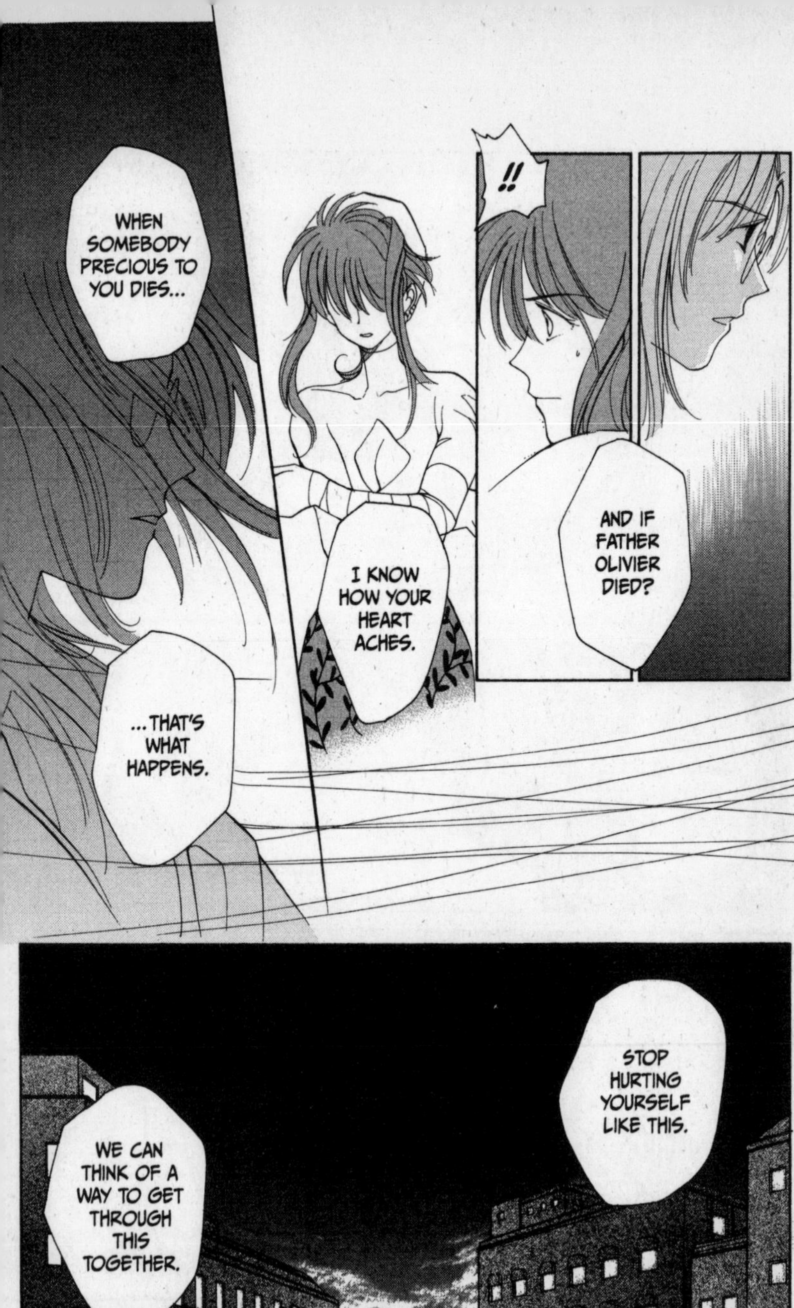
!!
AND IF FATHER OLIVIER DIED?
I KNOW HOW YOUR HEART ACHES.
WHEN SOMEBODY PRECIOUS TO YOU DIES...
...THAT'S WHAT HAPPENS.
STOP HURTING YOURSELF LIKE THIS.
WE CAN THINK OF A WAY TO GET THROUGH THIS TOGETHER.

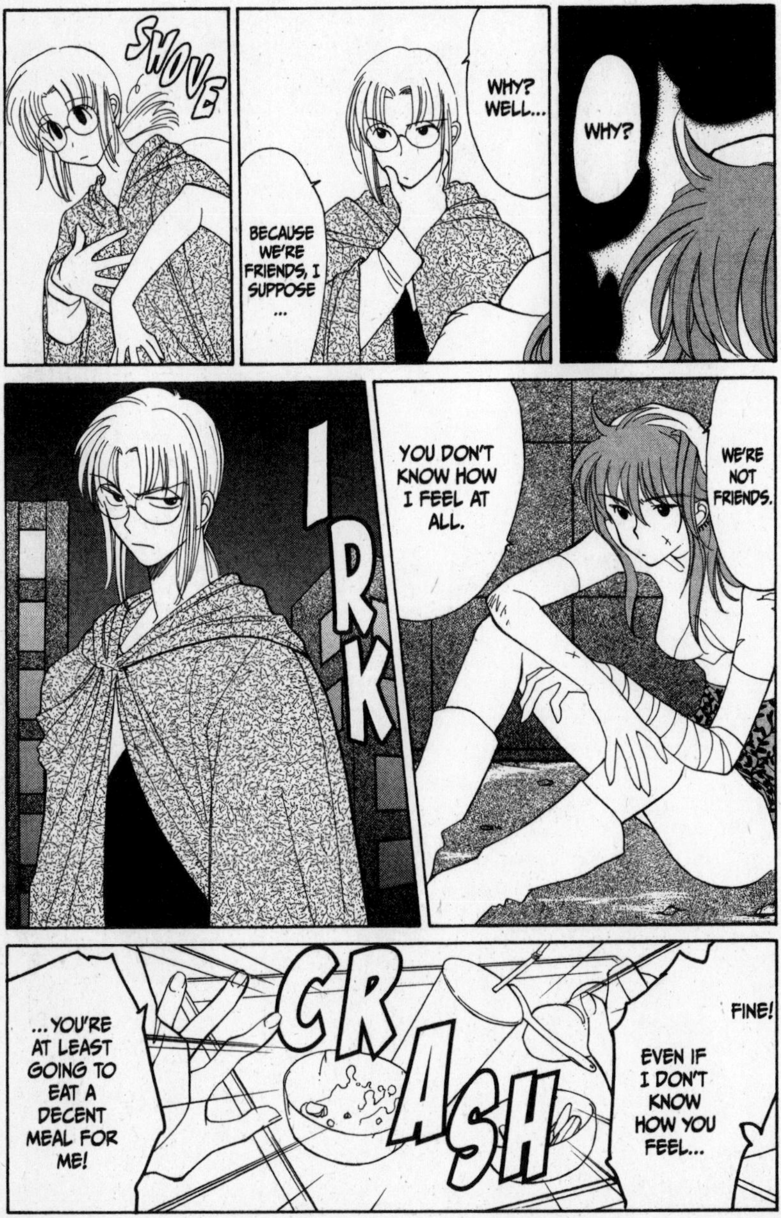
WHY?
WHY? WELL...
BECAUSE WE'RE FRIENDS, I SUPPOSE ...
SHOVE
WE'RE NOT FRIENDS.
YOU DON'T KNOW HOW I FEEL AT ALL.
IRK
FINE!
EVEN IF I DON'T KNOW HOW YOU FEEL...
CRASH
...YOU'RE AT LEAST GOING TO EAT A DECENT MEAL FOR ME!

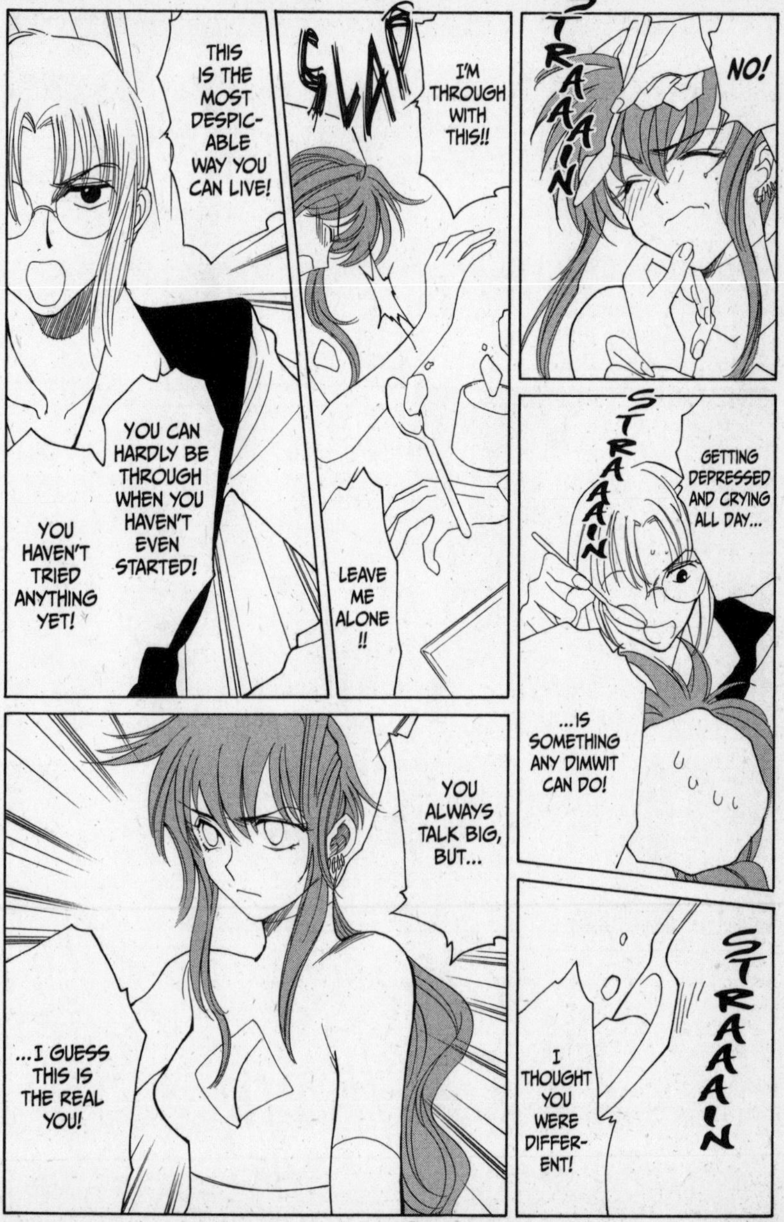
NO!
STRAAAIN
SLAP
I'M THROUGH WITH THIS!!
LEAVE ME ALONE!!
THIS IS THE MOST DESPIC-ABLE WAY YOU CAN LIVE!
YOU CAN HARDLY BE THROUGH WHEN YOU HAVEN'T EVEN STARTED!
YOU HAVEN'T TRIED ANYTHING YET!
STRAAAIN
GETTING DEPRESSED AND CRYING ALL DAY...
...IS SOMETHING ANY DIMWIT CAN DO!
YOU ALWAYS TALK BIG, BUT...
...I GUESS THIS IS THE REAL YOU!
STRAAAIN
I THOUGHT YOU WERE DIFFER-ENT!

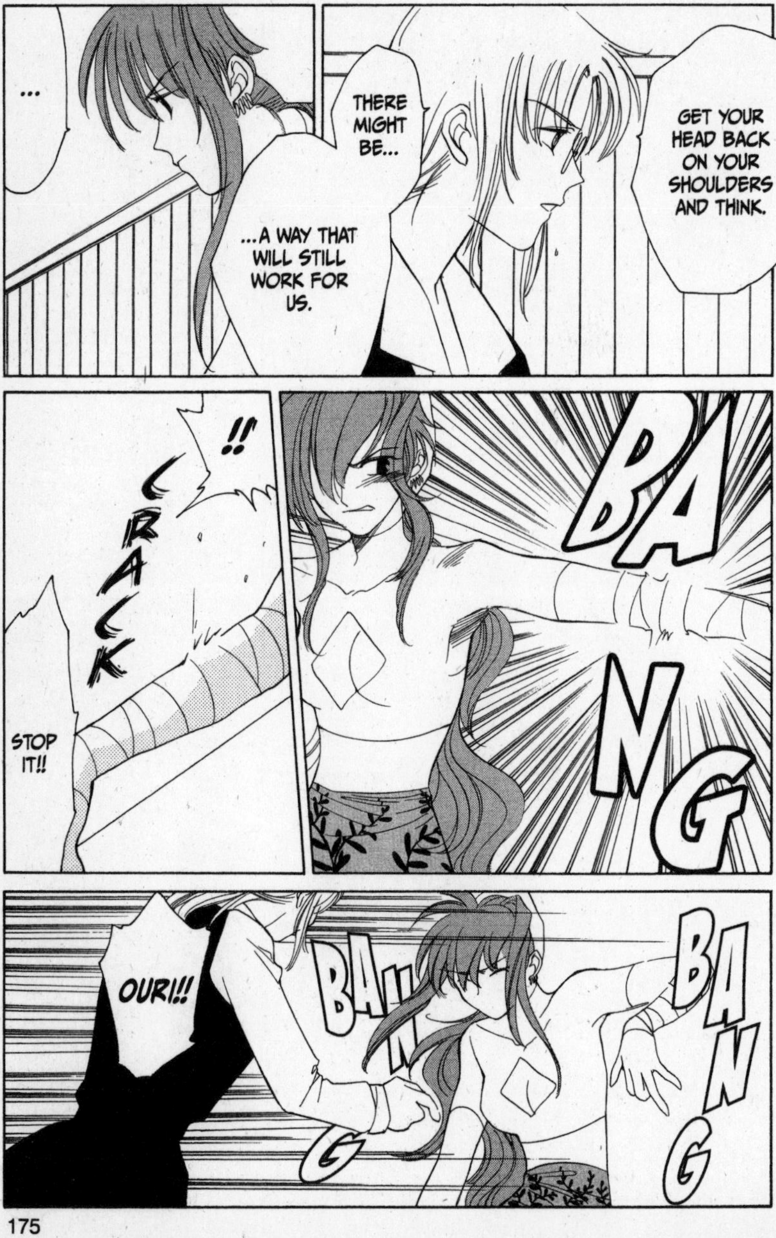
GET YOUR HEAD BACK ON YOUR SHOULDERS AND THINK.
THERE MIGHT BE...
...A WAY THAT WILL STILL WORK FOR US.
...
BANG
!!
CRACK
STOP IT!!
BANG
BANG
OURI!!

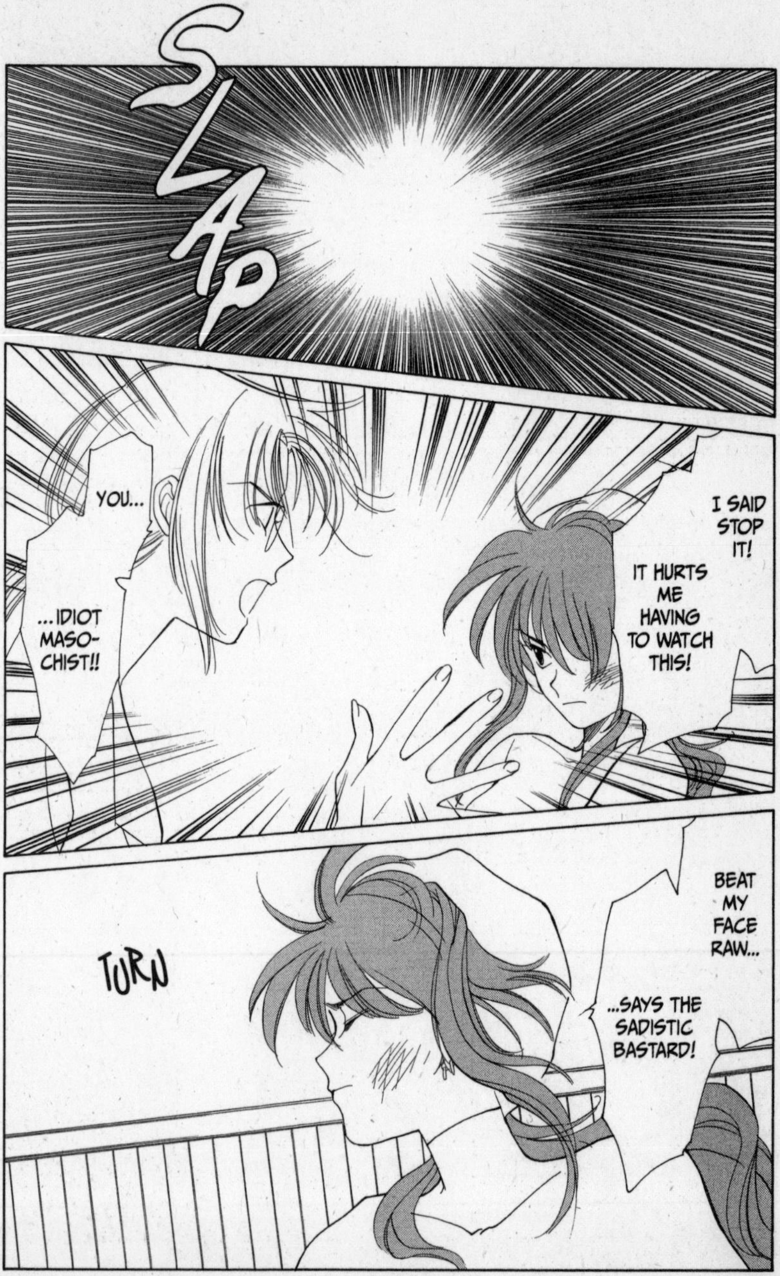
SLAP
I SAID STOP IT!
IT HURTS ME HAVING TO WATCH THIS!
YOU...
...IDIOT MASO-CHIST!!
BEAT MY FACE RAW...
...SAYS THE SADISTIC BASTARD!
TURN

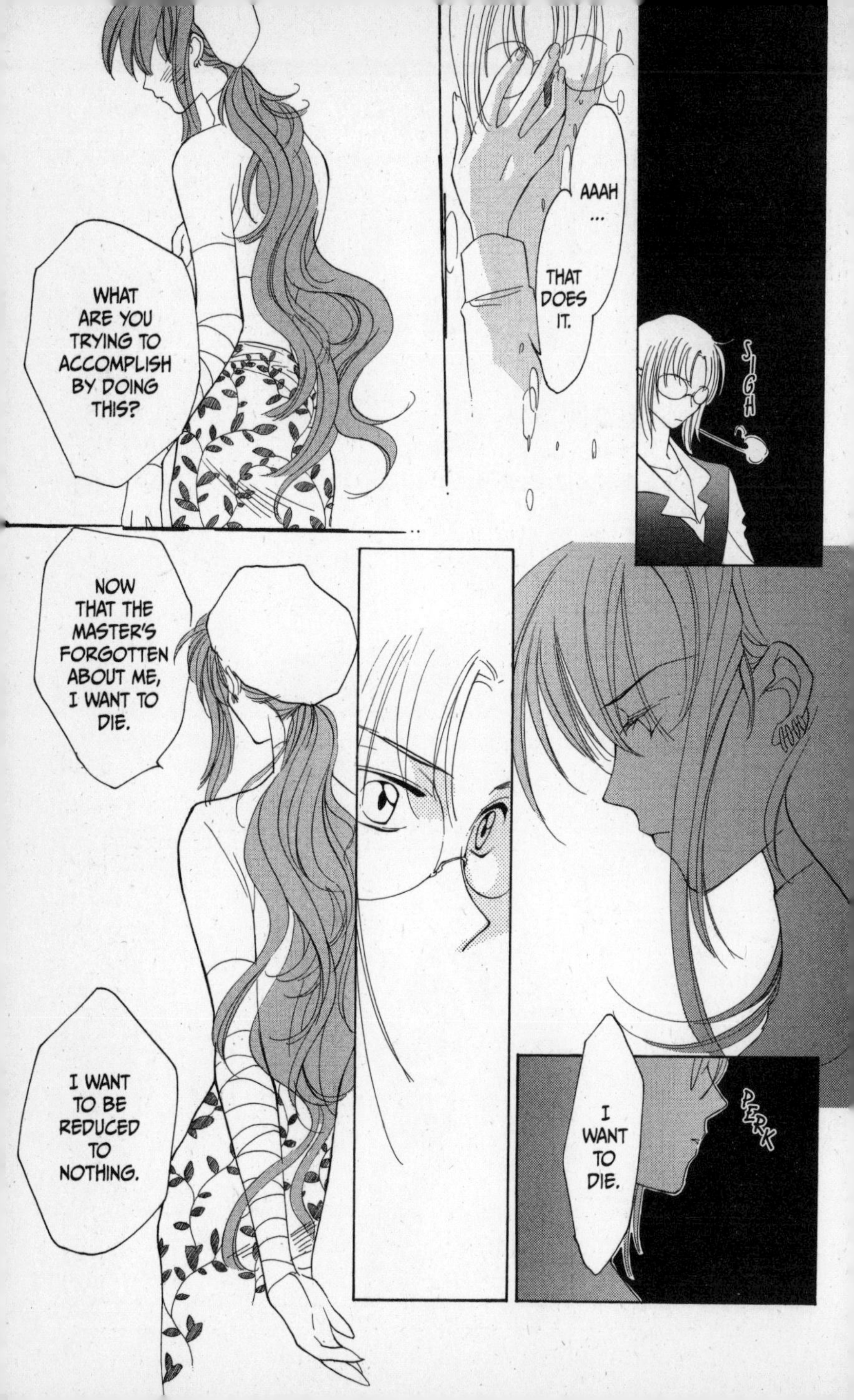
SIGH
AAAH ...
THAT DOES IT.
WHAT ARE YOU TRYING TO ACCOMPLISH BY DOING THIS?
I WANT TO DIE.
PERK
NOW THAT THE MASTER'S FORGOTTEN ABOUT ME, I WANT TO DIE.
I WANT TO BE REDUCED TO NOTHING.

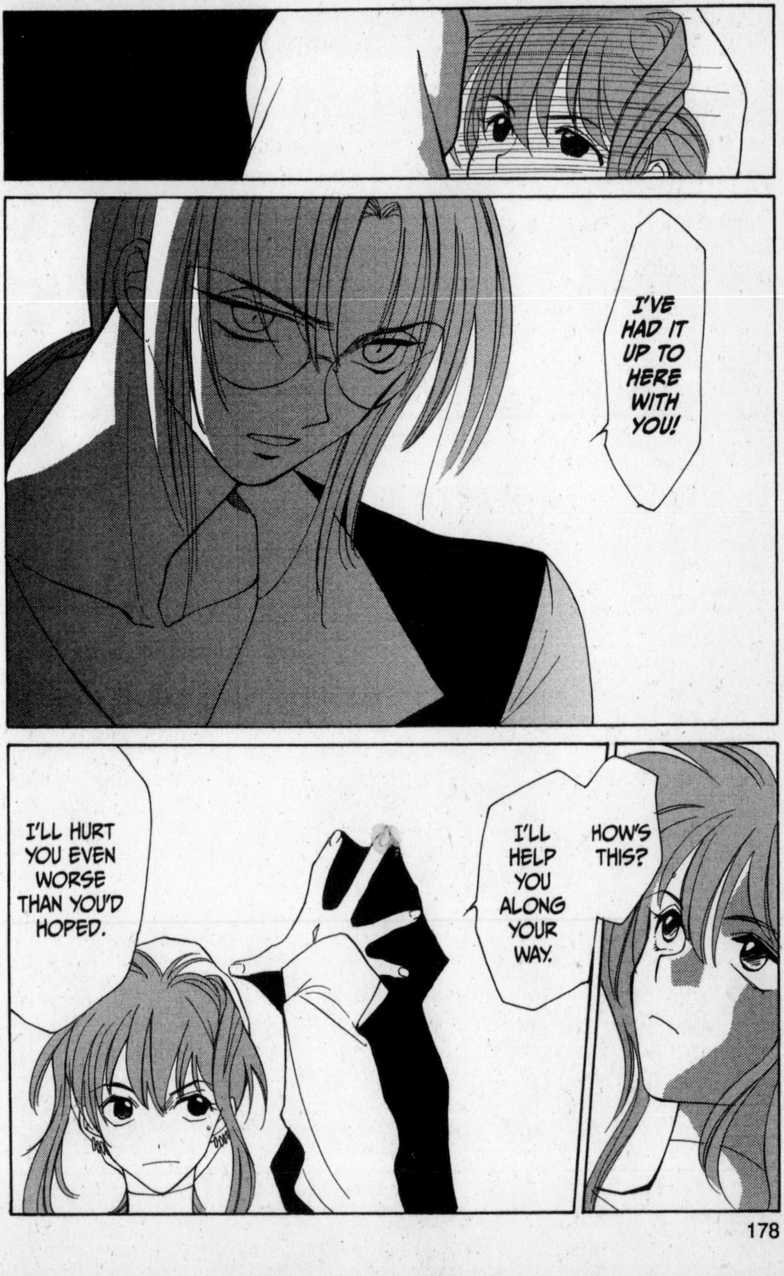
I'VE HAD IT UP TO HERE WITH YOU!
HOW'S THIS?
I'LL HELP YOU ALONG YOUR WAY.
I'LL HURT YOU EVEN WORSE THAN YOU'D HOPED.

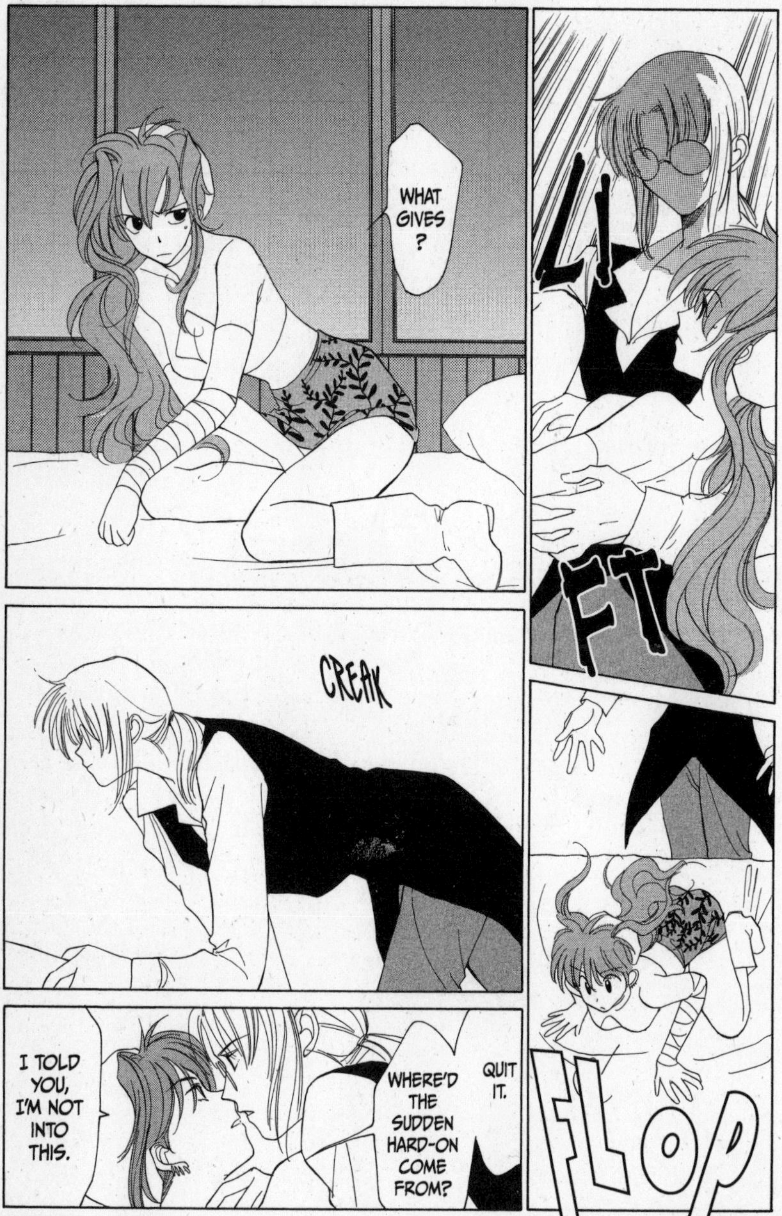
LIFT
WHAT GIVES ?
FLOP
CREAK
QUIT IT.
WHERE'D THE SUDDEN HARD-ON COME FROM?
I TOLD YOU, I'M NOT INTO THIS.

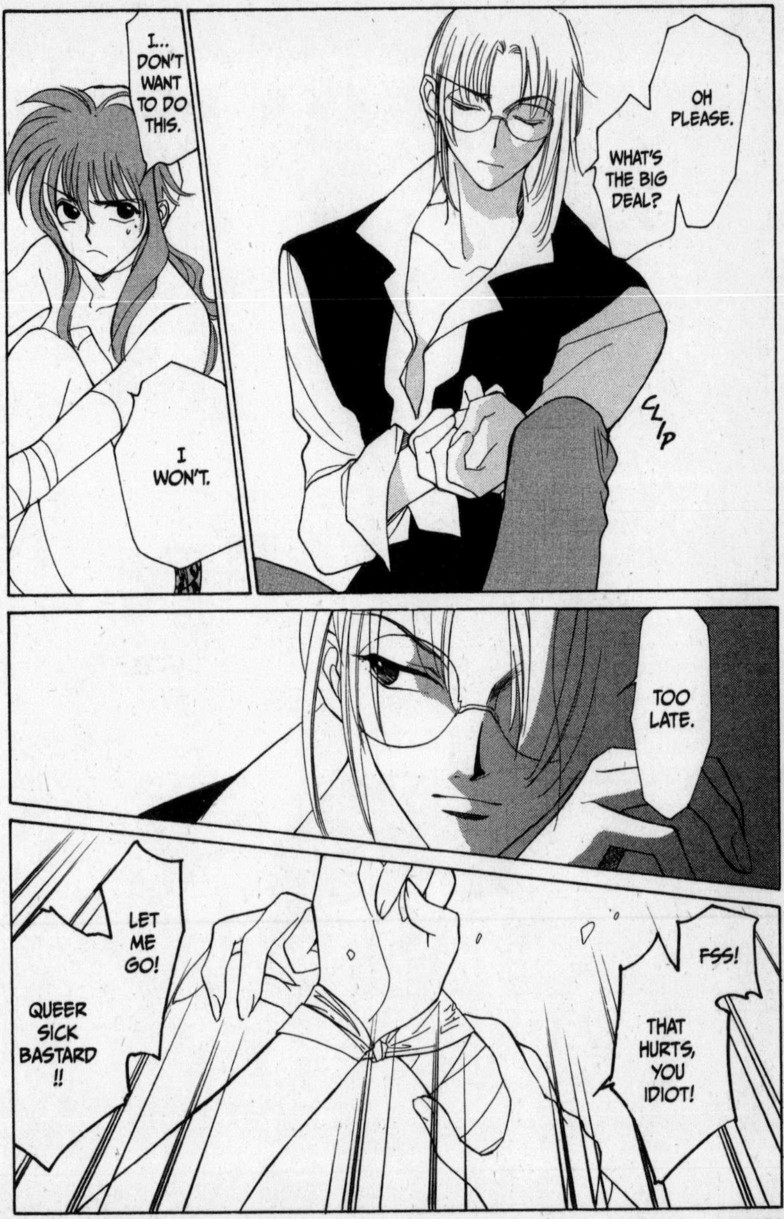
OH PLEASE.
WHAT'S THE BIG DEAL?
CLIP
I... DON'T WANT TO DO THIS.
I WON'T.
TOO LATE.
FSS!
THAT HURTS, YOU IDIOT!
LET ME GO!
QUEER SICK BASTARD!!

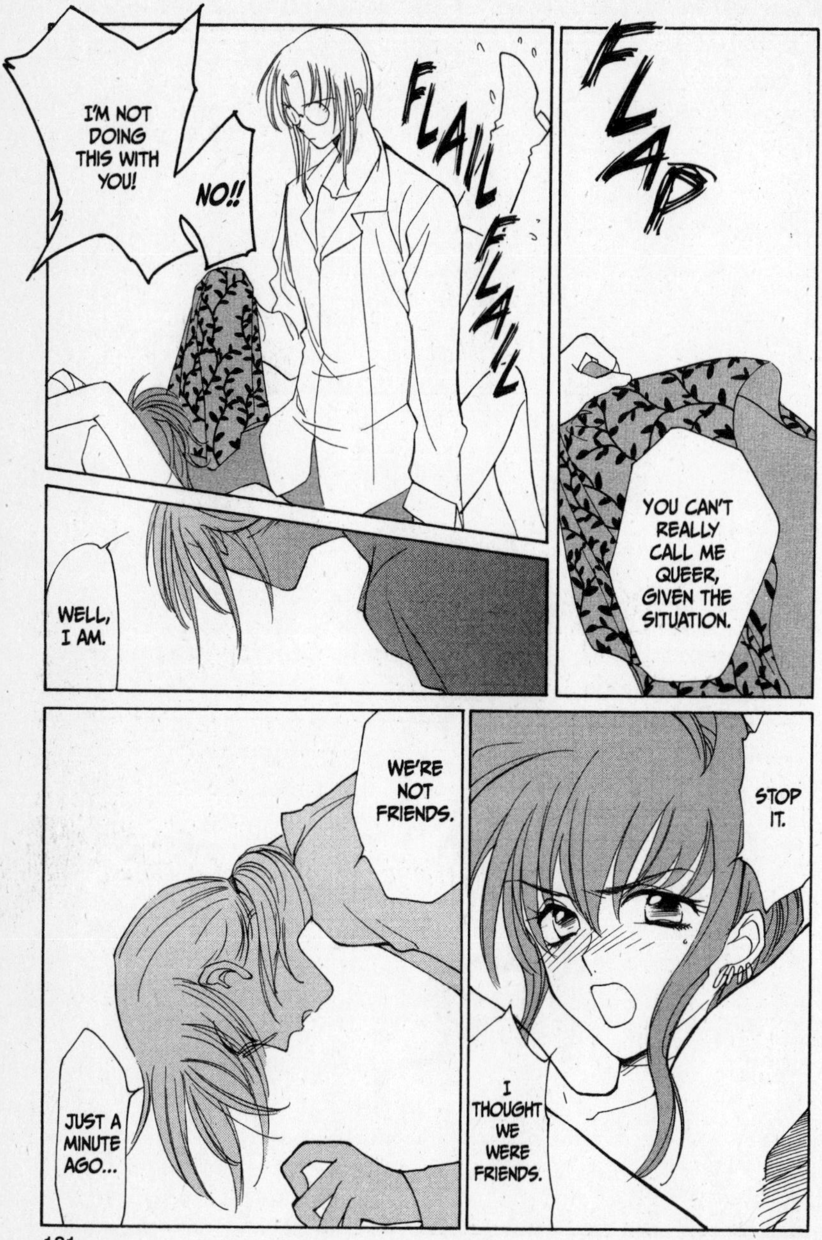

FLAP
YOU CAN'T REALLY CALL ME QUEER, GIVEN THE SITUATION.
I'M NOT DOING THIS WITH YOU!
NO!!
FLAIL FLAIL
WELL, I AM.
STOP IT.
I THOUGHT WE WERE FRIENDS.
WE'RE NOT FRIENDS.
JUST A MINUTE AGO...

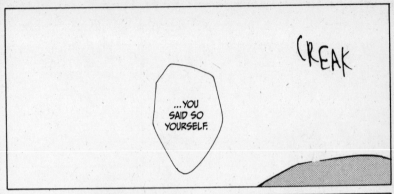

CREAK

...YOU SAID SO YOURSELF.

...WHAT I WAS TRYING TO SAY!

NO! THAT WASN'T...

I'D BE BETTER OFF DEAD.

MASTER...

I'M DONE!!

AND FATHER OLIVIER?

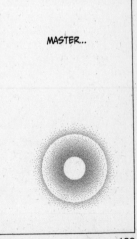

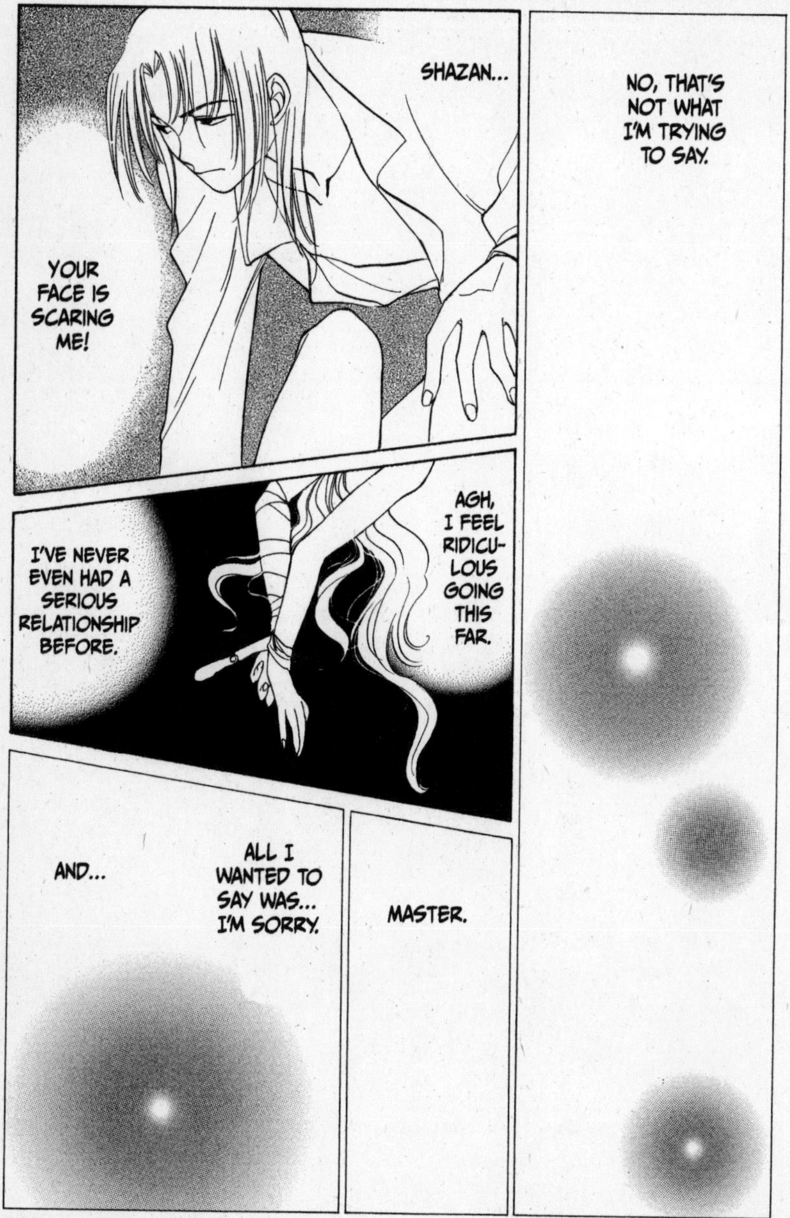
NO, THAT'S NOT WHAT I'M TRYING TO SAY.
SHAZAN...
YOUR FACE IS SCARING ME!
AGH, I FEEL RIDICULOUS GOING THIS FAR.
I'VE NEVER EVEN HAD A SERIOUS RELATIONSHIP BEFORE.
MASTER.
ALL I WANTED TO SAY WAS... I'M SORRY.
AND...

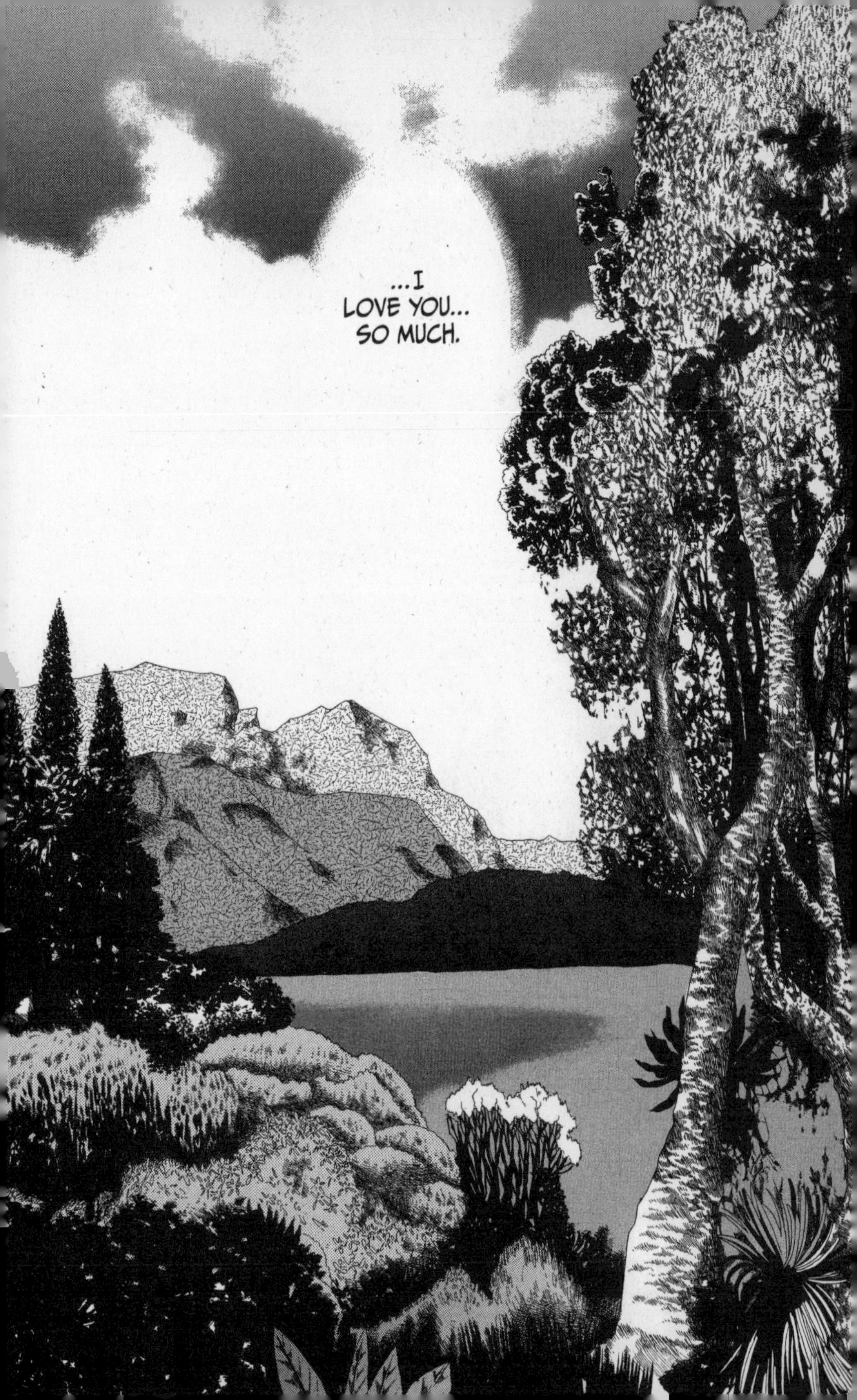
...I LOVE YOU... SO MUCH.

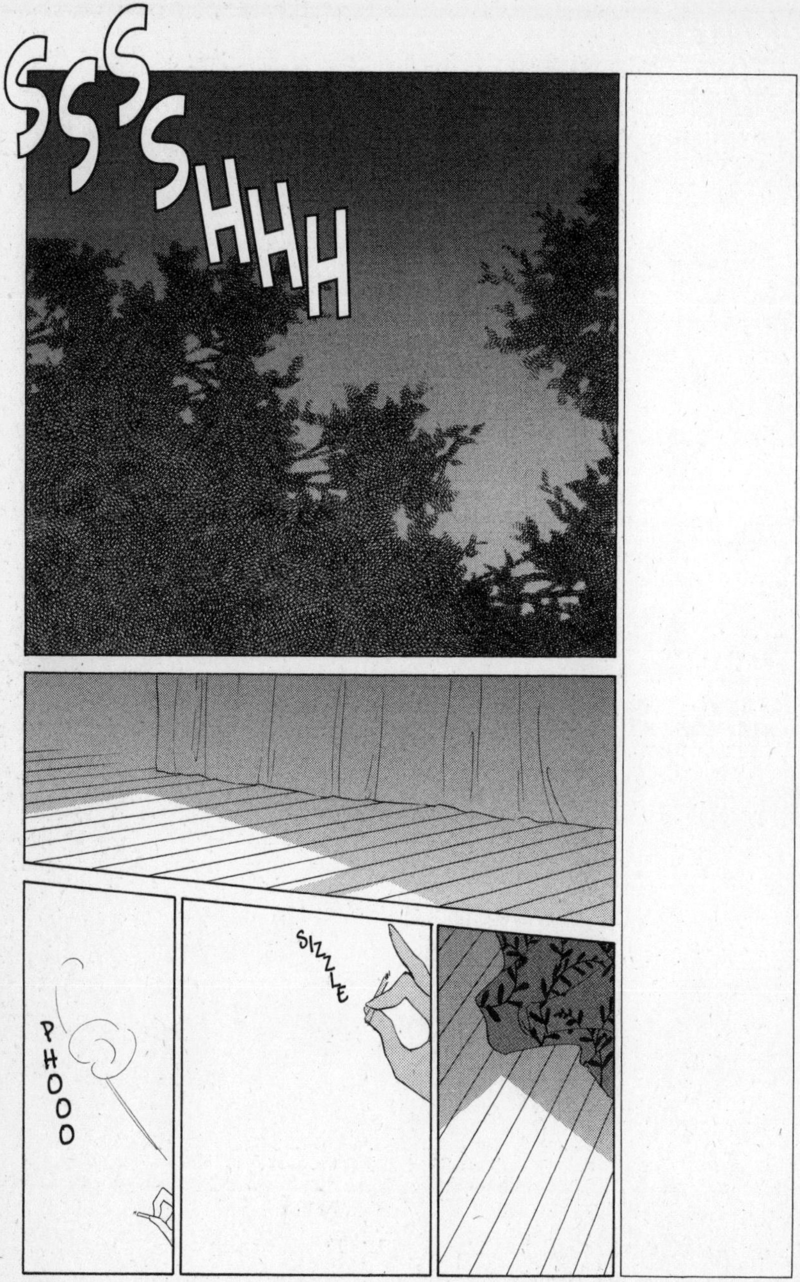
SSSSHHHH
SIZZLE
PHOOO

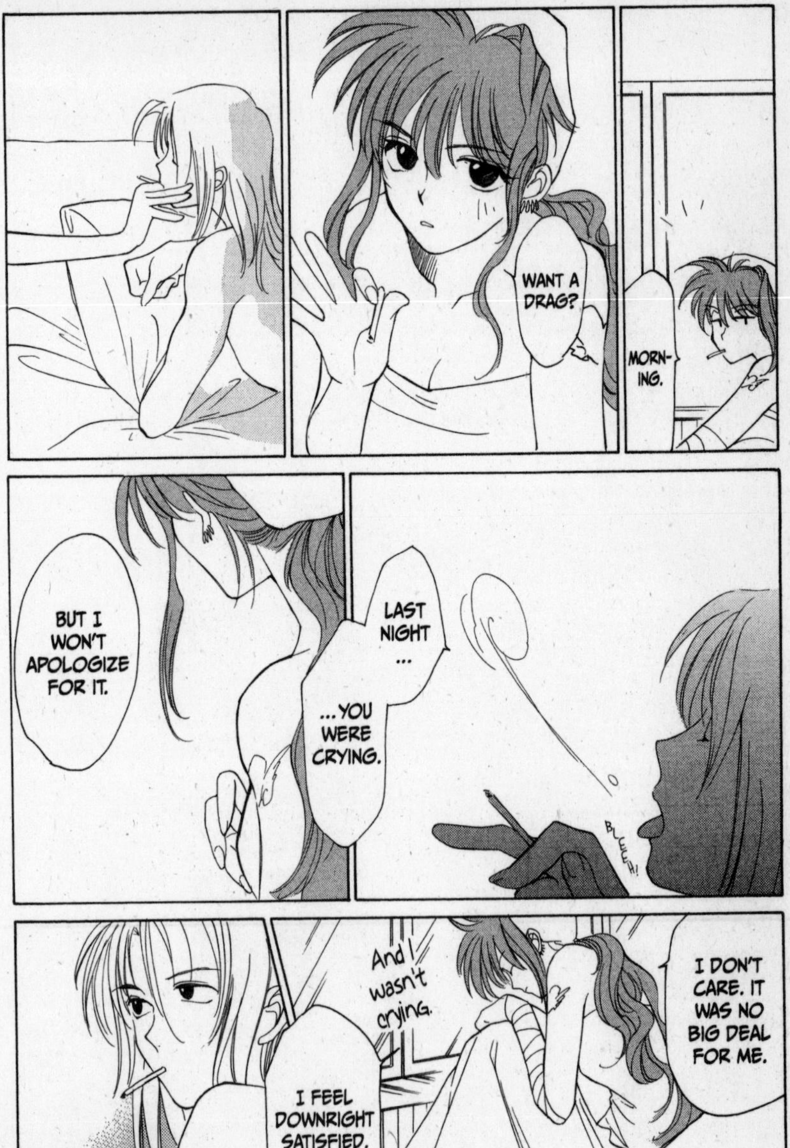
MORN-ING.
WANT A DRAG?
LAST NIGHT ...
...YOU WERE CRYING.
BLEEEH!
BUT I WON'T APOLOGIZE FOR IT.
I DON'T CARE. IT WAS NO BIG DEAL FOR ME.
And I wasn't crying.
I FEEL DOWNRIGHT SATISFIED.

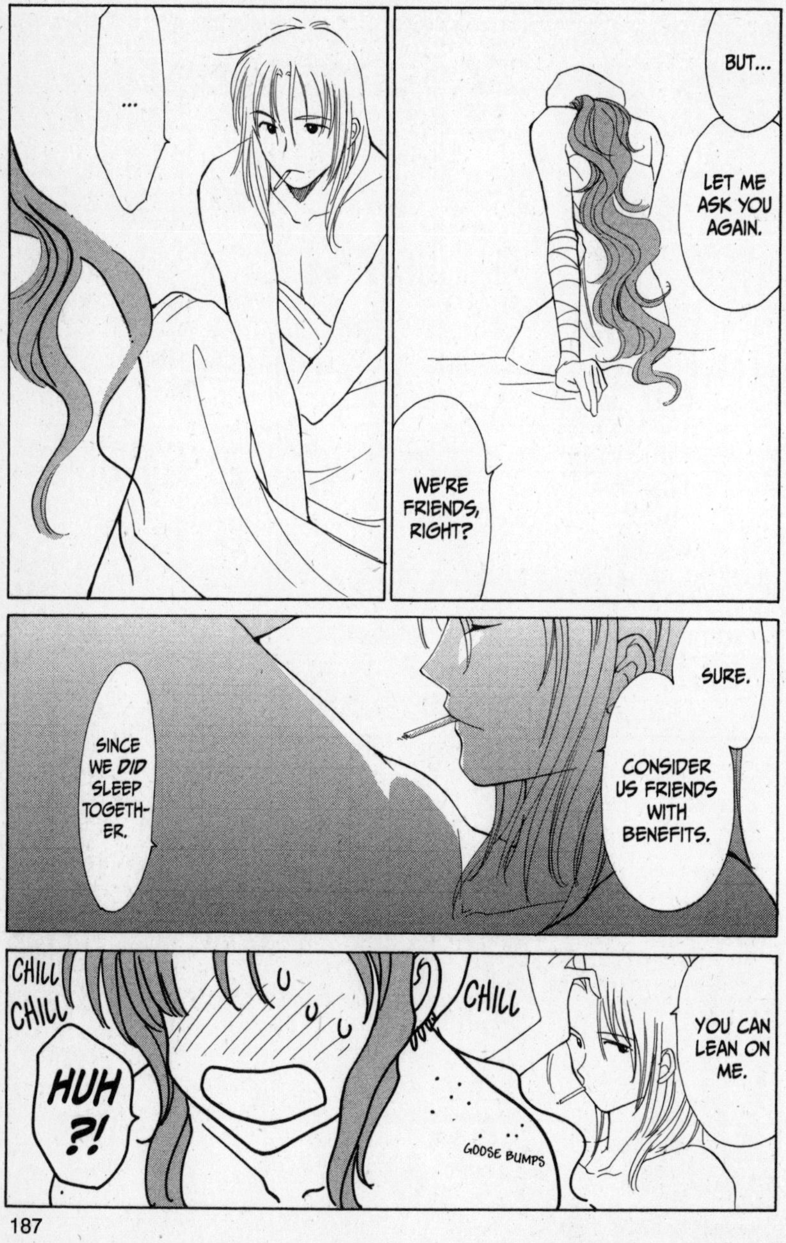
BUT...
LET ME ASK YOU AGAIN.
WE'RE FRIENDS, RIGHT?
...
SURE.
CONSIDER US FRIENDS WITH BENEFITS.
SINCE WE *DID* SLEEP TOGETHER.
YOU CAN LEAN ON ME.
GOOSE BUMPS
CHILL
HUH?!
CHILL CHILL

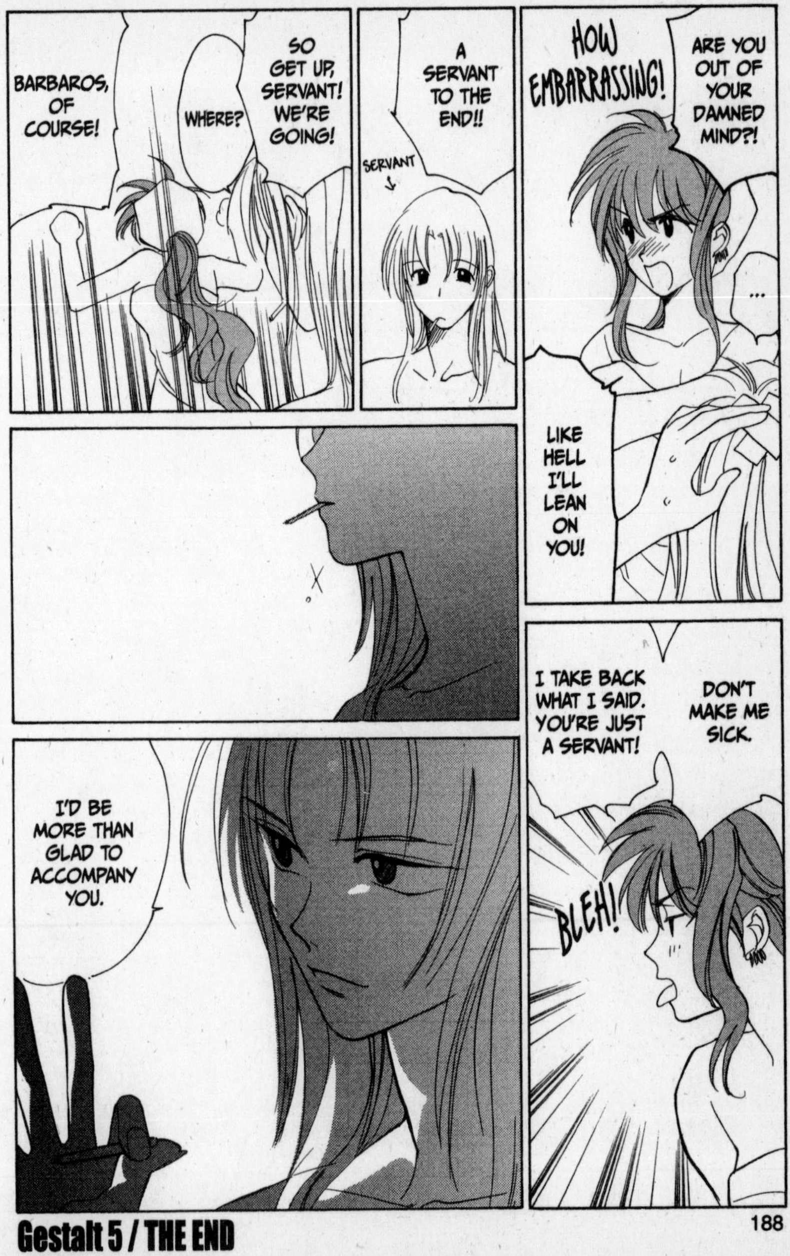
ARE YOU OUT OF YOUR DAMNED MIND?!
HOW EMBARRASSING!
...
LIKE HELL I'LL LEAN ON YOU!
A SERVANT TO THE END!!
SERVANT
SO GET UP, SERVANT! WE'RE GOING!
WHERE?
BARBAROS, OF COURSE!
DON'T MAKE ME SICK.
I TAKE BACK WHAT I SAID. YOU'RE JUST A SERVANT!
BLEH!
I'D BE MORE THAN GLAD TO ACCOMPANY YOU.

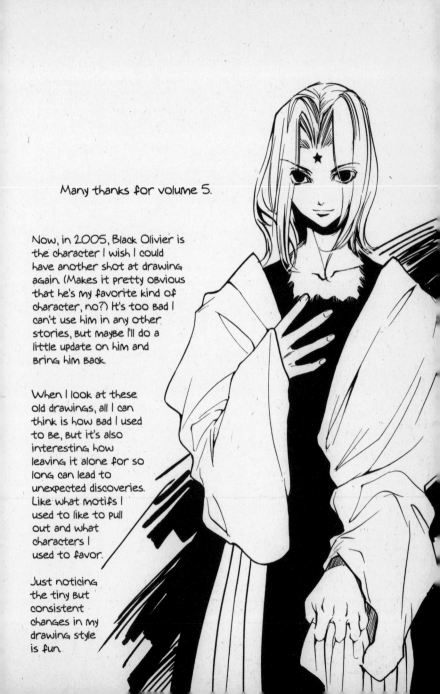

Many thanks for volume 5.

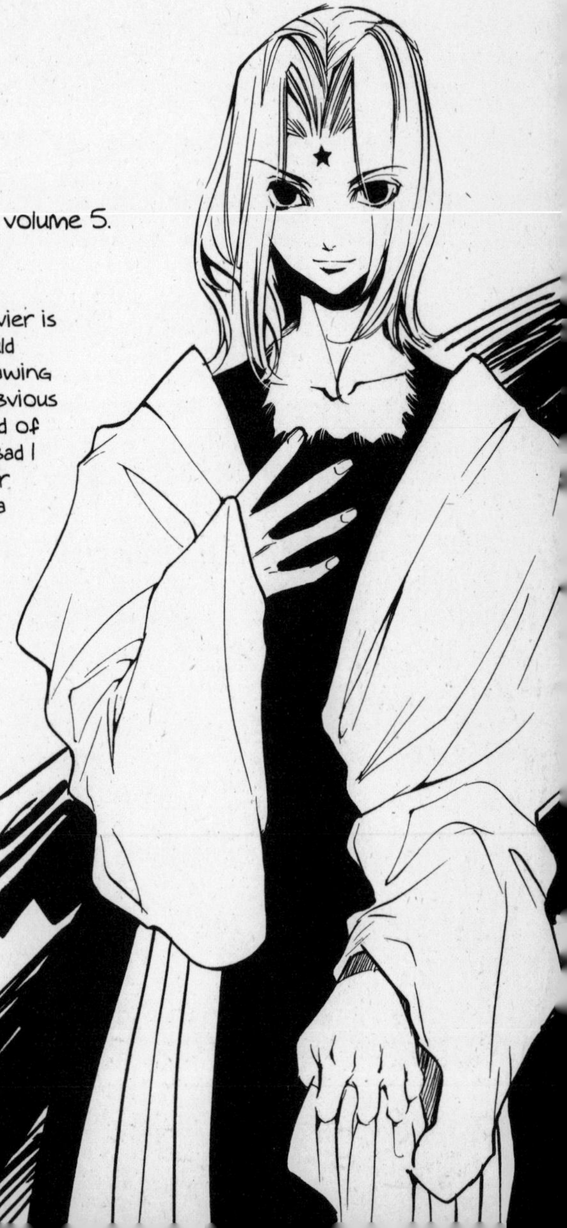

Now, in 2005, Black Olivier is the character I wish I could have another shot at drawing again. (Makes it pretty obvious that he's my favorite kind of character, no?) It's too bad I can't use him in any other stories, but maybe I'll do a little update on him and bring him back.

When I look at these old drawings, all I can think is how bad I used to be, but it's also interesting how leaving it alone for so long can lead to unexpected discoveries. Like what motifs I used to like to pull out and what characters I used to favor.

Just noticing the tiny but consistent changes in my drawing style is fun.

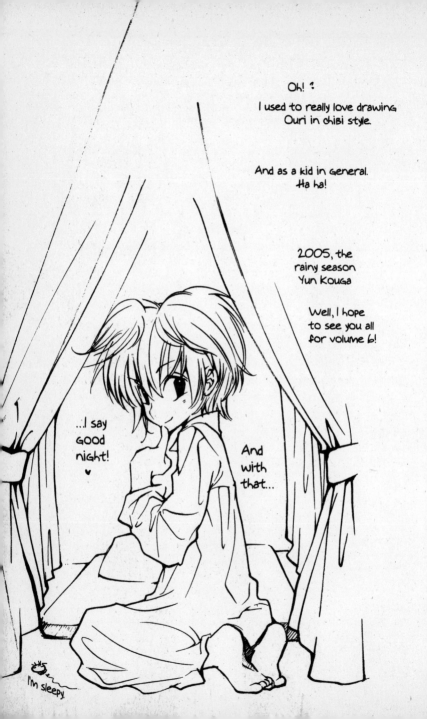

Oh! ?

I used to really love drawing Ouri in chibi style.

And as a kid in General. Ha ha!

2005, the rainy season Yun Kouga

Well, I hope to see you all for volume 6!

..I say GOOD night!
♥

And with that...

I'm sleepy.

I feel like flying toward the setting sun... not caring where I end up... until I sink into the horizon.
Sigh... I wish I could go to Africa or someplace like that.

Yun Kouga began her career as a doujinshi and debuted in 1986 with the original manga *Metal Heart*, serialized in *Comic VAL*. She is the creator of the popular series *Loveless* and *Earthian*, along with many manga and anime projects, including character design for *Gundam 00*.

Gestalt
Vol. 5
VIZ Media Edition

Story and Art by Yun Kouga

Translation & English Adaptation/Christine Schilling
Touch-up Art & Lettering/Mark McMurray
Design/Sean Lee
Editor/Chris Mackenzie

VP, Production/Alvin Lu
VP, Sales & Product Marketing/Gonzalo Ferreyra
VP, Creative/Linda Espinosa
Publisher/Hyoe Narita

Printed in the U.S.A.

Published by VIZ Media, LLC
P.O. Box 77010
San Francisco, CA 94107

10 9 8 7 6 5 4 3 2 1
First printing, February 2010

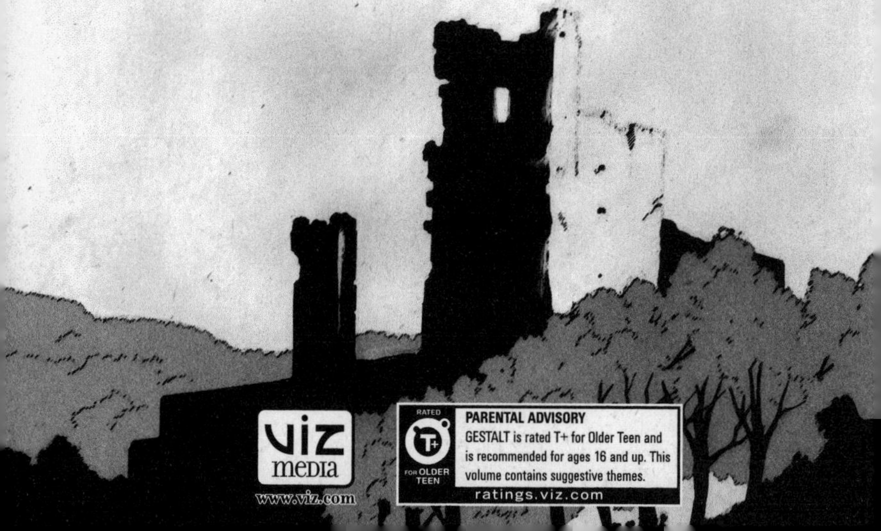
viz media
www.viz.com
RATED
T+
FOR OLDER TEEN
PARENTAL ADVISORY
GESTALT is rated T+ for Older Teen and is recommended for ages 16 and up. This volume contains suggestive themes.
ratings.viz.com

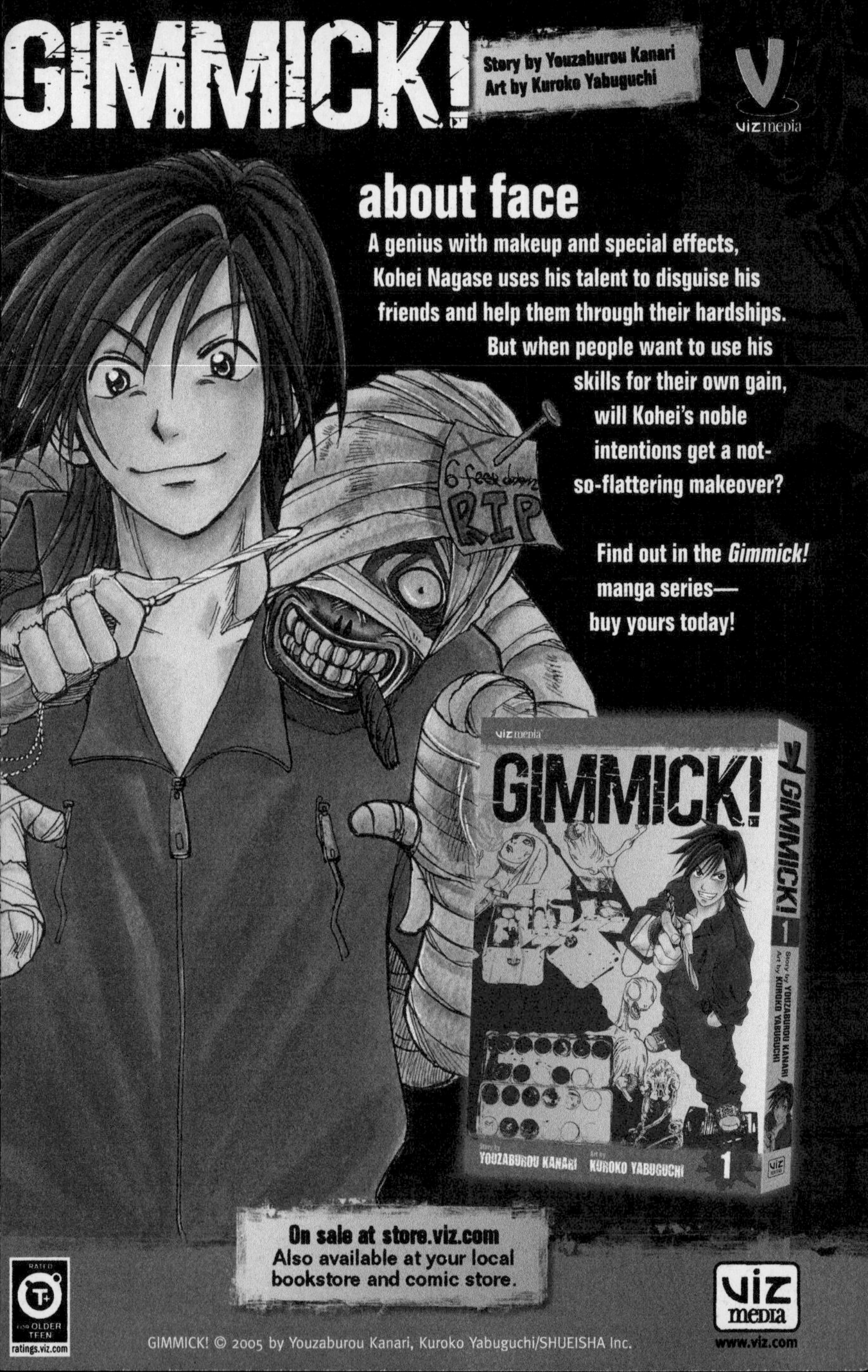
GIMMICK!
Story by Youzaburou Kanari
Art by Kuroko Yabuguchi
VIZ media
about face
A genius with makeup and special effects, Kohei Nagase uses his talent to disguise his friends and help them through their hardships. But when people want to use his skills for their own gain, will Kohei's noble intentions get a not-so-flattering makeover?
Find out in the Gimmick! manga series— buy yours today!
GIMMICK!
Story by Youzaburou Kanari
Art by Kuroko Yabuguchi
1
On sale at store.viz.com
Also available at your local bookstore and comic store.
RATED T+ FOR OLDER TEEN
ratings.viz.com
GIMMICK! © 2005 by Youzaburou Kanari, Kuroko Yabuguchi/SHUEISHA Inc.
VIZ media
www.viz.com

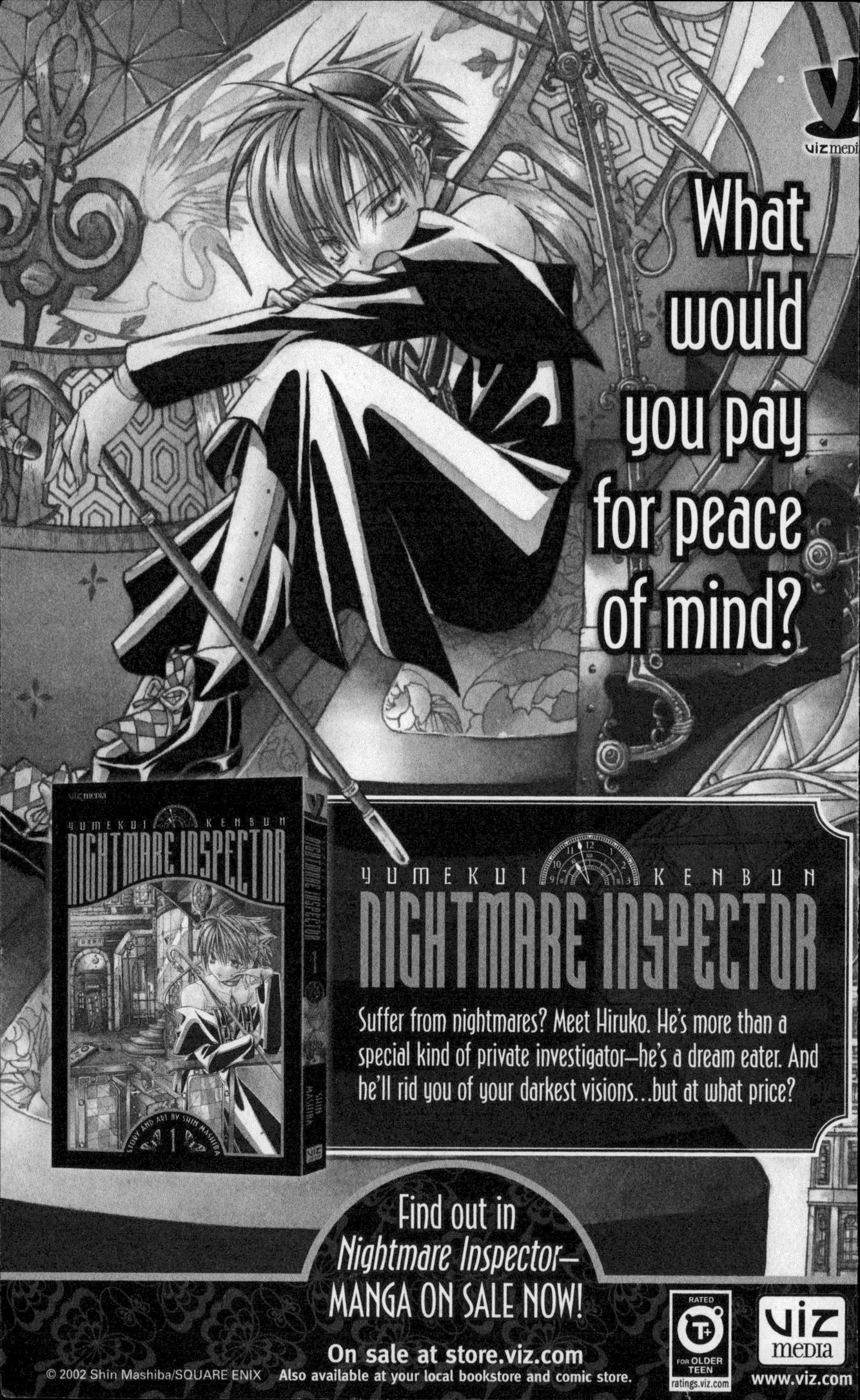
What would you pay for peace of mind?
YUMEKUI KENBUN
NIGHTMARE INSPECTOR
Suffer from nightmares? Meet Hiruko. He's more than a special kind of private investigator—he's a dream eater. And he'll rid you of your darkest visions...but at what price?
Find out in *Nightmare Inspector*—
MANGA ON SALE NOW!
On sale at store.viz.com
Also available at your local bookstore and comic store.
© 2002 Shin Mashiba/SQUARE ENIX
RATED T+ FOR OLDER TEEN
ratings.viz.com
VIZ MEDIA
www.viz.com

The Art of Fullmetal Alchemist

- Manga artwork and illustrations from 2001 to 2003
- Color title pages, Japanese tankobon and promotional artwork
- Main character portraits & character designs from the video games
- Special two-page message from series creator Hiromu Arakawa

The Art of Fullmetal Alchemist 2

- Original color manga artwork
- Illustrations presented in sequential order with commentary from creator from Hiromu Arakawa
- Character designs for the FMA PS2 video game
- Brand new manga pages

The Art of Fullmetal Alchemist: The Anime

- Initial character designs and artwork
- Cel art
- Production notes
- Interview with Yoshiyuki Itoh, character designer for the anime

ART OF

www.viz.com
store.viz.com

Fullmetal Alchemist Profiles

Get the background story and world history of the manga, plus:

- Character bios
- New, original artwork
- Interview with creator Hiromu Arakawa
- Bonus manga episode only available in this book

Fullmetal Alchemist Anime Profiles

Stay on top of your favorite episodes and characters with:

- Actual cel artwork from the TV series
- Summaries of all 51 TV episodes
- Definitive cast biographies
- Exclusive poster for your wall

FULLMETAL ALCHEMIST™

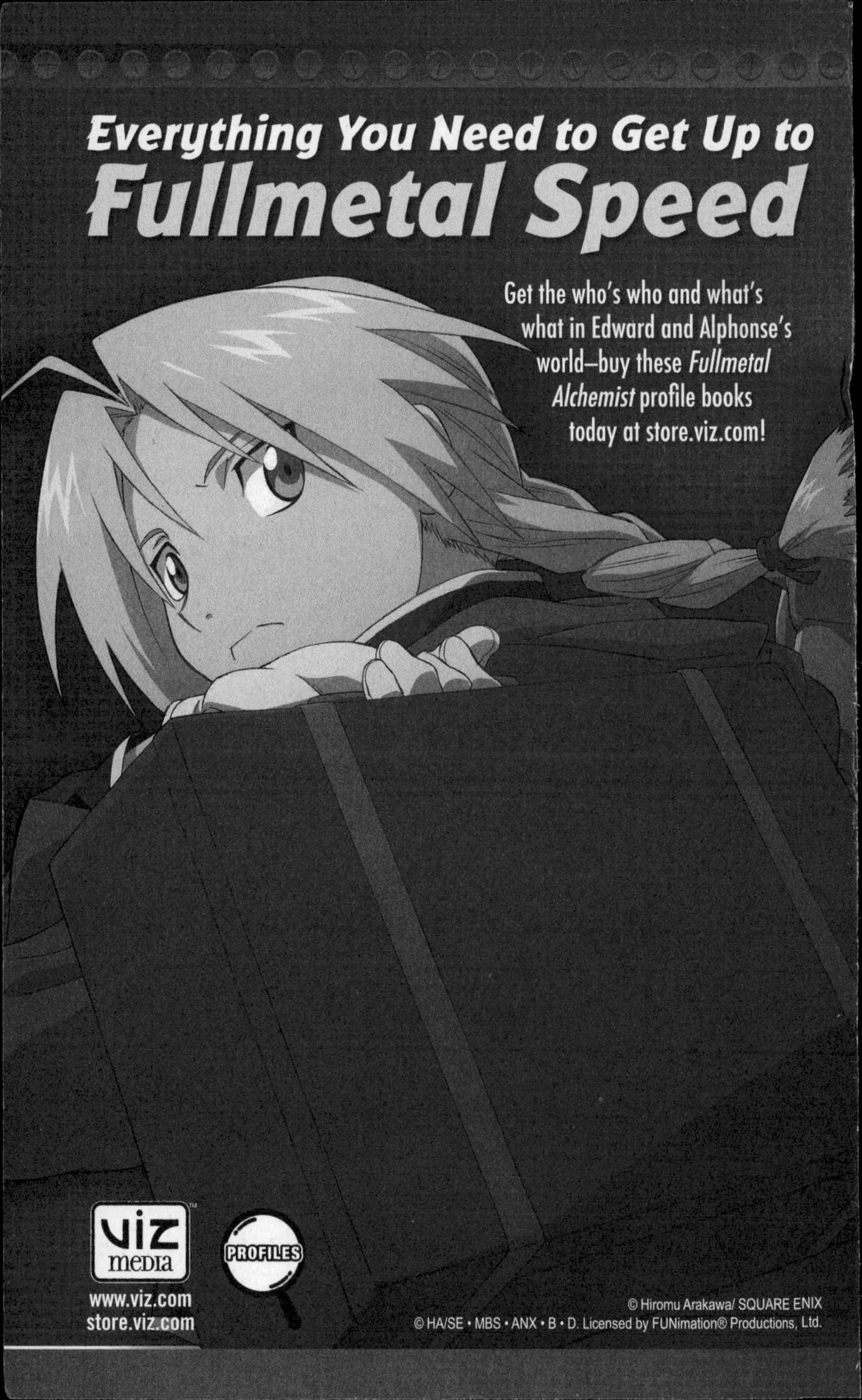
Everything You Need to Get Up to
Fullmetal Speed
Get the who's who and what's what in Edward and Alphonse's world—buy these Fullmetal Alchemist profile books today at store.viz.com!
viz media
PROFILES
www.viz.com
store.viz.com
© Hiromu Arakawa/ SQUARE ENIX
© HA/SE • MBS • ANX • B • D. Licensed by FUNimation® Productions, Ltd.